Becoming RBG

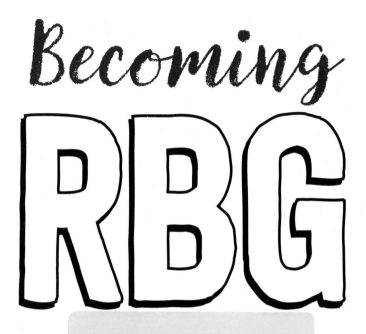

Fear not, Celia Bader!

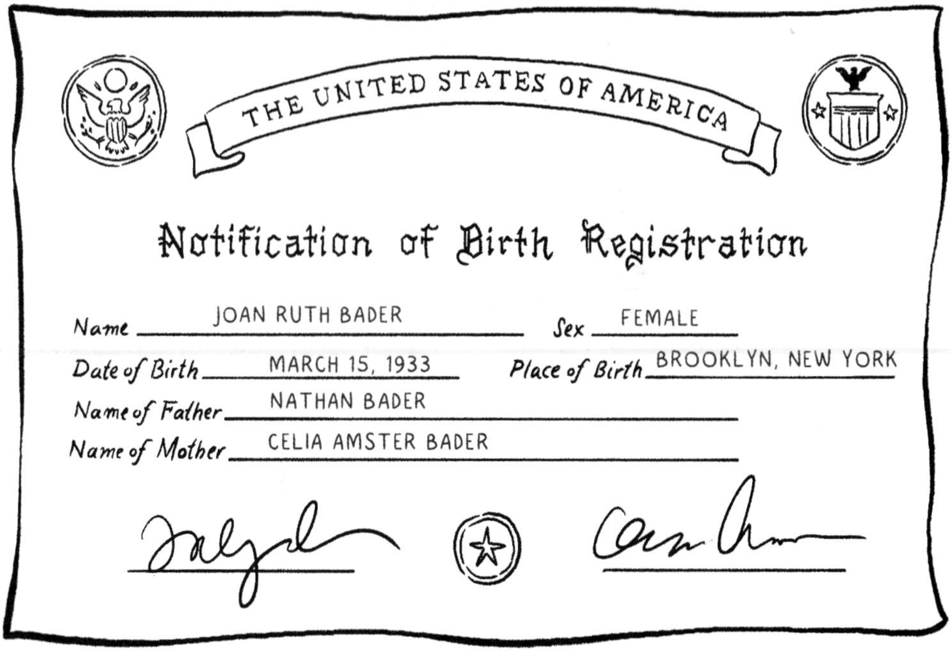
THE UNITED STATES OF AMERICA
Notification of Birth Registration
Name JOAN RUTH BADER
Sex FEMALE
Date of Birth MARCH 15, 1933
Place of Birth BROOKLYN, NEW YORK
Name of Father NATHAN BADER
Name of Mother CELIA AMSTER BADER

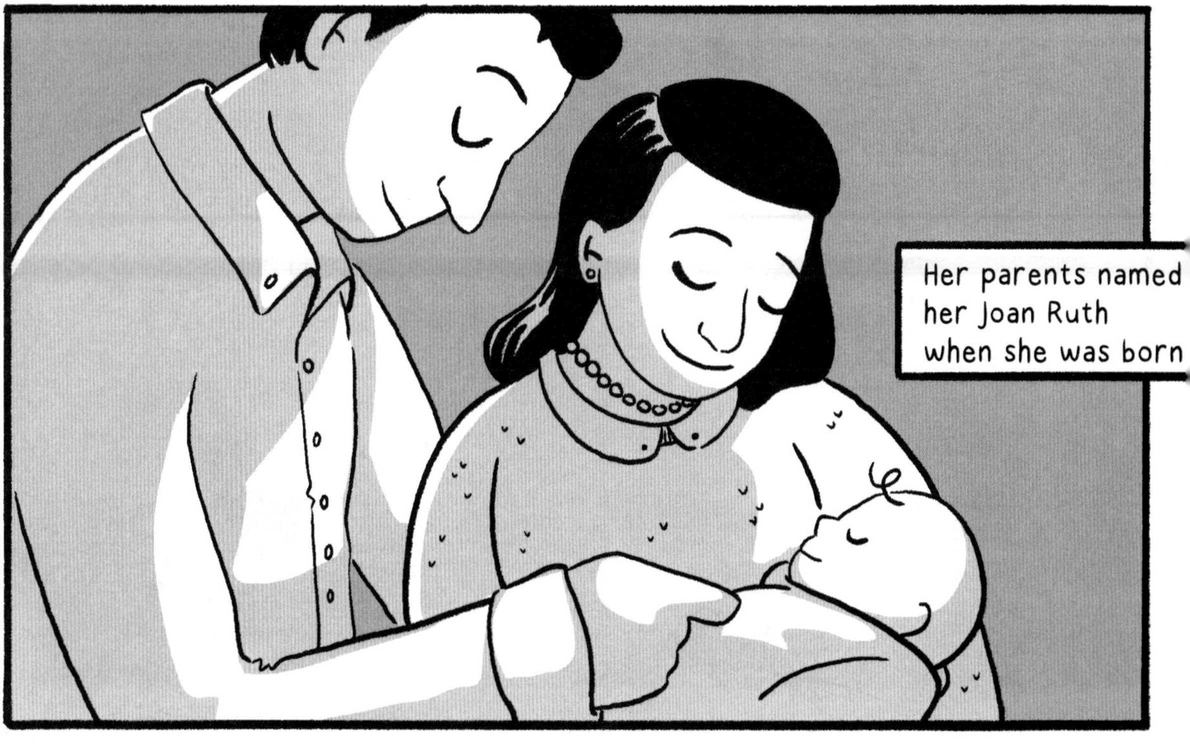
Her parents named her Joan Ruth when she was born

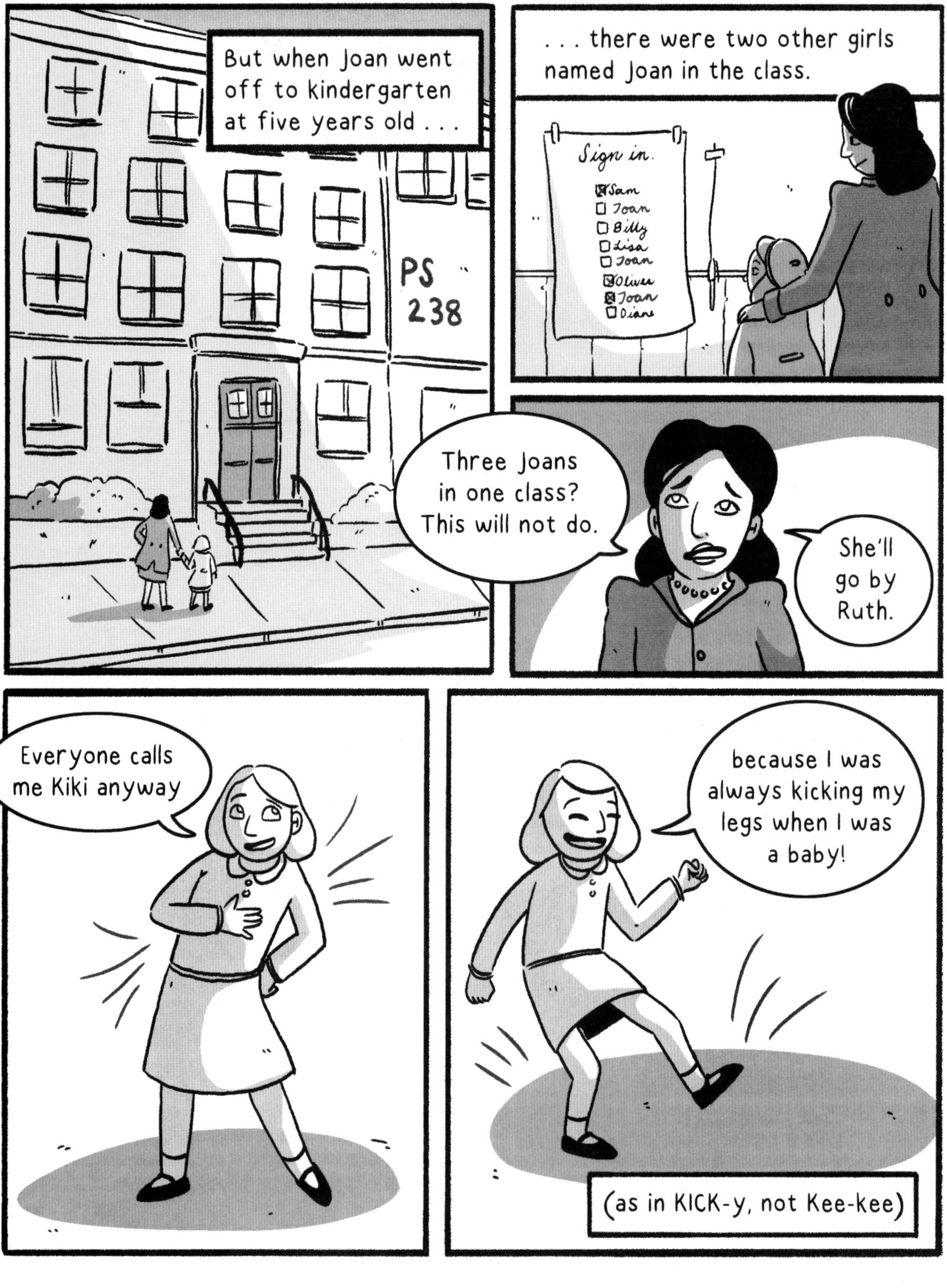

But when Joan went off to kindergarten at five years old . . .
PS 238
. . . there were two other girls named Joan in the class.
Sign in.
Sam
Joan
Billy
Lisa
Joan
Oliver
Joan
Diane
Three Joans in one class? This will not do.
She'll go by Ruth.
Everyone calls me Kiki anyway
because I was always kicking my legs when I was a baby!
(as in KICK-y, not Kee-kee)

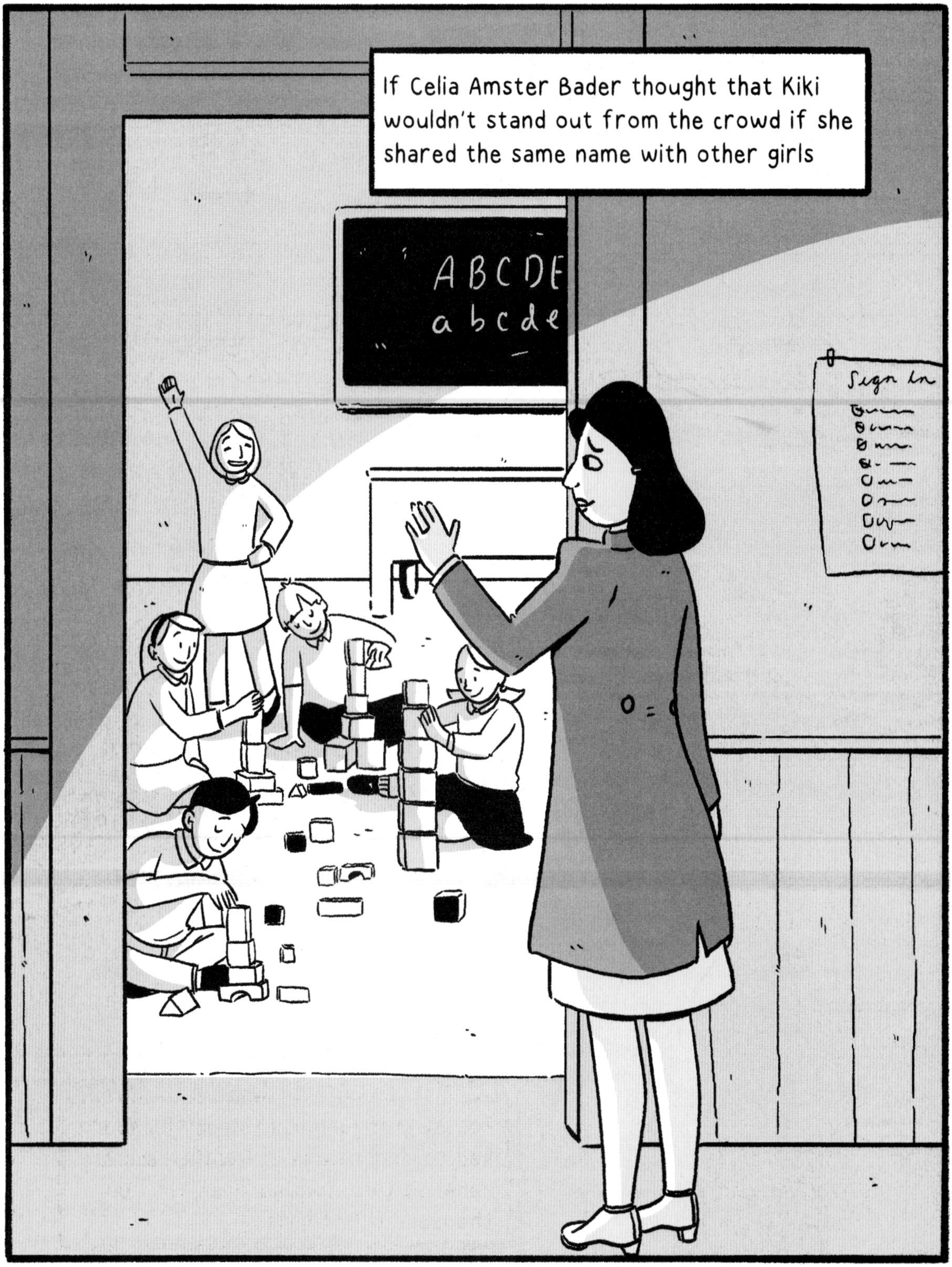
If Celia Amster Bader thought that Kiki wouldn't stand out from the crowd if she shared the same name with other girls
ABCDE
abcde
Sign In

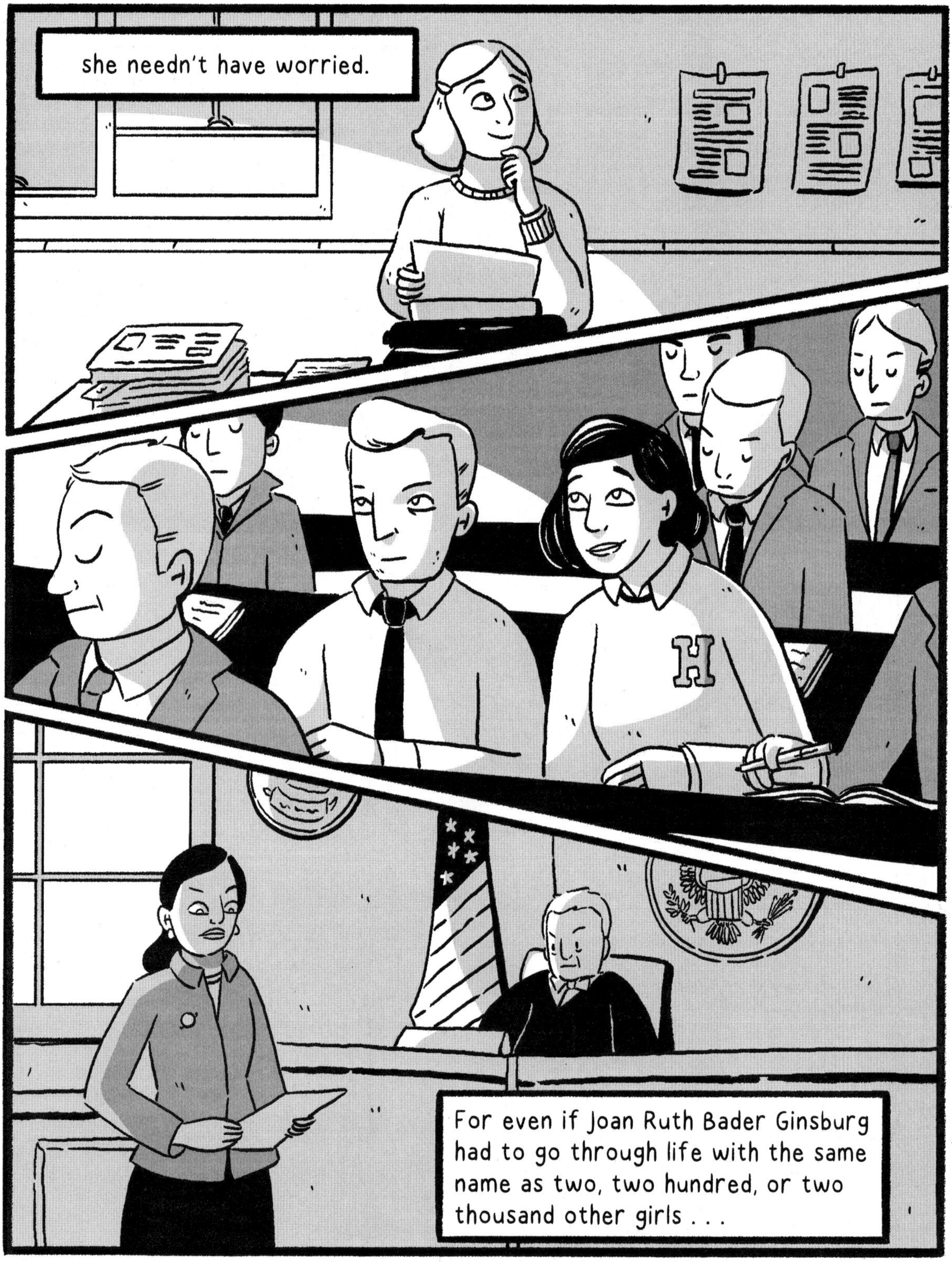
she needn't have worried.
For even if Joan Ruth Bader Ginsburg had to go through life with the same name as two, two hundred, or two thousand other girls . . .

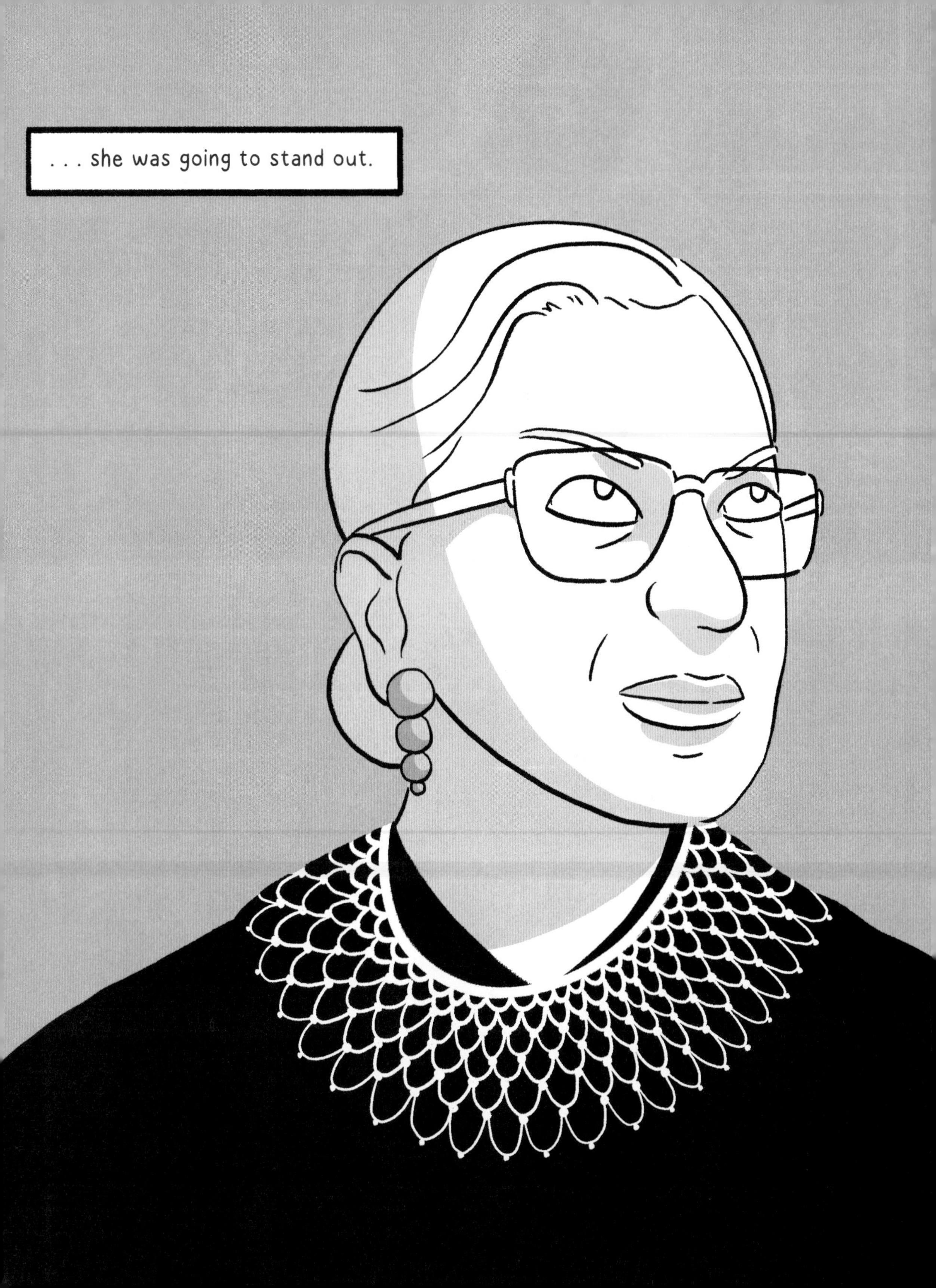
. . . she was going to stand out.

Becoming

RBG

RUTH BADER GINSBURG'S JOURNEY TO JUSTICE

DEBBIE LEVY

illustrated by
WHITNEY GARDNER

Simon & Schuster Books for Young Readers
New York London Toronto Sydney New Delhi

CHAPTER 1

Fun and Games, Family and Sorrow

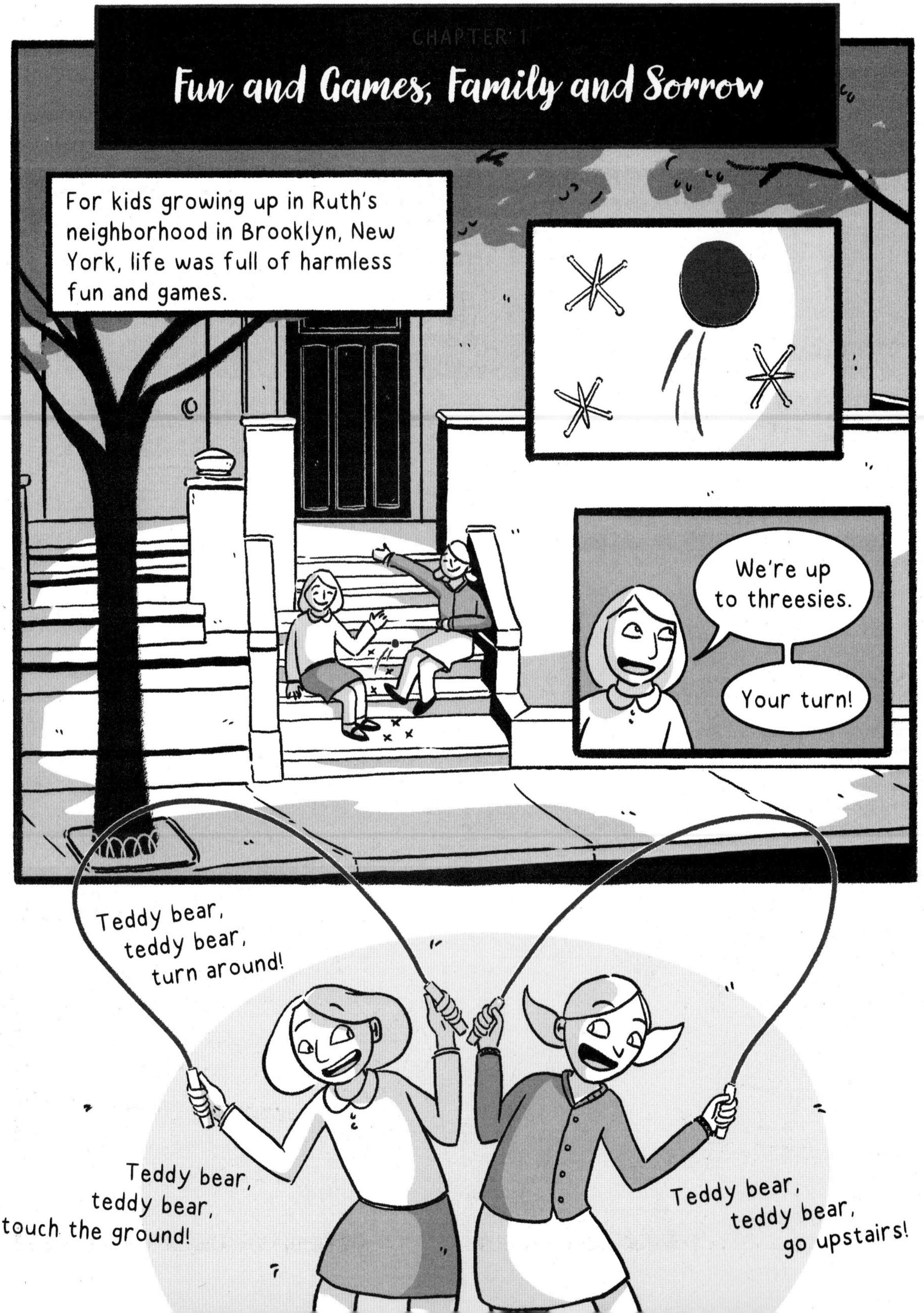
For kids growing up in Ruth's neighborhood in Brooklyn, New York, life was full of harmless fun and games.
We're up to threesies.
Your turn!
Teddy bear, teddy bear, turn around!
Teddy bear, teddy bear, touch the ground!
Teddy bear, teddy bear, go upstairs!

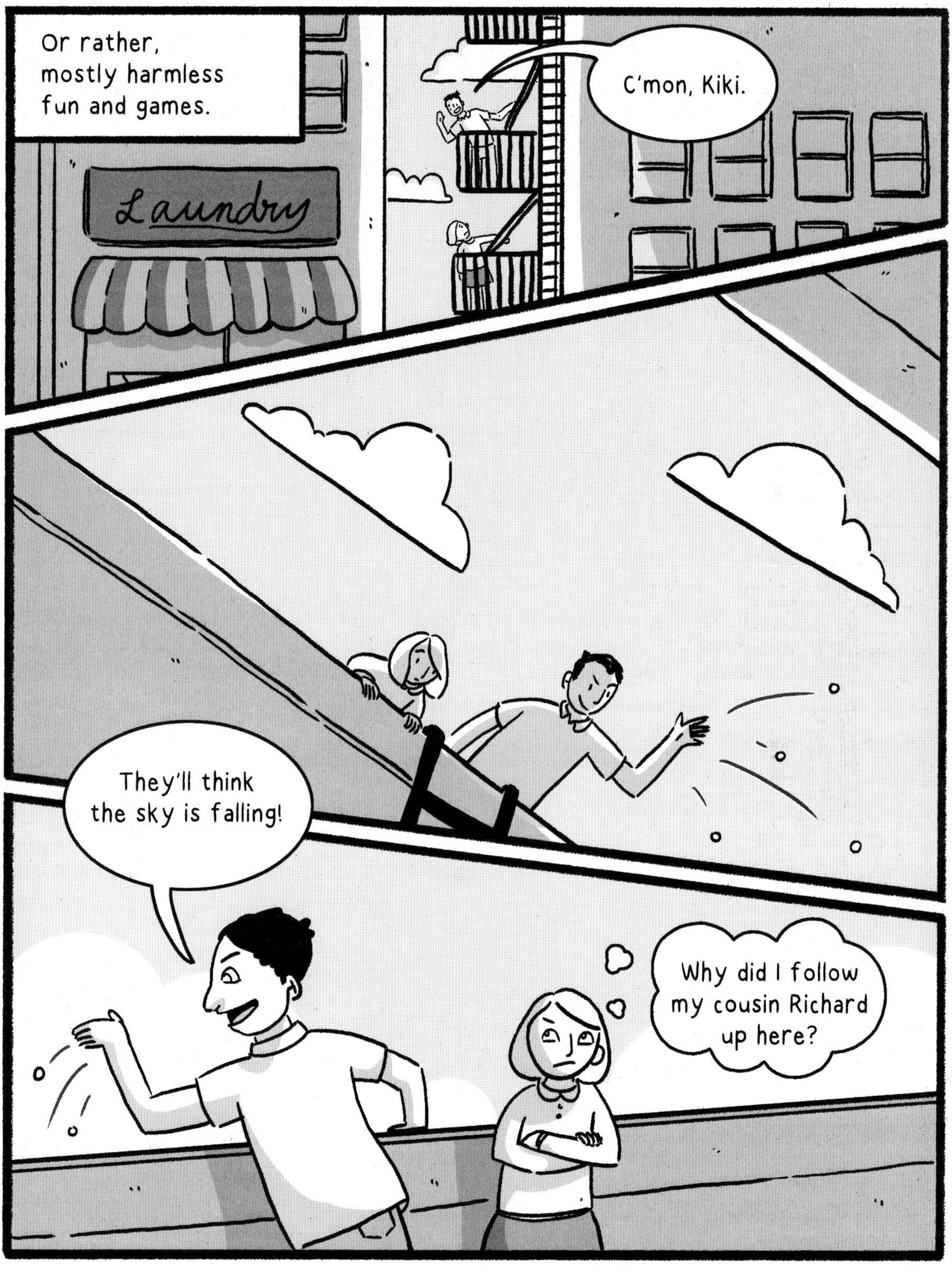
Or rather, mostly harmless fun and games.
Laundry
C'mon, Kiki.
They'll think the sky is falling!
Why did I follow my cousin Richard up here?

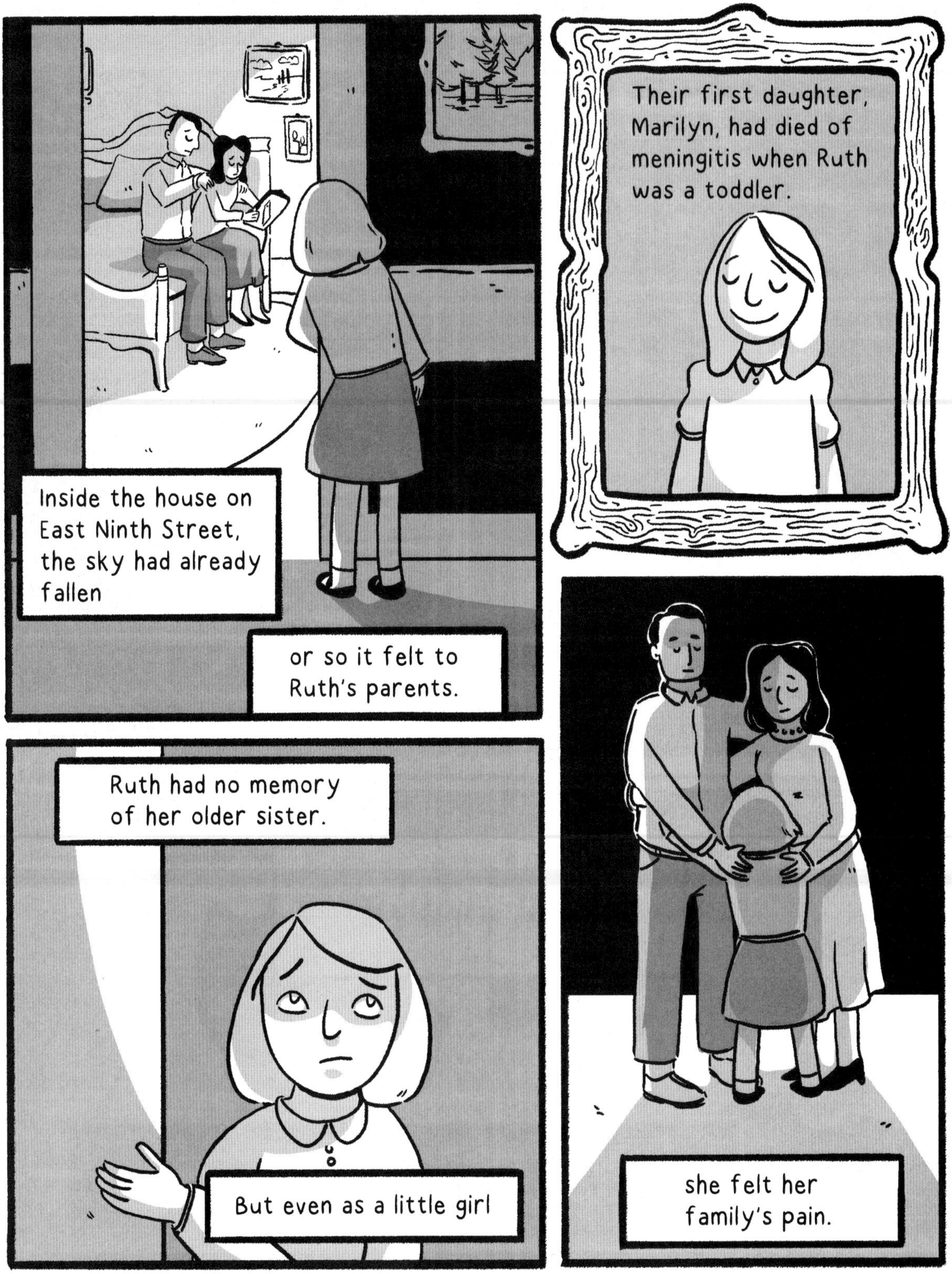
Inside the house on East Ninth Street, the sky had already fallen
or so it felt to Ruth's parents.
Their first daughter, Marilyn, had died of meningitis when Ruth was a toddler.
Ruth had no memory of her older sister.
But even as a little girl
she felt her family's pain.

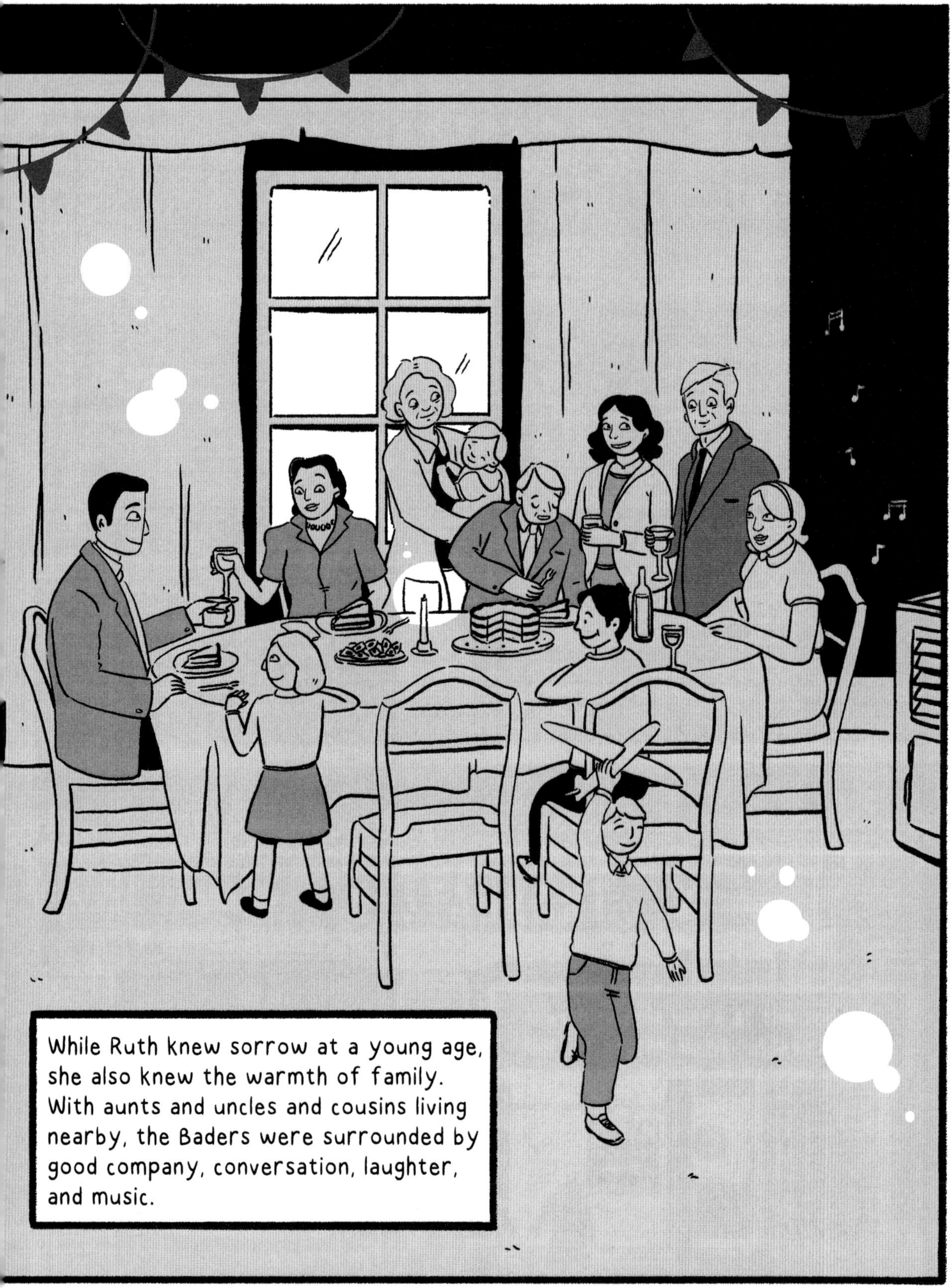
While Ruth knew sorrow at a young age, she also knew the warmth of family. With aunts and uncles and cousins living nearby, the Baders were surrounded by good company, conversation, laughter, and music.

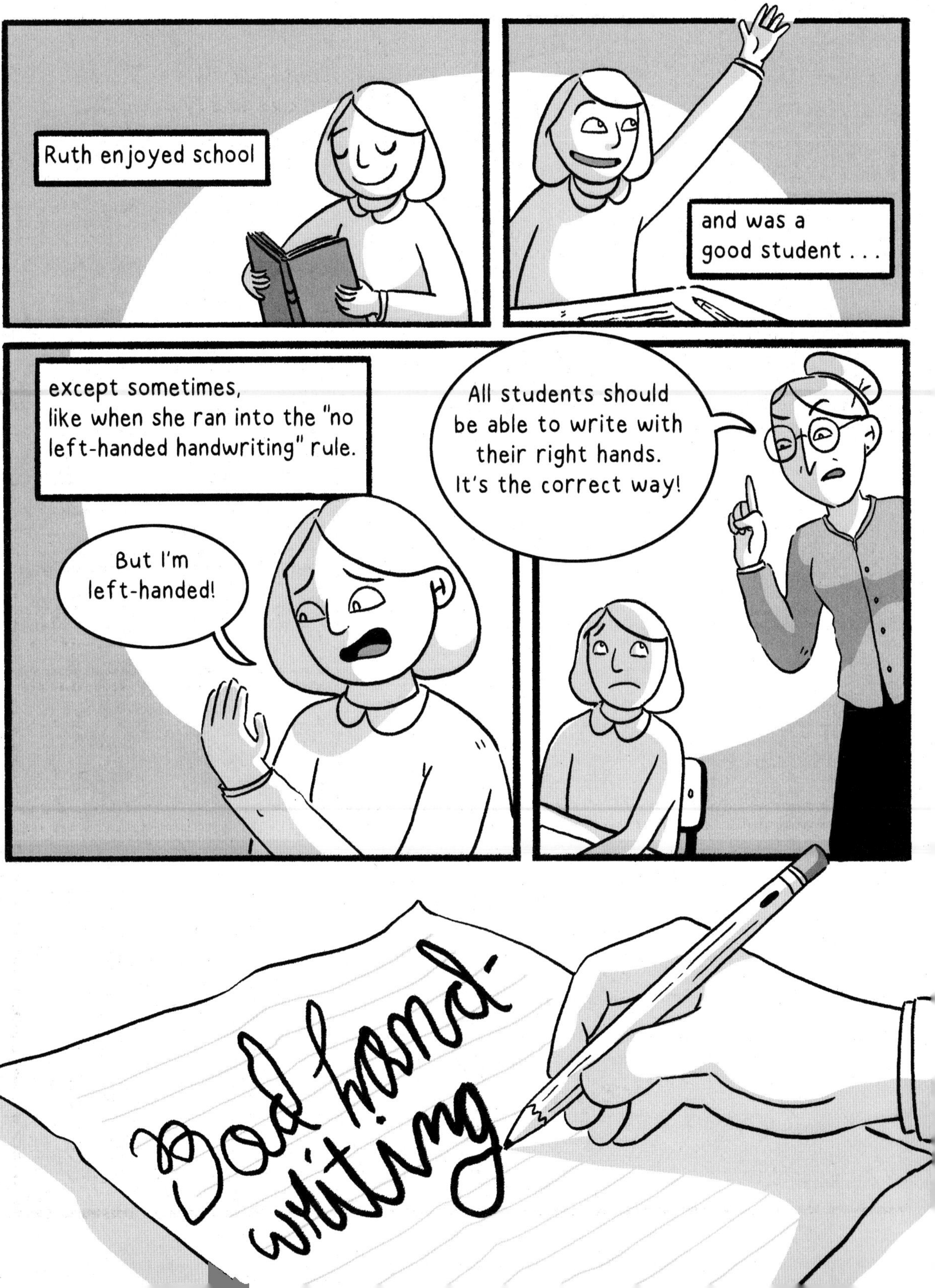
Ruth enjoyed school
and was a good student . . .
except sometimes, like when she ran into the "no left-handed handwriting" rule.
All students should be able to write with their right hands. It's the correct way!
But I'm left-handed!
Bad hand-writing

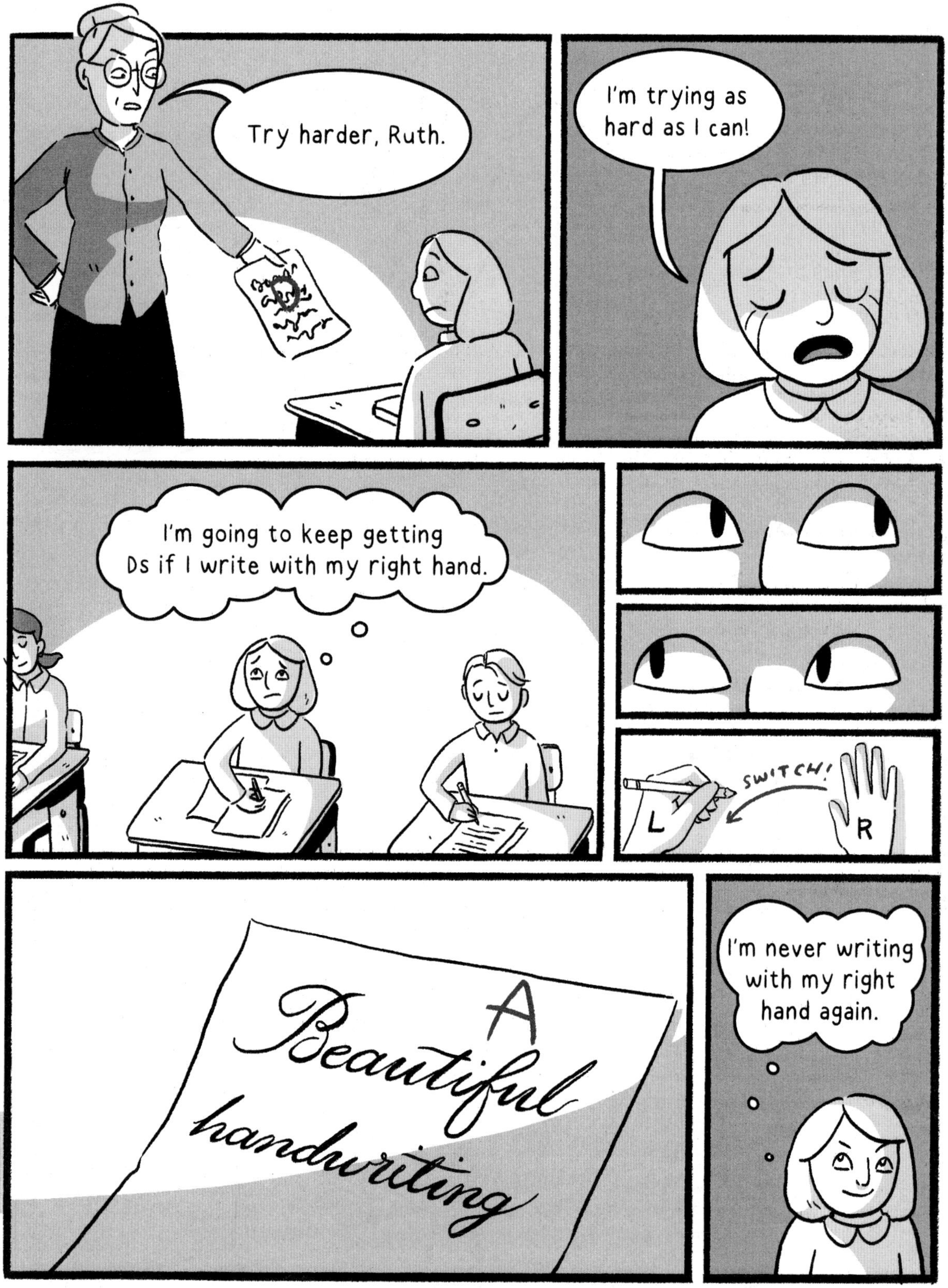
Try harder, Ruth.
I'm trying as hard as I can!
I'm going to keep getting Ds if I write with my right hand.
SWITCH!
L
R
A
Beautiful handwriting
I'm never writing with my right hand again.

CHAPTER 2

Its Ugly Head

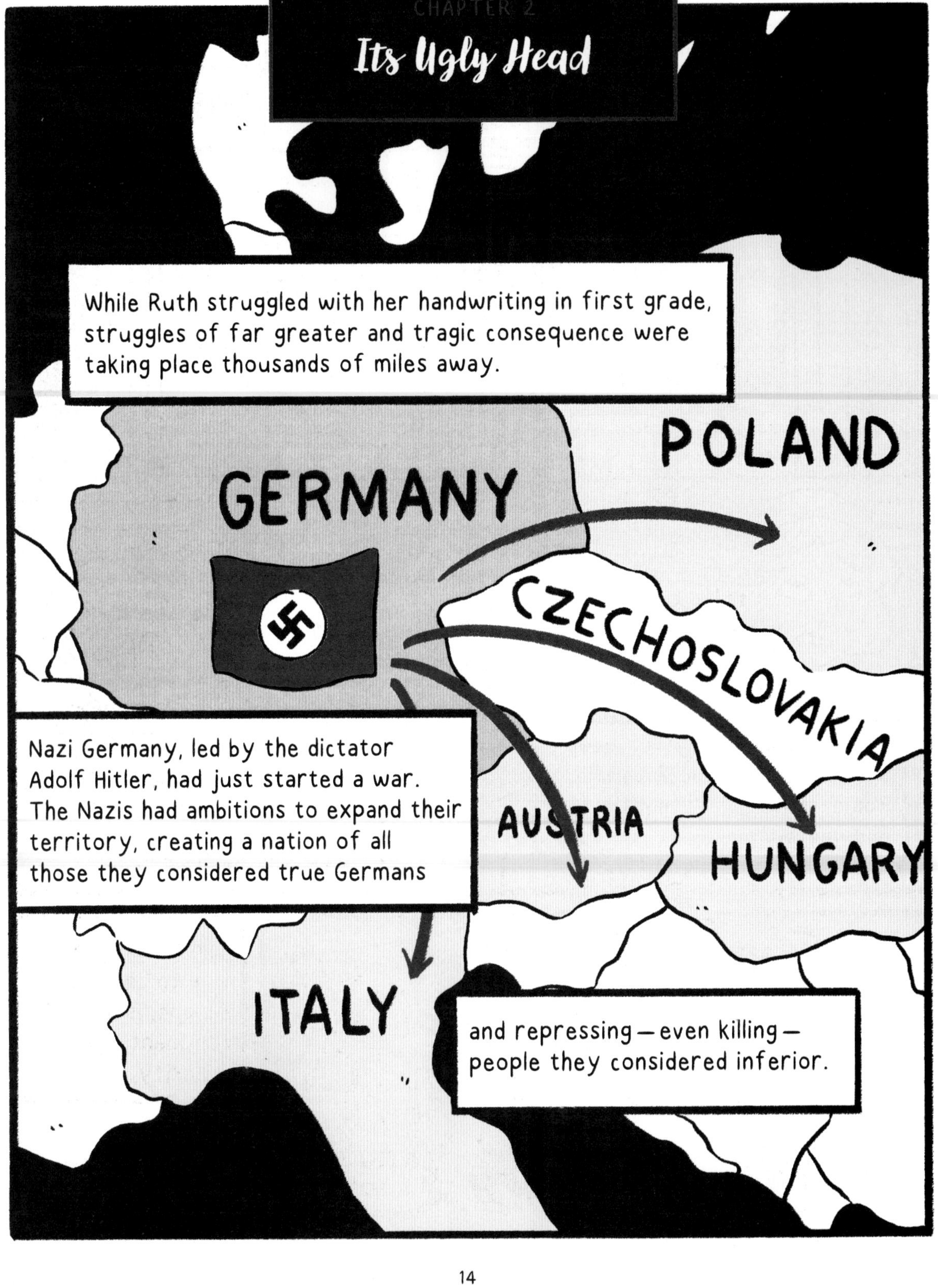

While Ruth struggled with her handwriting in first grade, struggles of far greater and tragic consequence were taking place thousands of miles away.
POLAND
GERMANY
CZECHOSLOVAKIA
Nazi Germany, led by the dictator Adolf Hitler, had just started a war. The Nazis had ambitions to expand their territory, creating a nation of all those they considered true Germans
AUSTRIA
HUNGARY
ITALY
and repressing—even killing—people they considered inferior.

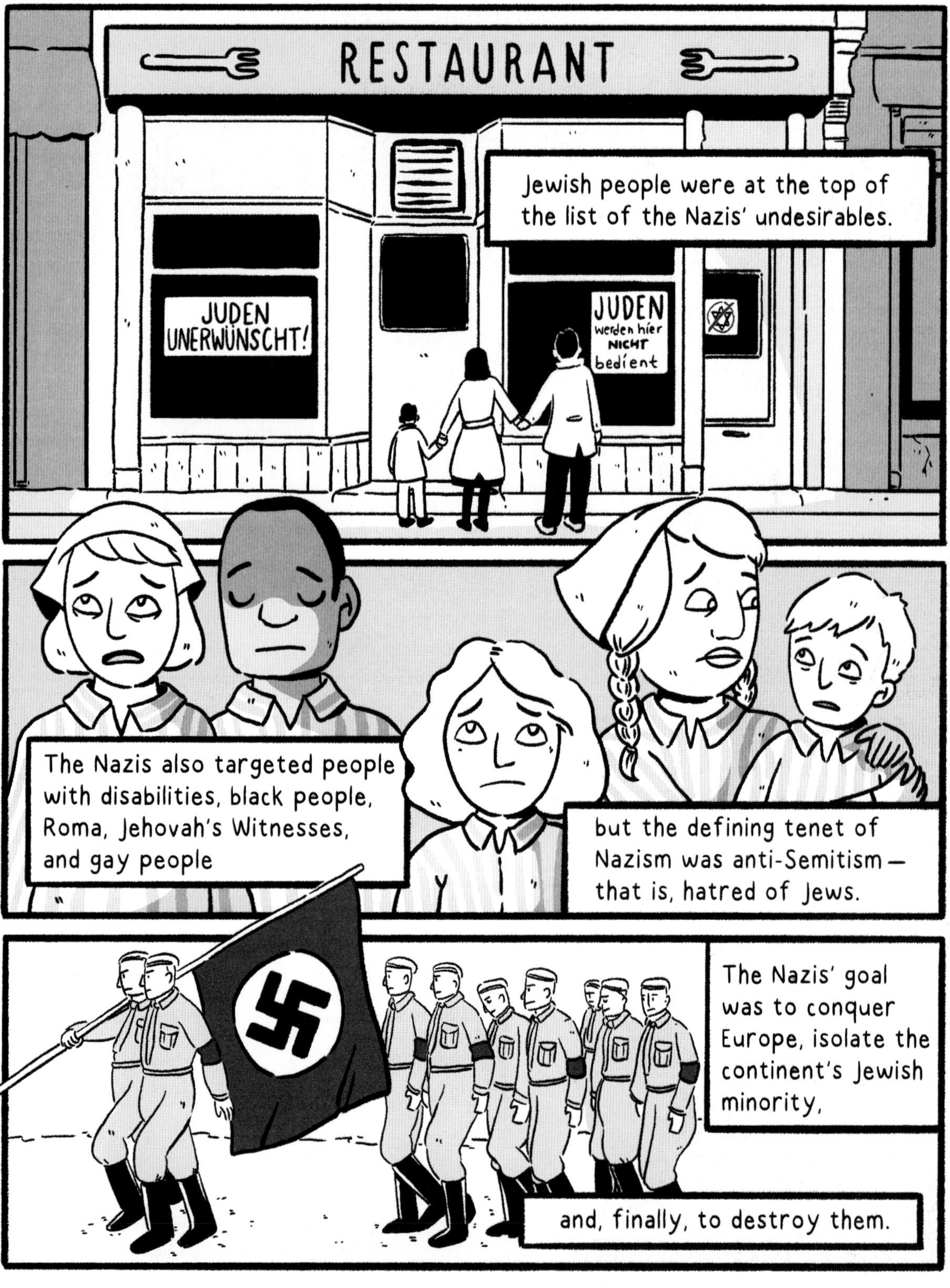
RESTAURANT
Jewish people were at the top of the list of the Nazis' undesirables.
JUDEN UNERWÜNSCHT!
JUDEN werden hier NICHT bedient
The Nazis also targeted people with disabilities, black people, Roma, Jehovah's Witnesses, and gay people
but the defining tenet of Nazism was anti-Semitism— that is, hatred of Jews.
The Nazis' goal was to conquer Europe, isolate the continent's Jewish minority,
and, finally, to destroy them.

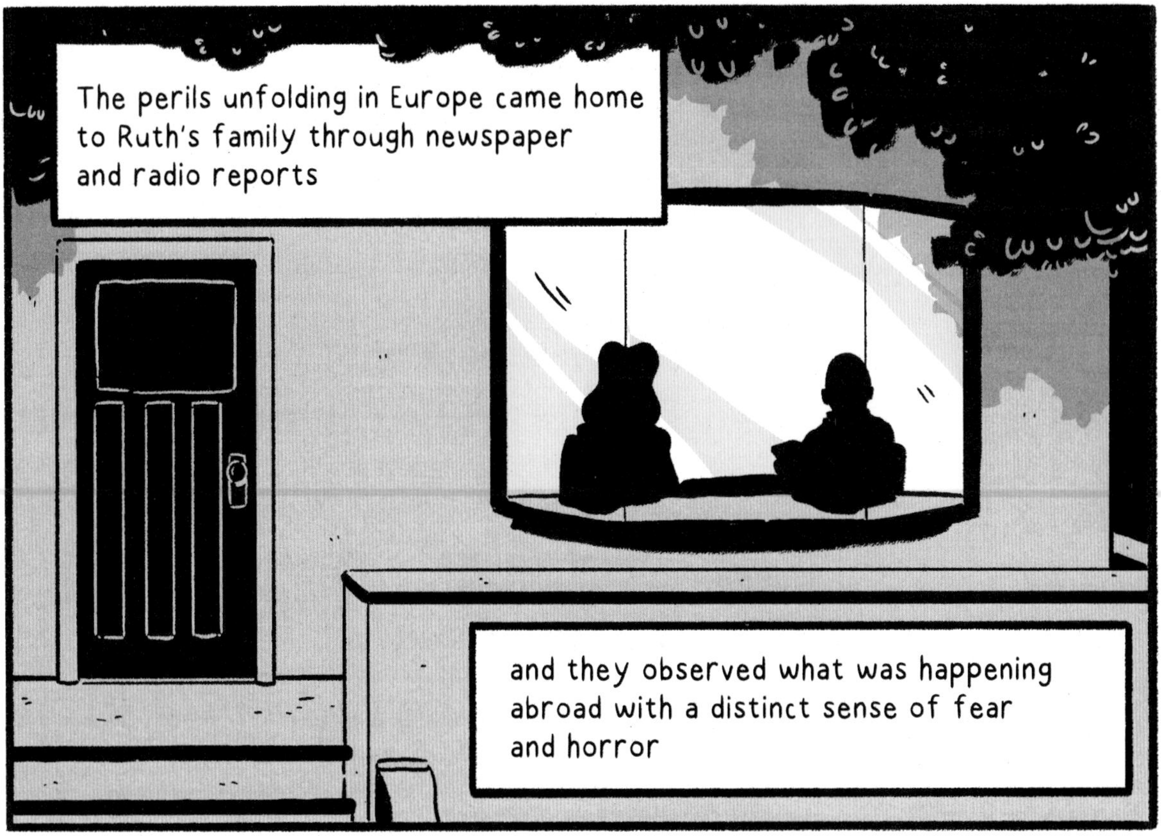
The perils unfolding in Europe came home to Ruth's family through newspaper and radio reports
and they observed what was happening abroad with a distinct sense of fear and horror

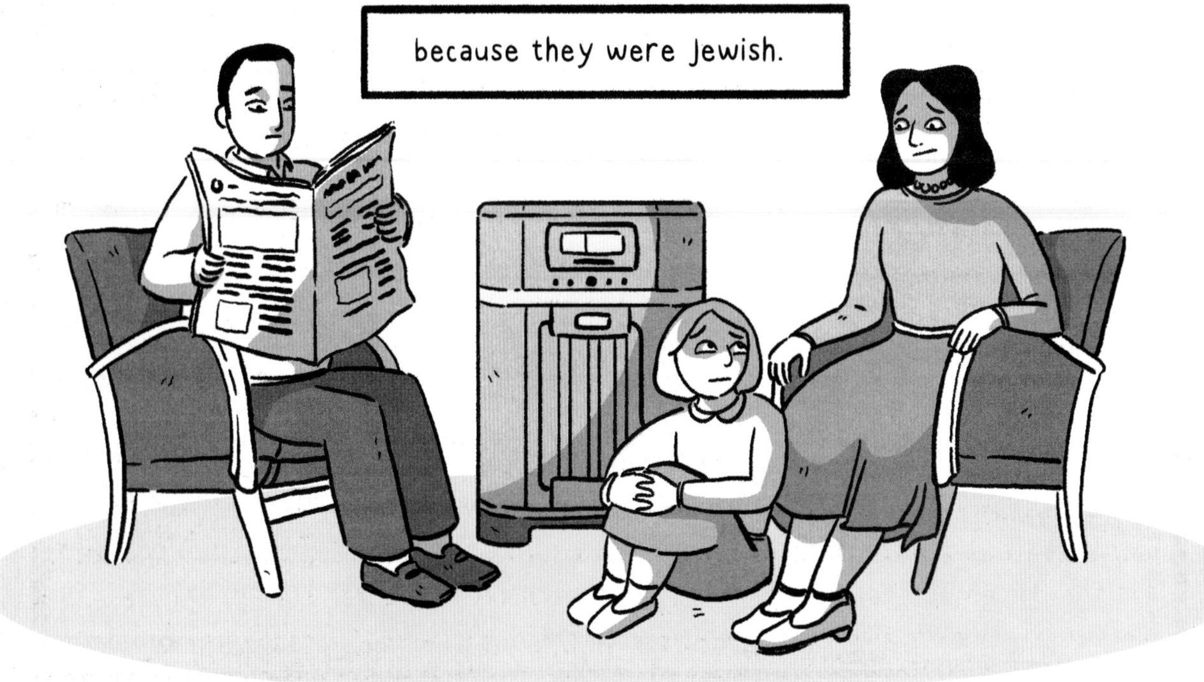
because they were Jewish.

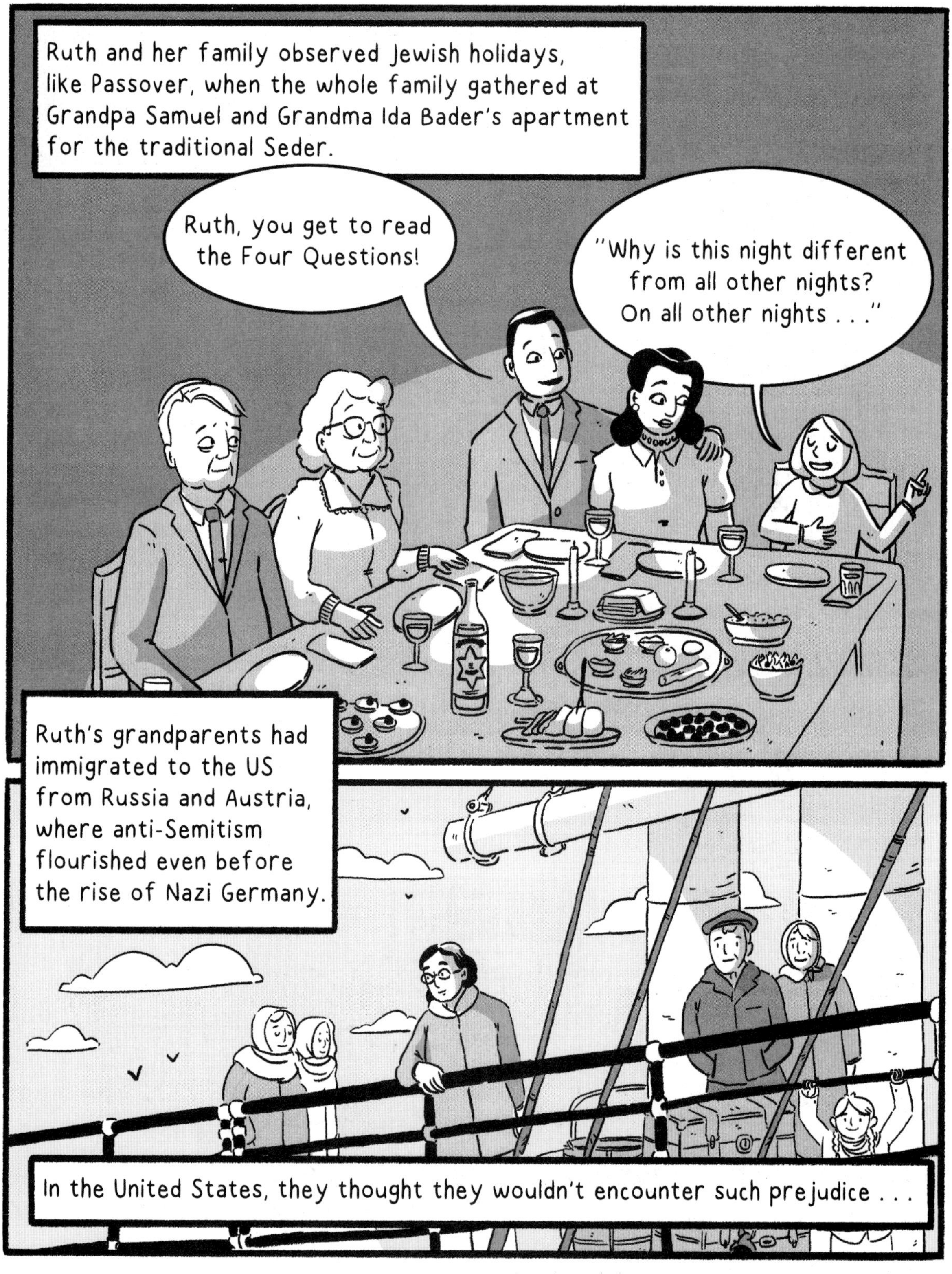
Ruth and her family observed Jewish holidays, like Passover, when the whole family gathered at Grandpa Samuel and Grandma Ida Bader's apartment for the traditional Seder.
Ruth, you get to read the Four Questions!
"Why is this night different from all other nights? On all other nights . . ."
Ruth's grandparents had immigrated to the US from Russia and Austria, where anti-Semitism flourished even before the rise of Nazi Germany.
In the United States, they thought they wouldn't encounter such prejudice . . .

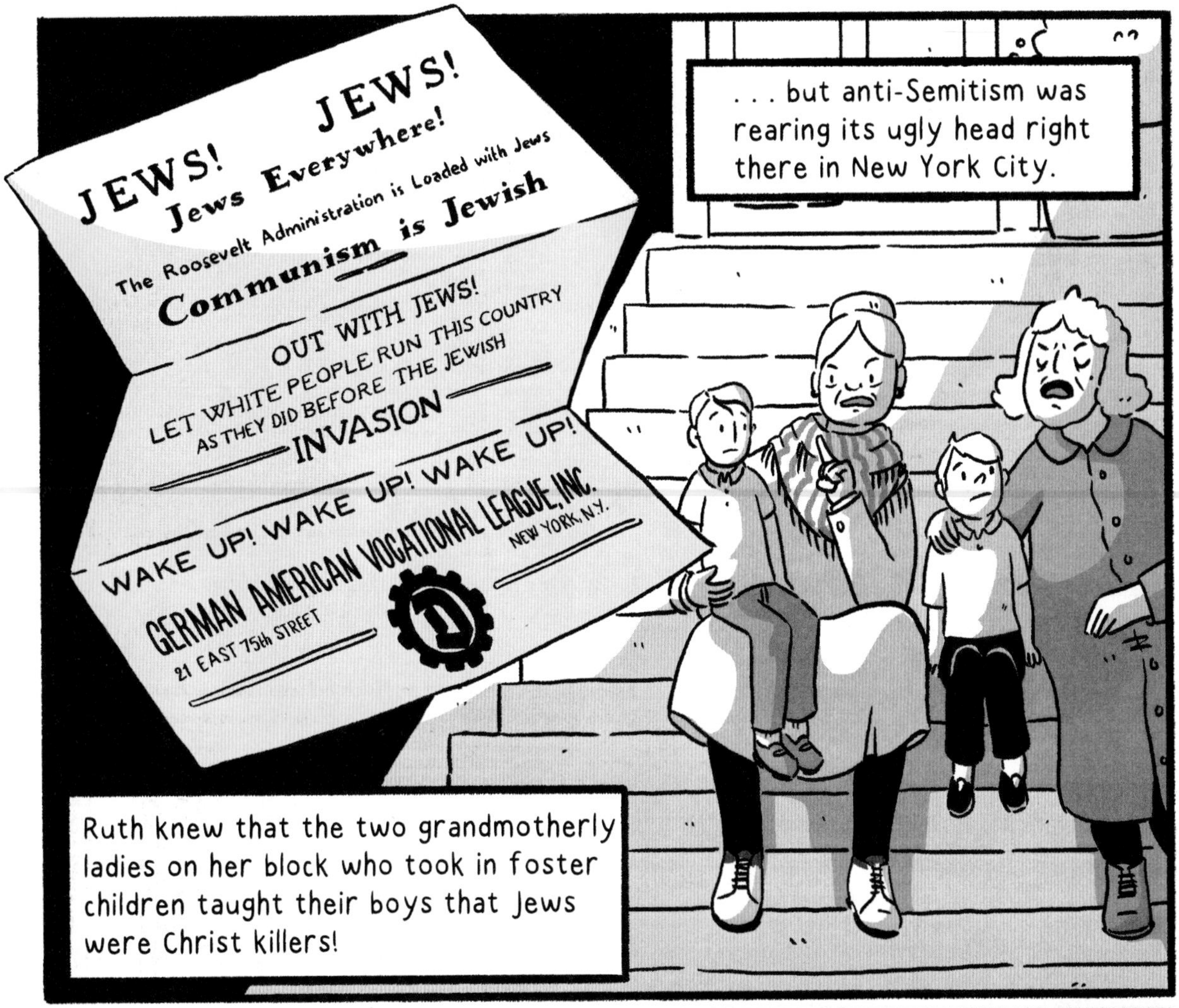
JEWS! JEWS!
Jews Everywhere!
The Roosevelt Administration is Loaded with Jews
Communism is Jewish
OUT WITH JEWS!
LET WHITE PEOPLE RUN THIS COUNTRY AS THEY DID BEFORE THE JEWISH
INVASION
WAKE UP! WAKE UP! WAKE UP! WAKE UP!
GERMAN AMERICAN VOCATIONAL LEAGUE, INC.
NEW YORK, N.Y.
21 EAST 75th STREET
. . . but anti-Semitism was rearing its ugly head right there in New York City.
Ruth knew that the two grandmotherly ladies on her block who took in foster children taught their boys that Jews were Christ killers!

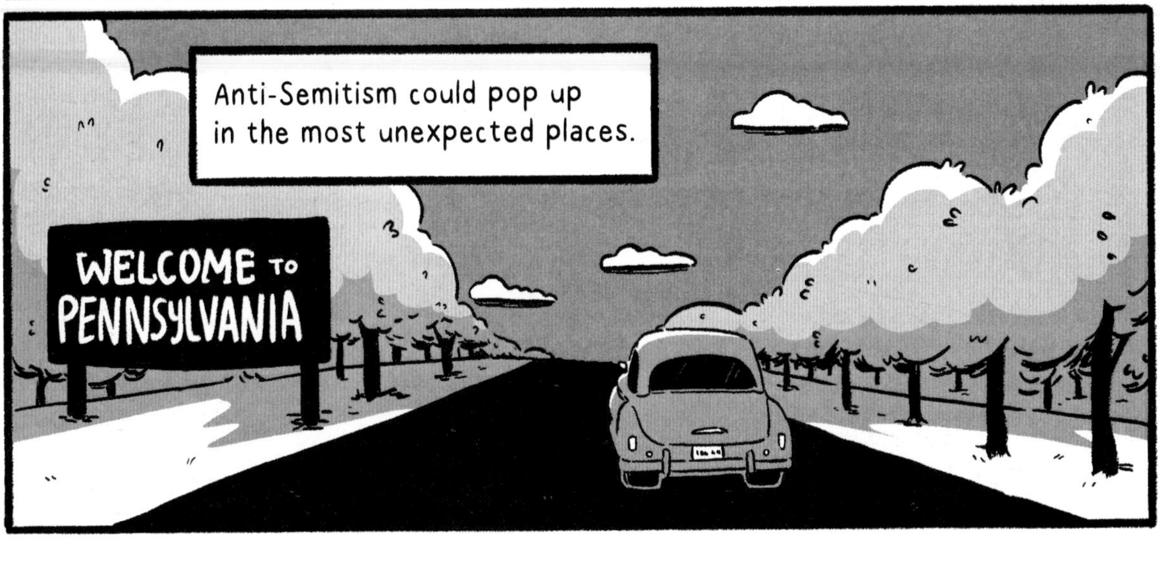
Anti-Semitism could pop up in the most unexpected places.
WELCOME TO PENNSYLVANIA

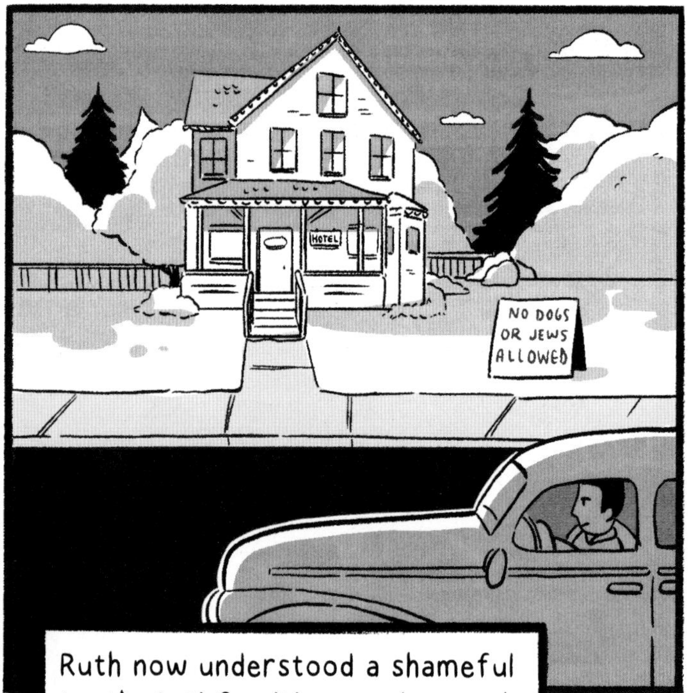

HOTEL
NO DOGS OR JEWS ALLOWED

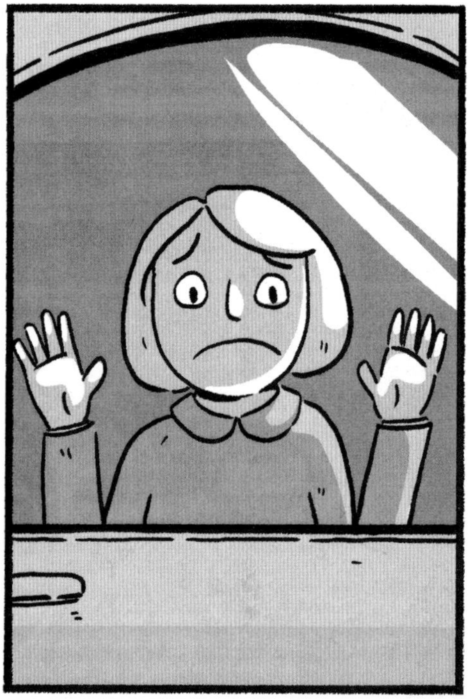

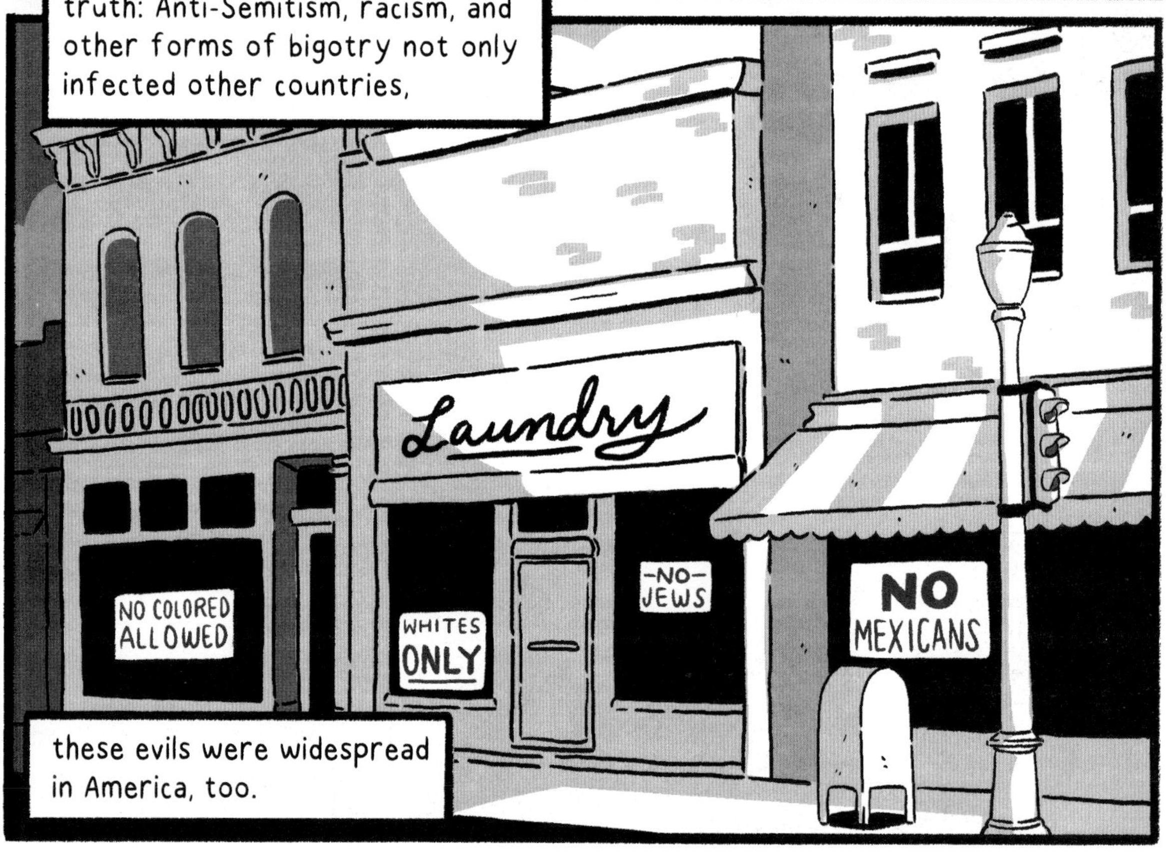

Ruth now understood a shameful truth: Anti-Semitism, racism, and other forms of bigotry not only infected other countries,
Laundry
NO COLORED ALLOWED
WHITES ONLY
-NO- JEWS
NO MEXICANS
these evils were widespread in America, too.

CHAPTER 3

We Do Not Allow Intolerance

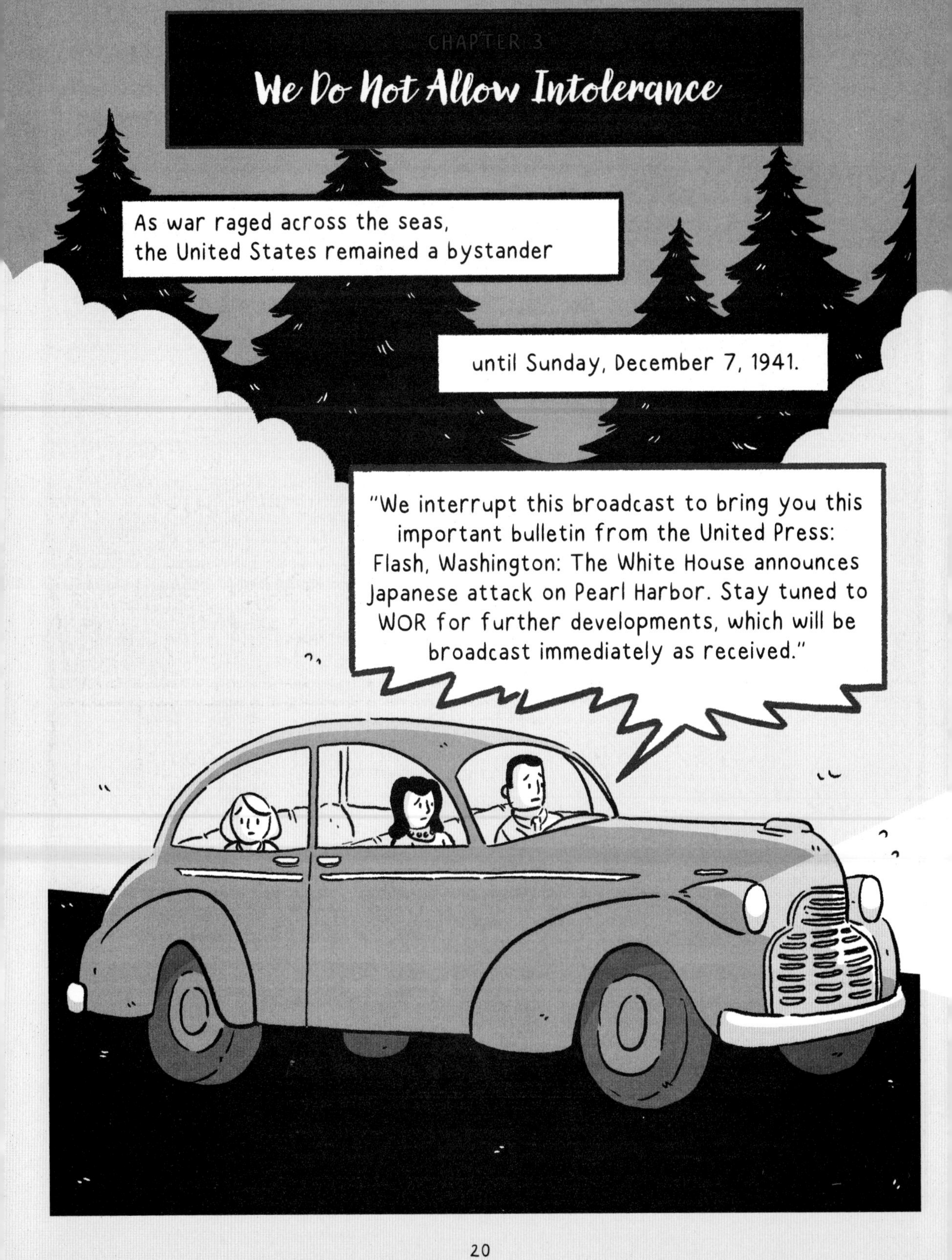
As war raged across the seas, the United States remained a bystander
until Sunday, December 7, 1941.
"We interrupt this broadcast to bring you this important bulletin from the United Press: Flash, Washington: The White House announces Japanese attack on Pearl Harbor. Stay tuned to WOR for further developments, which will be broadcast immediately as received."

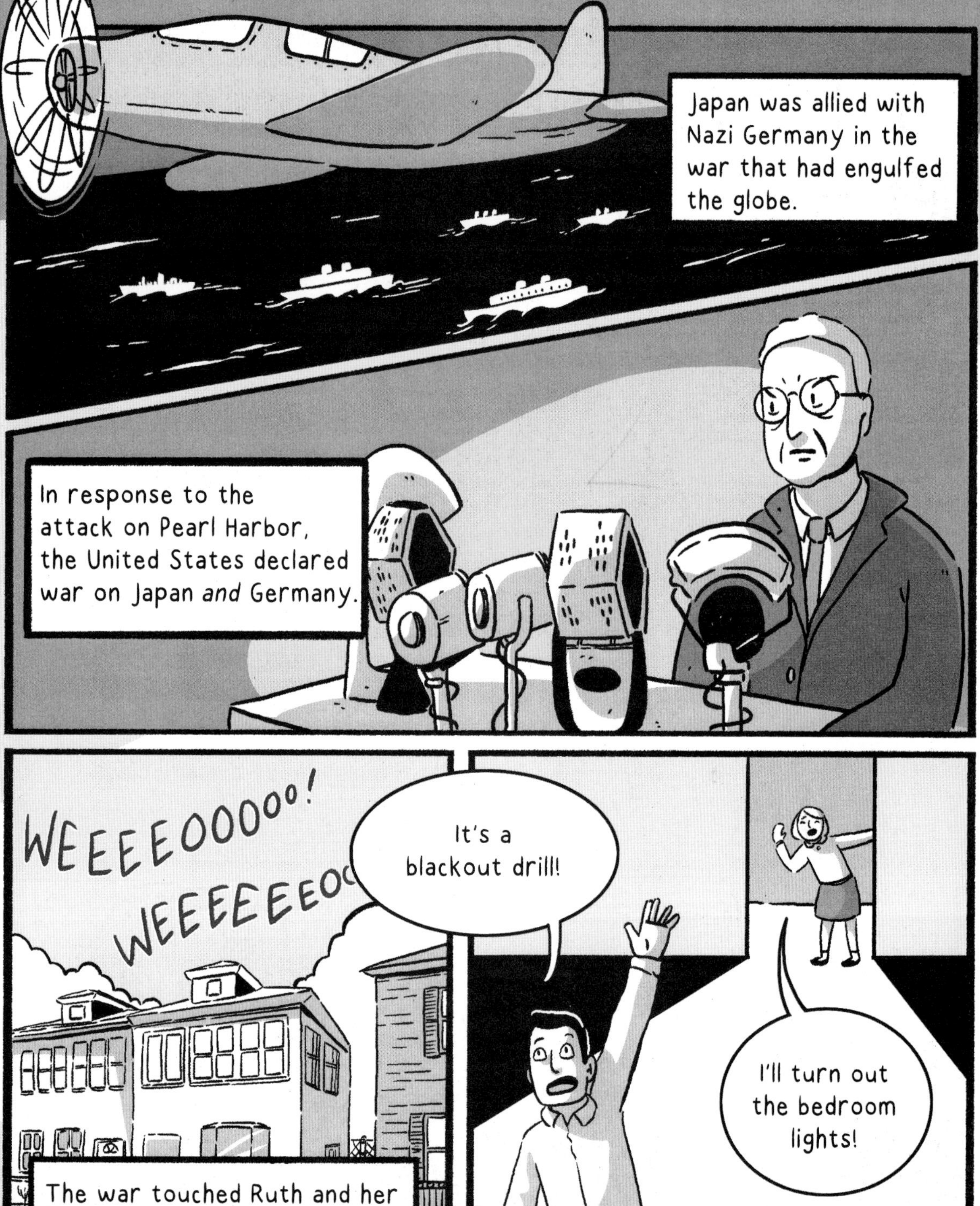
Japan was allied with Nazi Germany in the war that had engulfed the globe.
In response to the attack on Pearl Harbor, the United States declared war on Japan *and* Germany.
WEEEEOOOOo!
WEEEEEEO
It's a blackout drill!
I'll turn out the bedroom lights!
The war touched Ruth and her family, as it affected families everywhere.

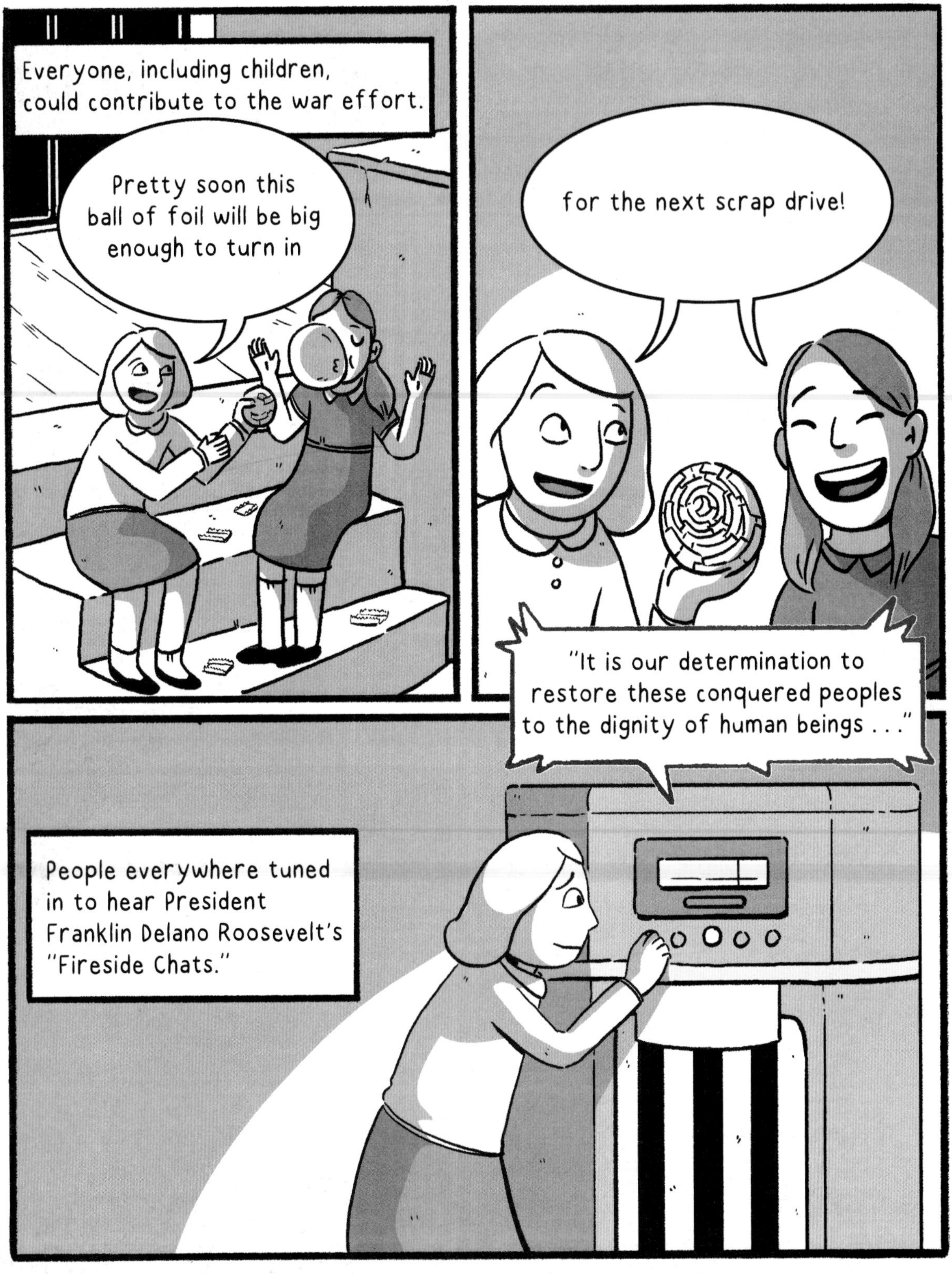
Everyone, including children, could contribute to the war effort.
Pretty soon this ball of foil will be big enough to turn in
for the next scrap drive!
"It is our determination to restore these conquered peoples to the dignity of human beings . . ."
People everywhere tuned in to hear President Franklin Delano Roosevelt's "Fireside Chats."

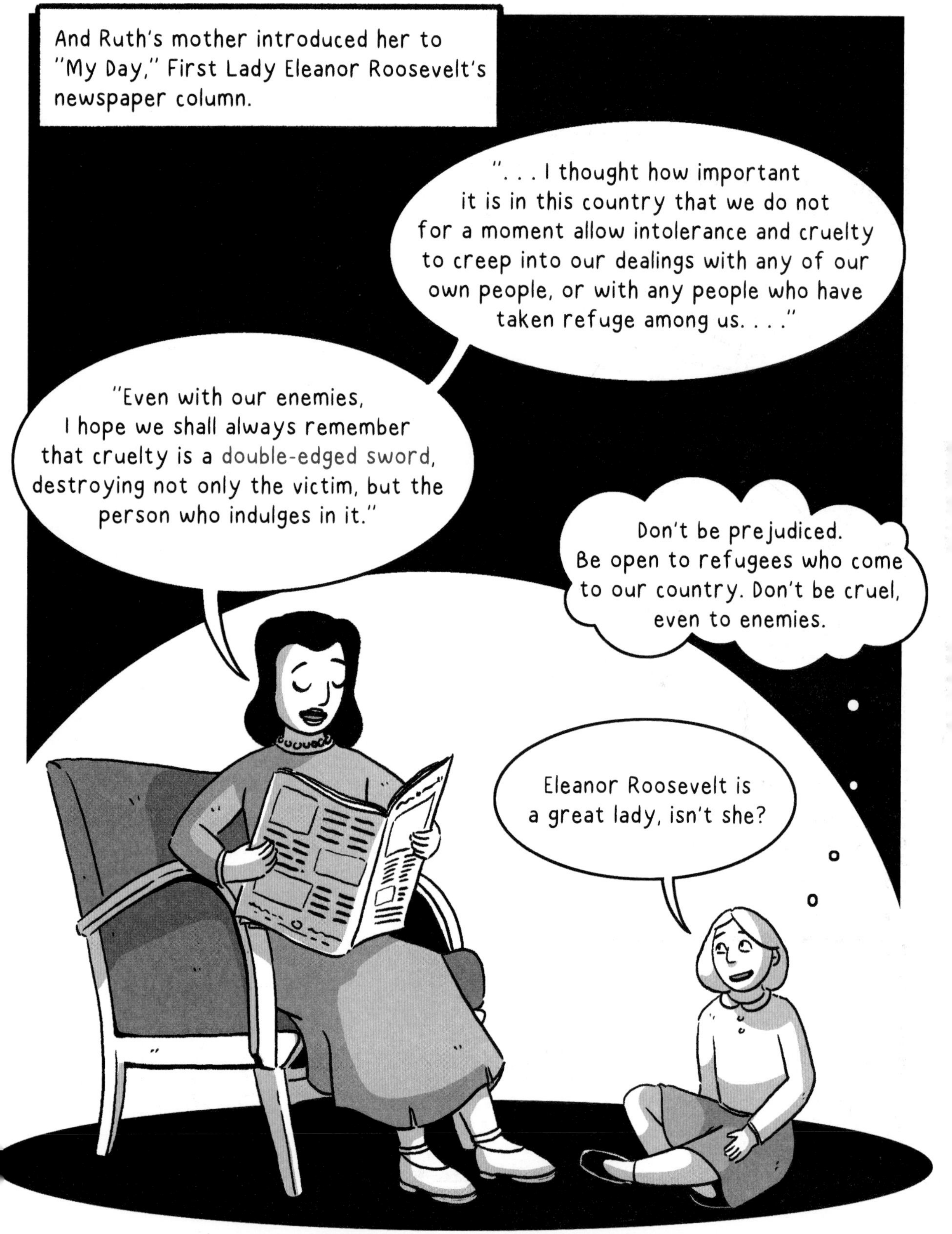
And Ruth's mother introduced her to "My Day," First Lady Eleanor Roosevelt's newspaper column.
". . . I thought how important it is in this country that we do not for a moment allow intolerance and cruelty to creep into our dealings with any of our own people, or with any people who have taken refuge among us. . . ."
"Even with our enemies, I hope we shall always remember that cruelty is a double-edged sword, destroying not only the victim, but the person who indulges in it."
Don't be prejudiced. Be open to refugees who come to our country. Don't be cruel, even to enemies.
Eleanor Roosevelt is a great lady, isn't she?

CHAPTER 4

What a Lady Is

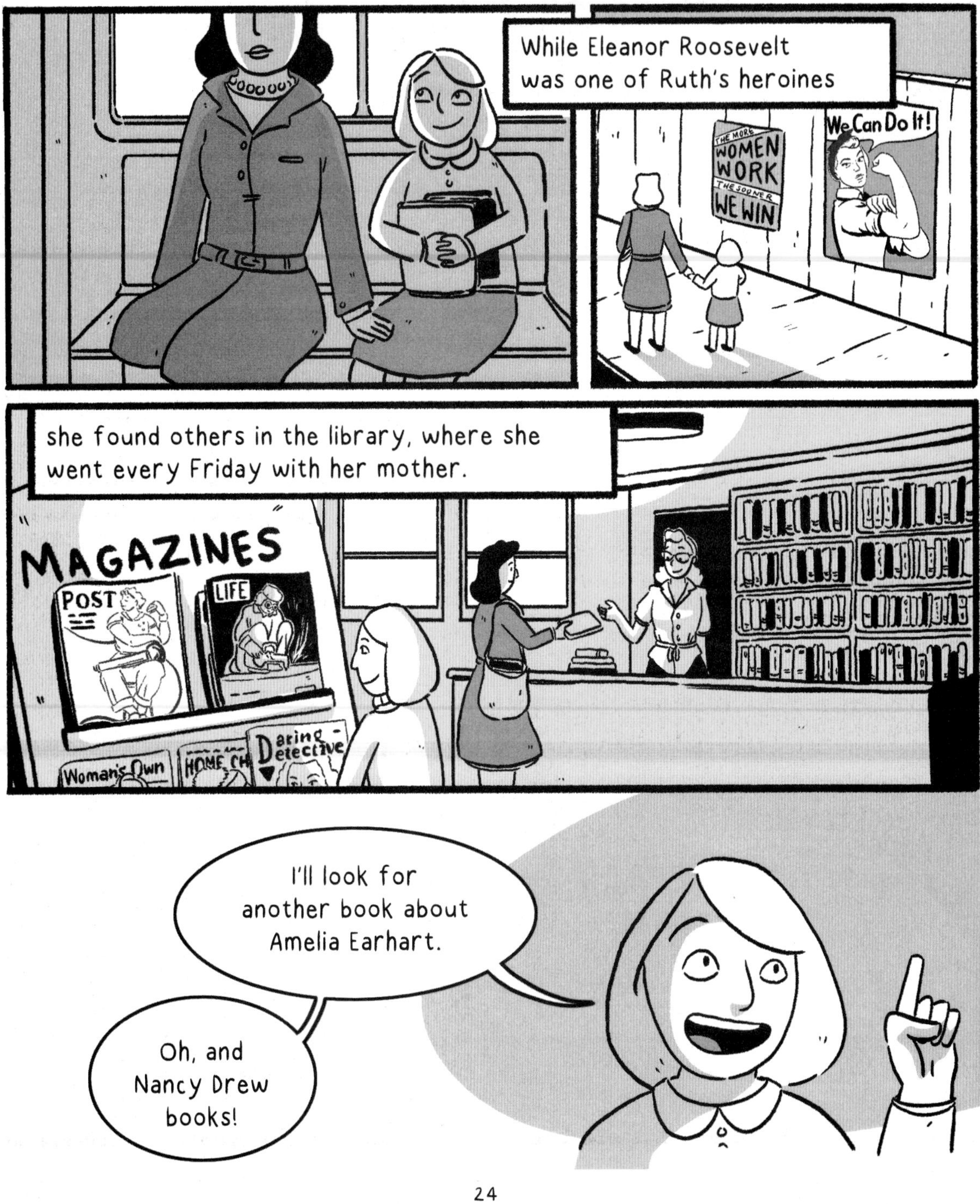
While Eleanor Roosevelt was one of Ruth's heroines
THE MORE WOMEN WORK THE SOONER WE WIN
We Can Do It!
she found others in the library, where she went every Friday with her mother.
MAGAZINES
POST
LIFE
Woman's Own
Daring Detective
I'll look for another book about Amelia Earhart.
Oh, and Nancy Drew books!

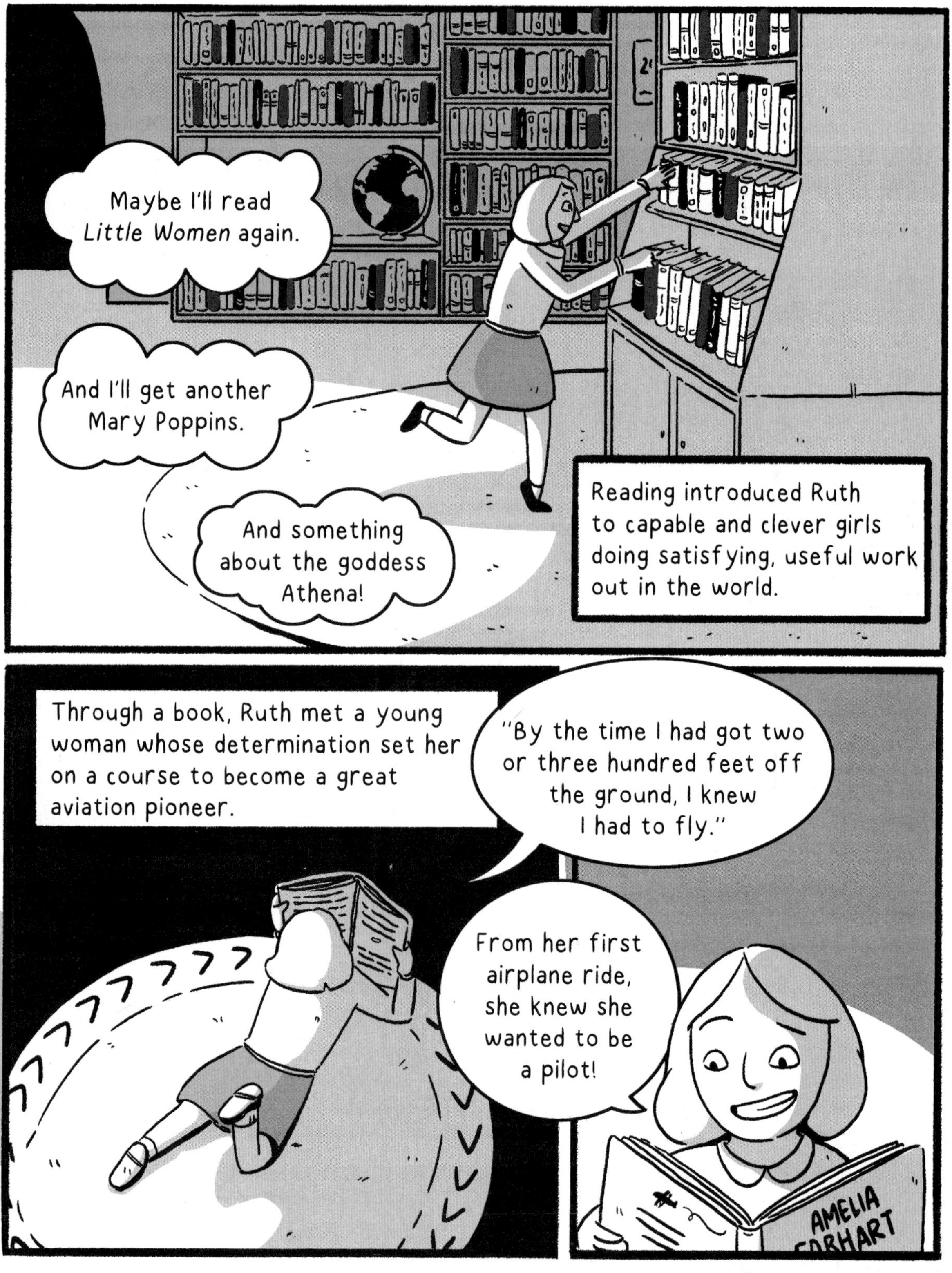
Maybe I'll read *Little Women* again.
And I'll get another Mary Poppins.
And something about the goddess Athena!
Reading introduced Ruth to capable and clever girls doing satisfying, useful work out in the world.
Through a book, Ruth met a young woman whose determination set her on a course to become a great aviation pioneer.
"By the time I had got two or three hundred feet off the ground, I knew I had to fly."
From her first airplane ride, she knew she wanted to be a pilot!

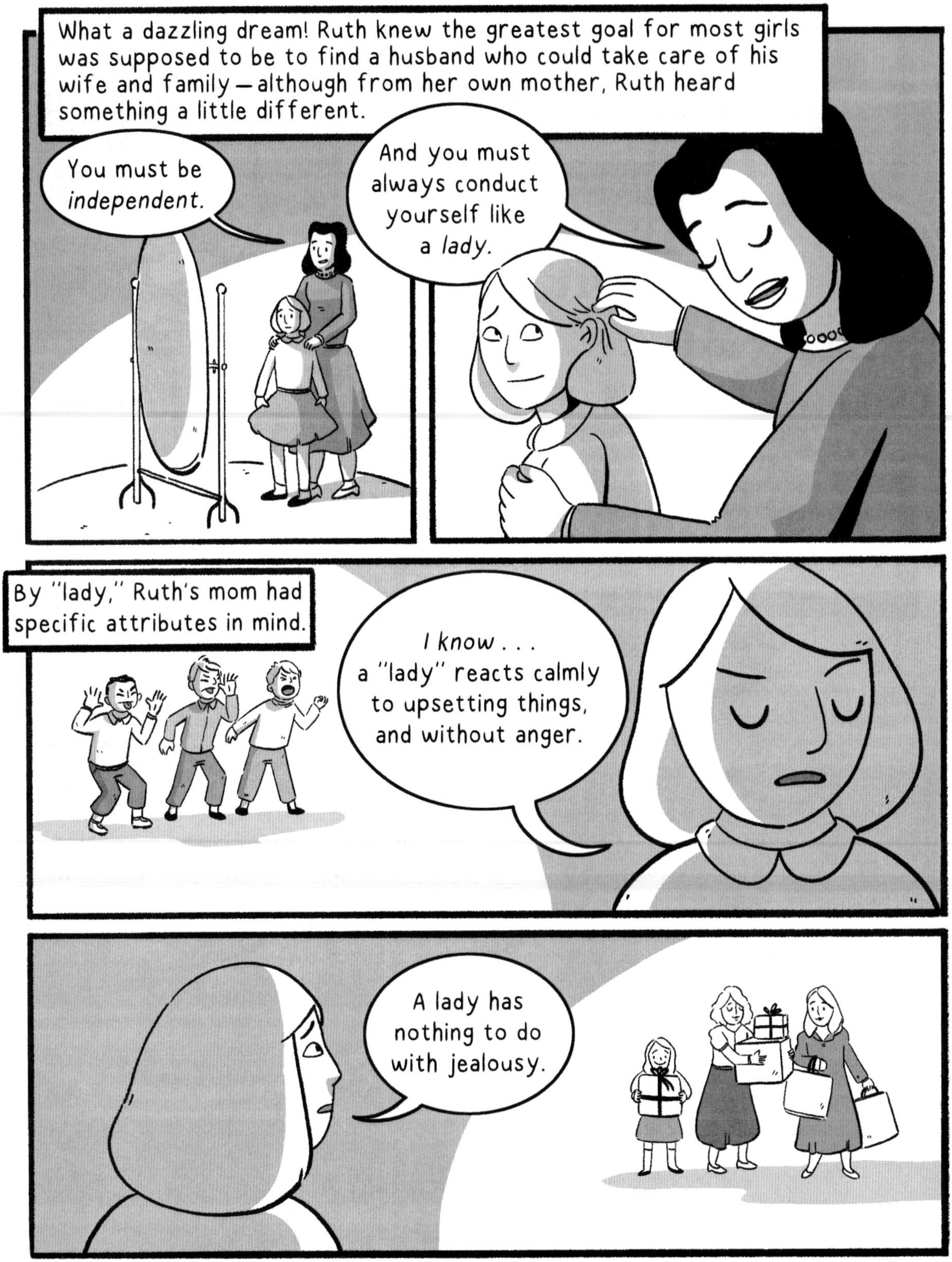
What a dazzling dream! Ruth knew the greatest goal for most girls was supposed to be to find a husband who could take care of his wife and family—although from her own mother, Ruth heard something a little different.
You must be *independent*.
And you must always conduct yourself like a *lady*.
By "lady," Ruth's mom had specific attributes in mind.
I know . . . a "lady" reacts calmly to upsetting things, and without anger.
A lady has nothing to do with jealousy.

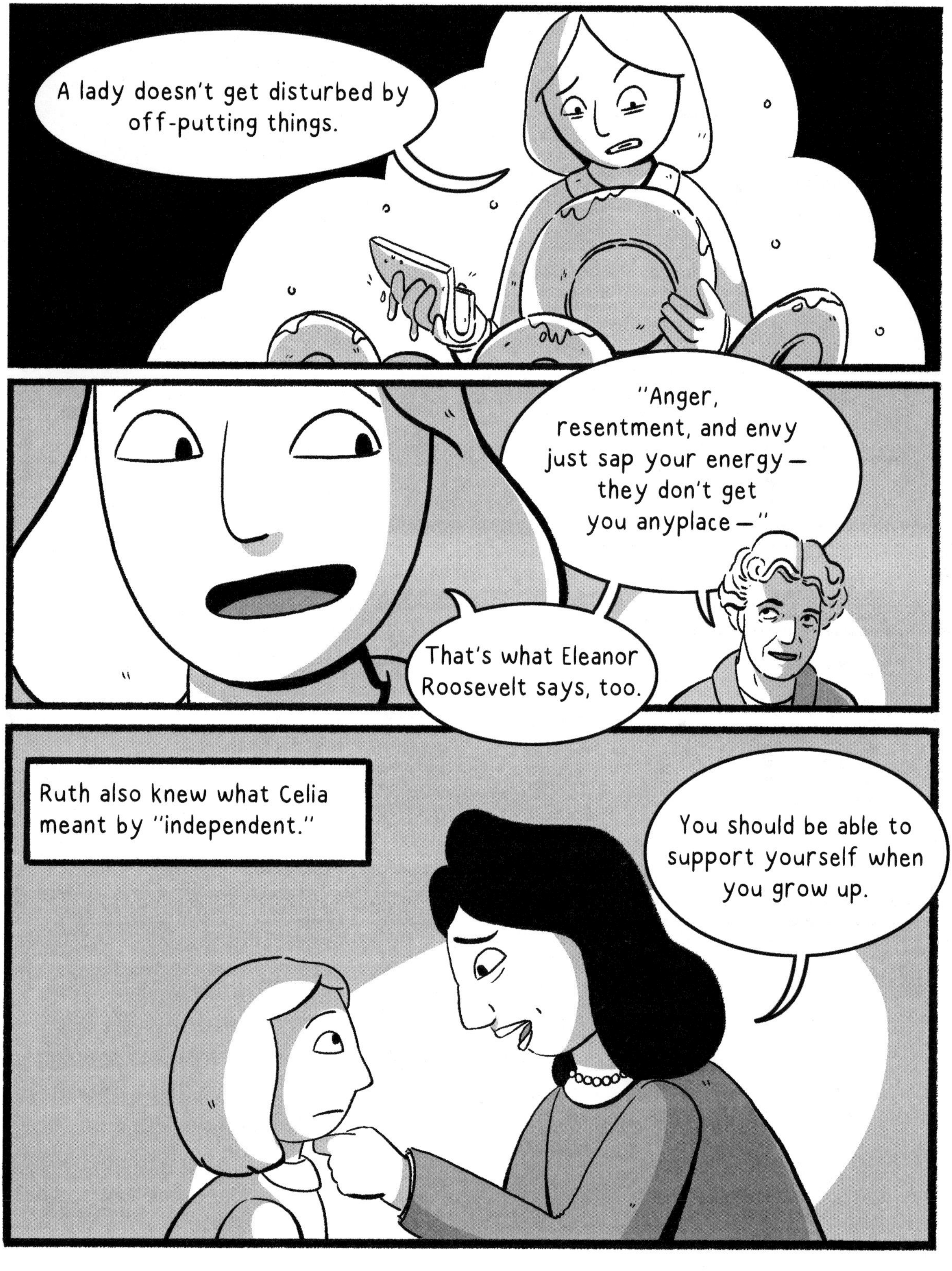
A lady doesn't get disturbed by off-putting things.
"Anger, resentment, and envy just sap your energy— they don't get you anyplace—"
That's what Eleanor Roosevelt says, too.
Ruth also knew what Celia meant by "independent."
You should be able to support yourself when you grow up.

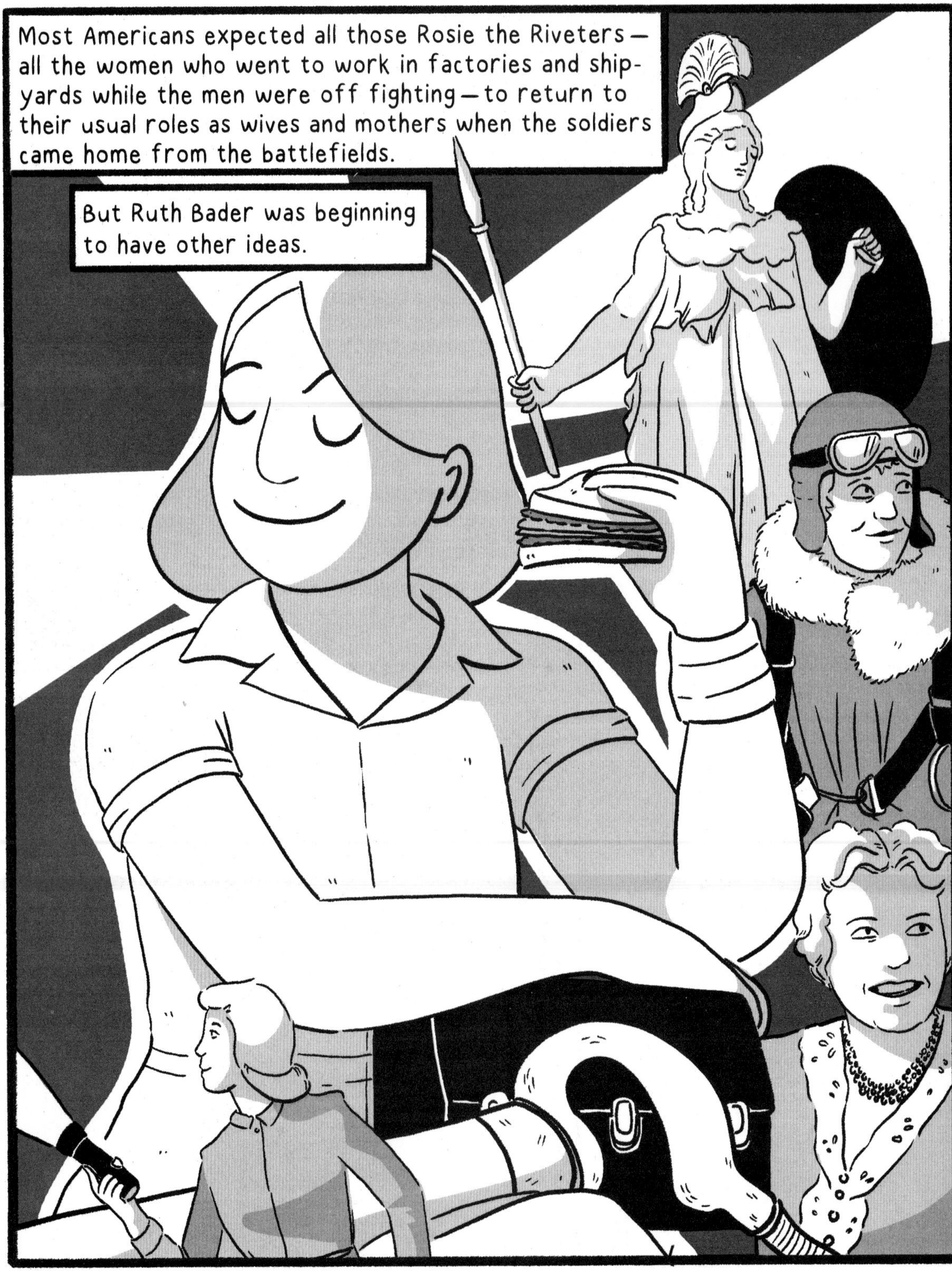
Most Americans expected all those Rosie the Riveters—all the women who went to work in factories and shipyards while the men were off fighting—to return to their usual roles as wives and mothers when the soldiers came home from the battlefields.
But Ruth Bader was beginning to have other ideas.

CHAPTER 5

If Not a Robin

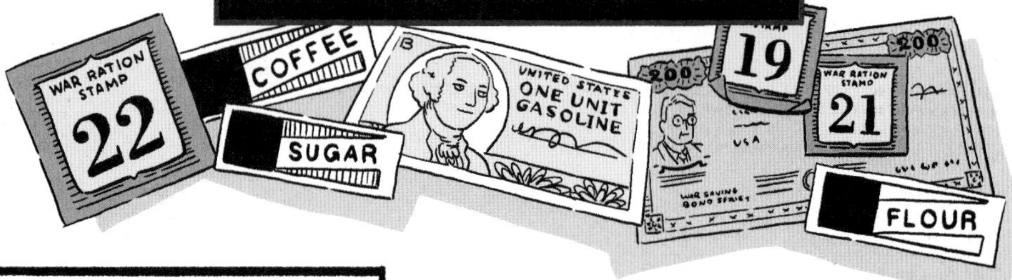
WAR RATION STAMP
22
COFFEE
SUGAR
UNITED STATES ONE UNIT GASOLINE
19
200
USA
WAR RATION STAMP
21
FLOUR

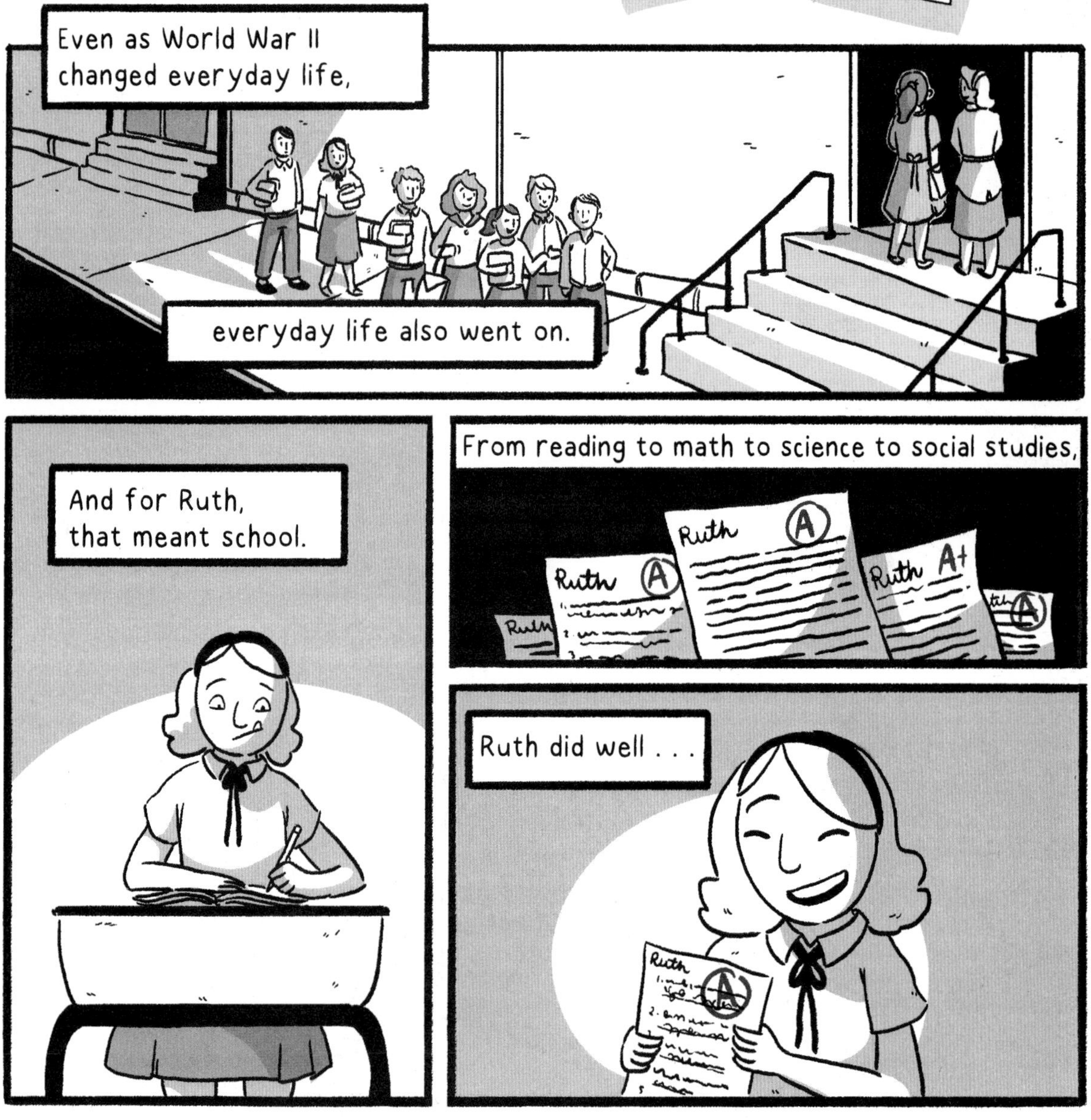
Even as World War II changed everyday life,
everyday life also went on.
And for Ruth, that meant school.
From reading to math to science to social studies,
Ruth
A
Ruth
A
Ruth
A+
Ruth did well . . .
Ruth

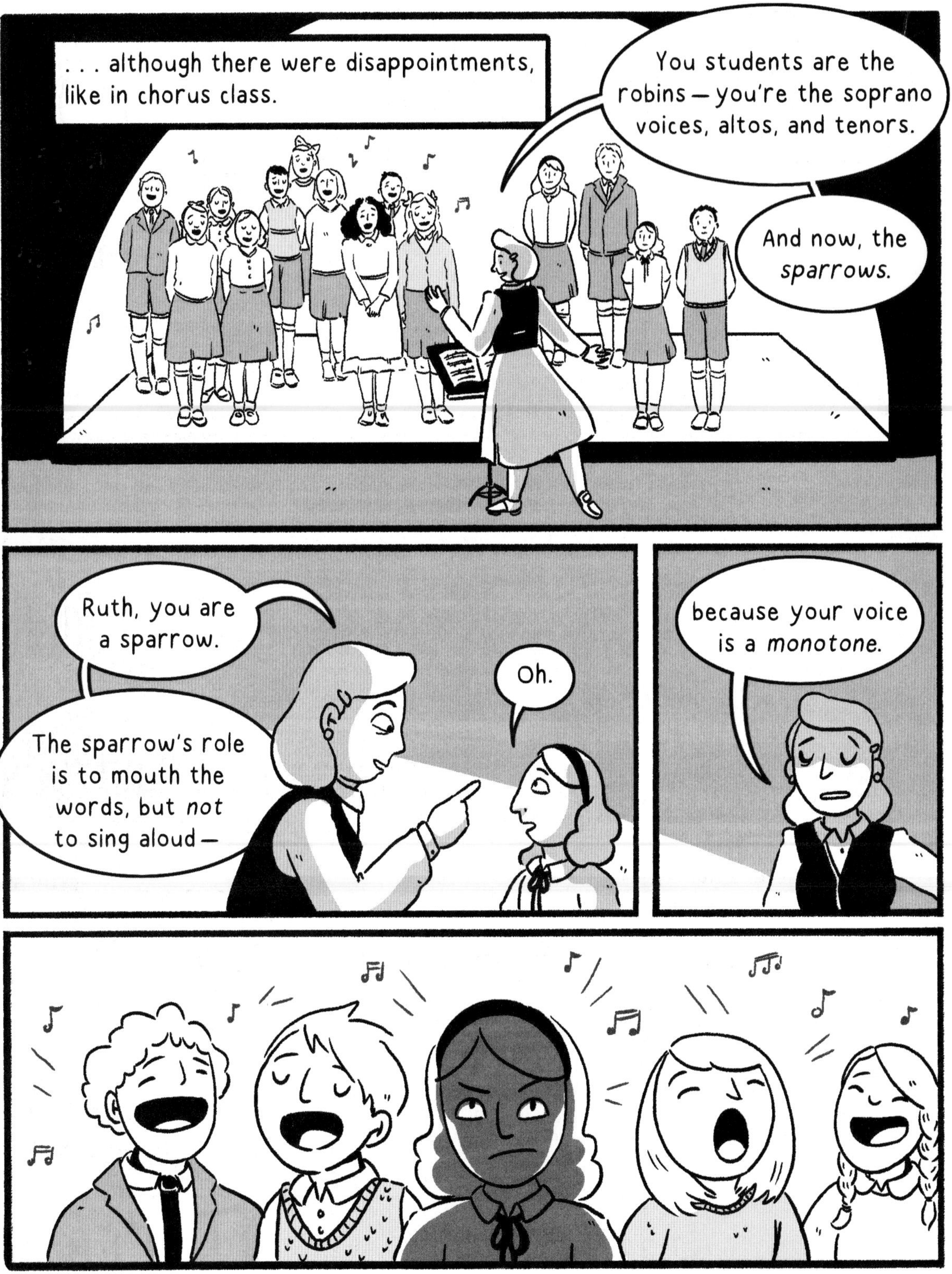
. . . although there were disappointments, like in chorus class.
You students are the robins — you're the soprano voices, altos, and tenors.
And now, the *sparrows.*
Ruth, you are a sparrow.
The sparrow's role is to mouth the words, but *not* to sing aloud —
Oh.
because your voice is a *monotone.*

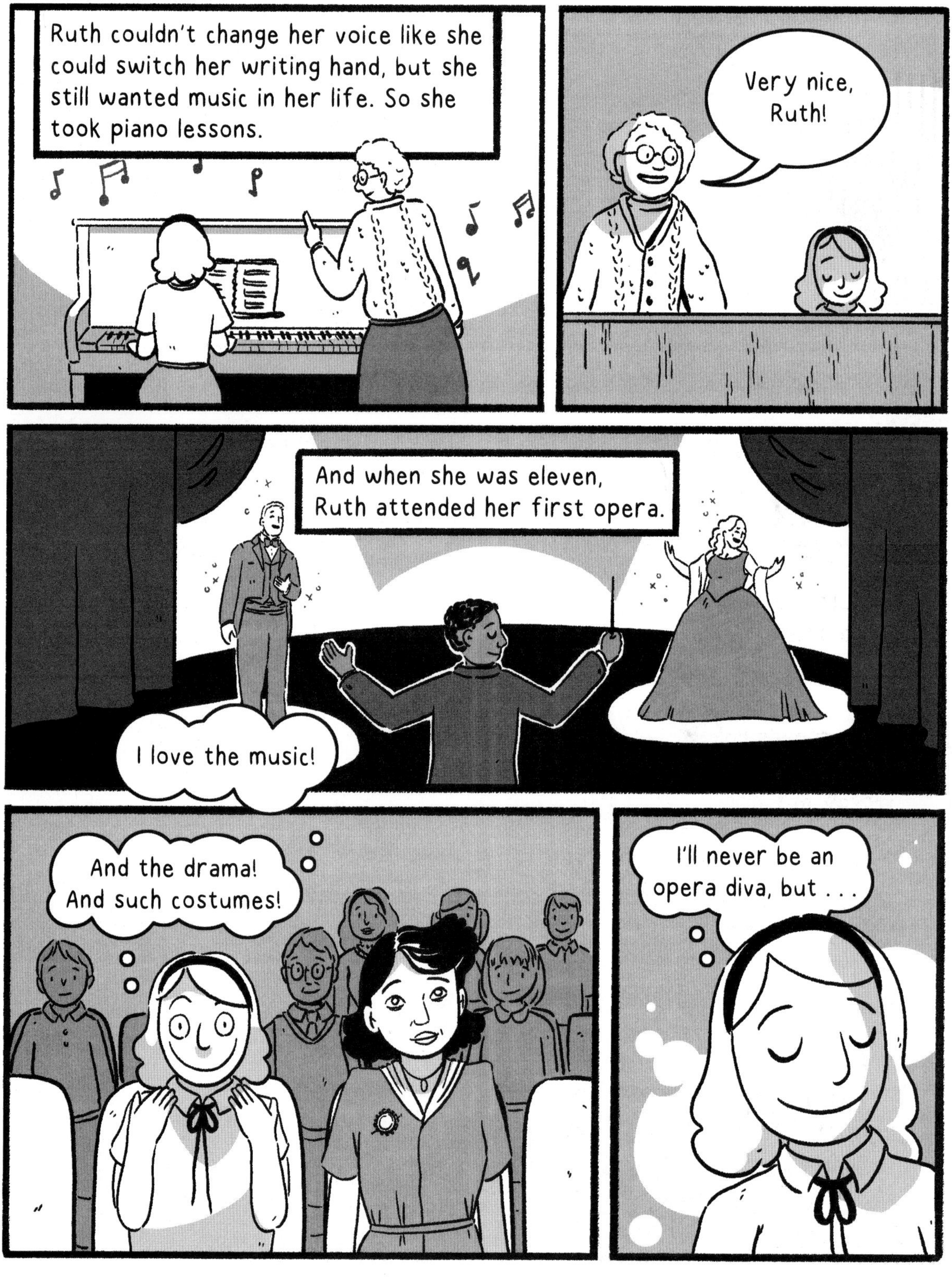
Ruth couldn't change her voice like she could switch her writing hand, but she still wanted music in her life. So she took piano lessons.
Very nice, Ruth!
And when she was eleven, Ruth attended her first opera.
I love the music!
And the drama! And such costumes!
I'll never be an opera diva, but . . .

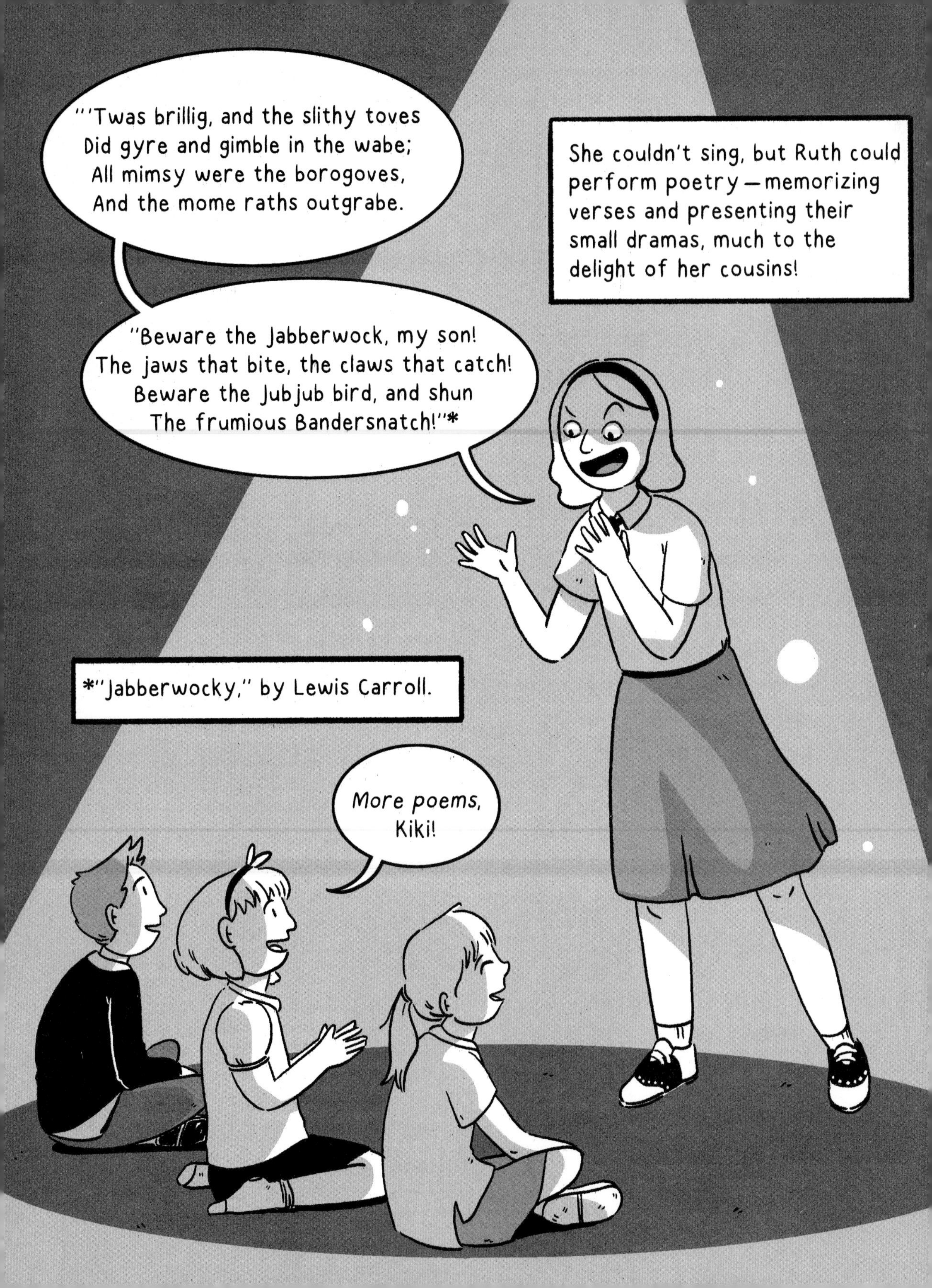
"'Twas brillig, and the slithy toves Did gyre and gimble in the wabe; All mimsy were the borogoves, And the mome raths outgrabe.
She couldn't sing, but Ruth could perform poetry—memorizing verses and presenting their small dramas, much to the delight of her cousins!
"Beware the Jabberwock, my son! The jaws that bite, the claws that catch! Beware the Jubjub bird, and shun The frumious Bandersnatch!"*
*"Jabberwocky," by Lewis Carroll.
More poems, Kiki!

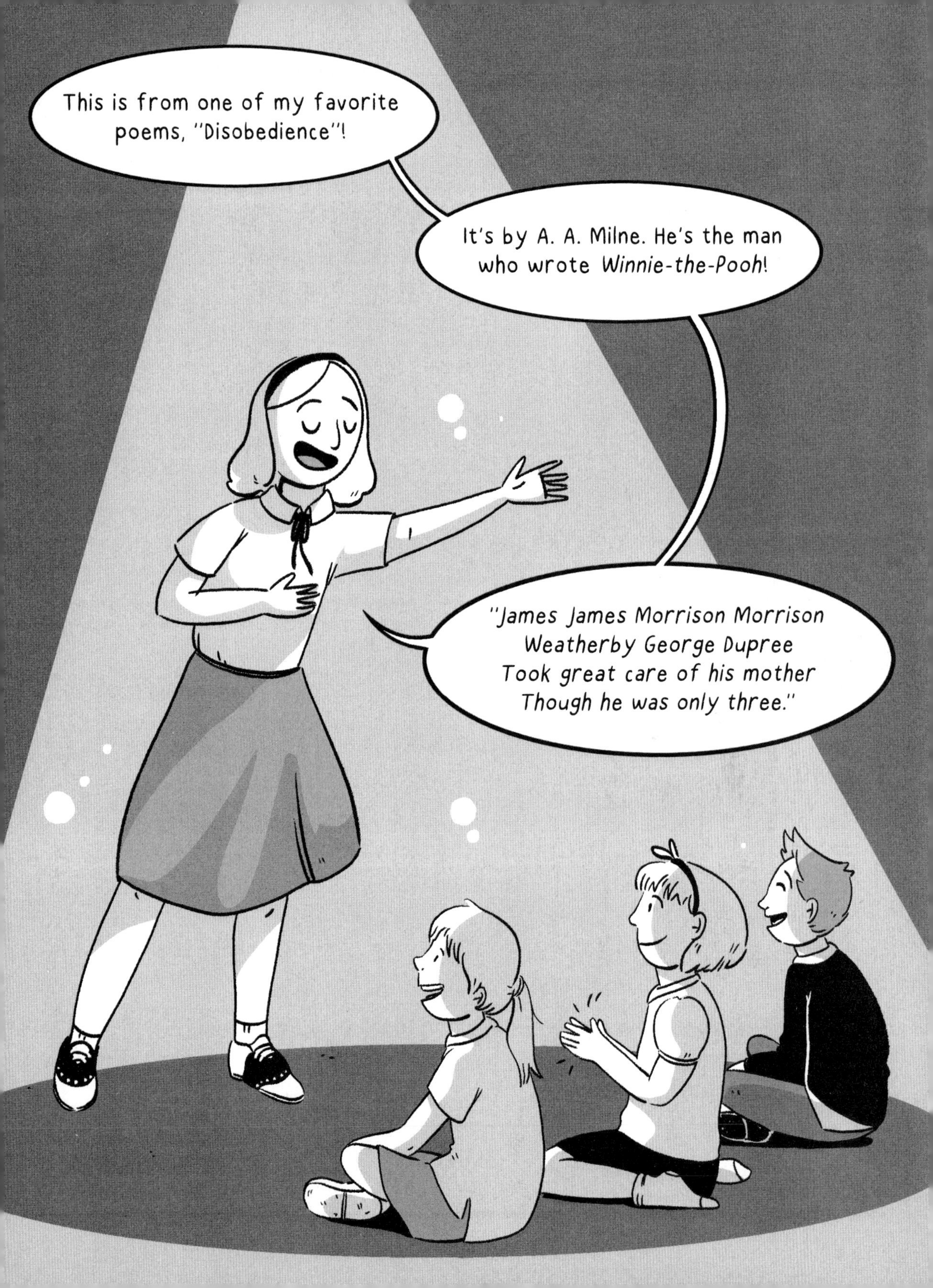

This is from one of my favorite poems, "Disobedience"!
It's by A. A. Milne. He's the man who wrote *Winnie-the-Pooh*!
"James James Morrison Morrison Weatherby George Dupree Took great care of his mother Though he was only three."

CHAPTER 6

Out of the Kitchen

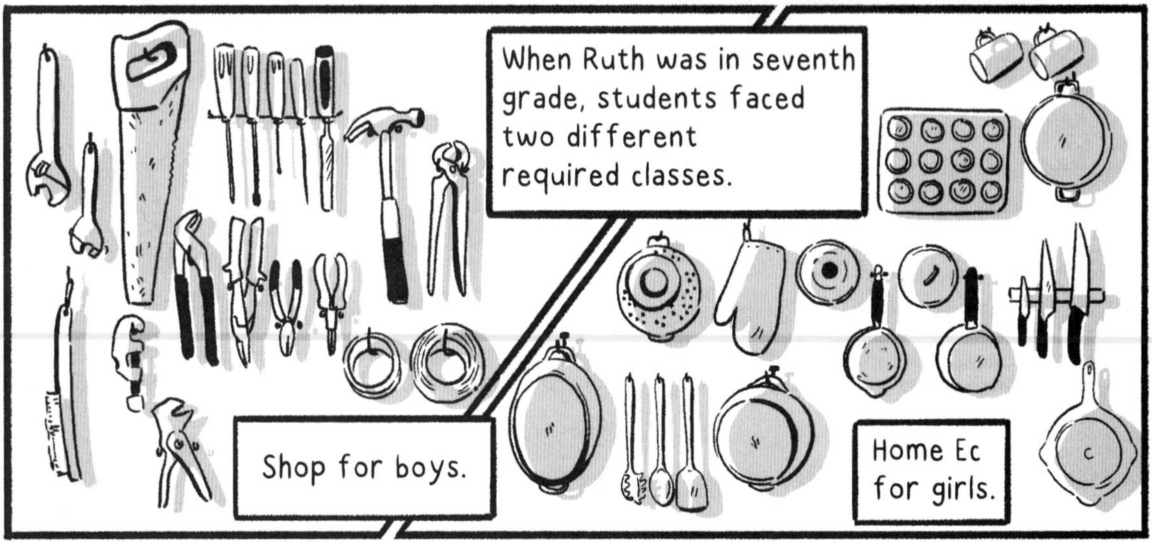
When Ruth was in seventh grade, students faced two different required classes.
Shop for boys.
Home Ec for girls.

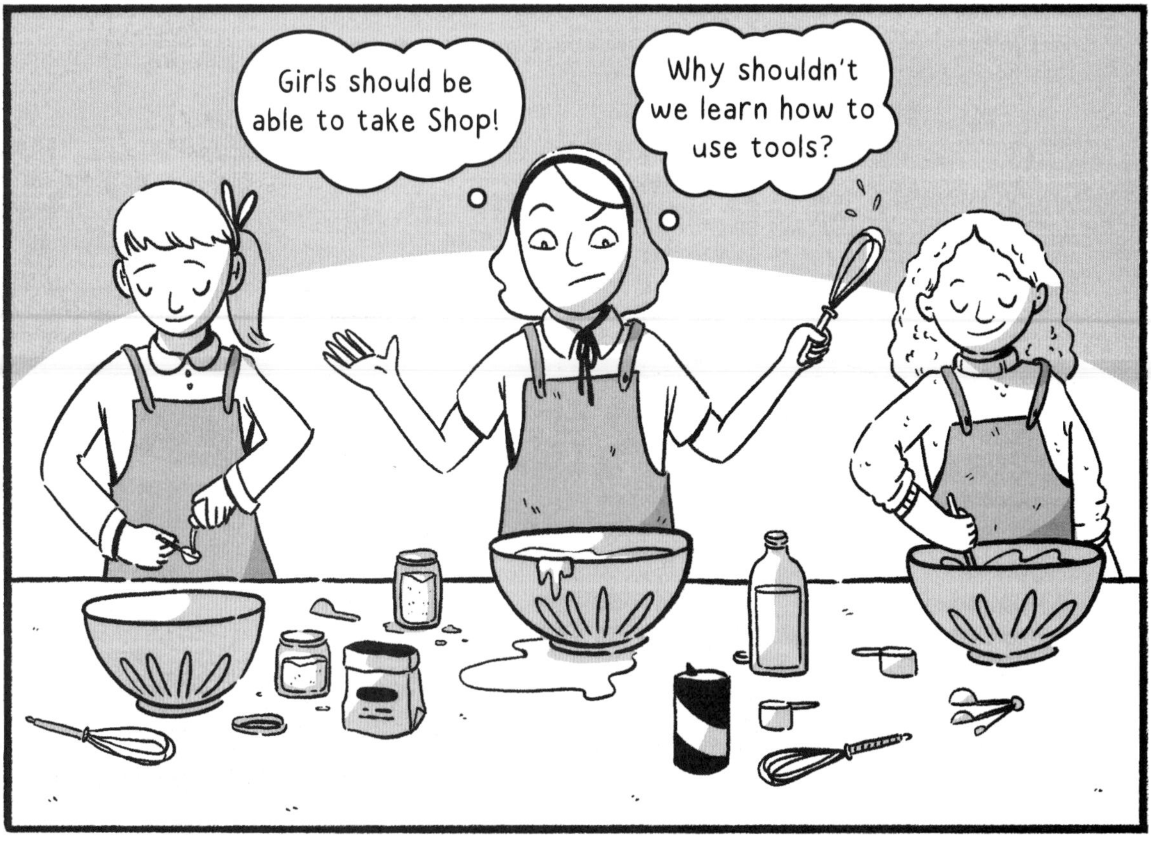
Girls should be able to take Shop!
Why shouldn't we learn how to use tools?

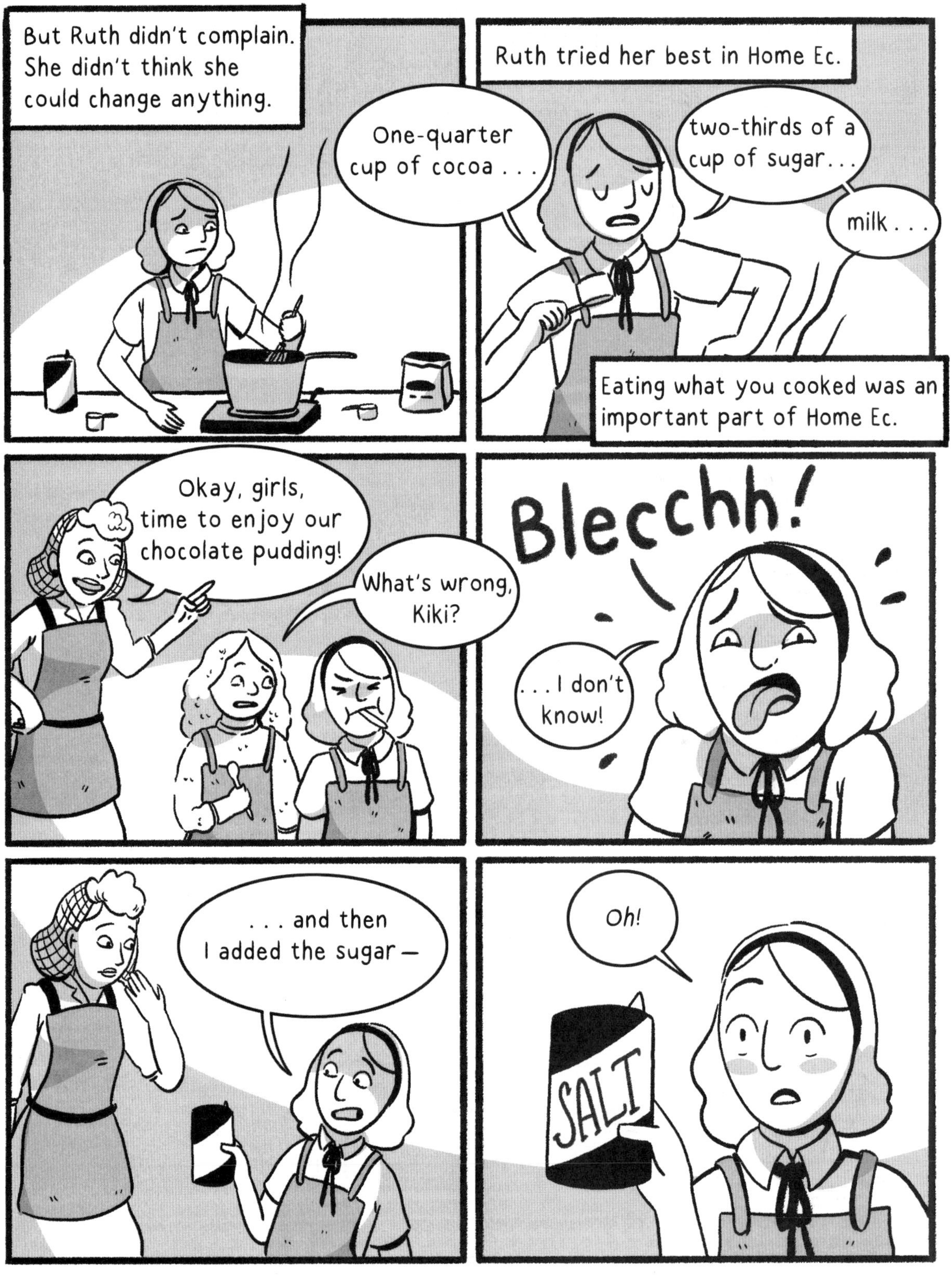

But Ruth didn't complain. She didn't think she could change anything.
Ruth tried her best in Home Ec.
One-quarter cup of cocoa . . .
two-thirds of a cup of sugar . . .
milk . . .
Eating what you cooked was an important part of Home Ec.
Okay, girls, time to enjoy our chocolate pudding!
What's wrong, Kiki?
Blecchh!
. . . I don't know!
. . . and then I added the sugar —
Oh!
SALT

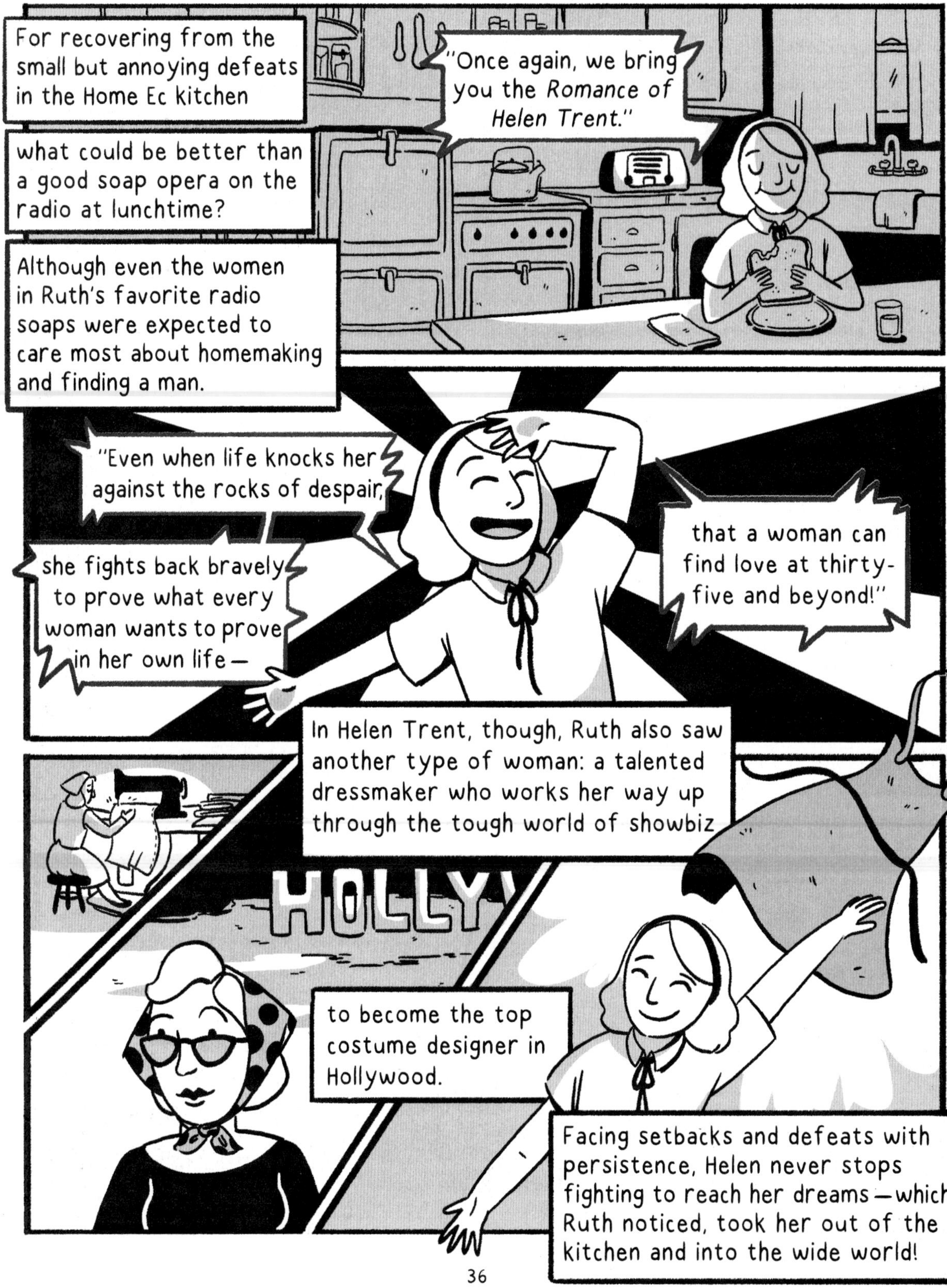
For recovering from the small but annoying defeats in the Home Ec kitchen
"Once again, we bring you the *Romance of Helen Trent.*"
what could be better than a good soap opera on the radio at lunchtime?
Although even the women in Ruth's favorite radio soaps were expected to care most about homemaking and finding a man.
"Even when life knocks her against the rocks of despair,
she fights back bravely to prove what every woman wants to prove in her own life—
that a woman can find love at thirty-five and beyond!"
In Helen Trent, though, Ruth also saw another type of woman: a talented dressmaker who works her way up through the tough world of showbiz
HOLLY
to become the top costume designer in Hollywood.
Facing setbacks and defeats with persistence, Helen never stops fighting to reach her dreams—which, Ruth noticed, took her out of the kitchen and into the wide world!

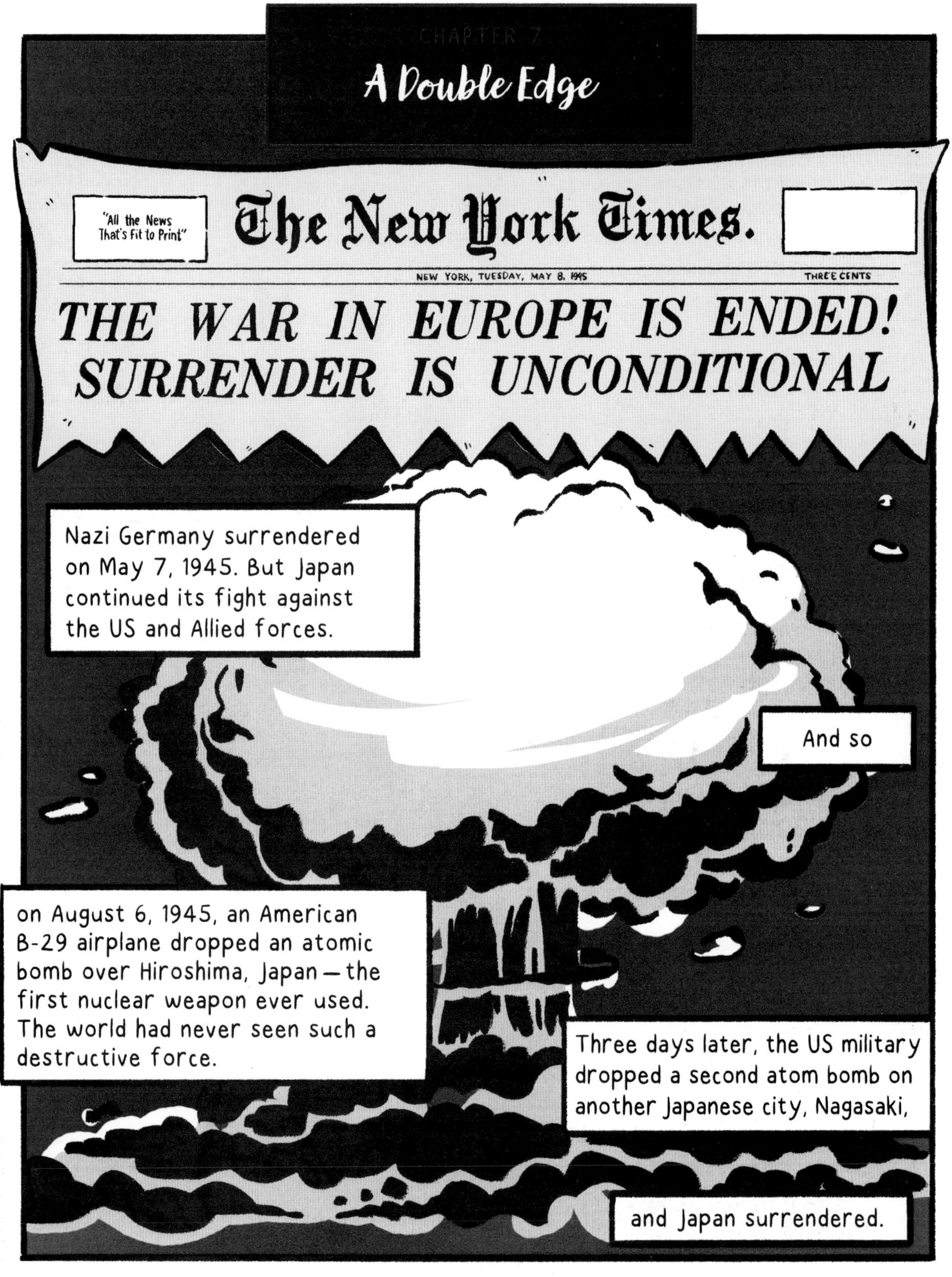
CHAPTER 7
A Double Edge
"All the News That's Fit to Print"
The New York Times.
NEW YORK, TUESDAY, MAY 8, 1945
THREE CENTS
THE WAR IN EUROPE IS ENDED! SURRENDER IS UNCONDITIONAL
Nazi Germany surrendered on May 7, 1945. But Japan continued its fight against the US and Allied forces.
And so
on August 6, 1945, an American B-29 airplane dropped an atomic bomb over Hiroshima, Japan—the first nuclear weapon ever used. The world had never seen such a destructive force.
Three days later, the US military dropped a second atom bomb on another Japanese city, Nagasaki,
and Japan surrendered.

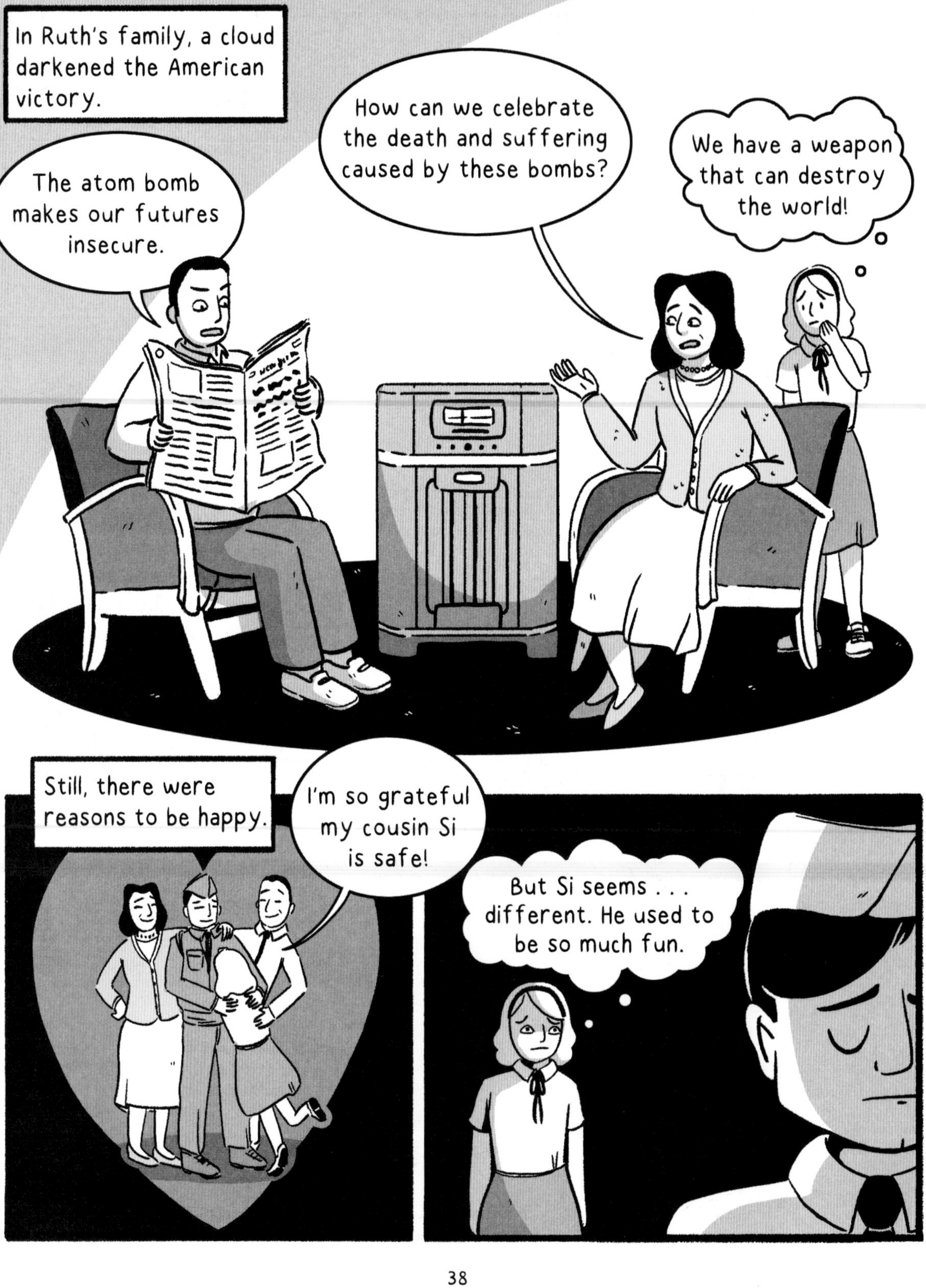
In Ruth's family, a cloud darkened the American victory.
The atom bomb makes our futures insecure.
How can we celebrate the death and suffering caused by these bombs?
We have a weapon that can destroy the world!
Still, there were reasons to be happy.
I'm so grateful my cousin Si is safe!
But Si seems . . . different. He used to be so much fun.

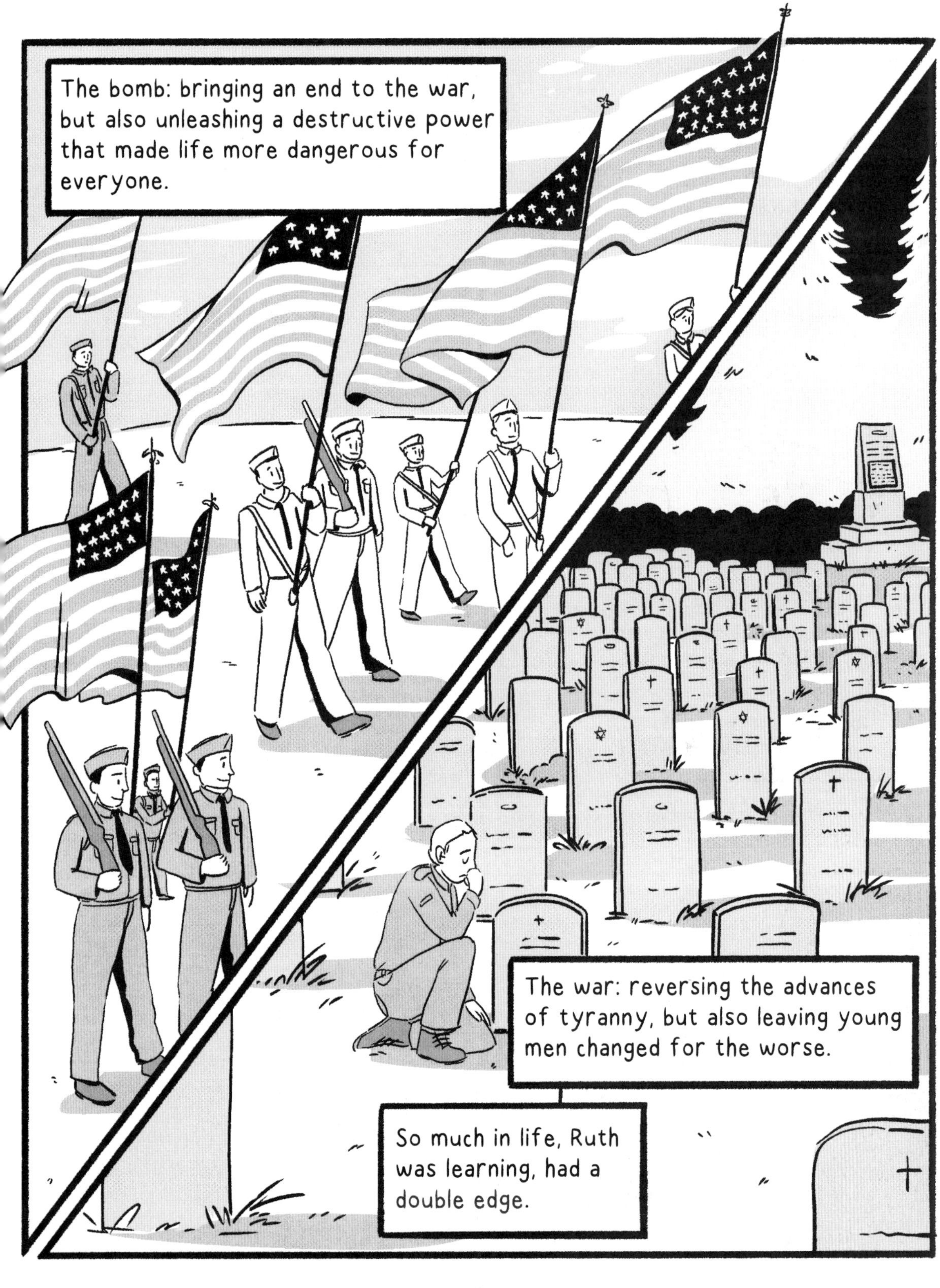
The bomb: bringing an end to the war, but also unleashing a destructive power that made life more dangerous for everyone.
The war: reversing the advances of tyranny, but also leaving young men changed for the worse.
So much in life, Ruth was learning, had a double edge.

CHAPTER 8

That Painful Trouble

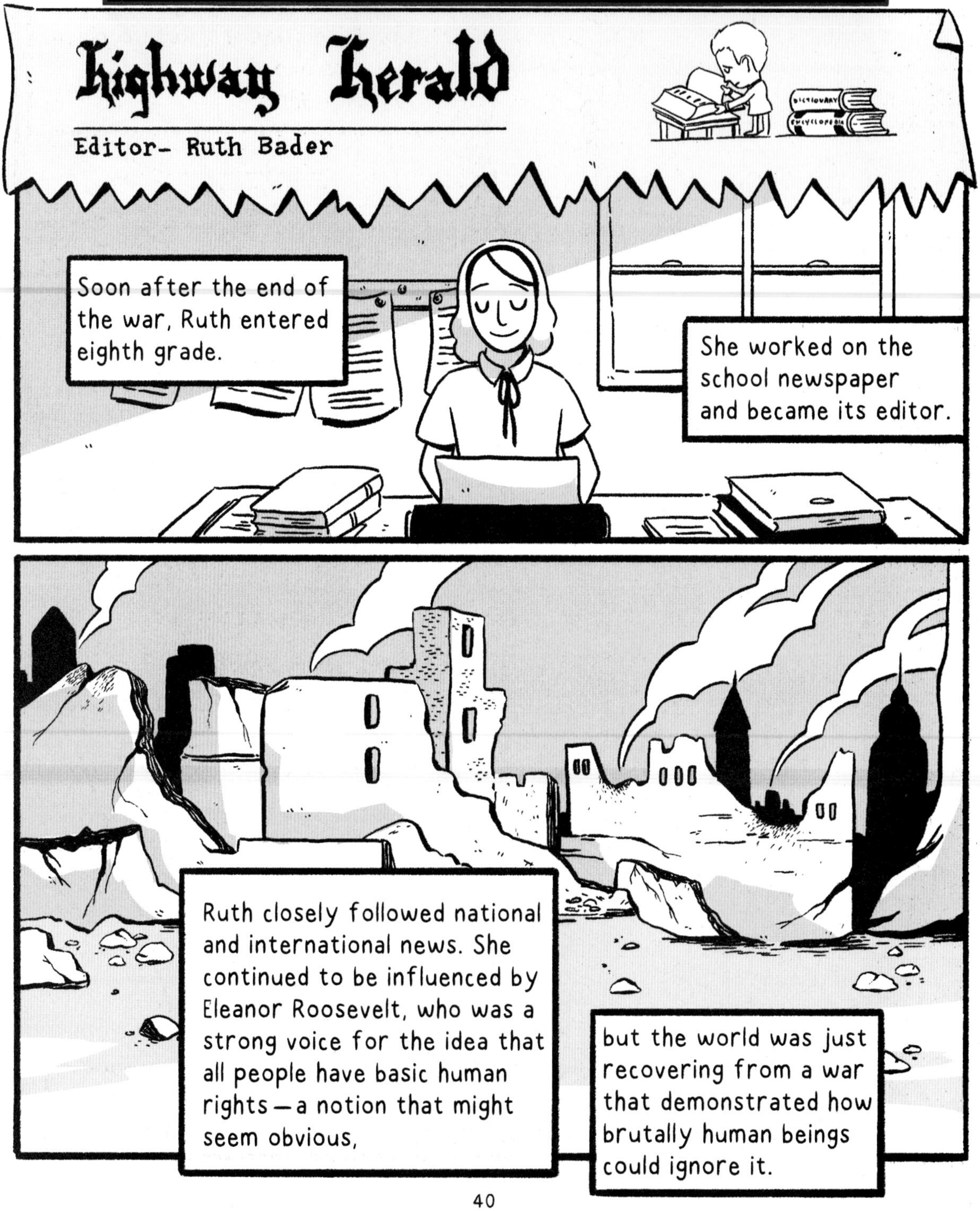
Highway Herald
Editor- Ruth Bader
Soon after the end of the war, Ruth entered eighth grade.
She worked on the school newspaper and became its editor.
Ruth closely followed national and international news. She continued to be influenced by Eleanor Roosevelt, who was a strong voice for the idea that all people have basic human rights—a notion that might seem obvious,
but the world was just recovering from a war that demonstrated how brutally human beings could ignore it.

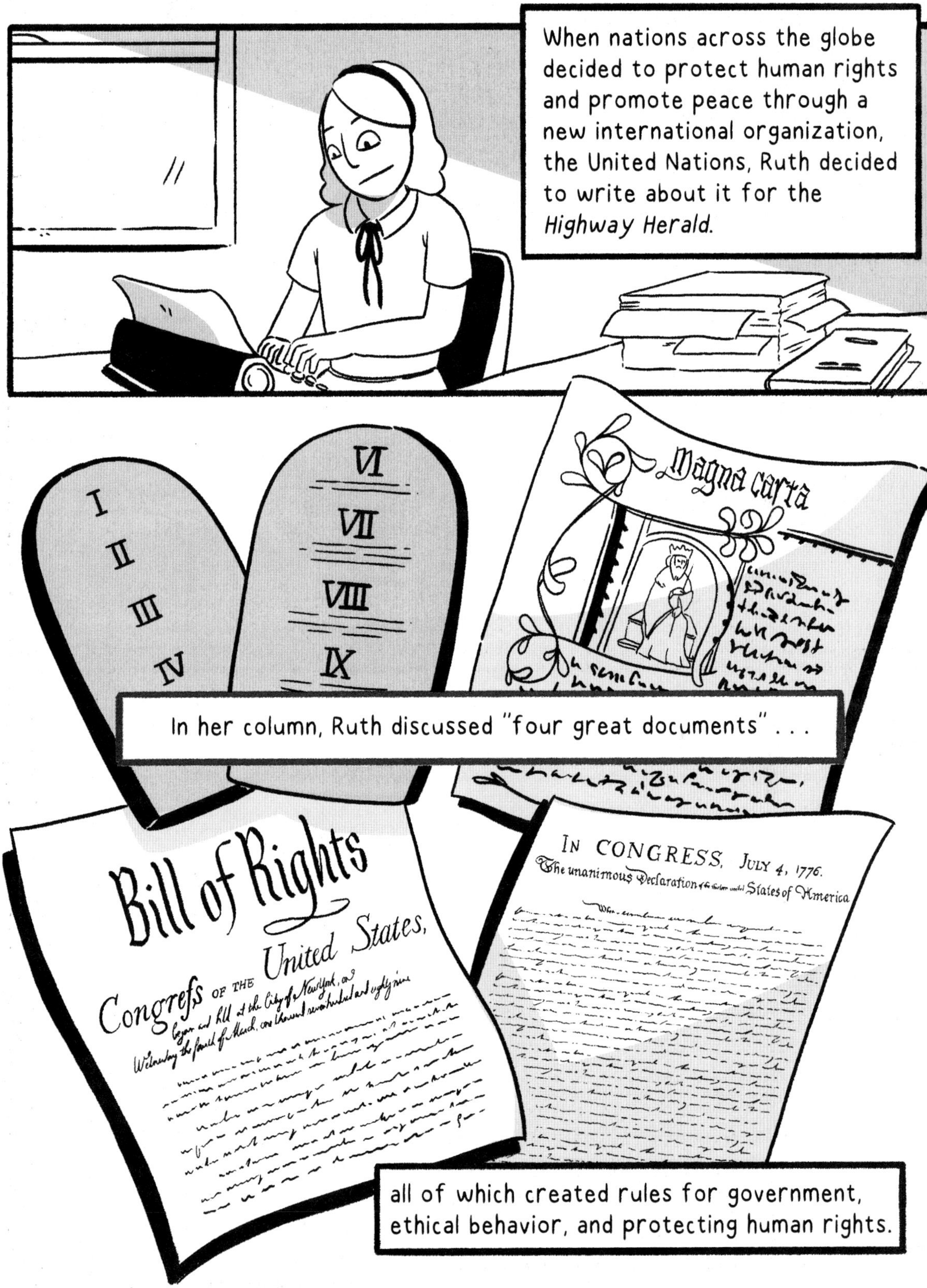
When nations across the globe decided to protect human rights and promote peace through a new international organization, the United Nations, Ruth decided to write about it for the *Highway Herald*.
I
II
III
IV
VI
VII
VIII
IX
Magna carta
In her column, Ruth discussed "four great documents" . . .
Bill of Rights
Congrefs OF THE United States,
IN CONGRESS, JULY 4, 1776.
The unanimous Declaration States of America
all of which created rules for government, ethical behavior, and protecting human rights.

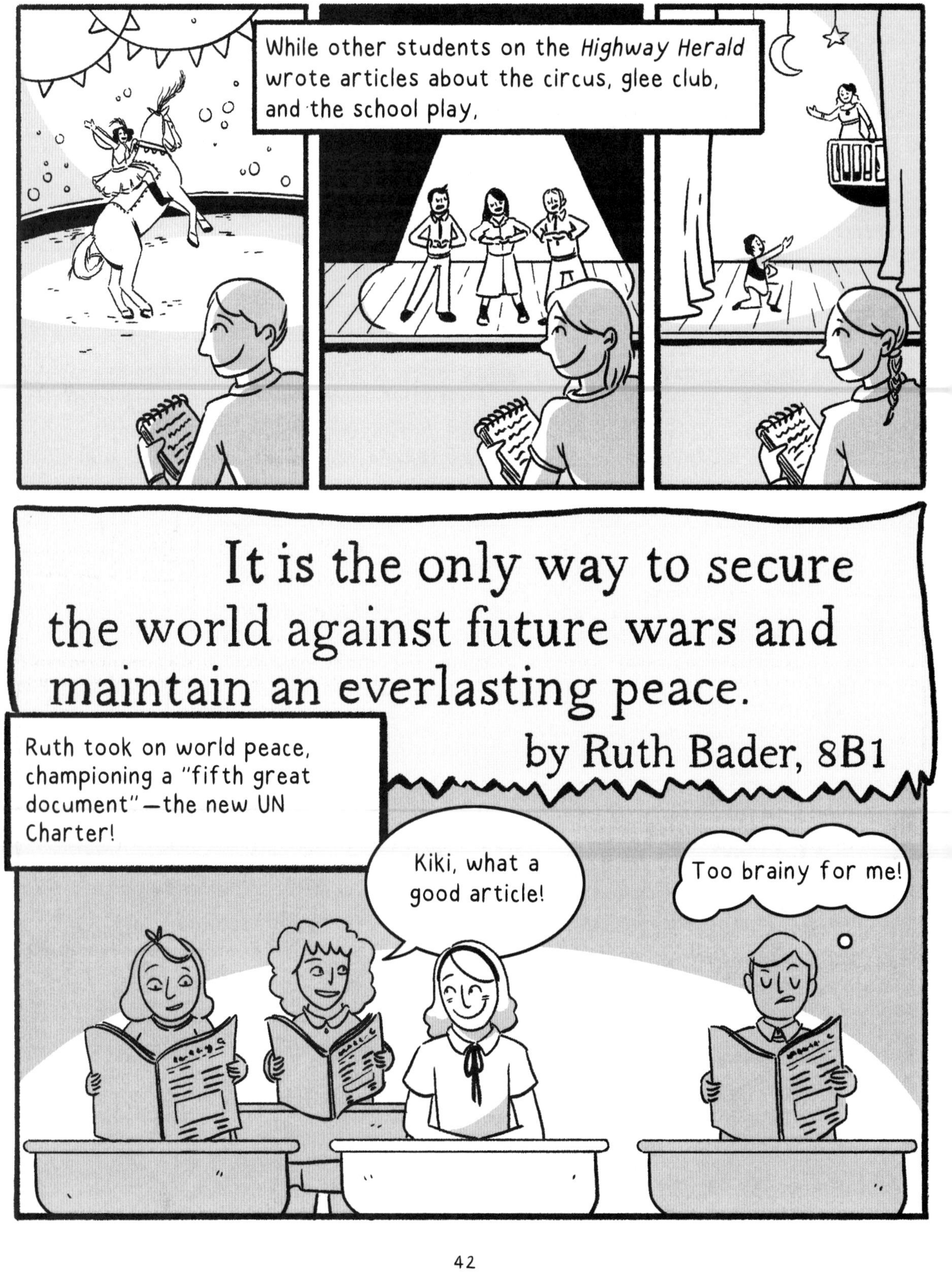
While other students on the *Highway Herald* wrote articles about the circus, glee club, and the school play,
It is the only way to secure the world against future wars and maintain an everlasting peace.
by Ruth Bader, 8B1
Ruth took on world peace, championing a "fifth great document"—the new UN Charter!
Kiki, what a good article!
Too brainy for me!

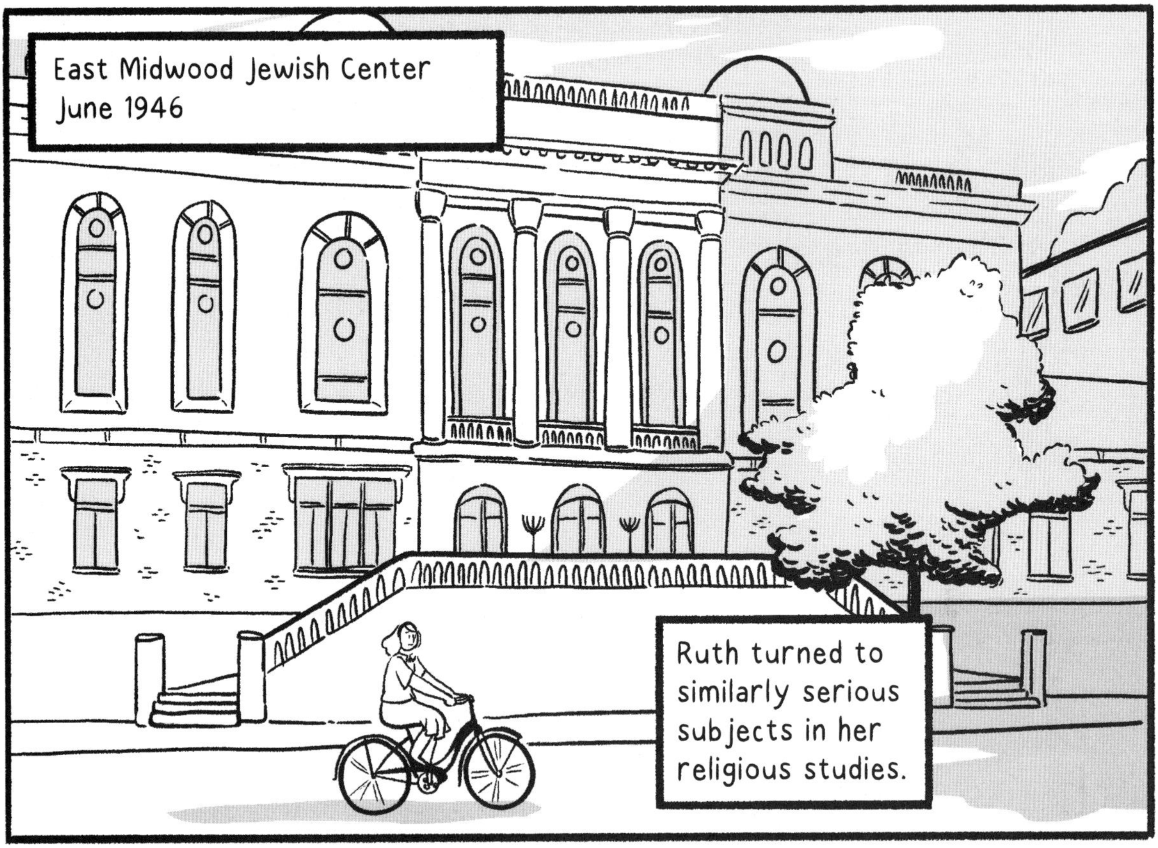
East Midwood Jewish Center
June 1946
Ruth turned to similarly serious subjects in her religious studies.

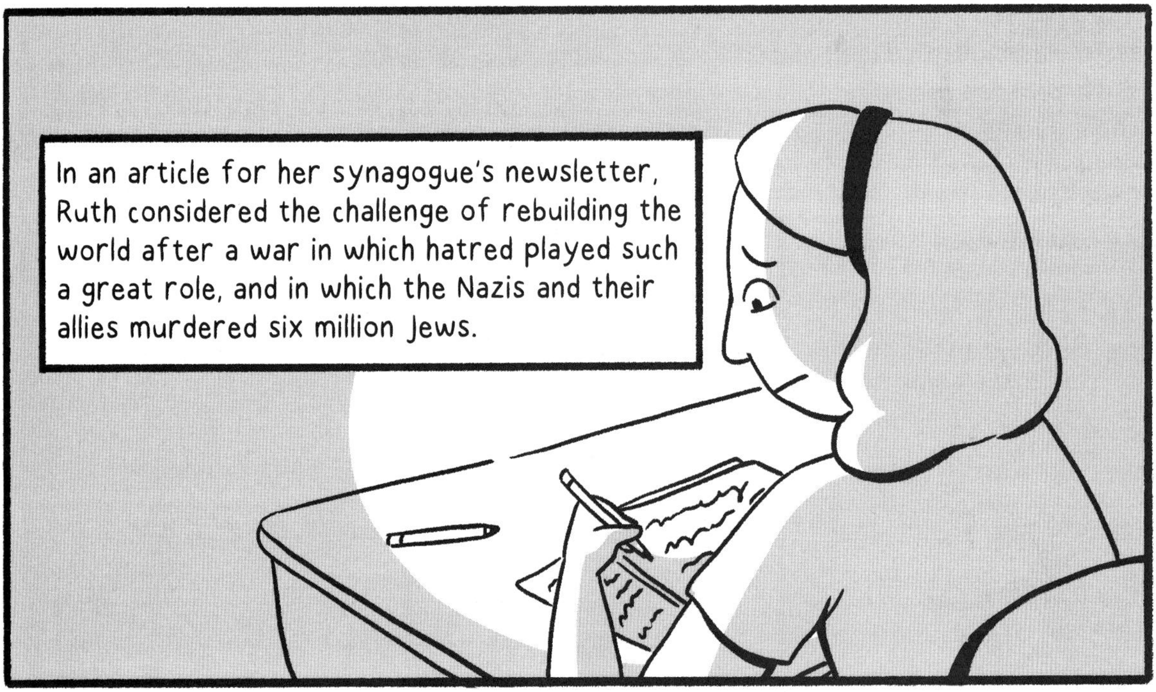
In an article for her synagogue's newsletter, Ruth considered the challenge of rebuilding the world after a war in which hatred played such a great role, and in which the Nazis and their allies murdered six million Jews.

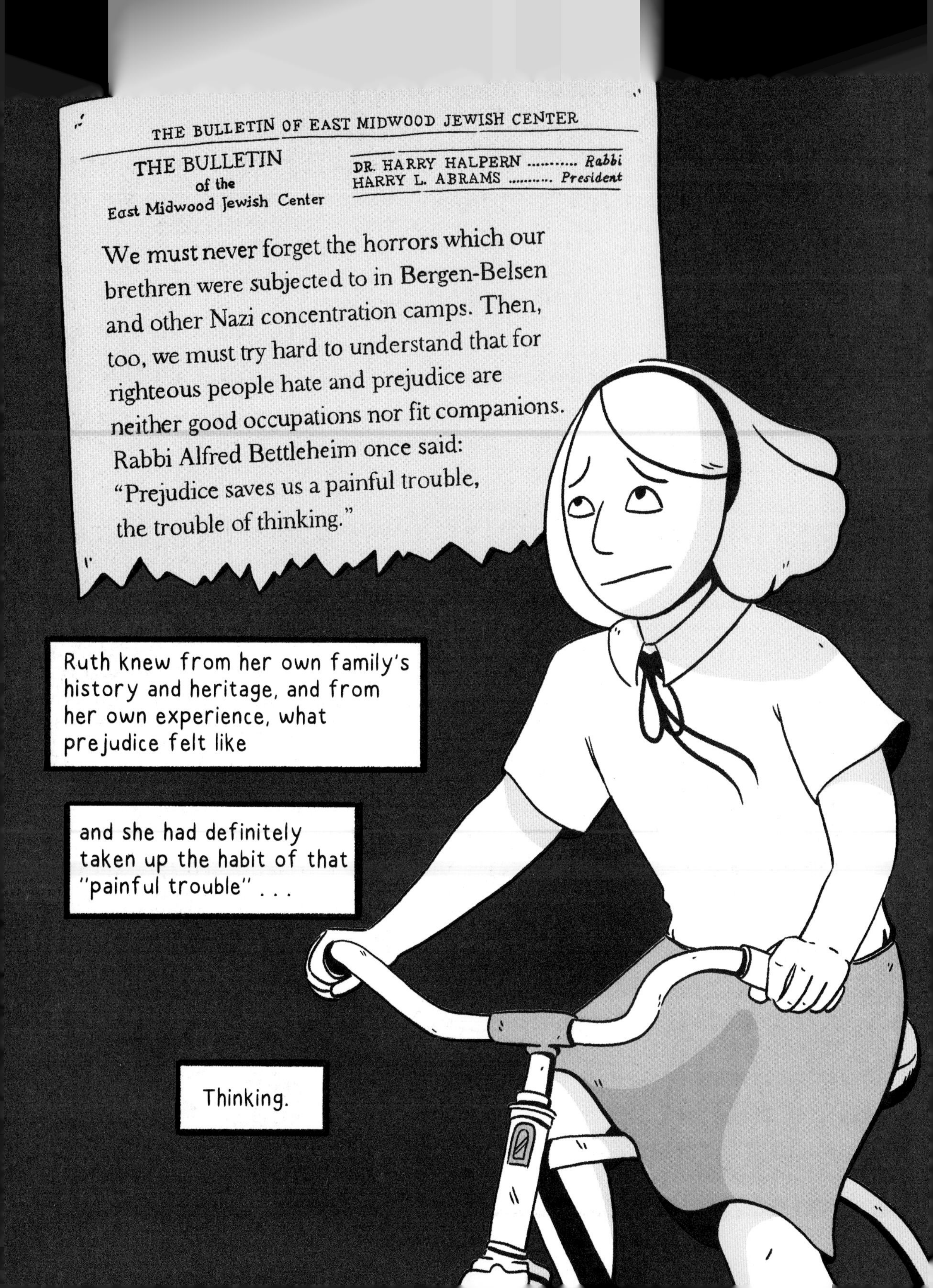
THE BULLETIN OF EAST MIDWOOD JEWISH CENTER
THE BULLETIN of the East Midwood Jewish Center
DR. HARRY HALPERN .... Rabbi
HARRY L. ABRAMS .... President
We must never forget the horrors which our brethren were subjected to in Bergen-Belsen and other Nazi concentration camps. Then, too, we must try hard to understand that for righteous people hate and prejudice are neither good occupations nor fit companions. Rabbi Alfred Bettleheim once said: "Prejudice saves us a painful trouble, the trouble of thinking."
Ruth knew from her own family's history and heritage, and from her own experience, what prejudice felt like
and she had definitely taken up the habit of that "painful trouble" . . .
Thinking.

CHAPTER 9

And Then

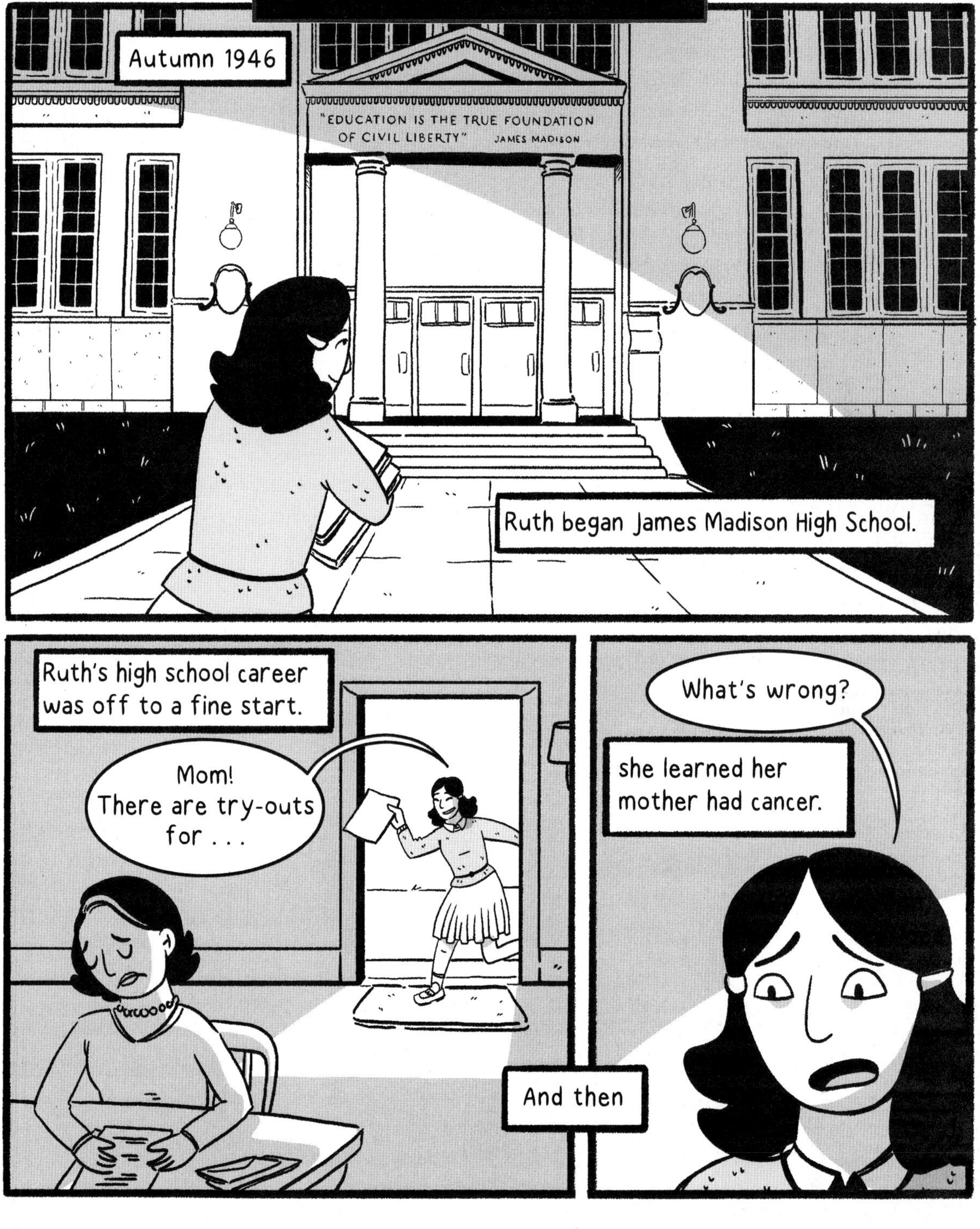
Autumn 1946
"EDUCATION IS THE TRUE FOUNDATION OF CIVIL LIBERTY" JAMES MADISON
Ruth began James Madison High School.
Ruth's high school career was off to a fine start.
Mom! There are try-outs for . . .
And then
she learned her mother had cancer.
What's wrong?

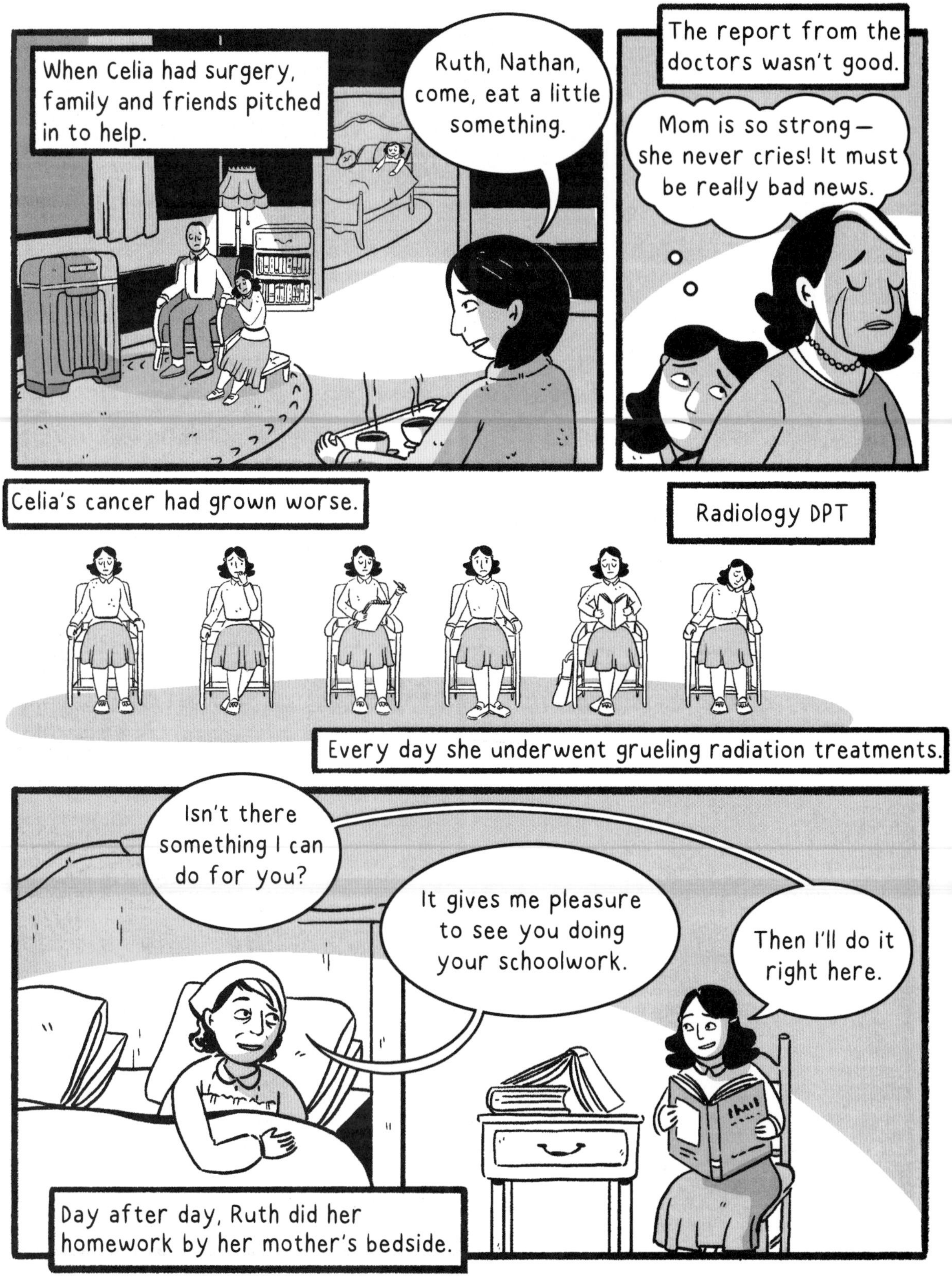
When Celia had surgery, family and friends pitched in to help.
Ruth, Nathan, come, eat a little something.
The report from the doctors wasn't good.
Mom is so strong— she never cries! It must be really bad news.
Celia's cancer had grown worse.
Radiology DPT
Every day she underwent grueling radiation treatments.
Isn't there something I can do for you?
It gives me pleasure to see you doing your schoolwork.
Then I'll do it right here.
Day after day, Ruth did her homework by her mother's bedside.

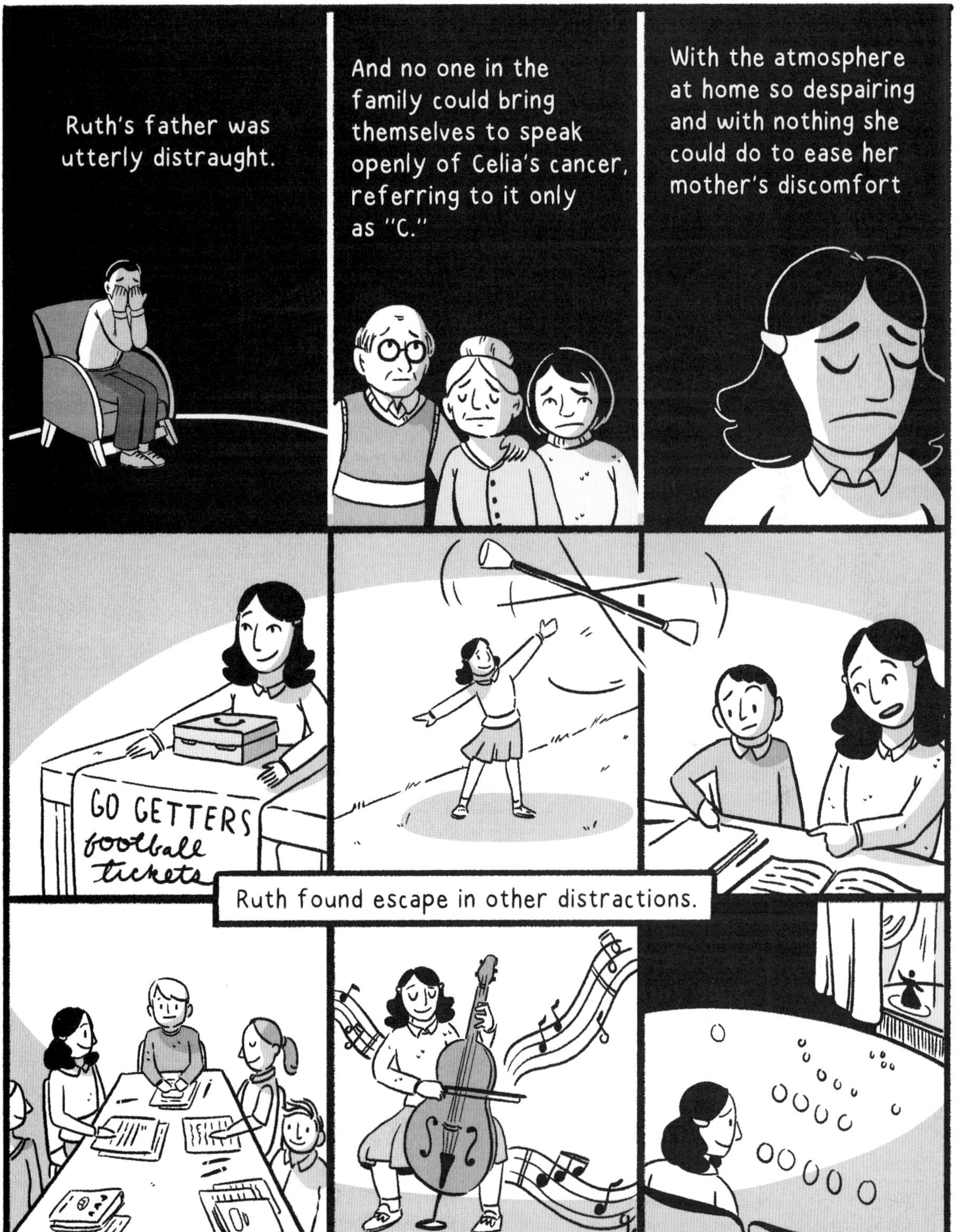
Ruth's father was utterly distraught.
And no one in the family could bring themselves to speak openly of Celia's cancer, referring to it only as "C."
With the atmosphere at home so despairing and with nothing she could do to ease her mother's discomfort
GO GETTERS
football tickets
Ruth found escape in other distractions.

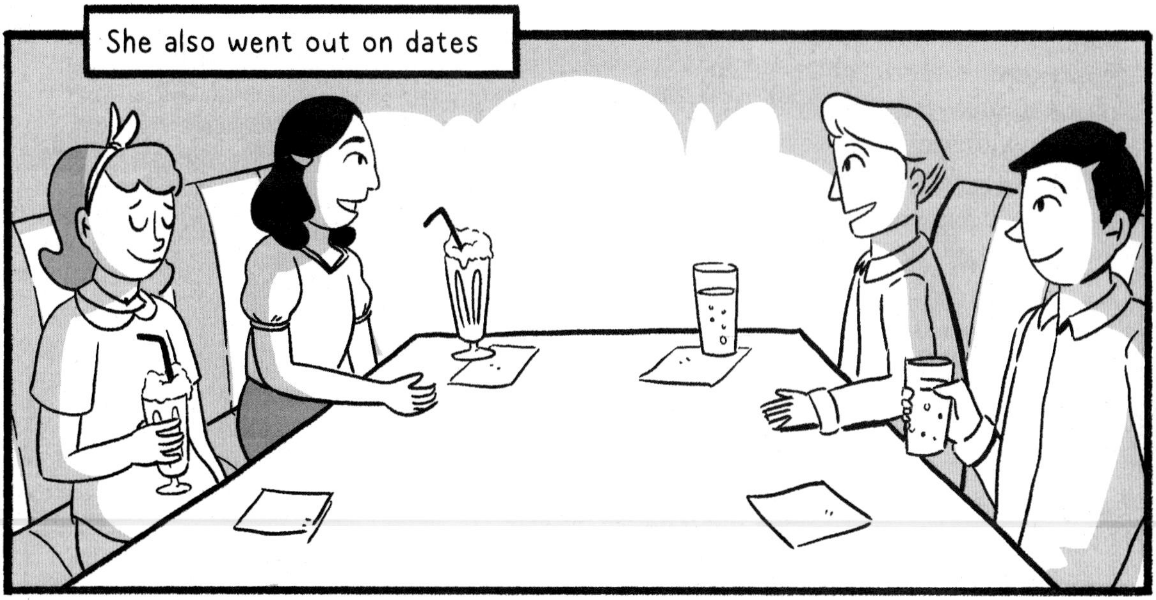
She also went out on dates

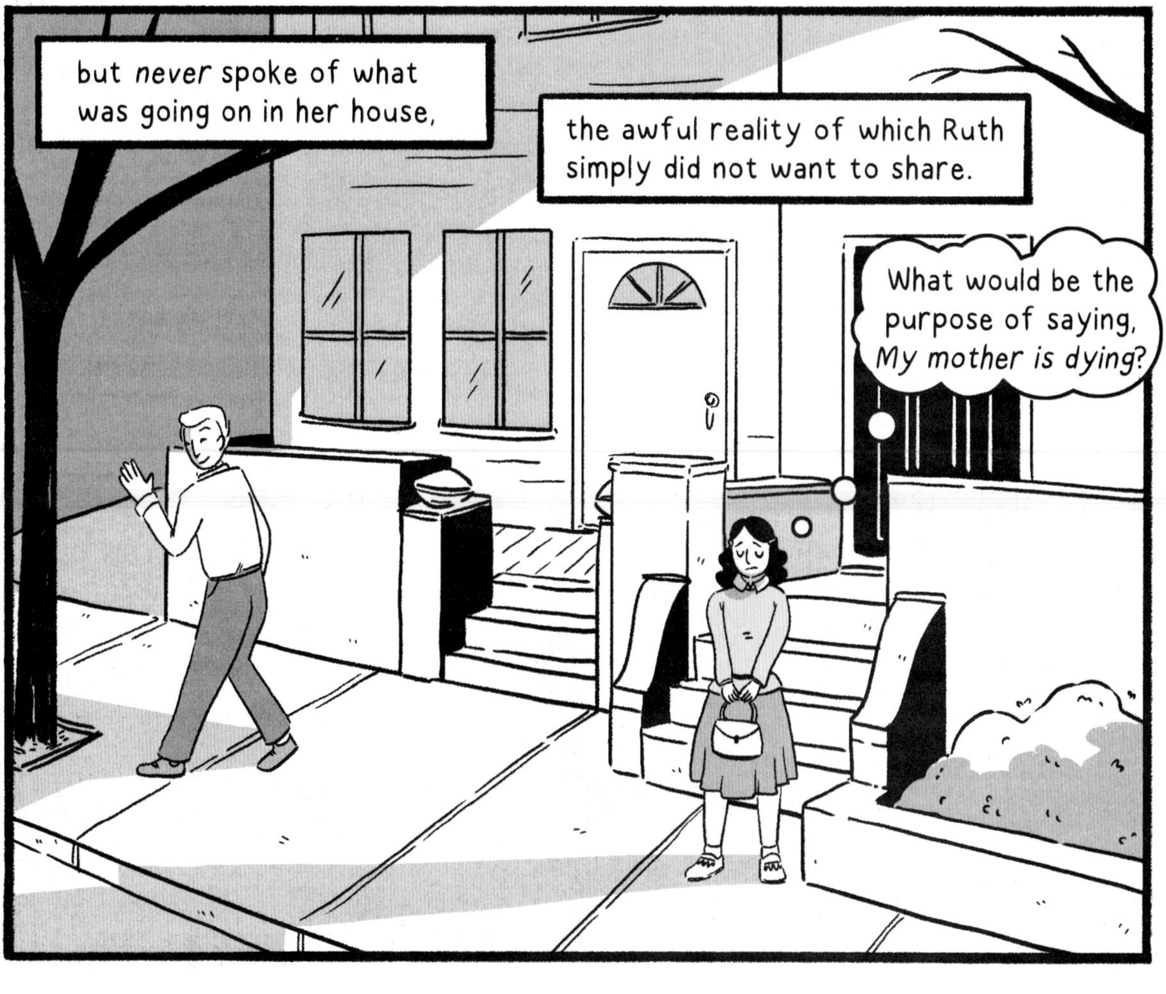
but *never* spoke of what was going on in her house,
the awful reality of which Ruth simply did not want to share.
What would be the purpose of saying, *My mother is dying*?

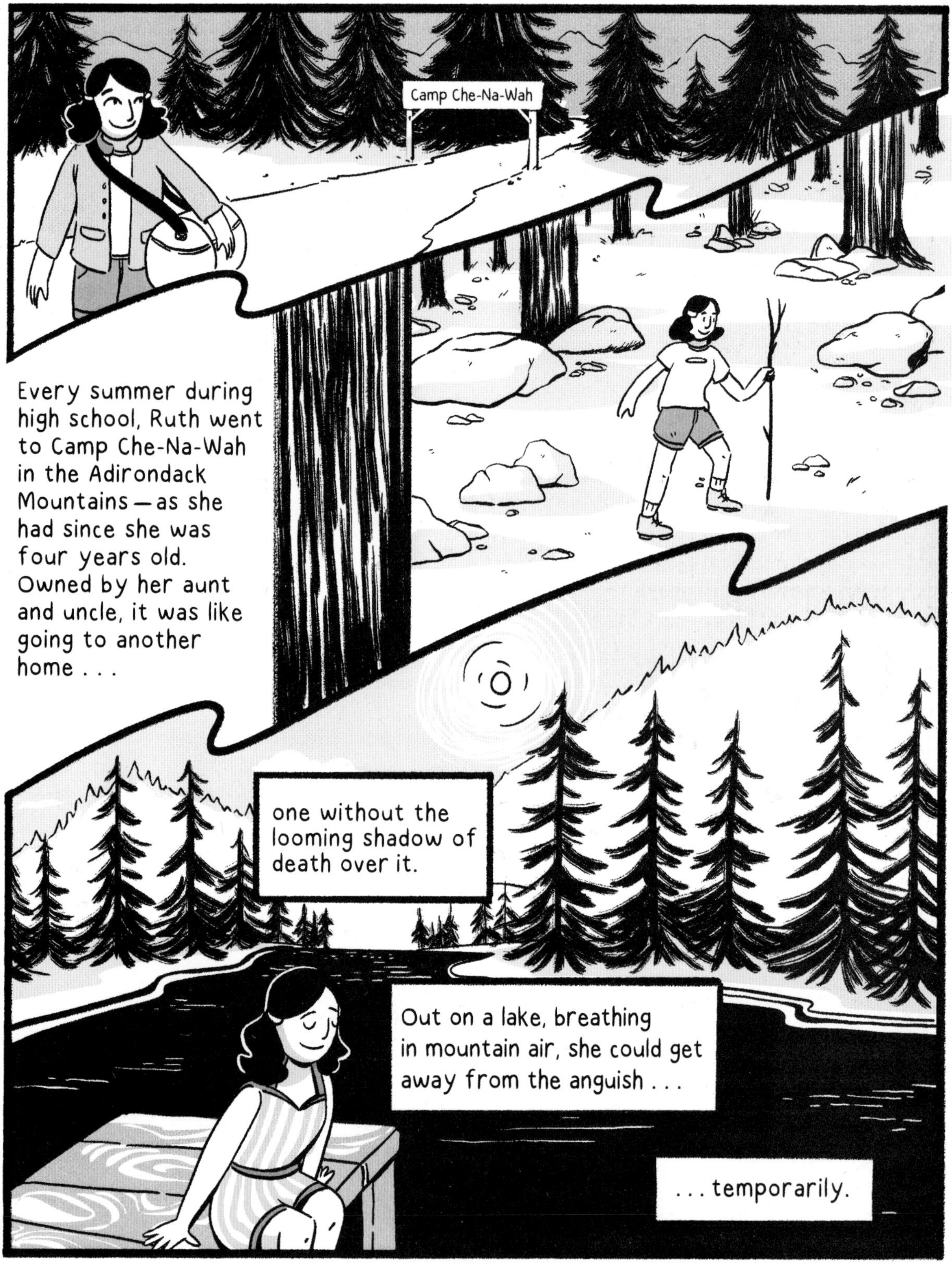

Camp Che-Na-Wah
Every summer during high school, Ruth went to Camp Che-Na-Wah in the Adirondack Mountains—as she had since she was four years old. Owned by her aunt and uncle, it was like going to another home . . .
one without the looming shadow of death over it.
Out on a lake, breathing in mountain air, she could get away from the anguish . . .
. . . temporarily.

CHAPTER 10

Gone

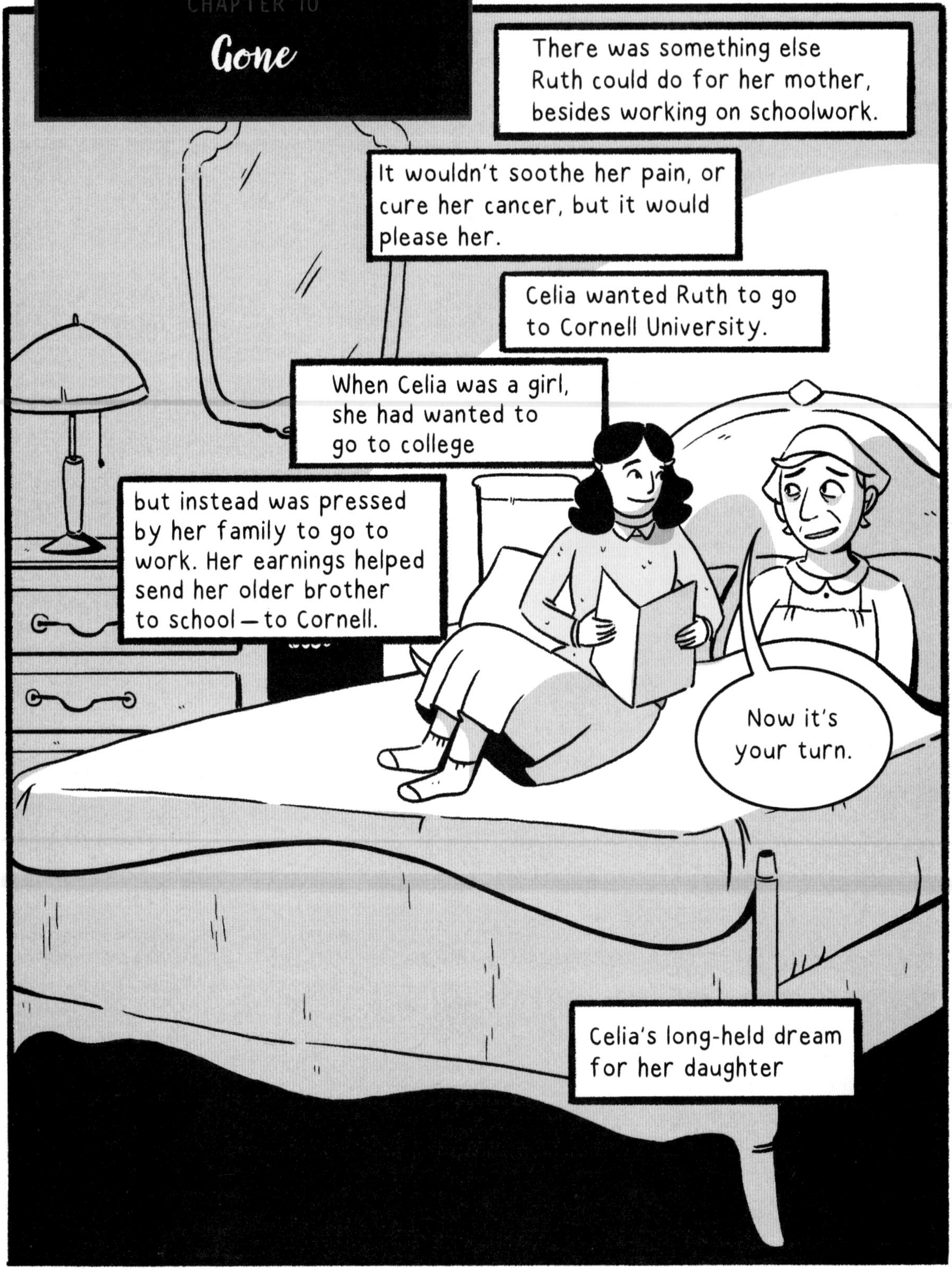

There was something else Ruth could do for her mother, besides working on schoolwork.
It wouldn't soothe her pain, or cure her cancer, but it would please her.
Celia wanted Ruth to go to Cornell University.
When Celia was a girl, she had wanted to go to college
but instead was pressed by her family to go to work. Her earnings helped send her older brother to school—to Cornell.
Now it's your turn.
Celia's long-held dream for her daughter

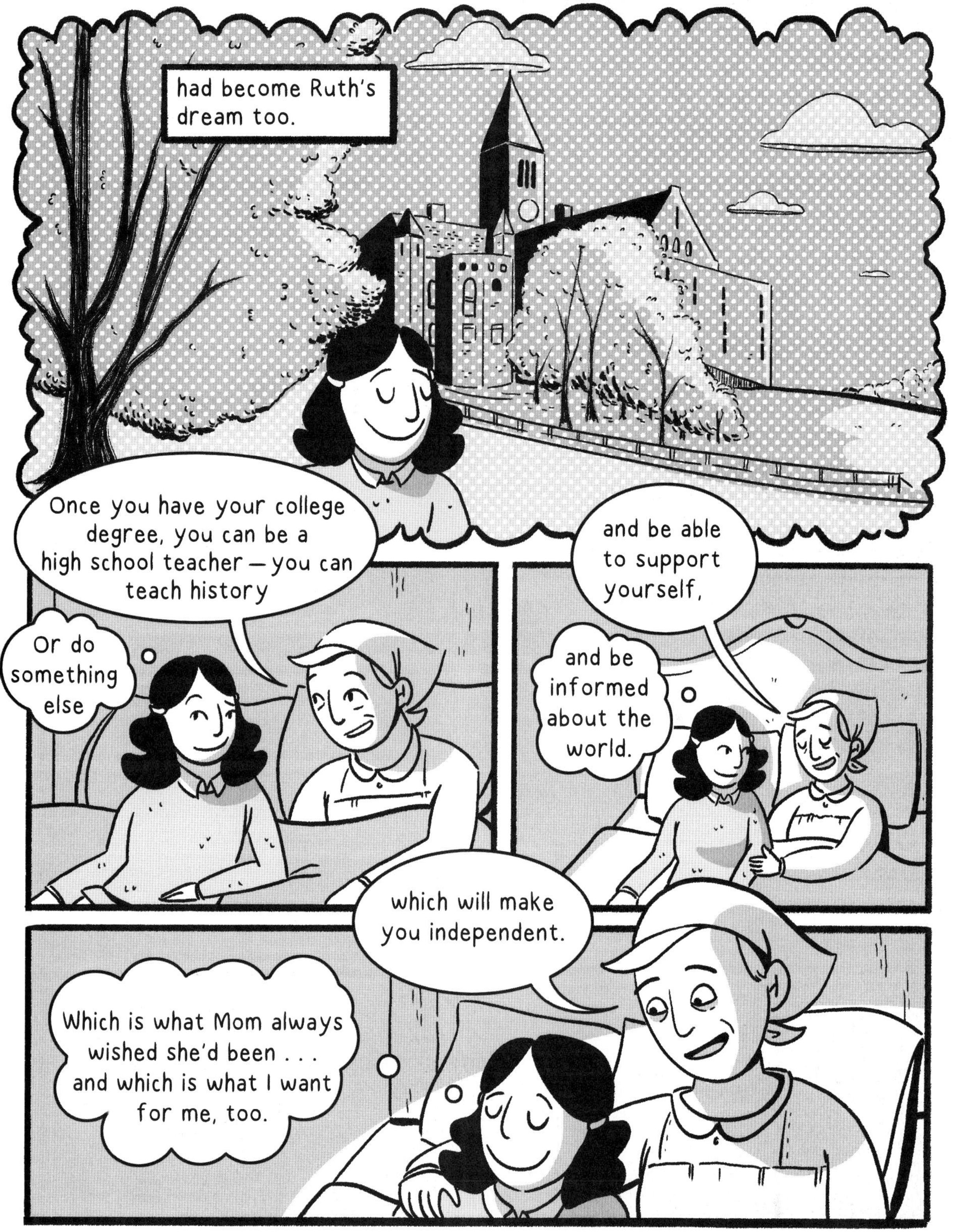
had become Ruth's dream too.
Once you have your college degree, you can be a high school teacher — you can teach history
Or do something else
and be able to support yourself,
and be informed about the world.
which will make you independent.
Which is what Mom always wished she'd been . . . and which is what I want for me, too.

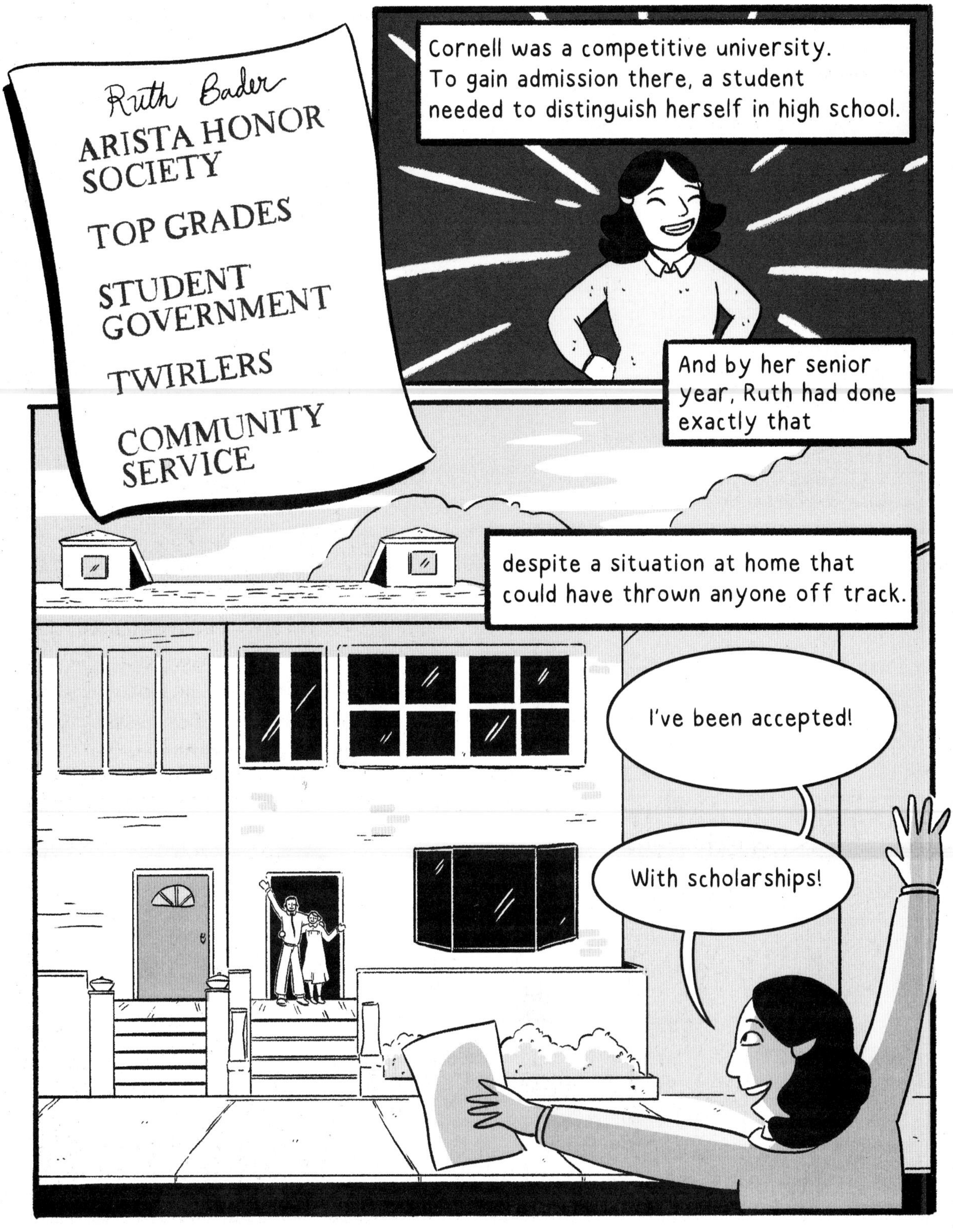
Ruth Bader
ARISTA HONOR SOCIETY
TOP GRADES
STUDENT GOVERNMENT
TWIRLERS
COMMUNITY SERVICE
Cornell was a competitive university. To gain admission there, a student needed to distinguish herself in high school.
And by her senior year, Ruth had done exactly that
despite a situation at home that could have thrown anyone off track.
I've been accepted!
With scholarships!

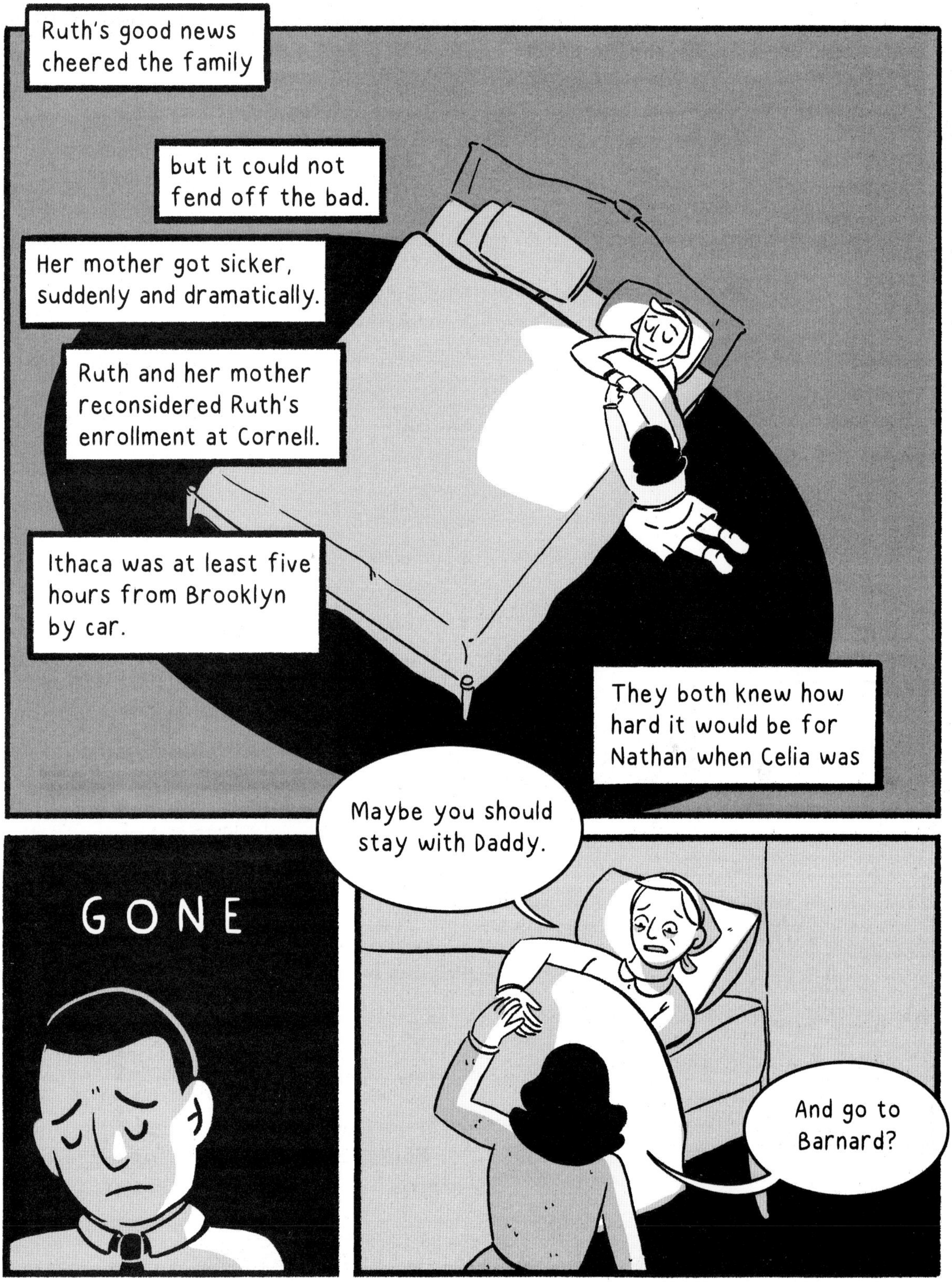
Ruth's good news cheered the family
but it could not fend off the bad.
Her mother got sicker, suddenly and dramatically.
Ruth and her mother reconsidered Ruth's enrollment at Cornell.
Ithaca was at least five hours from Brooklyn by car.
They both knew how hard it would be for Nathan when Celia was
GONE
Maybe you should stay with Daddy.
And go to Barnard?

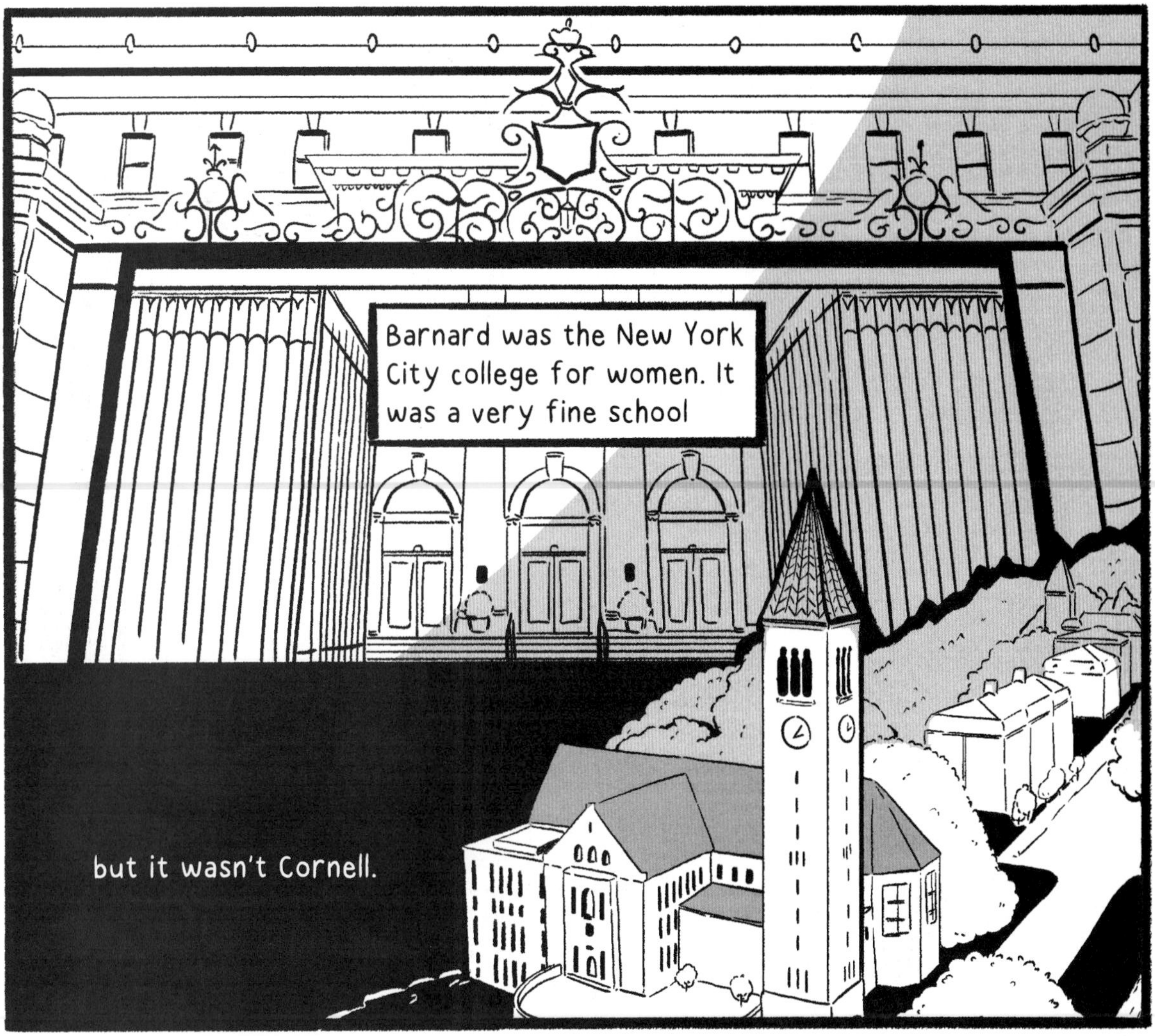
Barnard was the New York City college for women. It was a very fine school
but it wasn't Cornell.

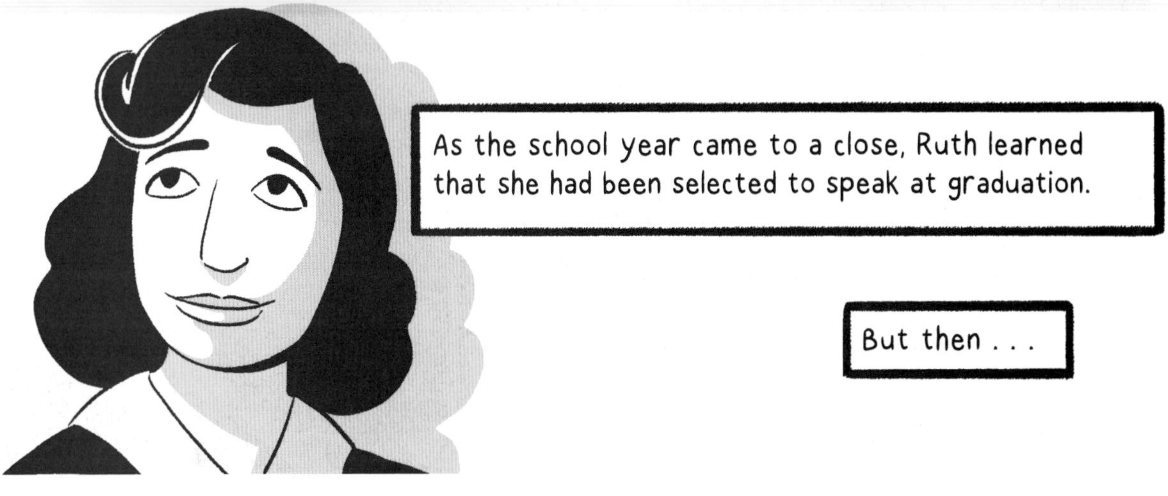
As the school year came to a close, Ruth learned that she had been selected to speak at graduation.
But then . . .

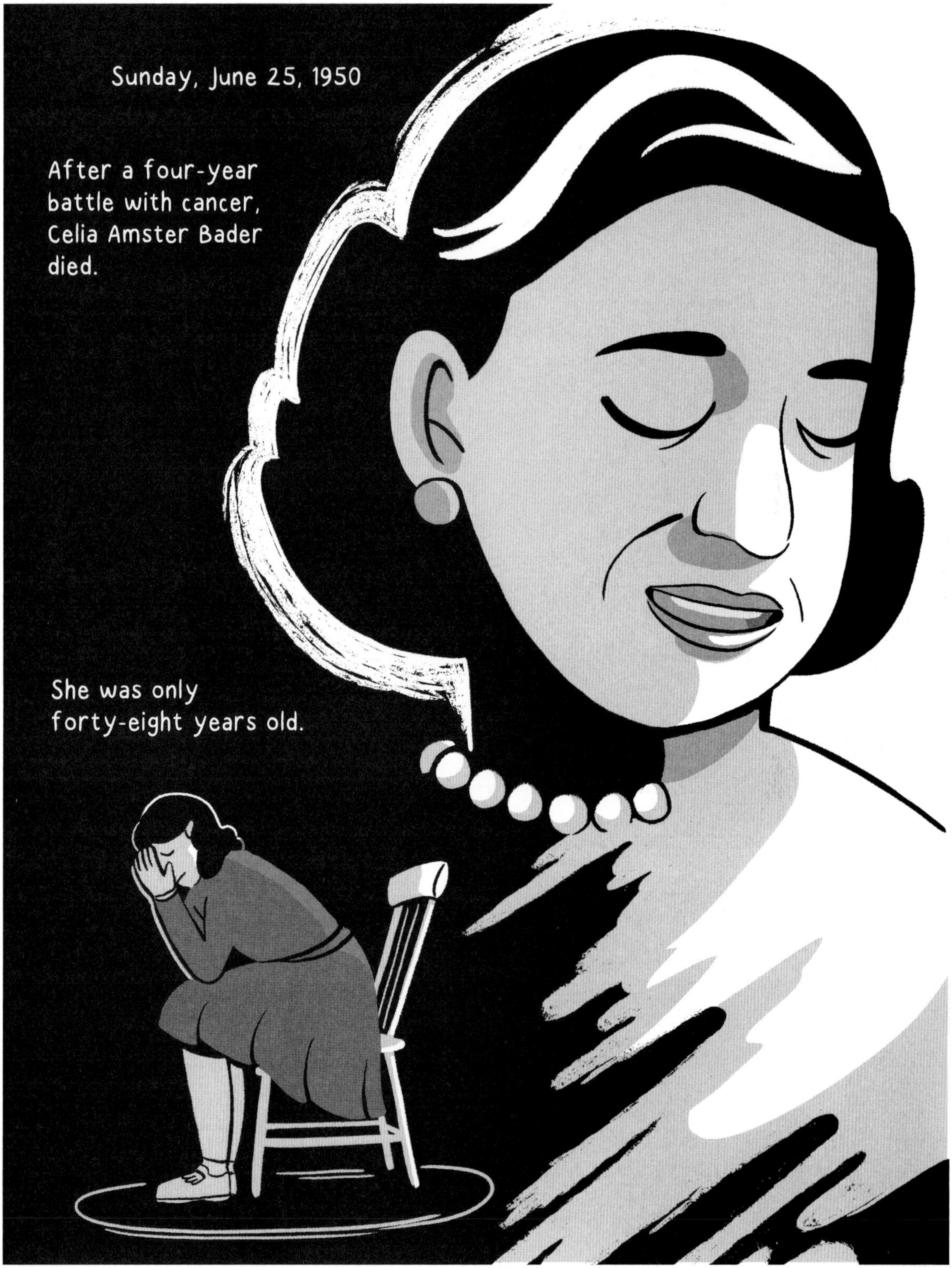
Sunday, June 25, 1950
After a four-year battle with cancer, Celia Amster Bader died.
She was only forty-eight years old.

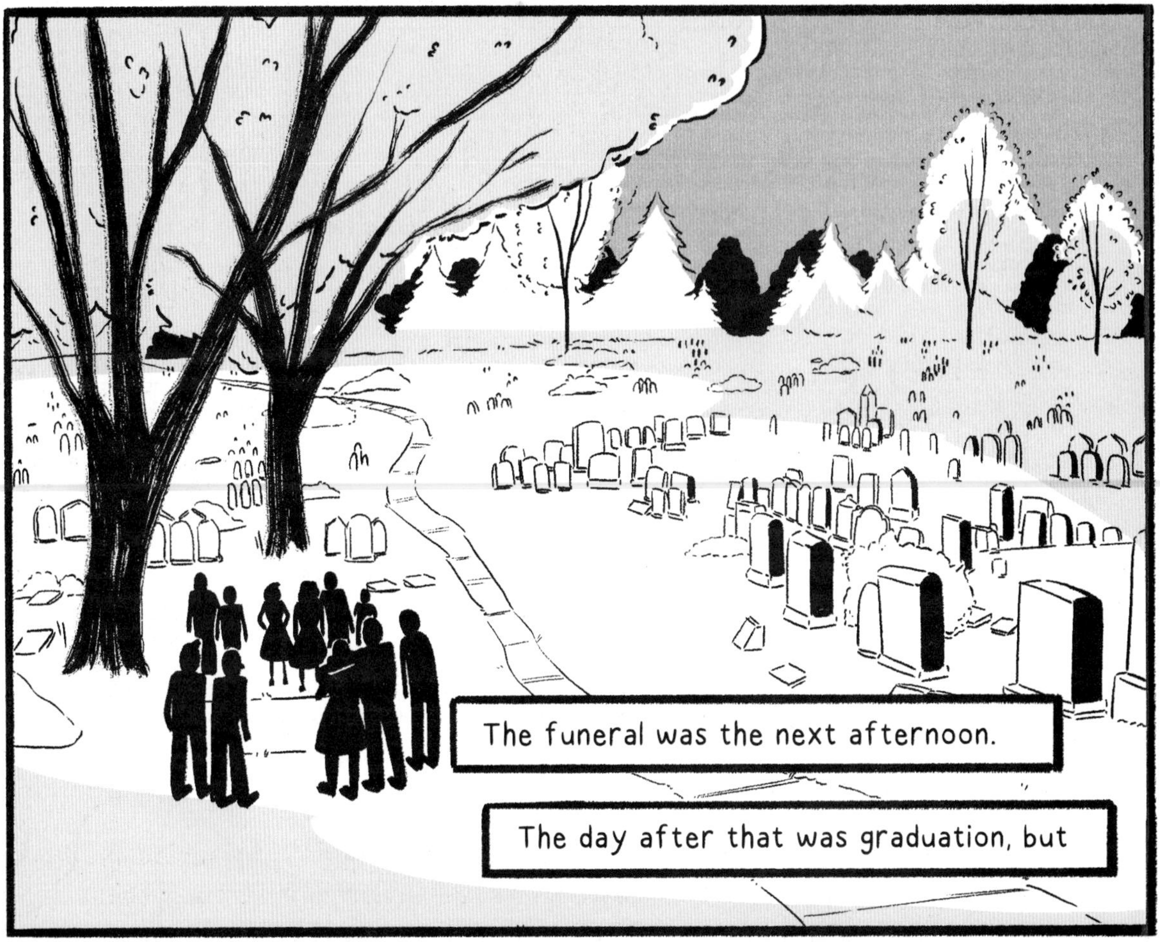
The funeral was the next afternoon.
The day after that was graduation, but

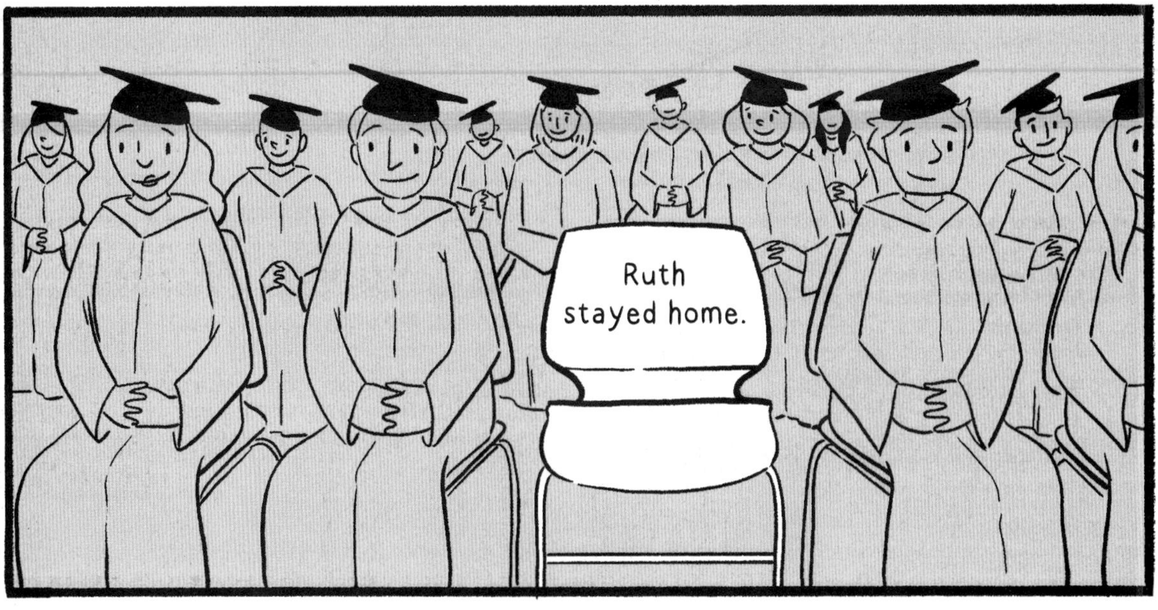
Ruth stayed home.

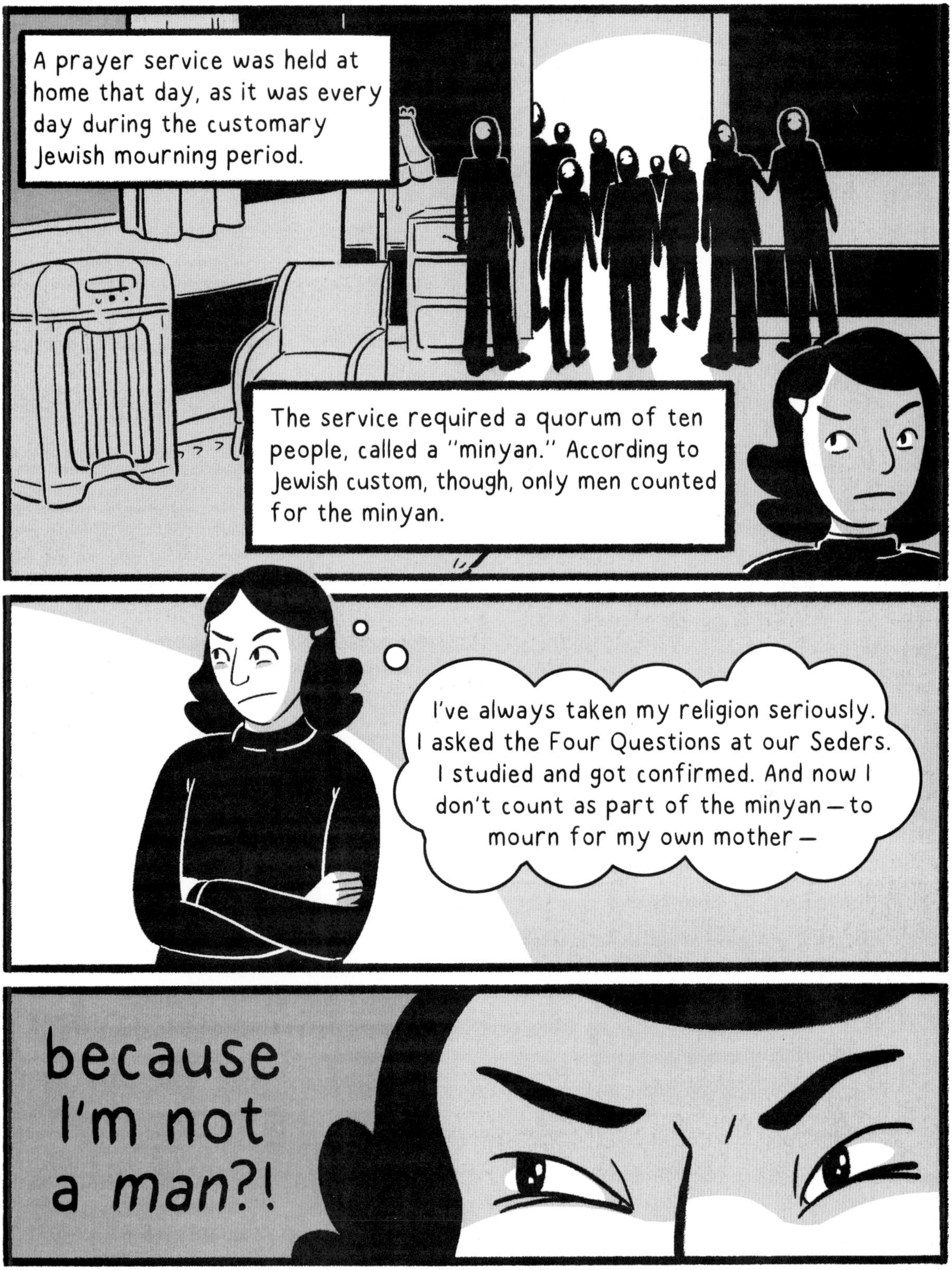

A prayer service was held at home that day, as it was every day during the customary Jewish mourning period.
The service required a quorum of ten people, called a "minyan." According to Jewish custom, though, only men counted for the minyan.
I've always taken my religion seriously. I asked the Four Questions at our Seders. I studied and got confirmed. And now I don't count as part of the minyan—to mourn for my own mother—
because I'm not a *man*?!

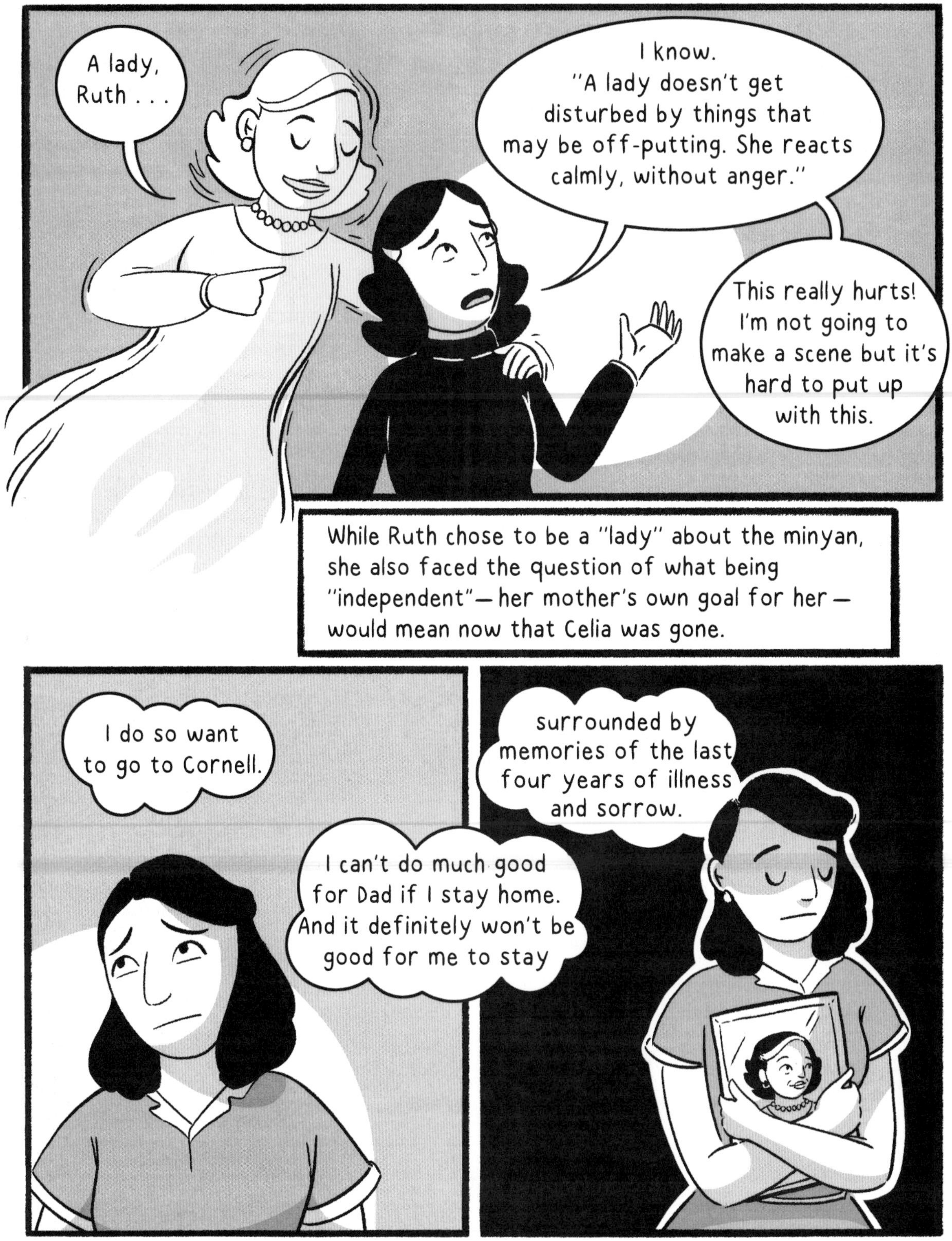
A lady, Ruth . . .
I know. "A lady doesn't get disturbed by things that may be off-putting. She reacts calmly, without anger."
This really hurts! I'm not going to make a scene but it's hard to put up with this.
While Ruth chose to be a "lady" about the minyan, she also faced the question of what being "independent"—her mother's own goal for her—would mean now that Celia was gone.
I do so want to go to Cornell.
I can't do much good for Dad if I stay home. And it definitely won't be good for me to stay
surrounded by memories of the last four years of illness and sorrow.

CHAPTER 11
Finding Her Place

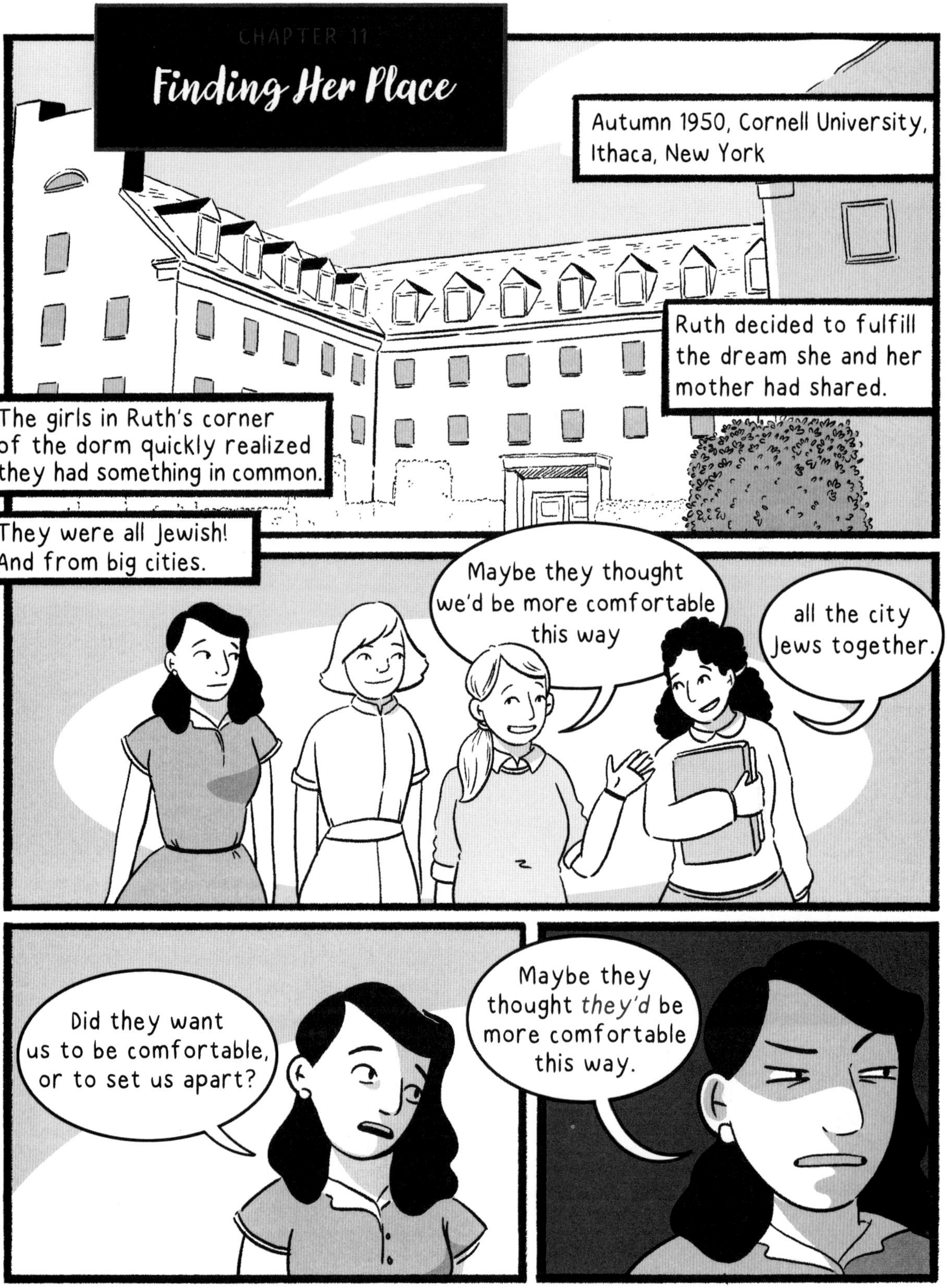

Autumn 1950, Cornell University, Ithaca, New York
Ruth decided to fulfill the dream she and her mother had shared.
The girls in Ruth's corner of the dorm quickly realized they had something in common.
They were all Jewish! And from big cities.
Maybe they thought we'd be more comfortable this way
all the city Jews together.
Did they want us to be comfortable, or to set us apart?
Maybe they thought *they'd* be more comfortable this way.

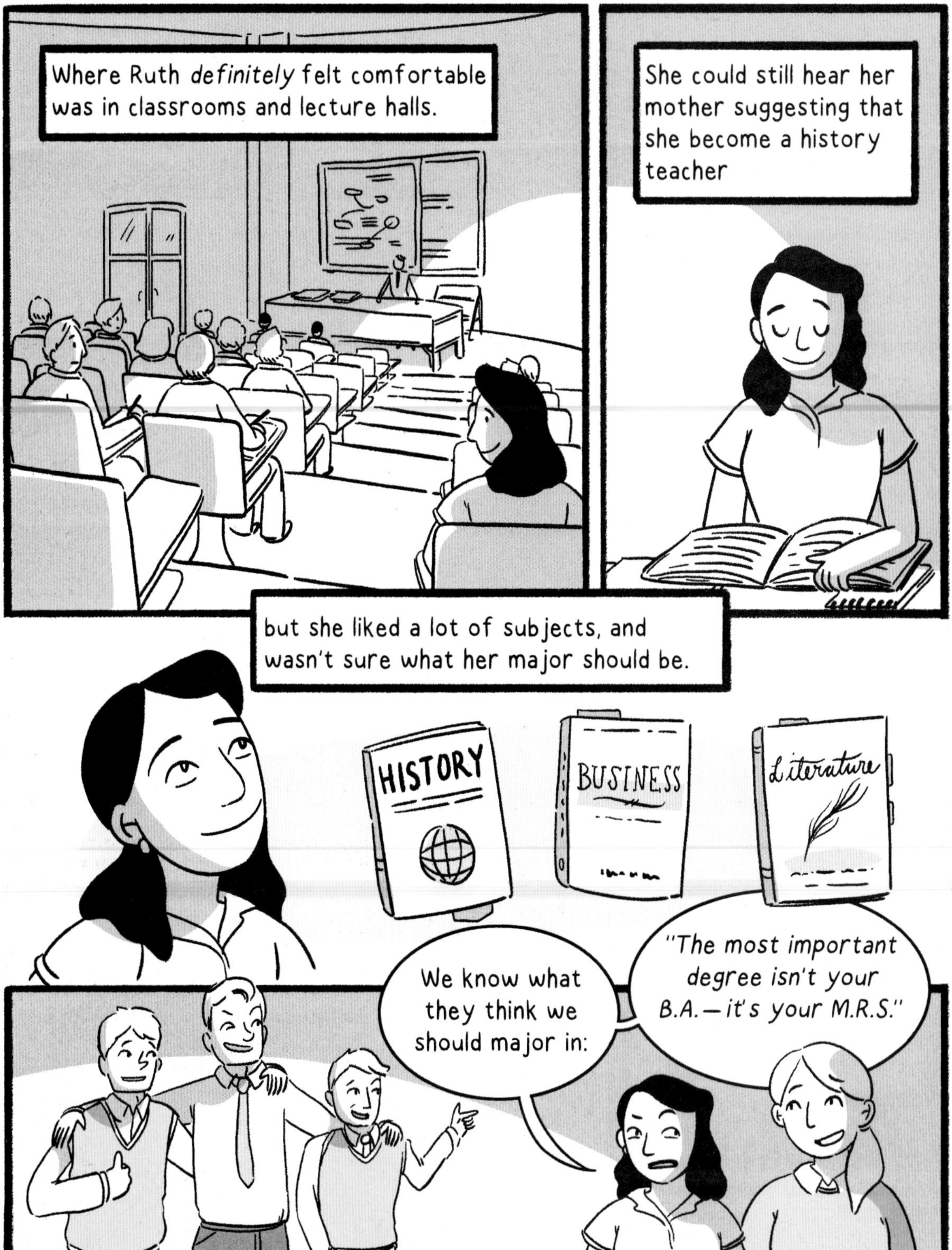
Where Ruth *definitely* felt comfortable was in classrooms and lecture halls.
She could still hear her mother suggesting that she become a history teacher
but she liked a lot of subjects, and wasn't sure what her major should be.
HISTORY
BUSINESS
Literature
We know what they think we should major in:
"The most important degree isn't your B.A.—it's your M.R.S."

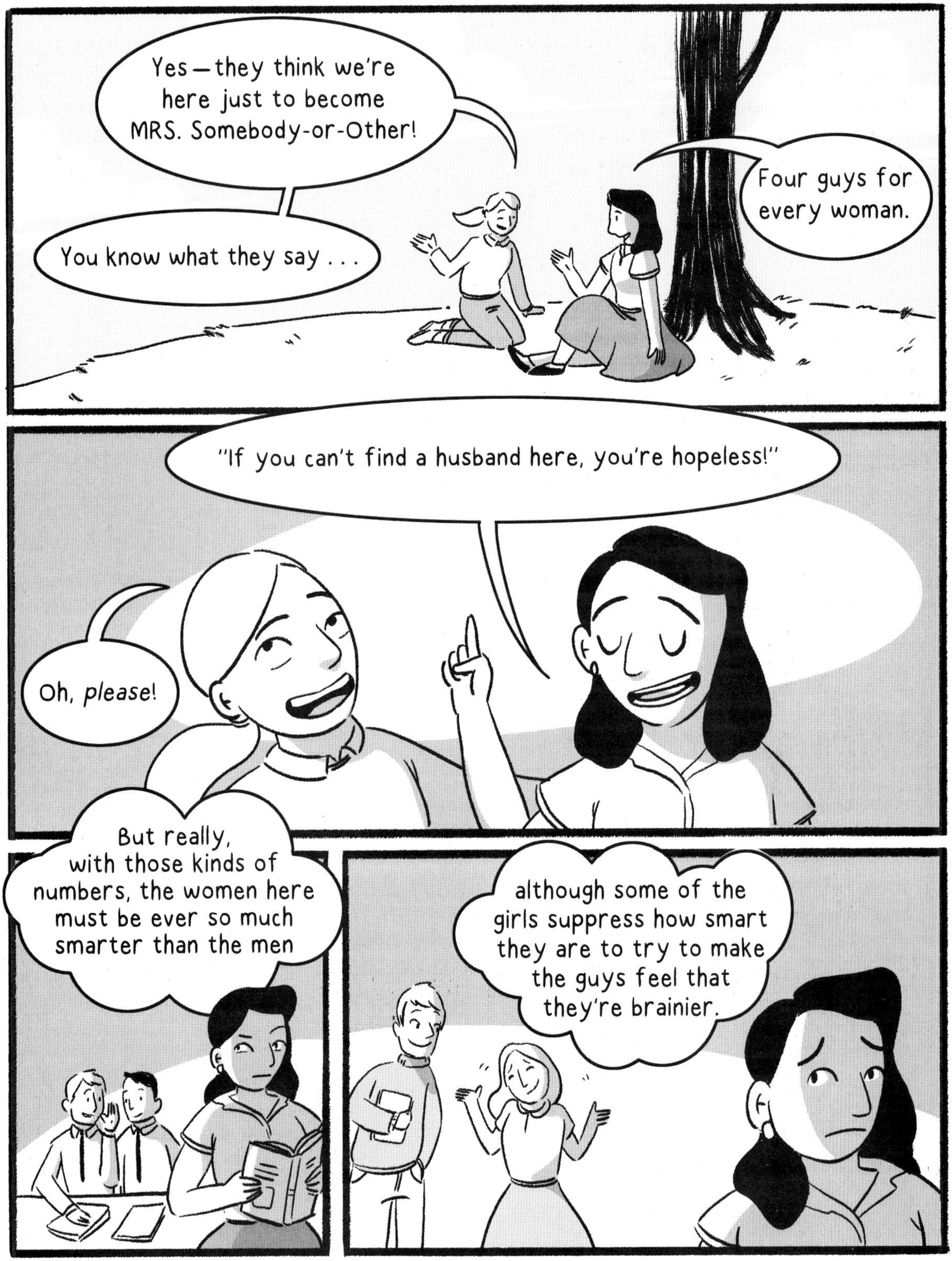
You know what they say . . .
Yes—they think we're here just to become MRS. Somebody-or-Other!
Four guys for every woman.
"If you can't find a husband here, you're hopeless!"
Oh, *please*!
But really, with those kinds of numbers, the women here must be ever so much smarter than the men
although some of the girls suppress how smart they are to try to make the guys feel that they're brainier.

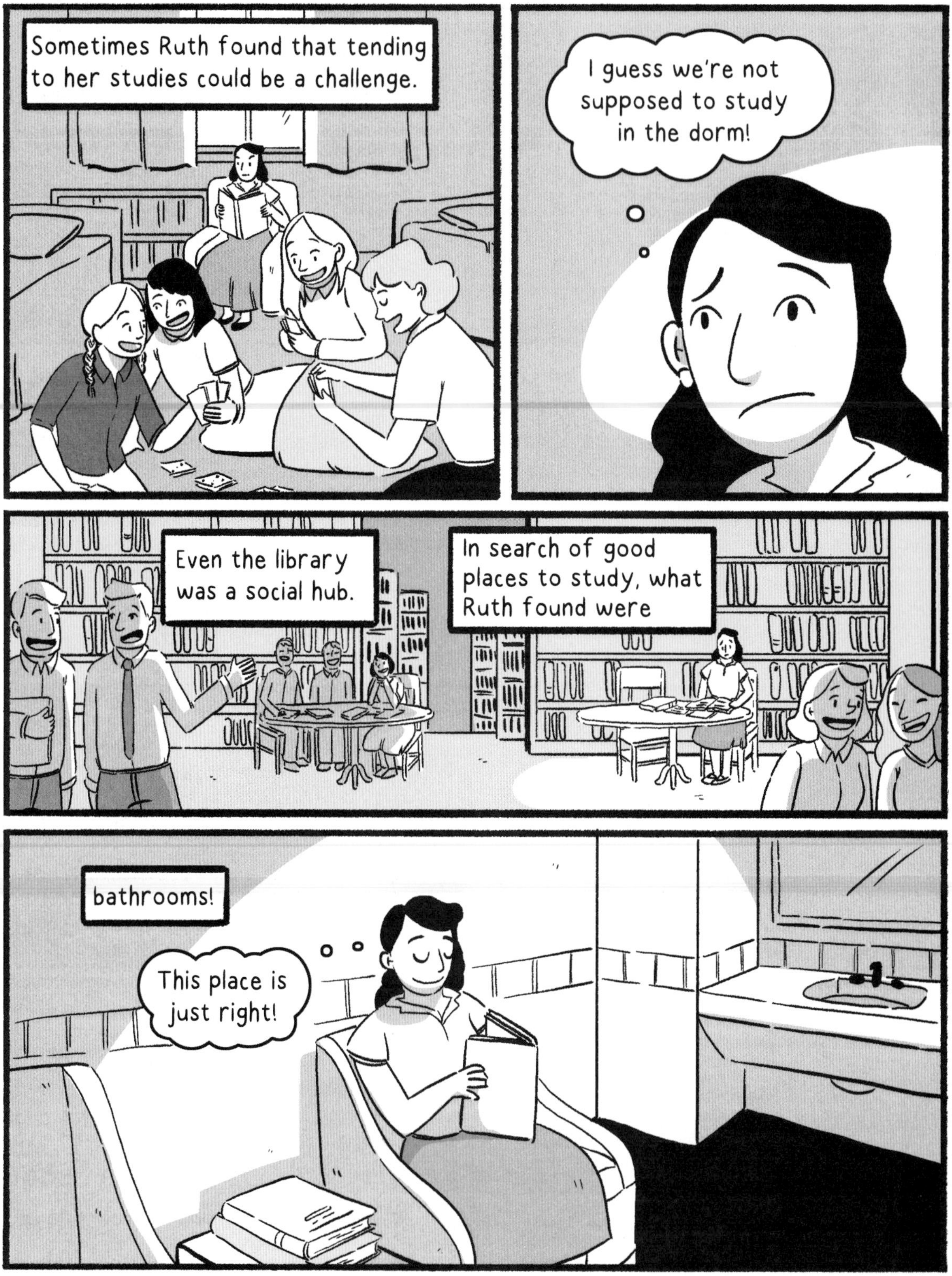
Sometimes Ruth found that tending to her studies could be a challenge.
I guess we're not supposed to study in the dorm!
Even the library was a social hub.
In search of good places to study, what Ruth found were
bathrooms!
This place is just right!

CHAPTER 12

Friends at First Sight

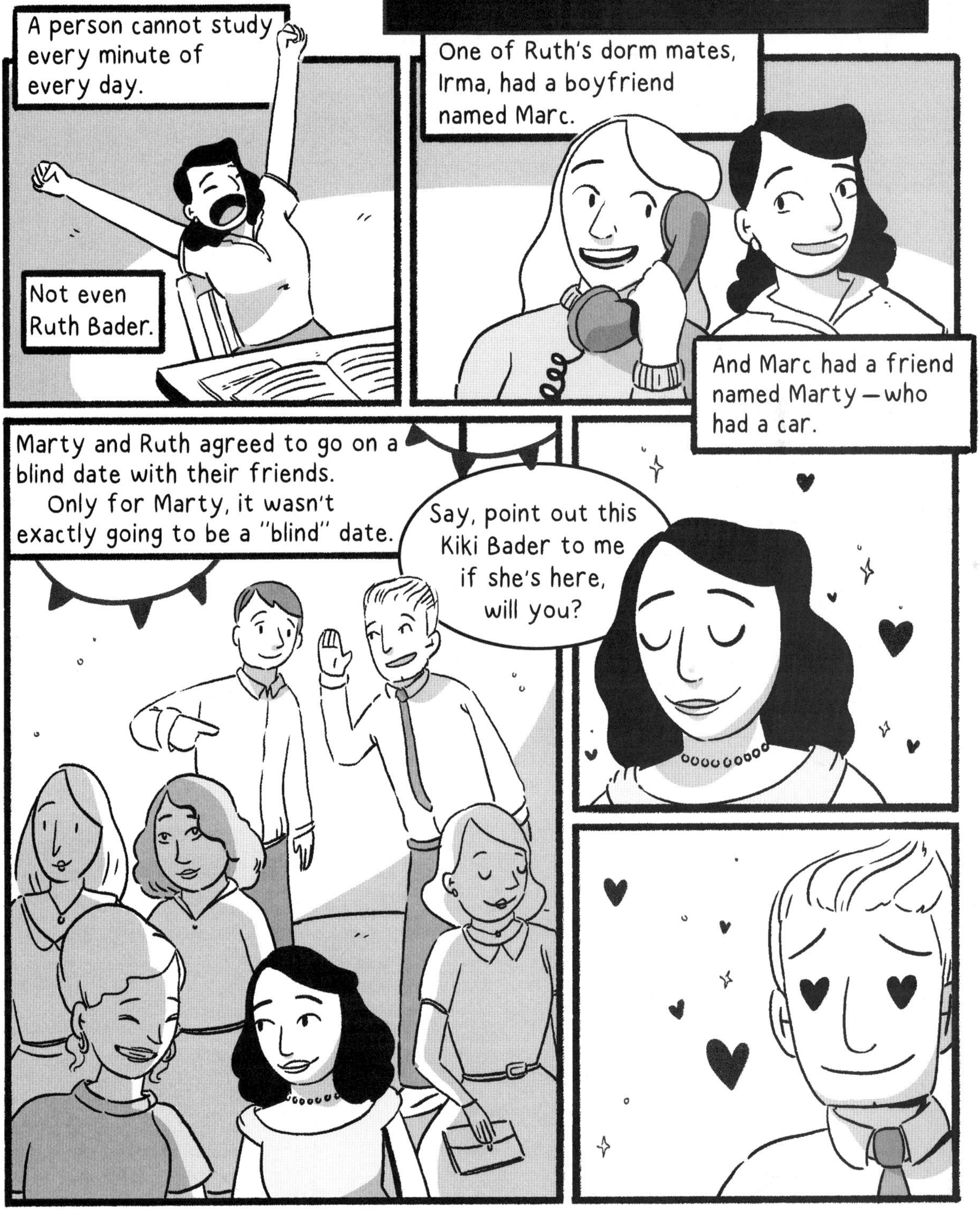
A person cannot study every minute of every day.
Not even Ruth Bader.
One of Ruth's dorm mates, Irma, had a boyfriend named Marc.
And Marc had a friend named Marty—who had a car.
Marty and Ruth agreed to go on a blind date with their friends.
Only for Marty, it wasn't exactly going to be a "blind" date.
Say, point out this Kiki Bader to me if she's here, will you?

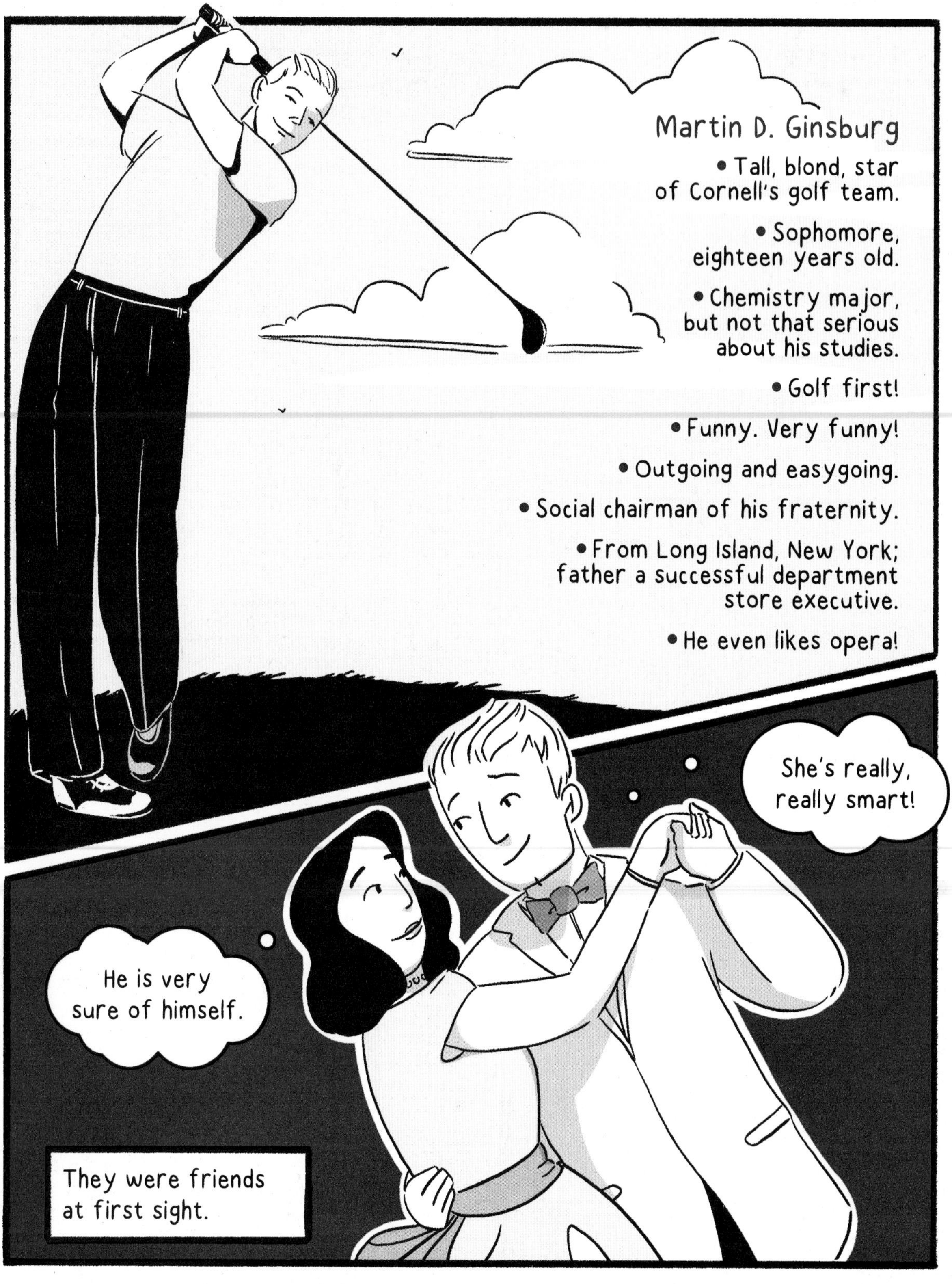
Martin D. Ginsburg
• Tall, blond, star of Cornell's golf team.
• Sophomore, eighteen years old.
• Chemistry major, but not that serious about his studies.
• Golf first!
• Funny. Very funny!
• Outgoing and easygoing.
• Social chairman of his fraternity.
• From Long Island, New York; father a successful department store executive.
• He even likes opera!
She's really, really smart!
He is very sure of himself.
They were friends at first sight.

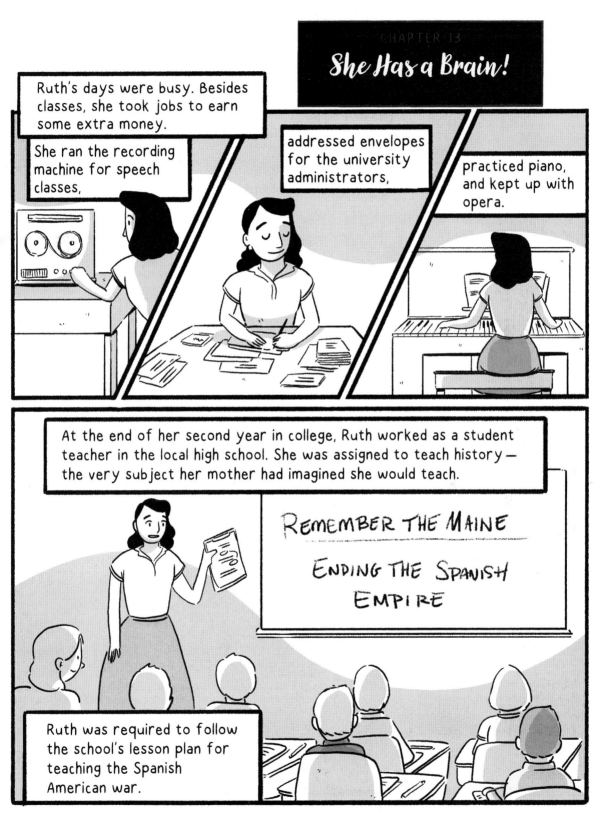

CHAPTER 13

She Has a Brain!

Ruth's days were busy. Besides classes, she took jobs to earn some extra money.

She ran the recording machine for speech classes,

addressed envelopes for the university administrators,

practiced piano, and kept up with opera.

At the end of her second year in college, Ruth worked as a student teacher in the local high school. She was assigned to teach history — the very subject her mother had imagined she would teach.

REMEMBER THE MAINE

ENDING THE SPANISH EMPIRE

Ruth was required to follow the school's lesson plan for teaching the Spanish American war.

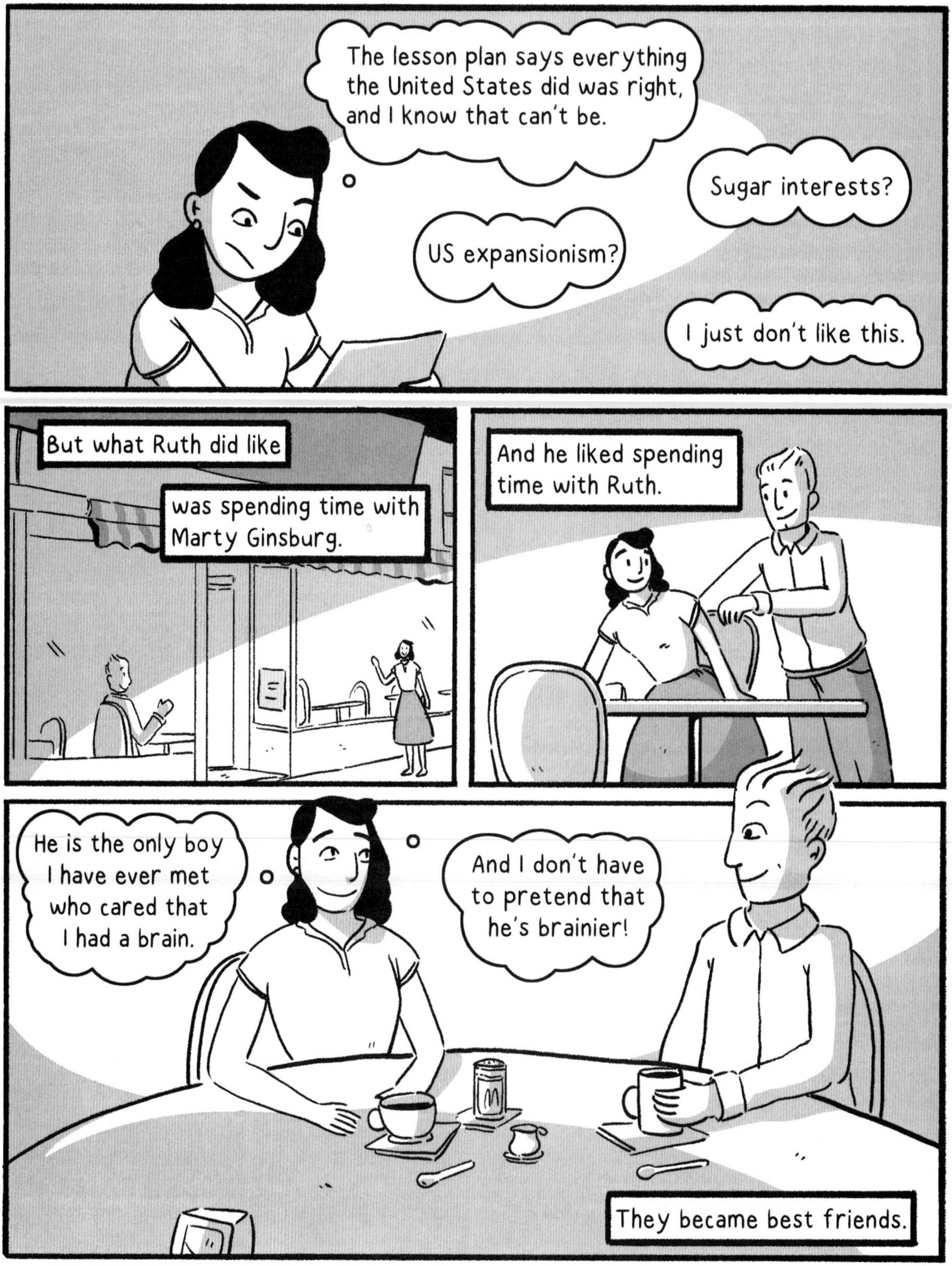
The lesson plan says everything the United States did was right, and I know that can't be.
US expansionism?
Sugar interests?
I just don't like this.
But what Ruth did like
was spending time with Marty Ginsburg.
And he liked spending time with Ruth.
He is the only boy I have ever met who cared that I had a brain.
And I don't have to pretend that he's brainier!
They became best friends.

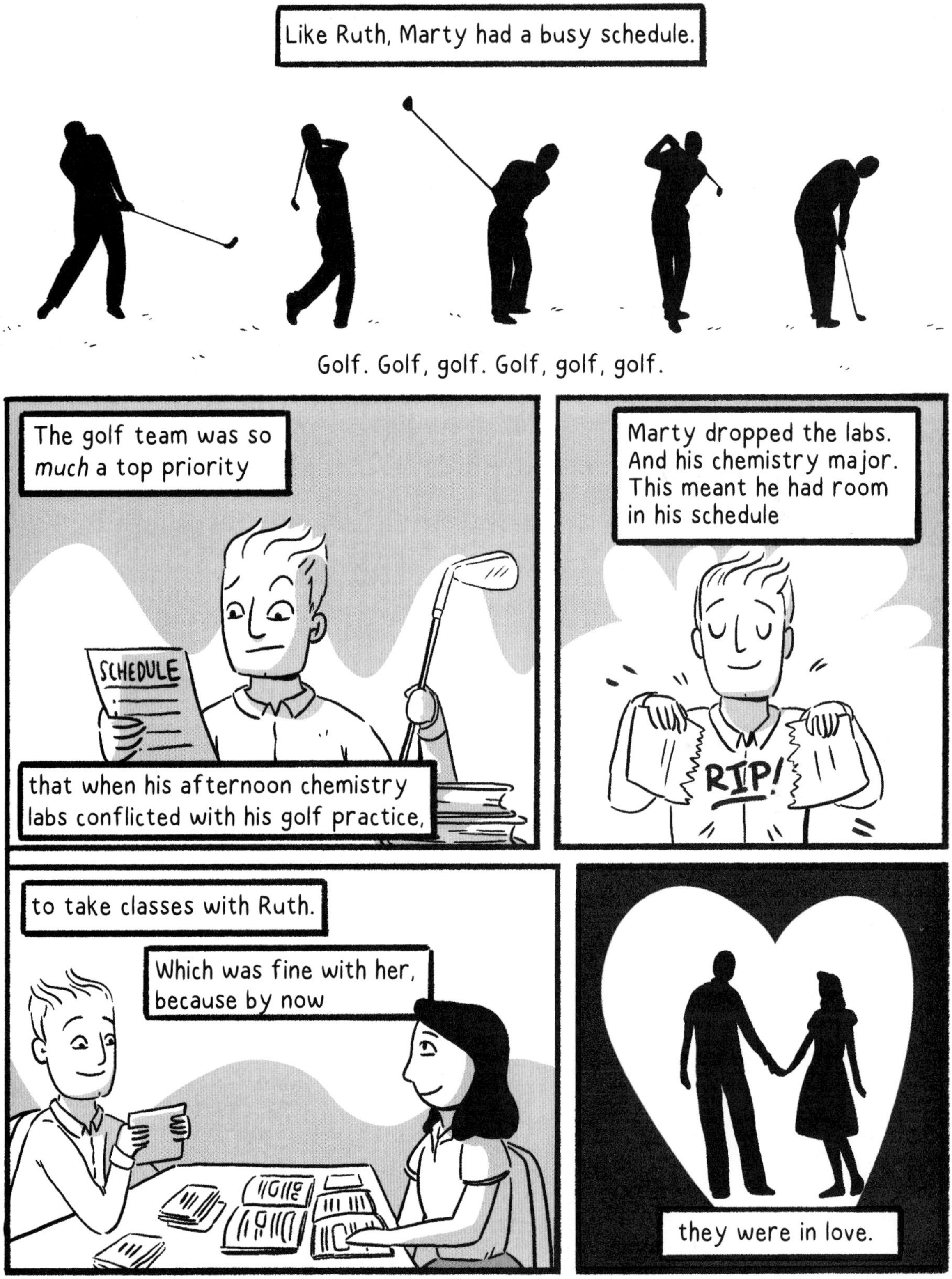
Like Ruth, Marty had a busy schedule.
Golf. Golf, golf. Golf, golf, golf.
The golf team was so *much* a top priority
SCHEDULE
that when his afternoon chemistry labs conflicted with his golf practice,
Marty dropped the labs. And his chemistry major. This meant he had room in his schedule
RIP!
to take classes with Ruth.
Which was fine with her, because by now
they were in love.

CHAPTER 14

Deep Impressions

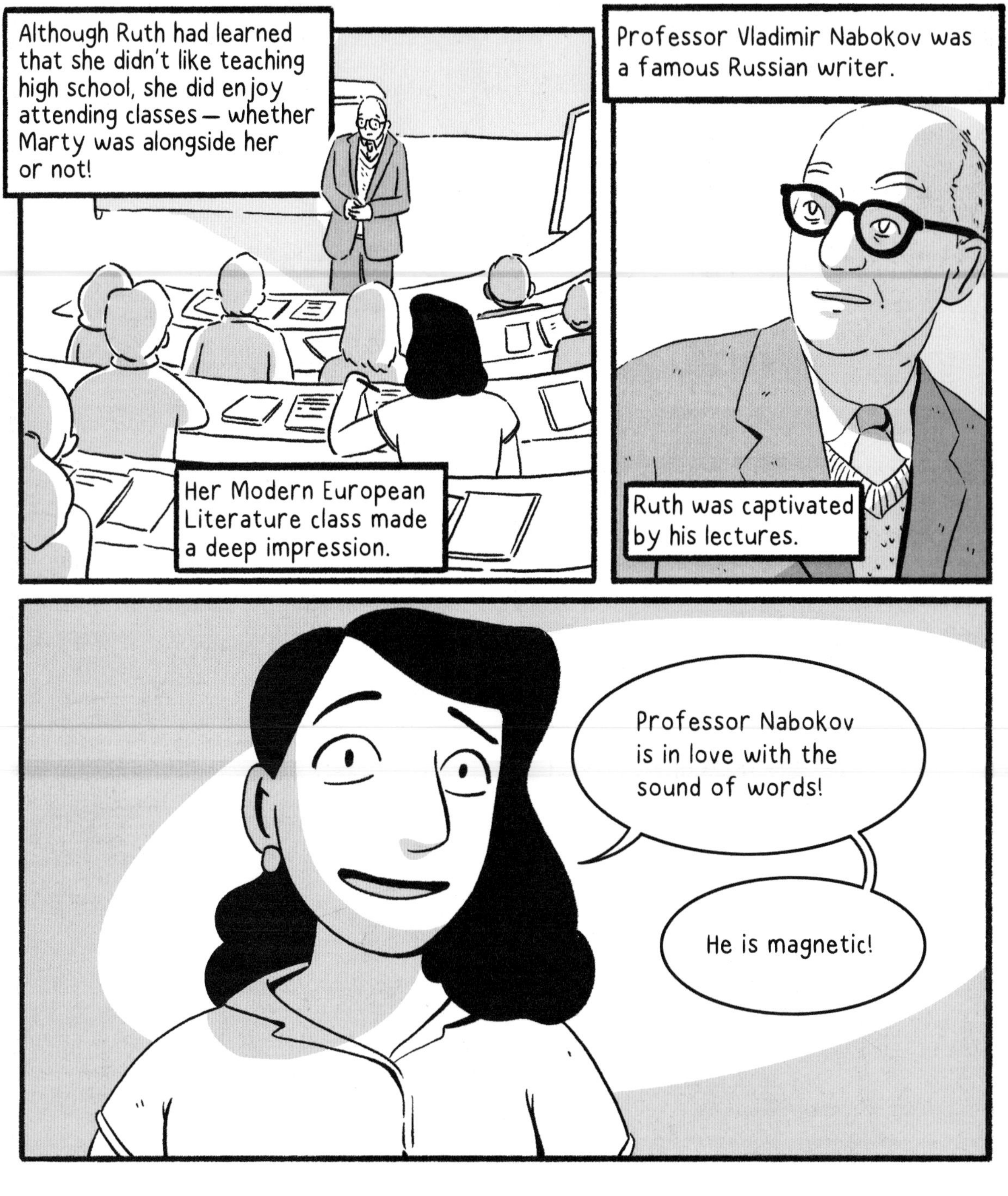

Although Ruth had learned that she didn't like teaching high school, she did enjoy attending classes — whether Marty was alongside her or not!
Her Modern European Literature class made a deep impression.
Professor Vladimir Nabokov was a famous Russian writer.
Ruth was captivated by his lectures.
Professor Nabokov is in love with the sound of words!
He is magnetic!

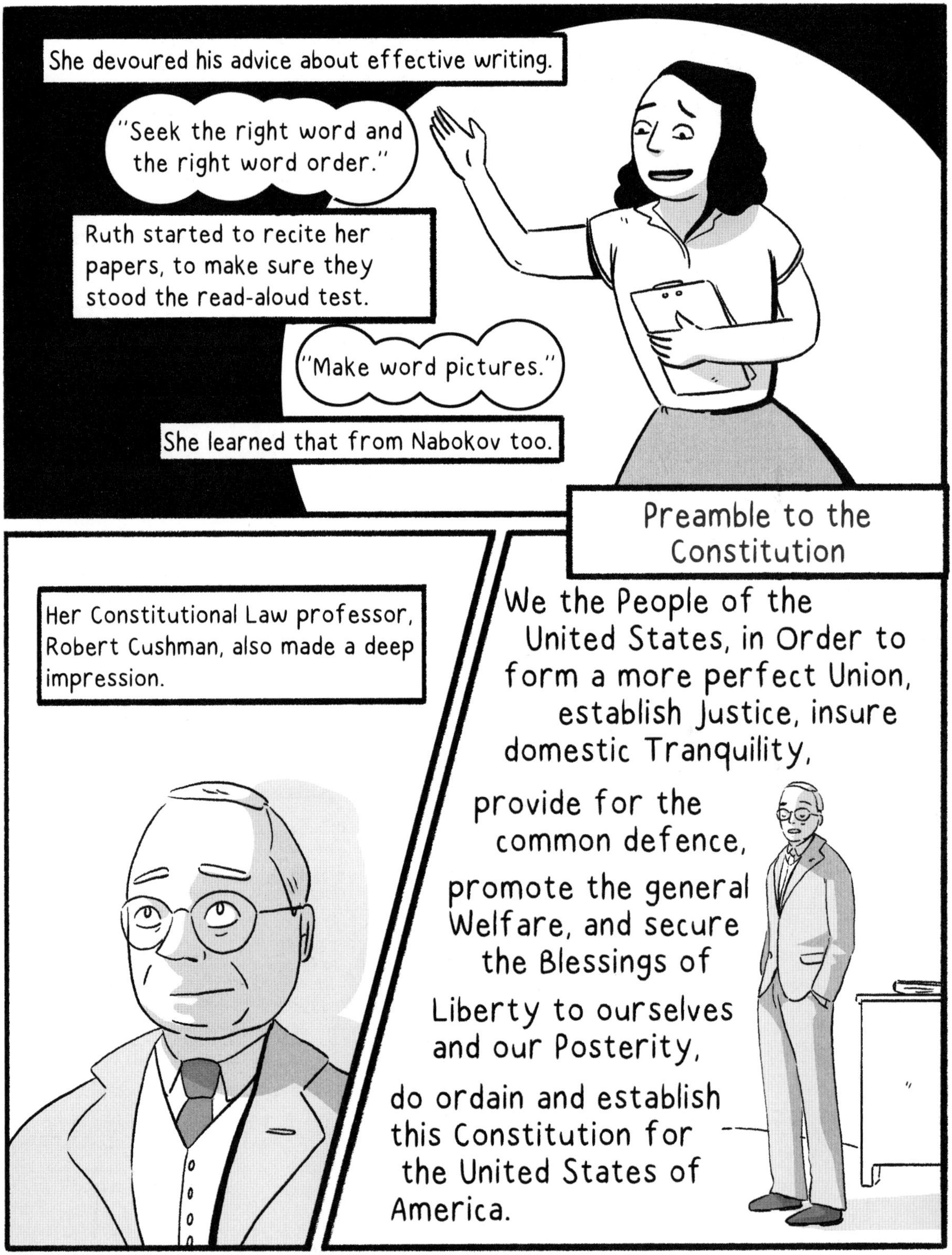

She devoured his advice about effective writing.
"Seek the right word and the right word order."
Ruth started to recite her papers, to make sure they stood the read-aloud test.
"Make word pictures."
She learned that from Nabokov too.
Her Constitutional Law professor, Robert Cushman, also made a deep impression.
Preamble to the Constitution
We the People of the United States, in Order to form a more perfect Union, establish Justice, insure domestic Tranquility,
provide for the common defence,
promote the general Welfare, and secure the Blessings of
Liberty to ourselves and our Posterity,
do ordain and establish this Constitution for the United States of America.

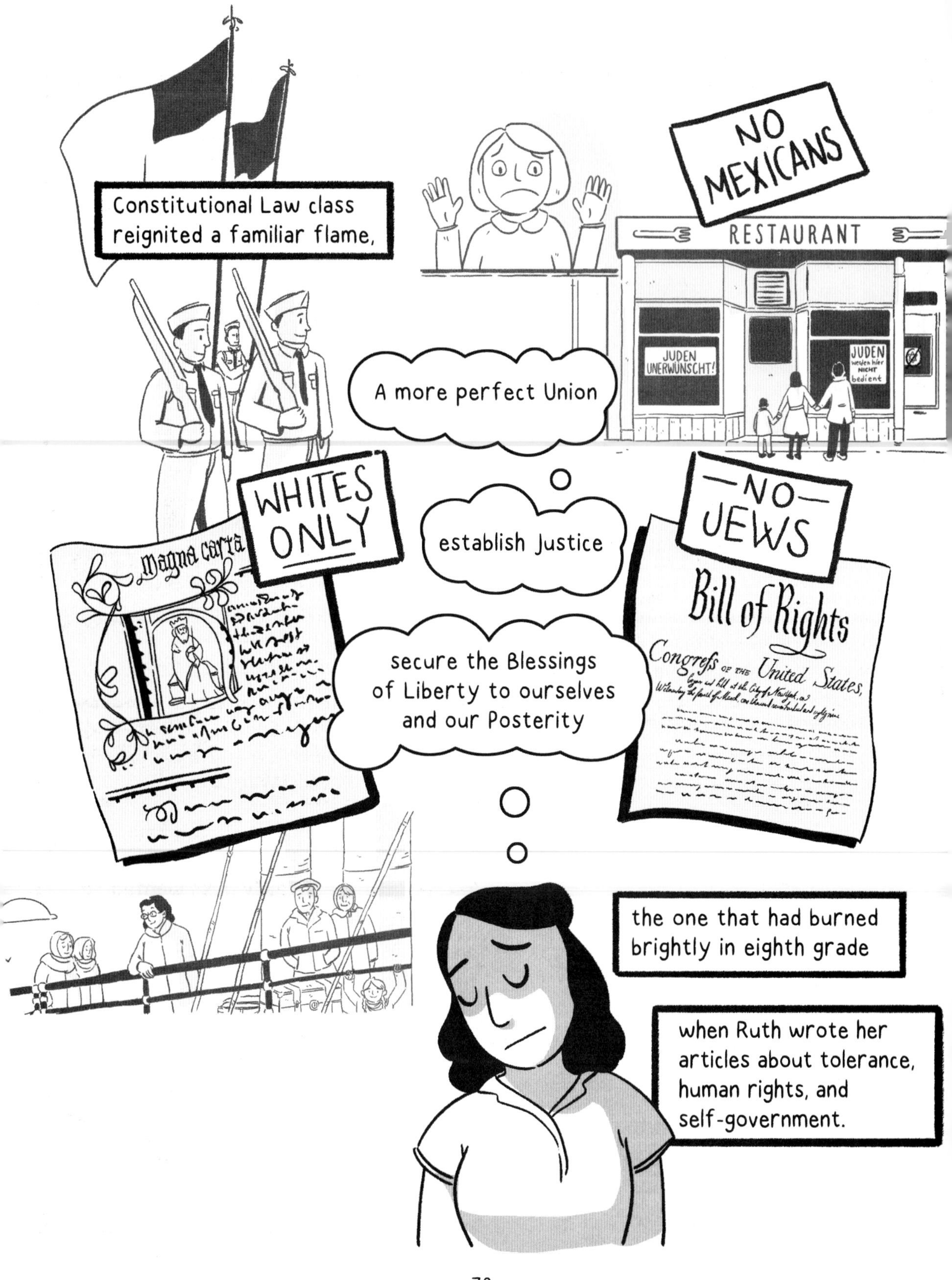
Constitutional Law class reignited a familiar flame,
NO MEXICANS
RESTAURANT
JUDEN UNERWÜNSCHT!
JUDEN werden hier NICHT bedient
A more perfect Union
WHITES ONLY
Magna Carta
establish Justice
—NO— JEWS
Bill of Rights
Congress OF THE United States,
secure the Blessings of Liberty to ourselves and our Posterity
the one that had burned brightly in eighth grade
when Ruth wrote her articles about tolerance, human rights, and self-government.

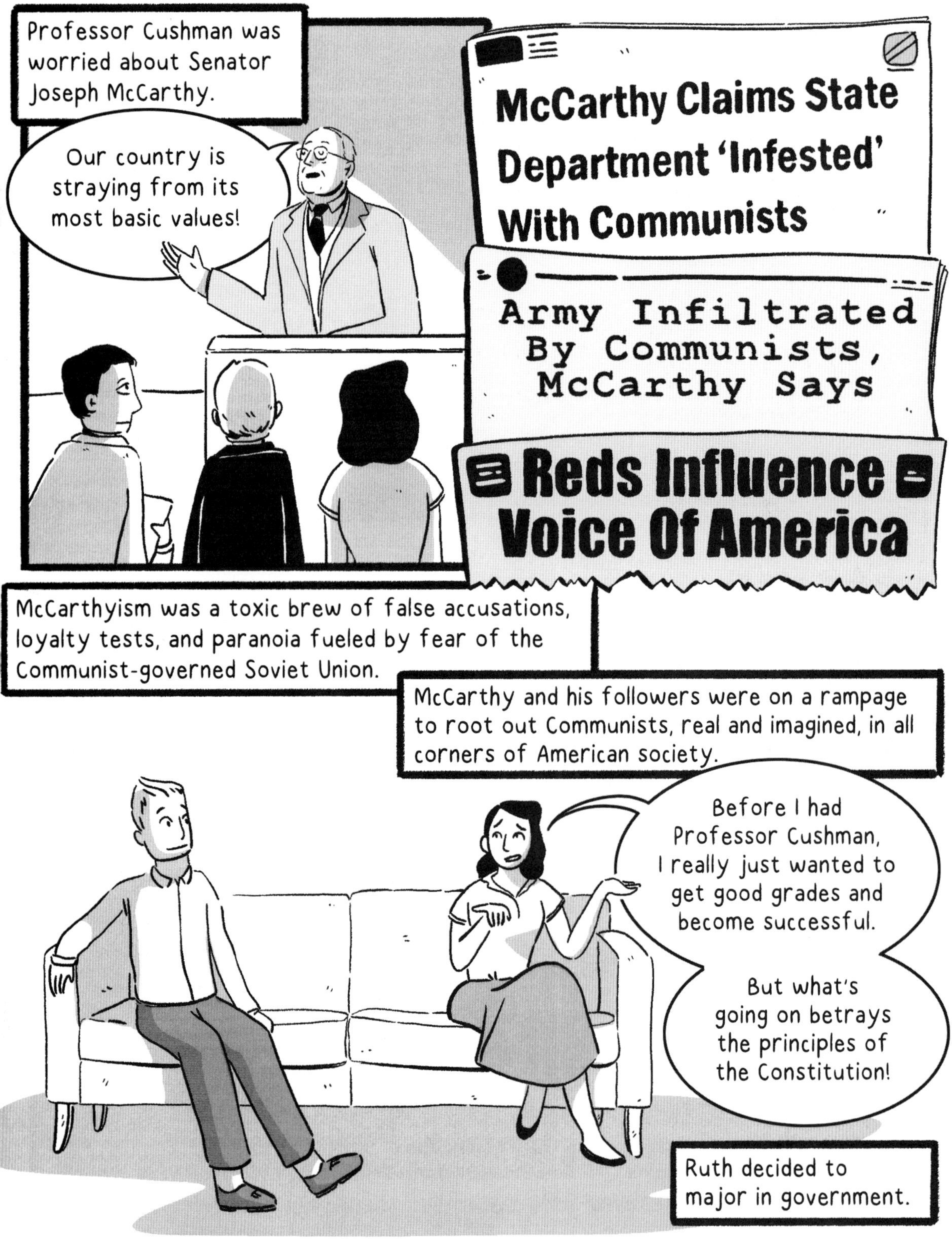
Professor Cushman was worried about Senator Joseph McCarthy.
Our country is straying from its most basic values!
McCarthy Claims State Department 'Infested' With Communists
Army Infiltrated By Communists, McCarthy Says
Reds Influence Voice Of America
McCarthyism was a toxic brew of false accusations, loyalty tests, and paranoia fueled by fear of the Communist-governed Soviet Union.
McCarthy and his followers were on a rampage to root out Communists, real and imagined, in all corners of American society.
Before I had Professor Cushman, I really just wanted to get good grades and become successful.
But what's going on betrays the principles of the Constitution!
Ruth decided to major in government.

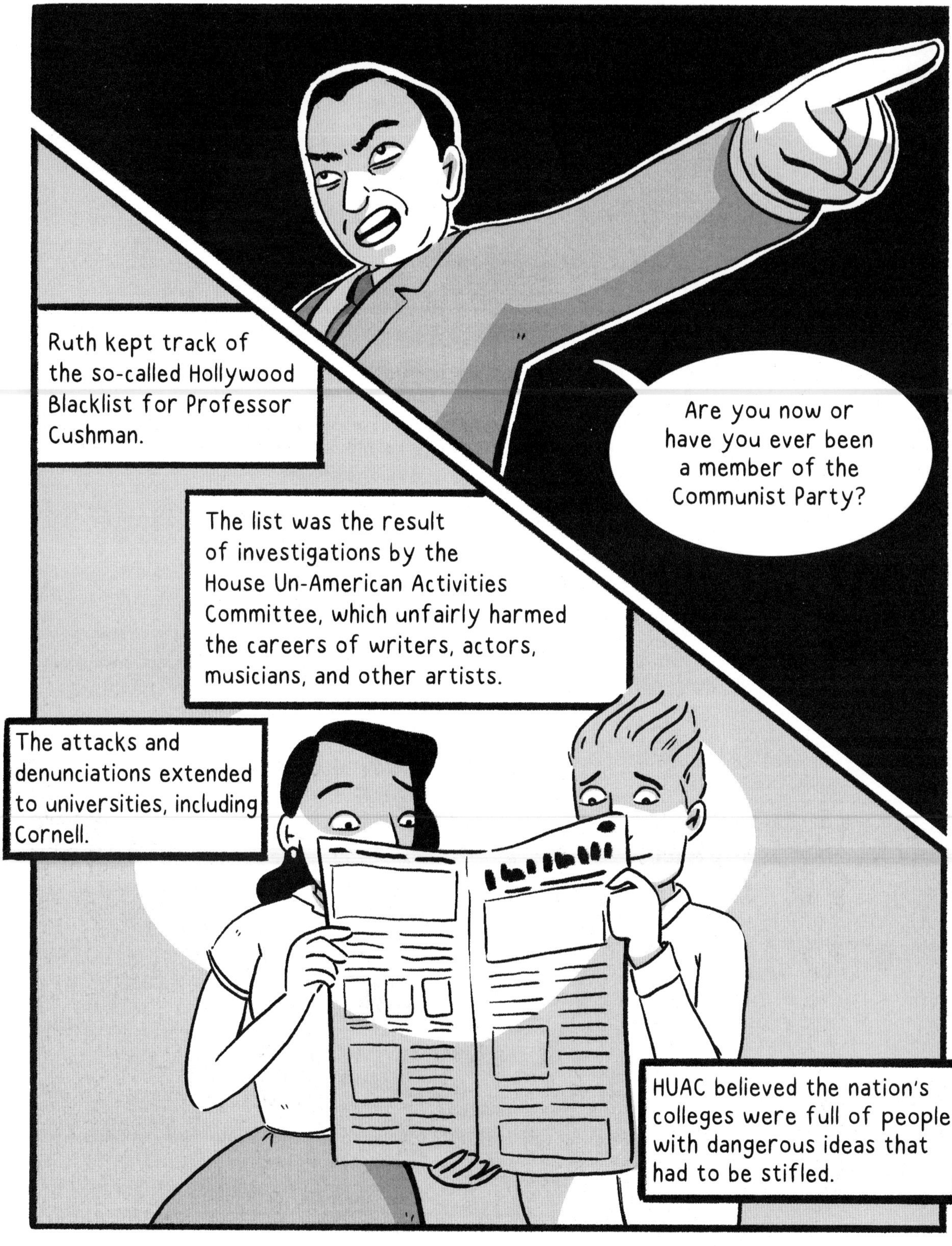
Ruth kept track of the so-called Hollywood Blacklist for Professor Cushman.
Are you now or have you ever been a member of the Communist Party?
The list was the result of investigations by the House Un-American Activities Committee, which unfairly harmed the careers of writers, actors, musicians, and other artists.
The attacks and denunciations extended to universities, including Cornell.
HUAC believed the nation's colleges were full of people with dangerous ideas that had to be stifled.

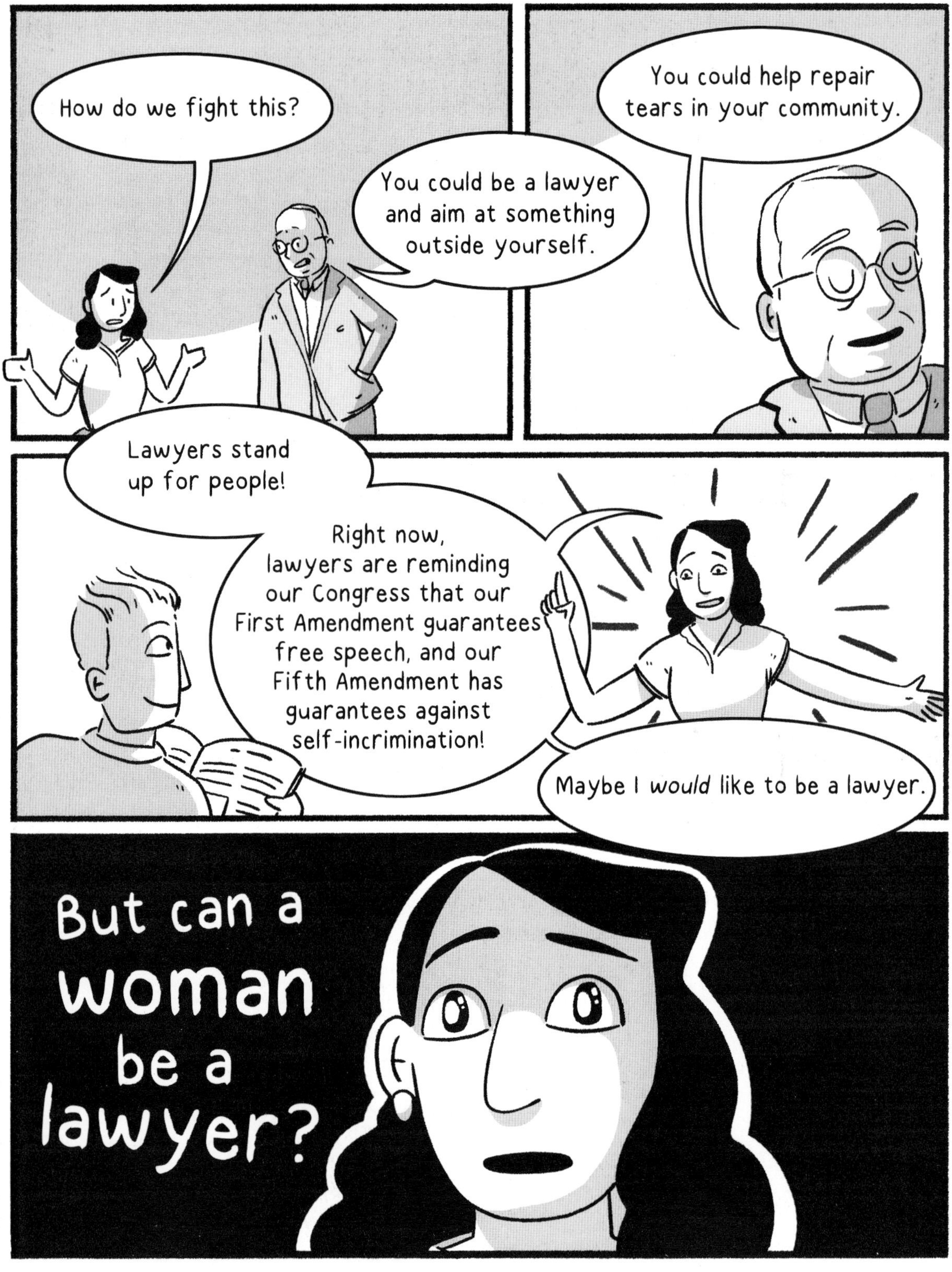
How do we fight this?
You could be a lawyer and aim at something outside yourself.
You could help repair tears in your community.
Lawyers stand up for people!
Right now, lawyers are reminding our Congress that our First Amendment guarantees free speech, and our Fifth Amendment has guarantees against self-incrimination!
Maybe I *would* like to be a lawyer.
But can a woman be a lawyer?

CHAPTER 15

Let Her Try

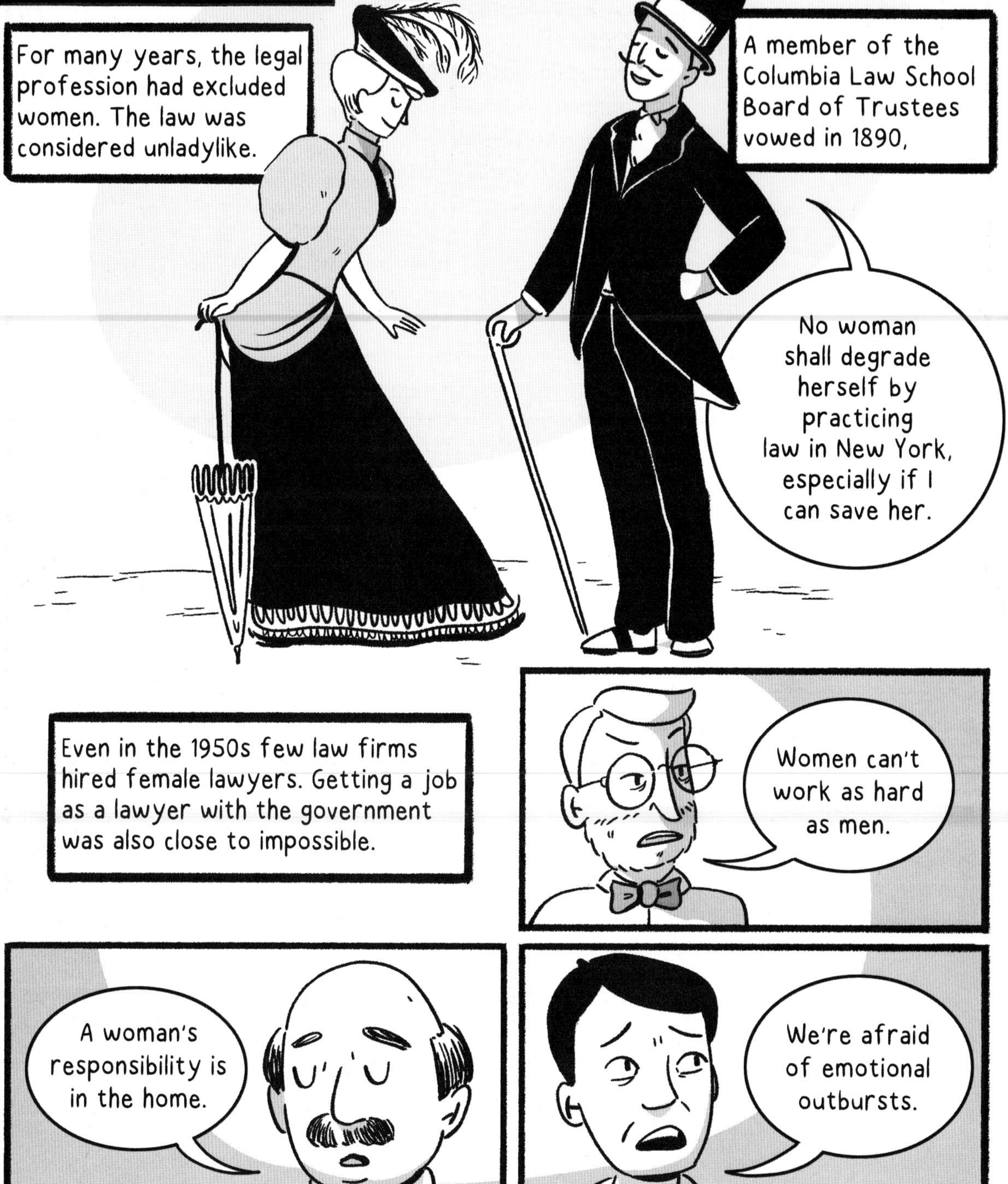
For many years, the legal profession had excluded women. The law was considered unladylike.
A member of the Columbia Law School Board of Trustees vowed in 1890,
No woman shall degrade herself by practicing law in New York, especially if I can save her.
Even in the 1950s few law firms hired female lawyers. Getting a job as a lawyer with the government was also close to impossible.
Women can't work as hard as men.
A woman's responsibility is in the home.
We're afraid of emotional outbursts.

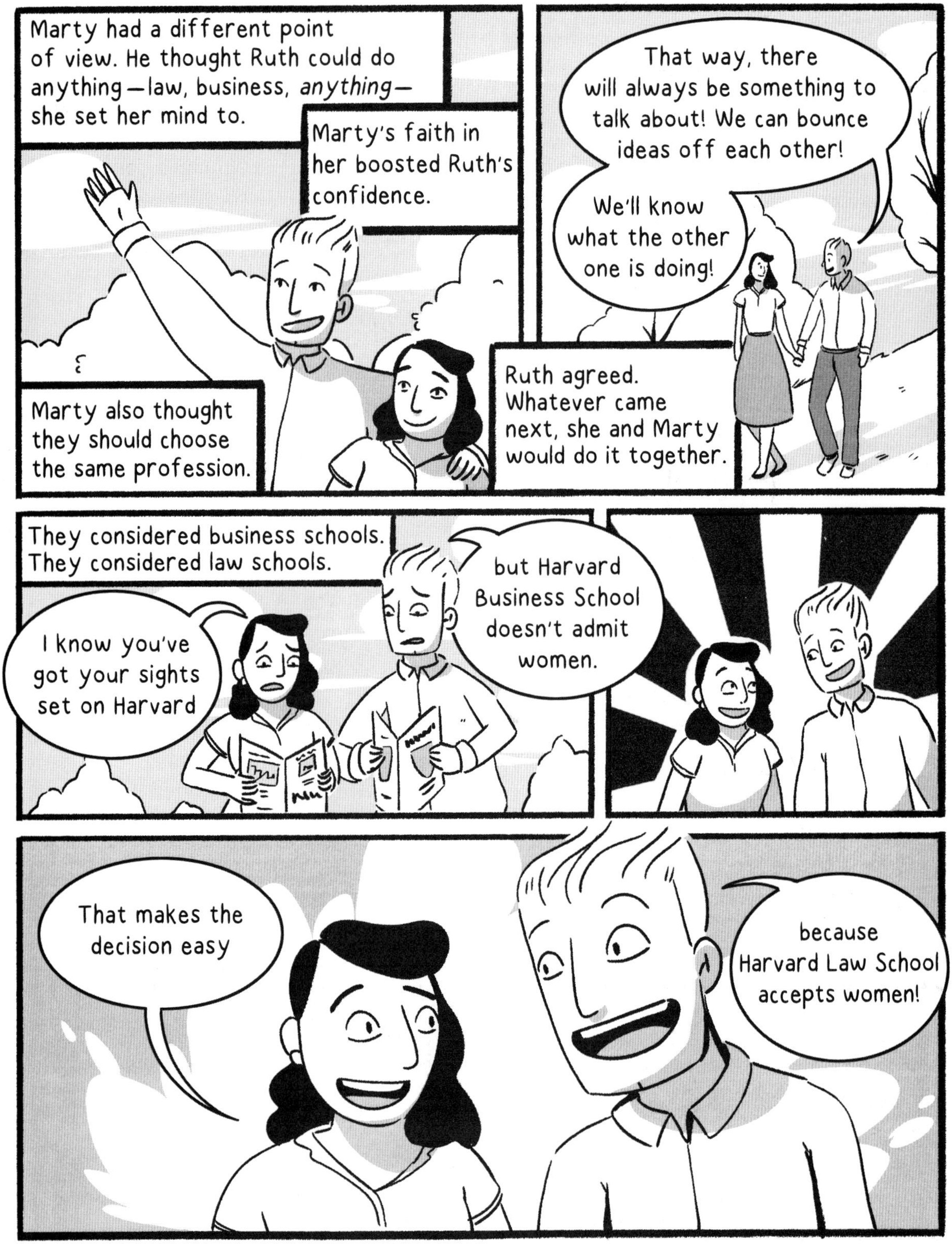

Marty had a different point of view. He thought Ruth could do anything—law, business, *anything*—she set her mind to.
Marty's faith in her boosted Ruth's confidence.
Marty also thought they should choose the same profession.
That way, there will always be something to talk about! We can bounce ideas off each other!
We'll know what the other one is doing!
Ruth agreed. Whatever came next, she and Marty would do it together.
They considered business schools. They considered law schools.
I know you've got your sights set on Harvard
but Harvard Business School doesn't admit women.
That makes the decision easy
because Harvard Law School accepts women!

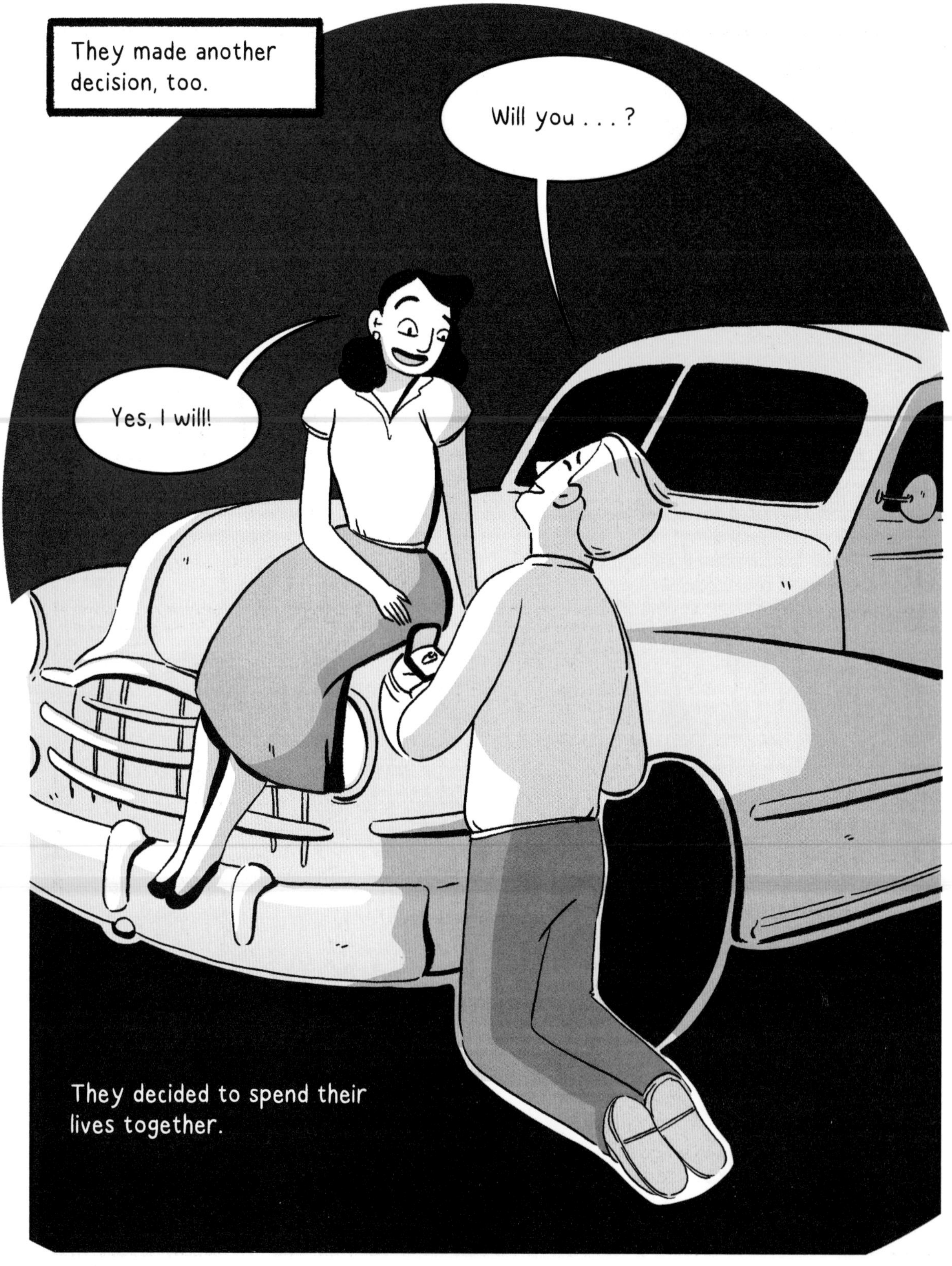
They made another decision, too.
Will you . . . ?
Yes, I will!
They decided to spend their lives together.

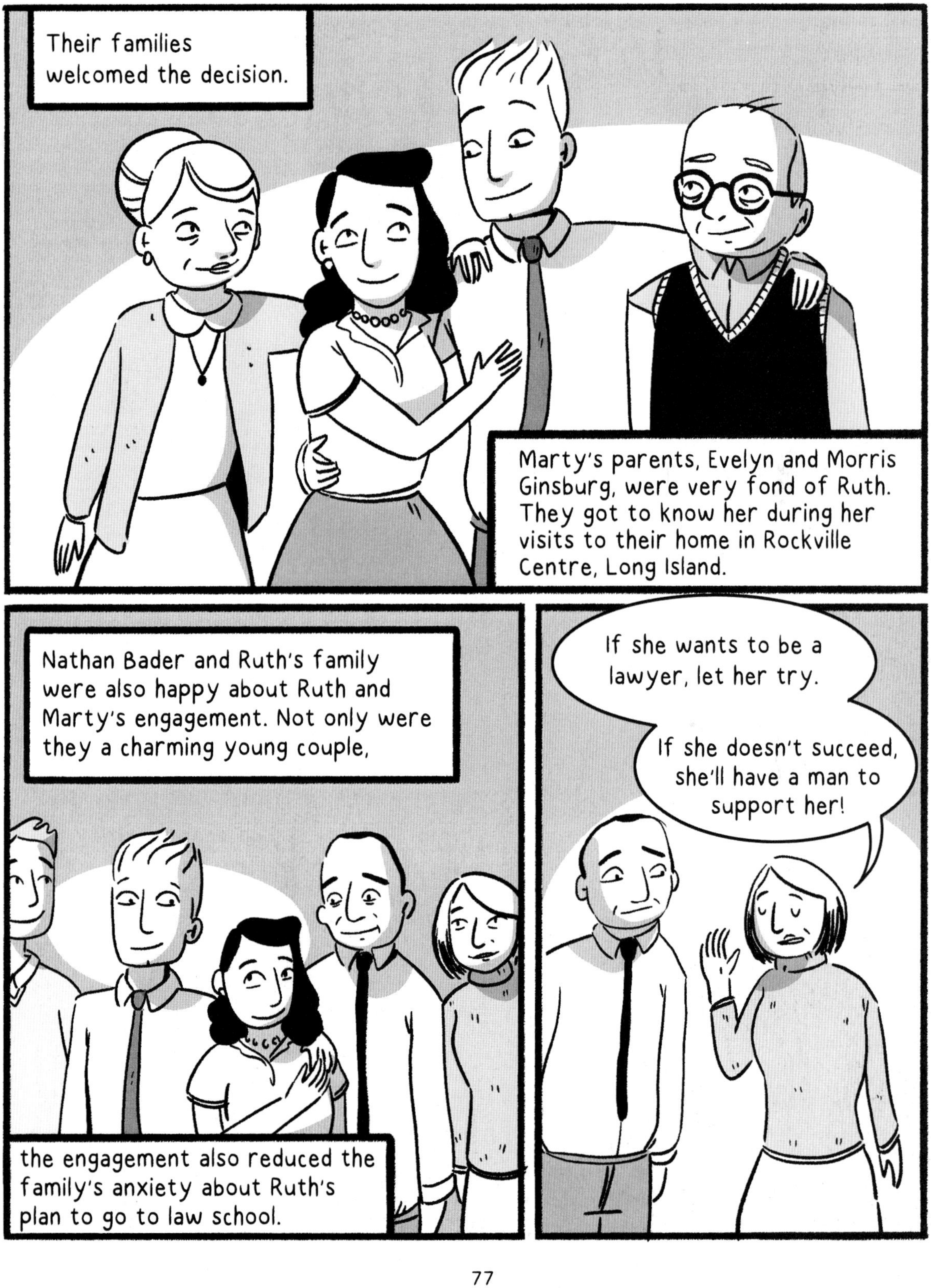
Their families welcomed the decision.
Marty's parents, Evelyn and Morris Ginsburg, were very fond of Ruth. They got to know her during her visits to their home in Rockville Centre, Long Island.
Nathan Bader and Ruth's family were also happy about Ruth and Marty's engagement. Not only were they a charming young couple,
the engagement also reduced the family's anxiety about Ruth's plan to go to law school.
If she wants to be a lawyer, let her try.
If she doesn't succeed, she'll have a man to support her!

CHAPTER 16
Advice

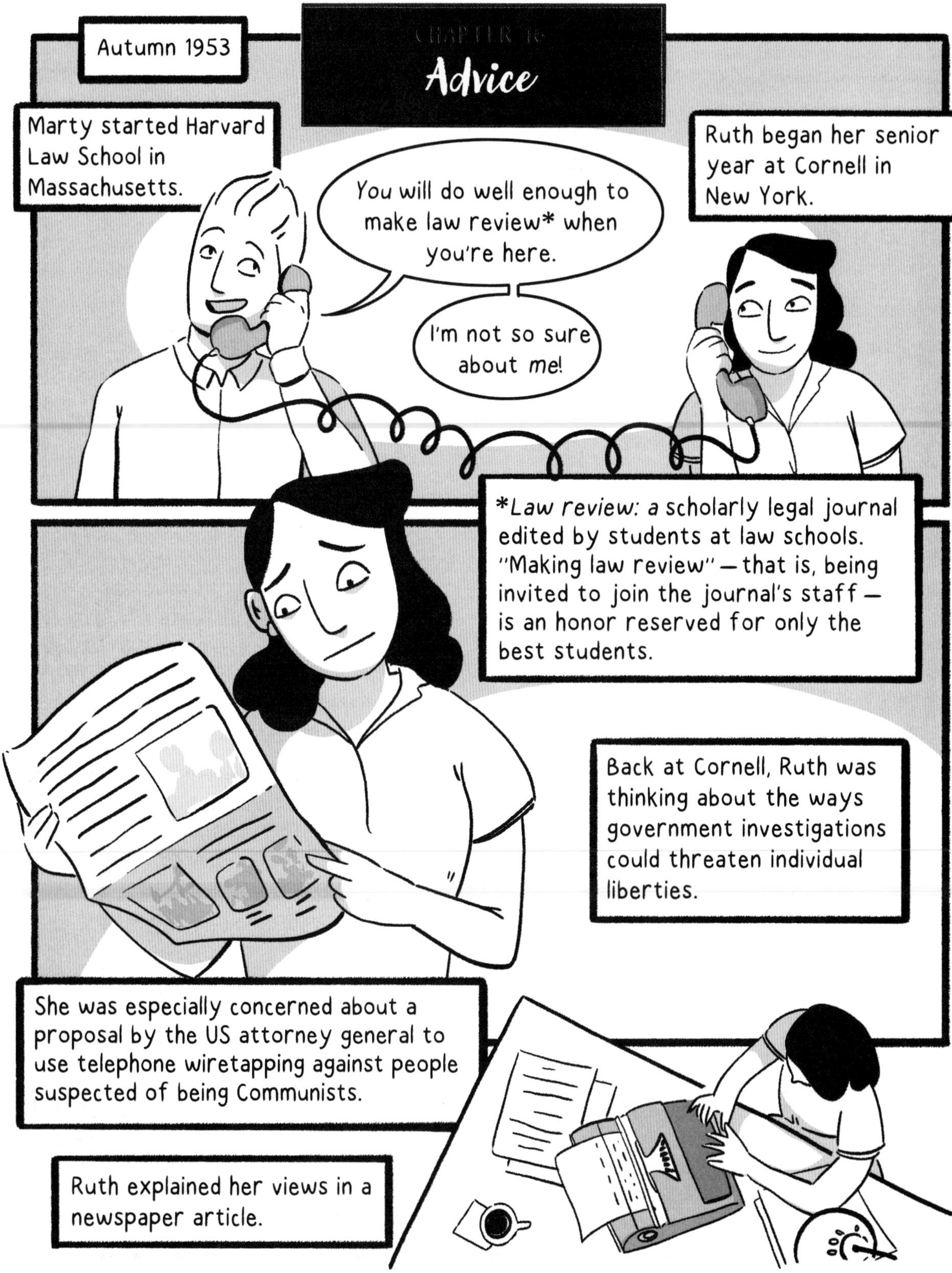

Autumn 1953
Marty started Harvard Law School in Massachusetts.
Ruth began her senior year at Cornell in New York.
You will do well enough to make law review* when you're here.
I'm not so sure about *me*!
**Law review:* a scholarly legal journal edited by students at law schools. "Making law review" — that is, being invited to join the journal's staff — is an honor reserved for only the best students.
Back at Cornell, Ruth was thinking about the ways government investigations could threaten individual liberties.
She was especially concerned about a proposal by the US attorney general to use telephone wiretapping against people suspected of being Communists.
Ruth explained her views in a newspaper article.

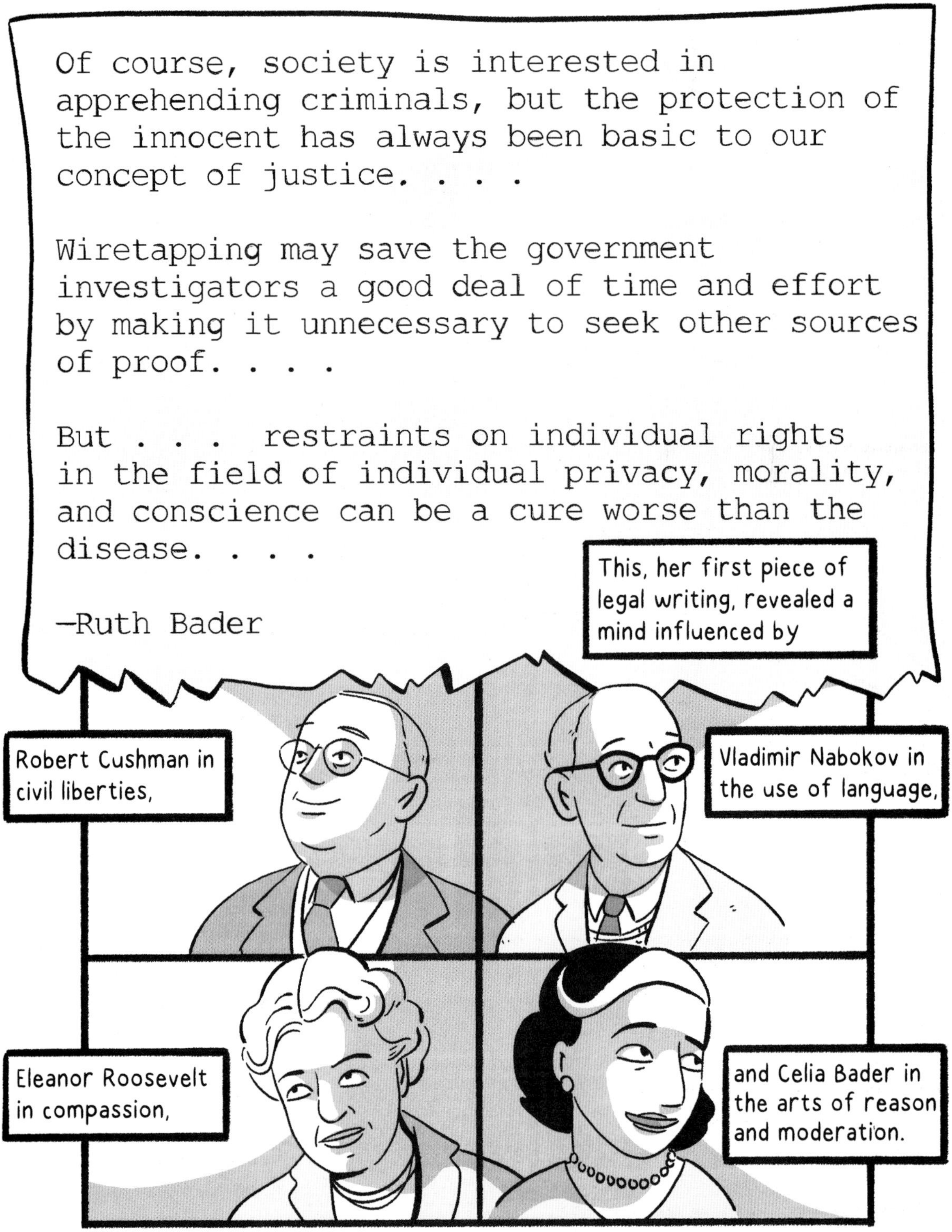
Of course, society is interested in apprehending criminals, but the protection of the innocent has always been basic to our concept of justice. . . .
Wiretapping may save the government investigators a good deal of time and effort by making it unnecessary to seek other sources of proof. . . .
But . . . restraints on individual rights in the field of individual privacy, morality, and conscience can be a cure worse than the disease. . . .
—Ruth Bader
This, her first piece of legal writing, revealed a mind influenced by
Robert Cushman in civil liberties,
Vladimir Nabokov in the use of language,
Eleanor Roosevelt in compassion,
and Celia Bader in the arts of reason and moderation.

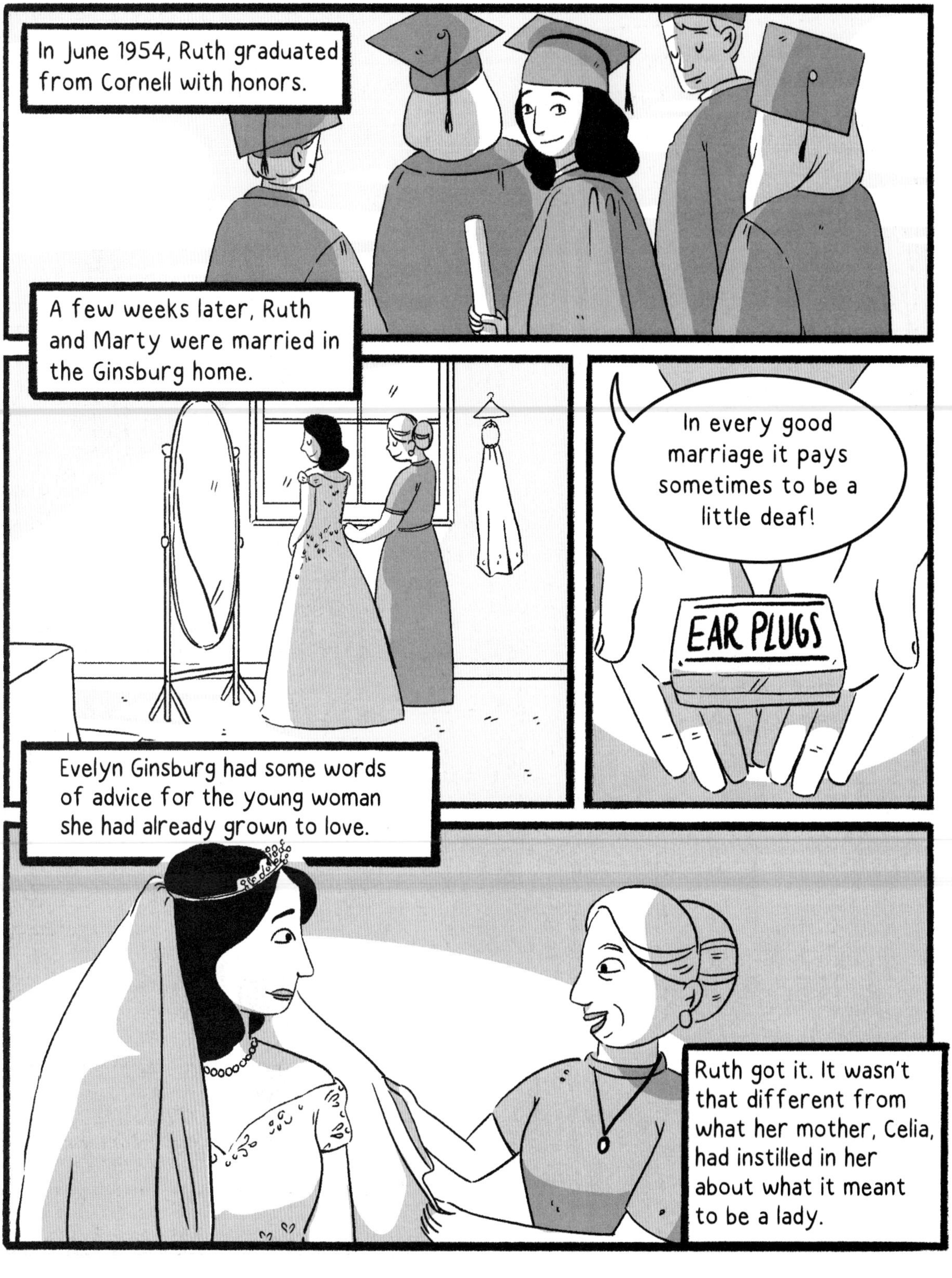
In June 1954, Ruth graduated from Cornell with honors.
A few weeks later, Ruth and Marty were married in the Ginsburg home.
In every good marriage it pays sometimes to be a little deaf!
EAR PLUGS
Evelyn Ginsburg had some words of advice for the young woman she had already grown to love.
Ruth got it. It wasn't that different from what her mother, Celia, had instilled in her about what it meant to be a lady.

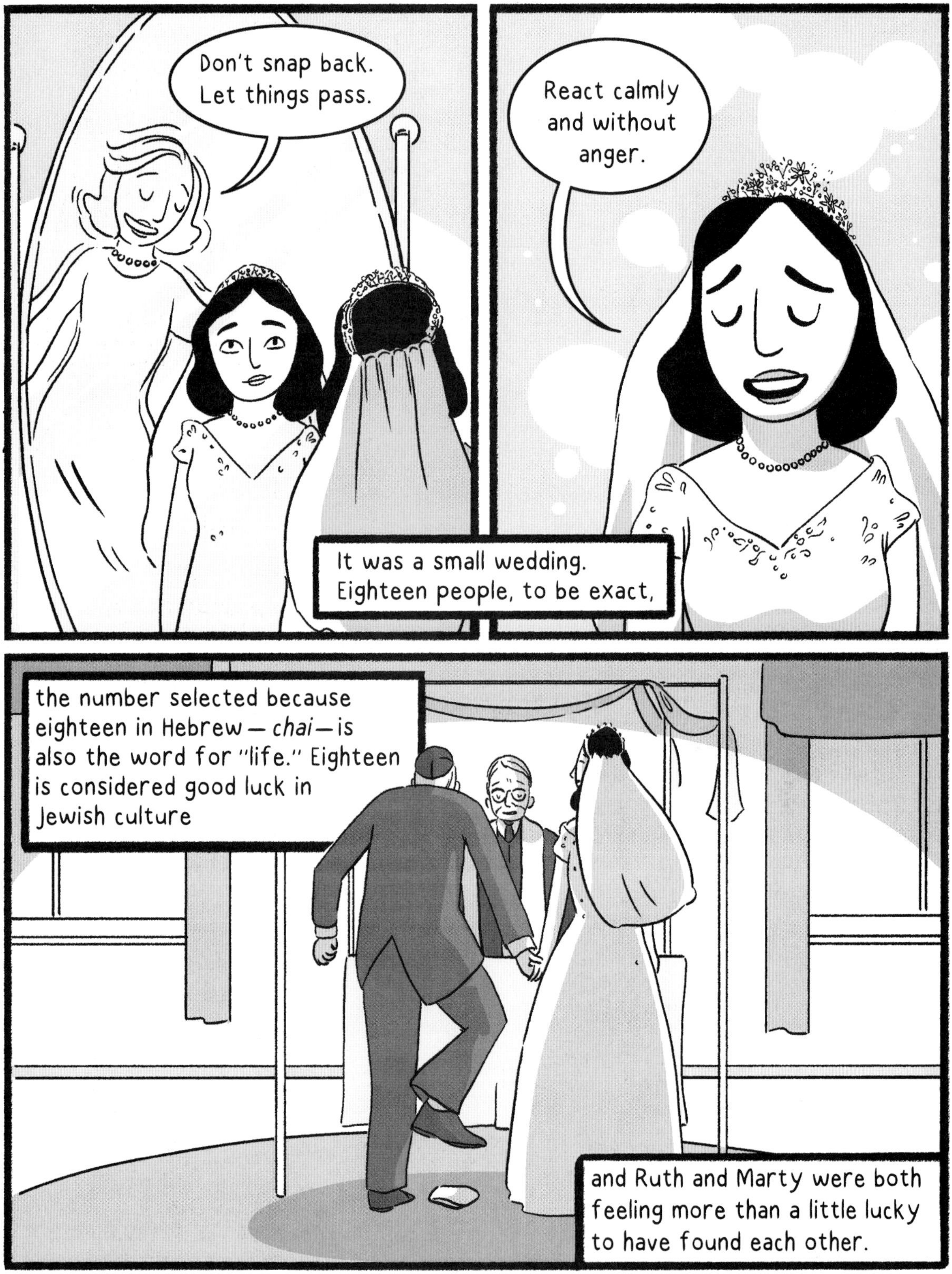
Don't snap back. Let things pass.
React calmly and without anger.
It was a small wedding. Eighteen people, to be exact,
the number selected because eighteen in Hebrew — *chai* — is also the word for "life." Eighteen is considered good luck in Jewish culture
and Ruth and Marty were both feeling more than a little lucky to have found each other.

CHAPTER 17

Detour

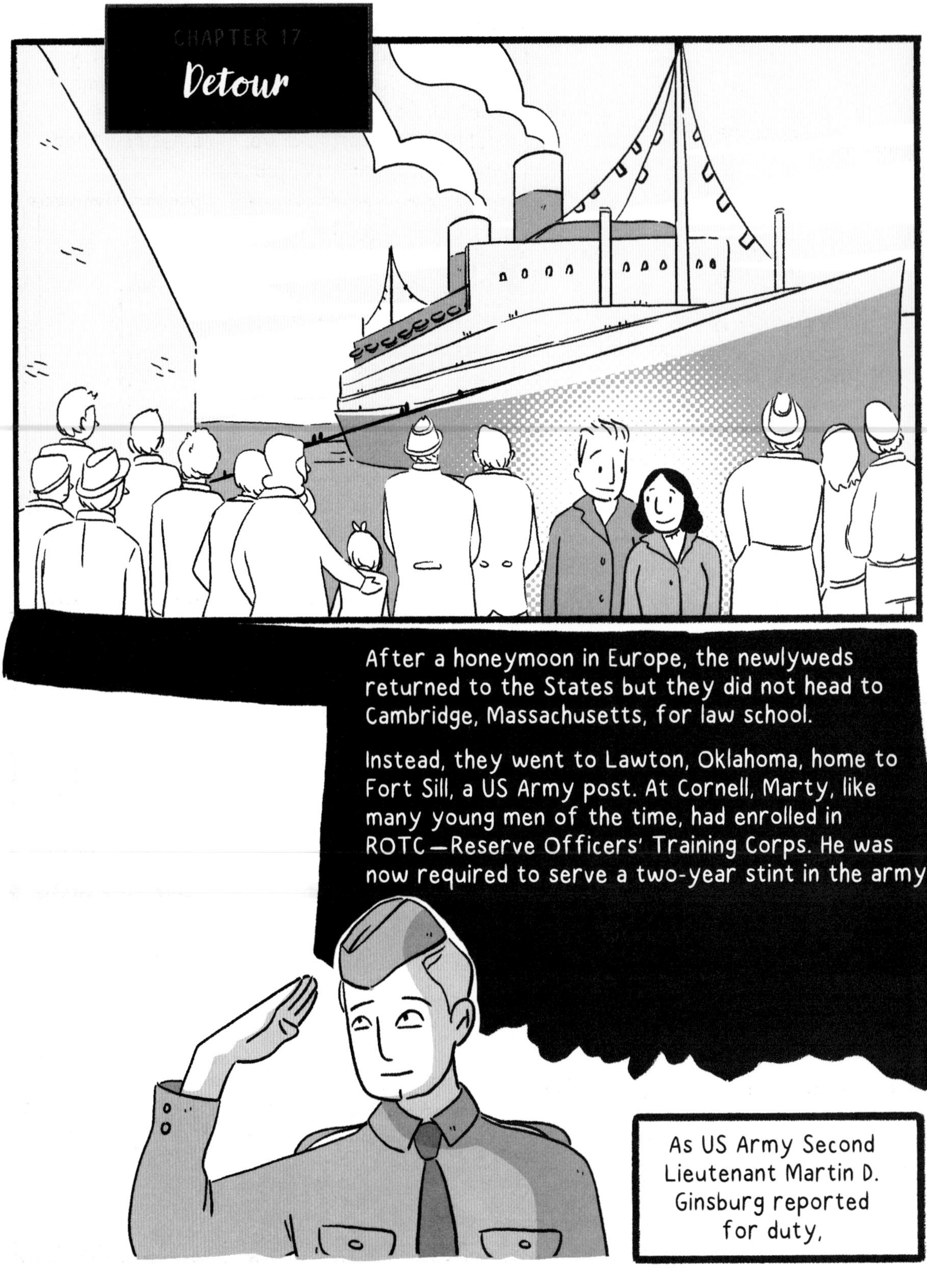
After a honeymoon in Europe, the newlyweds returned to the States but they did not head to Cambridge, Massachusetts, for law school.
Instead, they went to Lawton, Oklahoma, home to Fort Sill, a US Army post. At Cornell, Marty, like many young men of the time, had enrolled in ROTC—Reserve Officers' Training Corps. He was now required to serve a two-year stint in the army.
As US Army Second Lieutenant Martin D. Ginsburg reported for duty,

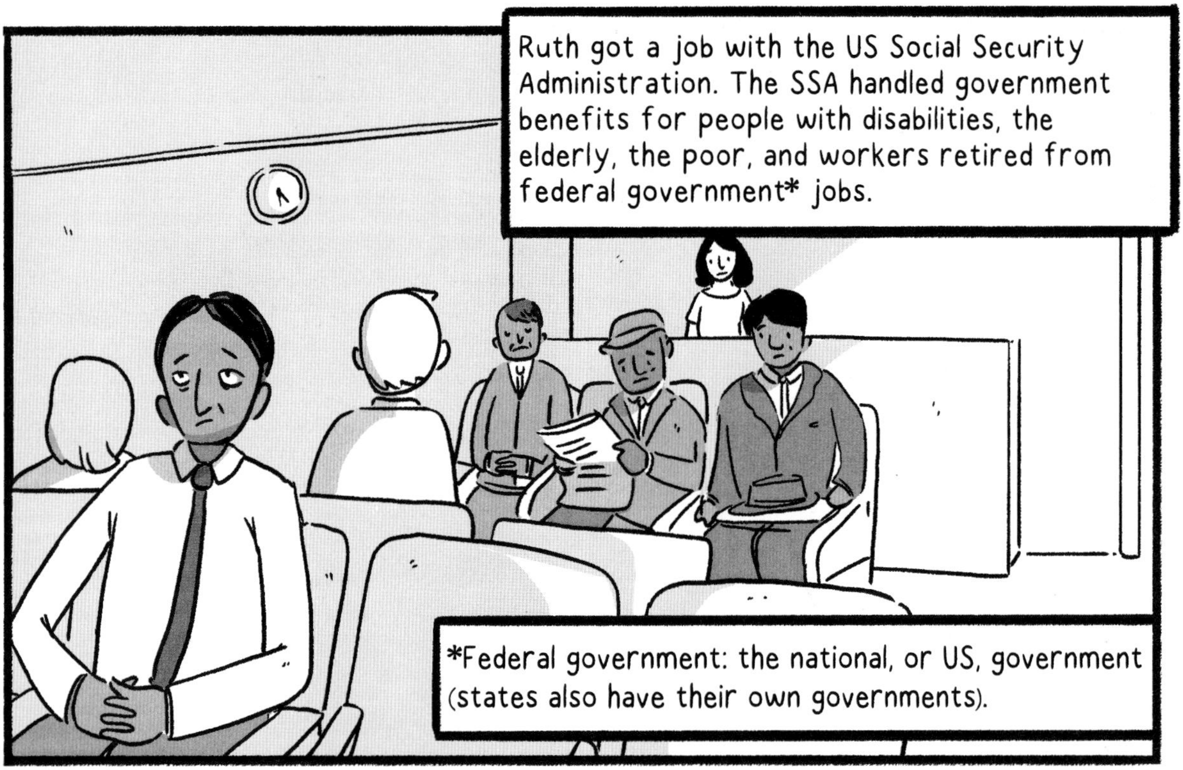
Ruth got a job with the US Social Security Administration. The SSA handled government benefits for people with disabilities, the elderly, the poor, and workers retired from federal government* jobs.
*Federal government: the national, or US, government (states also have their own governments).

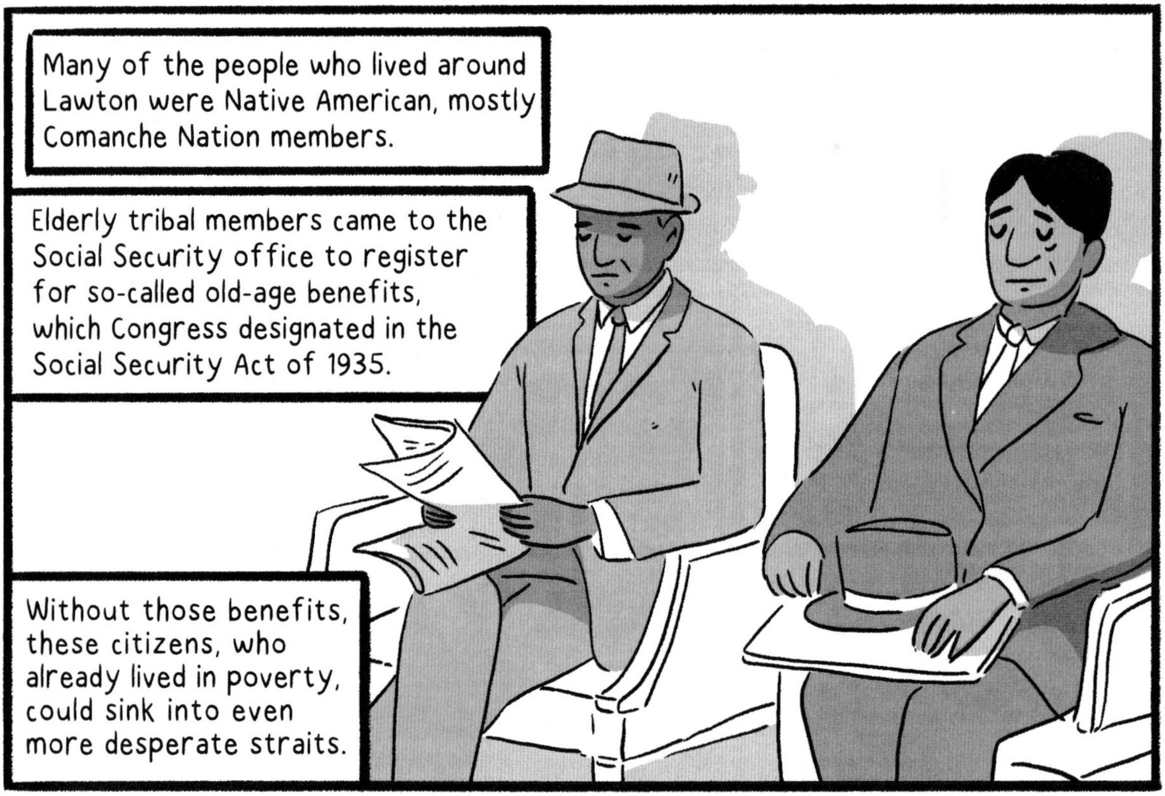
Many of the people who lived around Lawton were Native American, mostly Comanche Nation members.
Elderly tribal members came to the Social Security office to register for so-called old-age benefits, which Congress designated in the Social Security Act of 1935.
Without those benefits, these citizens, who already lived in poverty, could sink into even more desperate straits.

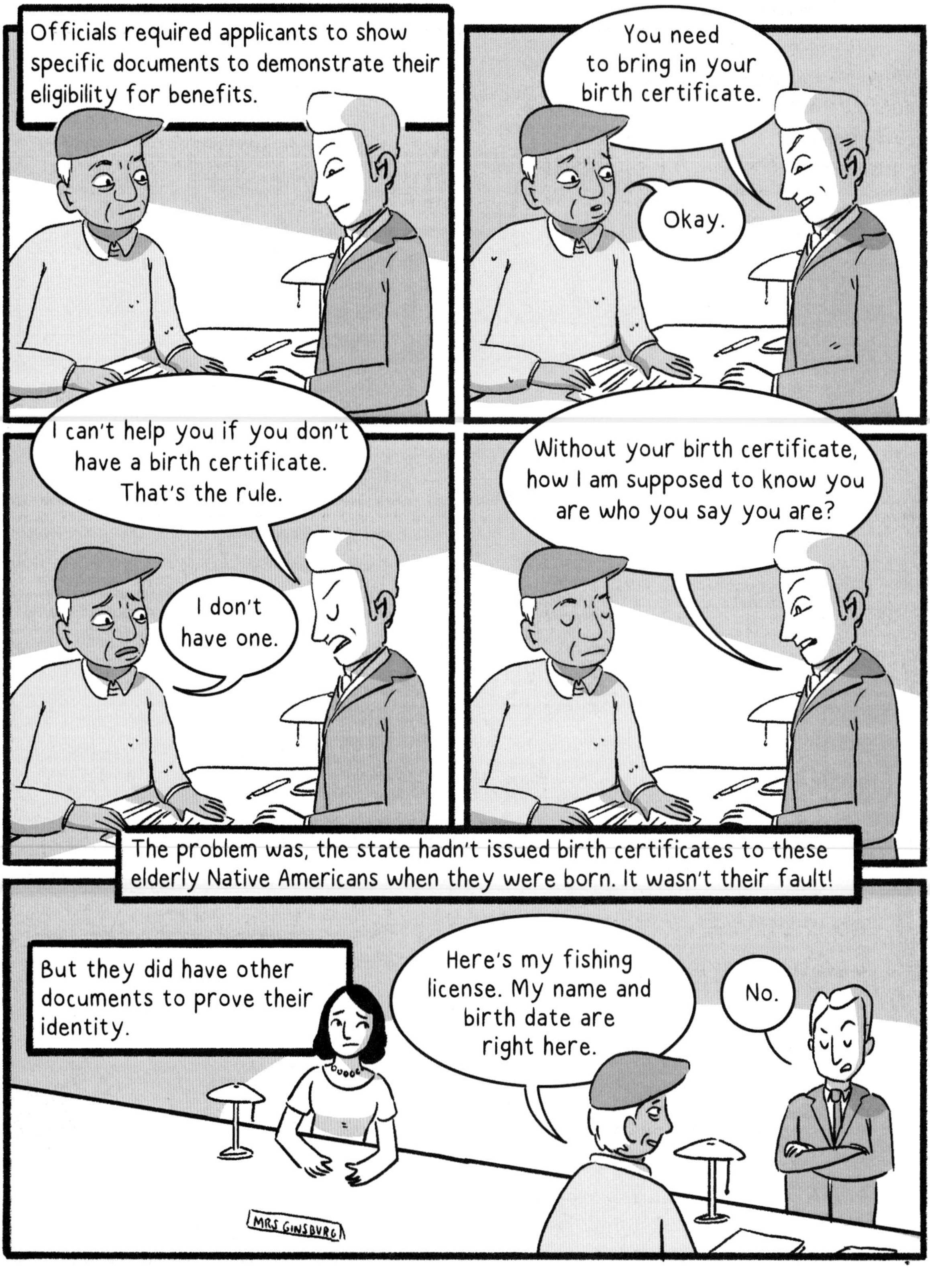
Officials required applicants to show specific documents to demonstrate their eligibility for benefits.
You need to bring in your birth certificate.
Okay.
I can't help you if you don't have a birth certificate. That's the rule.
I don't have one.
Without your birth certificate, how I am supposed to know you are who you say you are?
The problem was, the state hadn't issued birth certificates to these elderly Native Americans when they were born. It wasn't their fault!
But they did have other documents to prove their identity.
Here's my fishing license. My name and birth date are right here.
No.
MRS GINSBURG

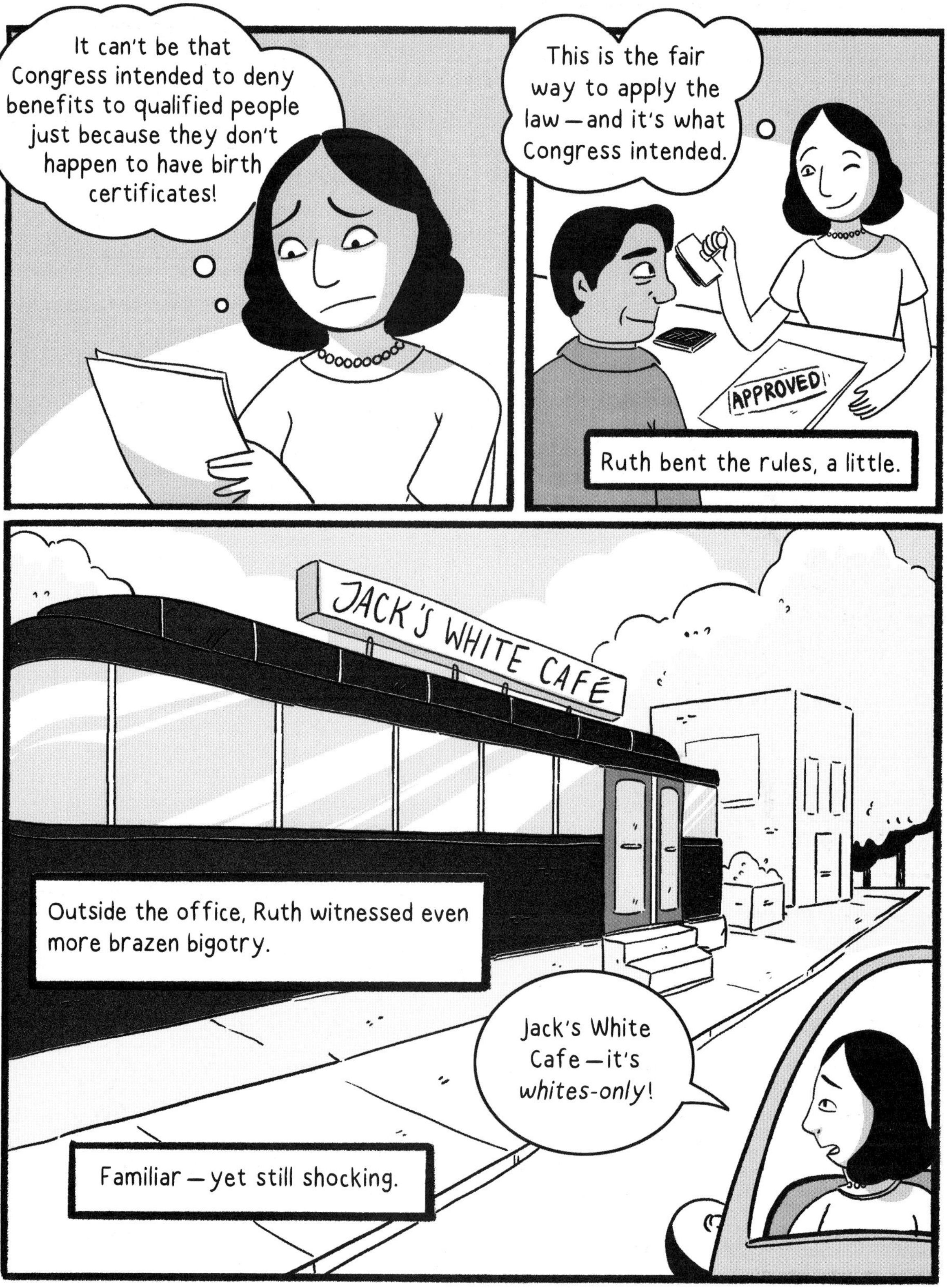
It can't be that Congress intended to deny benefits to qualified people just because they don't happen to have birth certificates!
This is the fair way to apply the law—and it's what Congress intended.
APPROVED
Ruth bent the rules, a little.
JACK'S WHITE CAFÉ
Outside the office, Ruth witnessed even more brazen bigotry.
Jack's White Cafe—it's *whites-only*!
Familiar—yet still shocking.

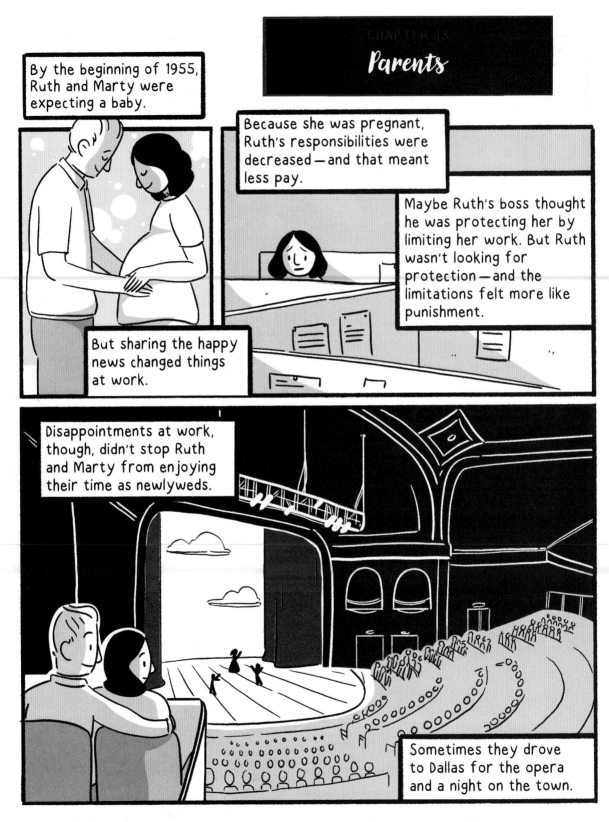

By the beginning of 1955, Ruth and Marty were expecting a baby.

Because she was pregnant, Ruth's responsibilities were decreased—and that meant less pay.

Maybe Ruth's boss thought he was protecting her by limiting her work. But Ruth wasn't looking for protection—and the limitations felt more like punishment.

But sharing the happy news changed things at work.

Disappointments at work, though, didn't stop Ruth and Marty from enjoying their time as newlyweds.

Sometimes they drove to Dallas for the opera and a night on the town.

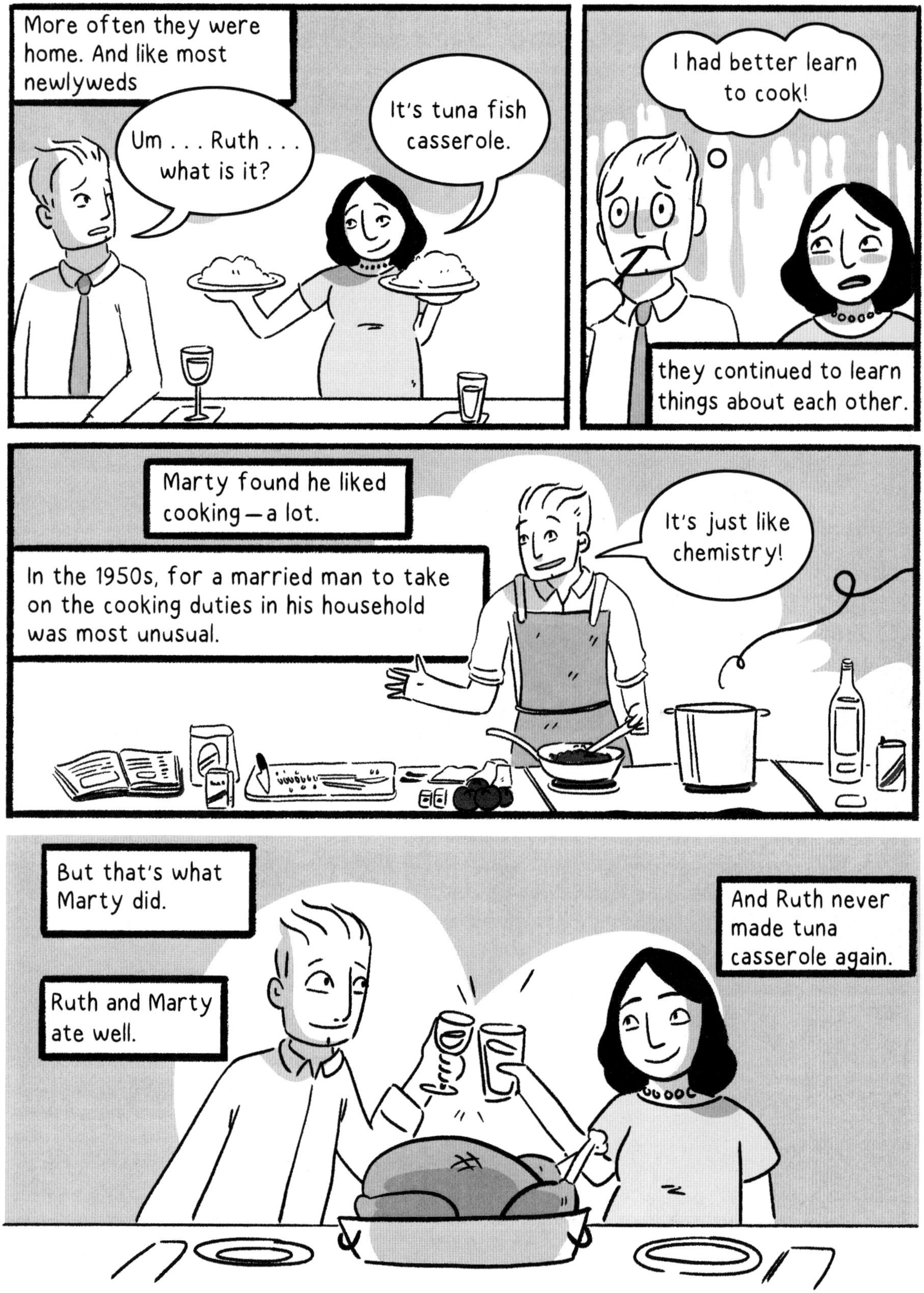
More often they were home. And like most newlyweds
Um . . . Ruth . . . what is it?
It's tuna fish casserole.
I had better learn to cook!
they continued to learn things about each other.
Marty found he liked cooking—a lot.
In the 1950s, for a married man to take on the cooking duties in his household was most unusual.
It's just like chemistry!
But that's what Marty did.
Ruth and Marty ate well.
And Ruth never made tuna casserole again.

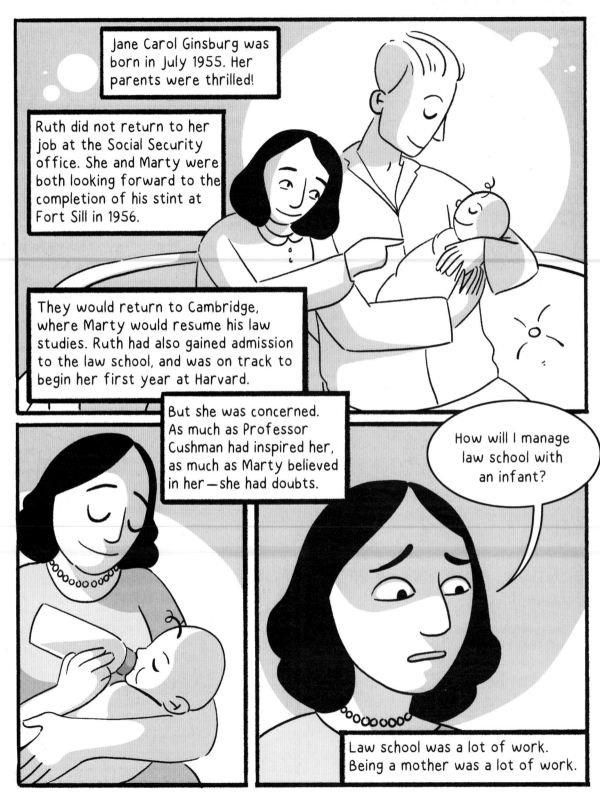

Jane Carol Ginsburg was born in July 1955. Her parents were thrilled!

Ruth did not return to her job at the Social Security office. She and Marty were both looking forward to the completion of his stint at Fort Sill in 1956.

They would return to Cambridge, where Marty would resume his law studies. Ruth had also gained admission to the law school, and was on track to begin her first year at Harvard.

But she was concerned. As much as Professor Cushman had inspired her, as much as Marty believed in her—she had doubts.

How will I manage law school with an infant?

Law school was a lot of work. Being a mother was a lot of work.

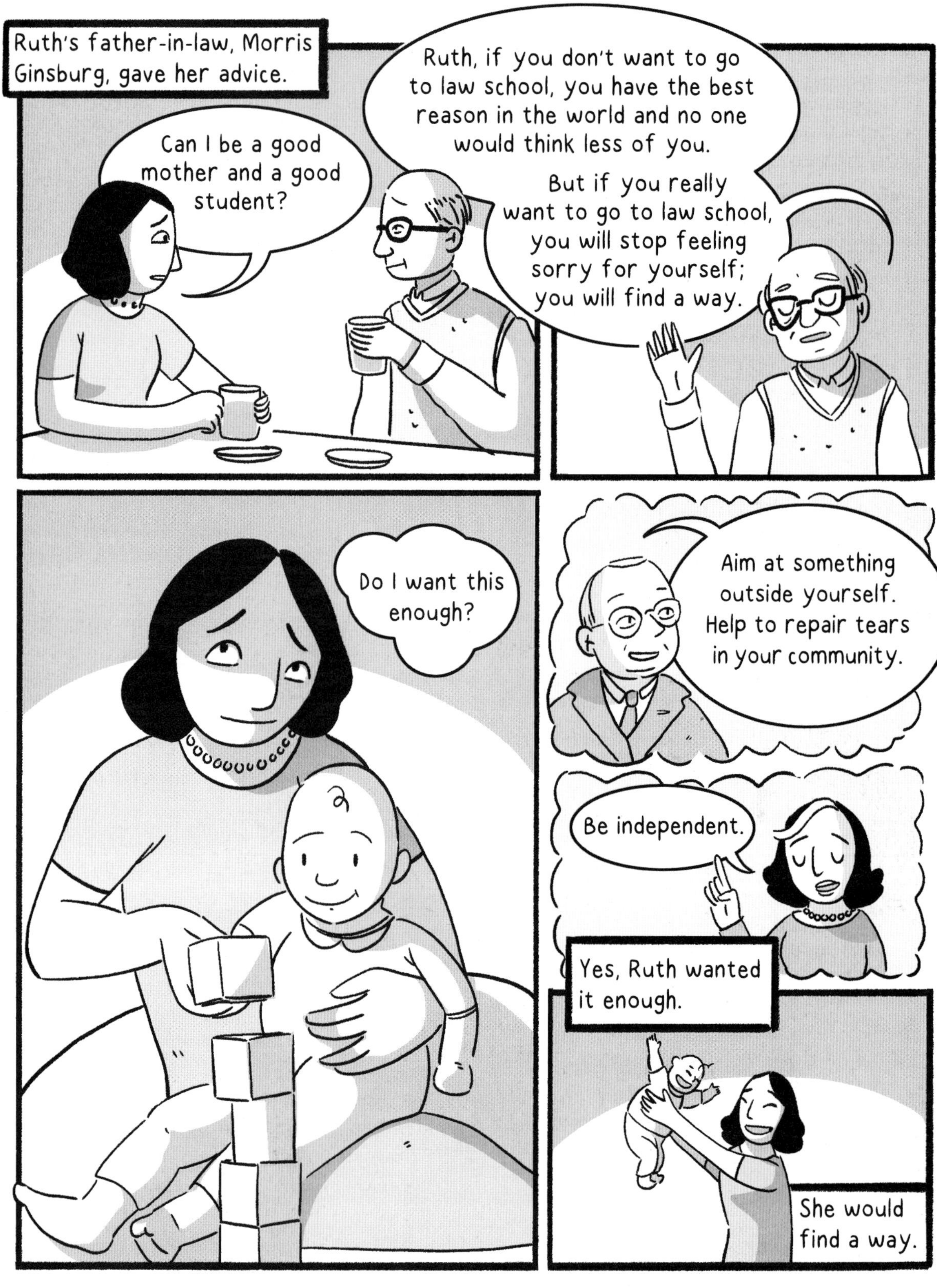
Ruth's father-in-law, Morris Ginsburg, gave her advice.
Can I be a good mother and a good student?
Ruth, if you don't want to go to law school, you have the best reason in the world and no one would think less of you.
But if you really want to go to law school, you will stop feeling sorry for yourself; you will find a way.
Do I want this enough?
Aim at something outside yourself. Help to repair tears in your community.
Be independent.
Yes, Ruth wanted it enough.
She would find a way.

CHAPTER 19

The Way Things Are

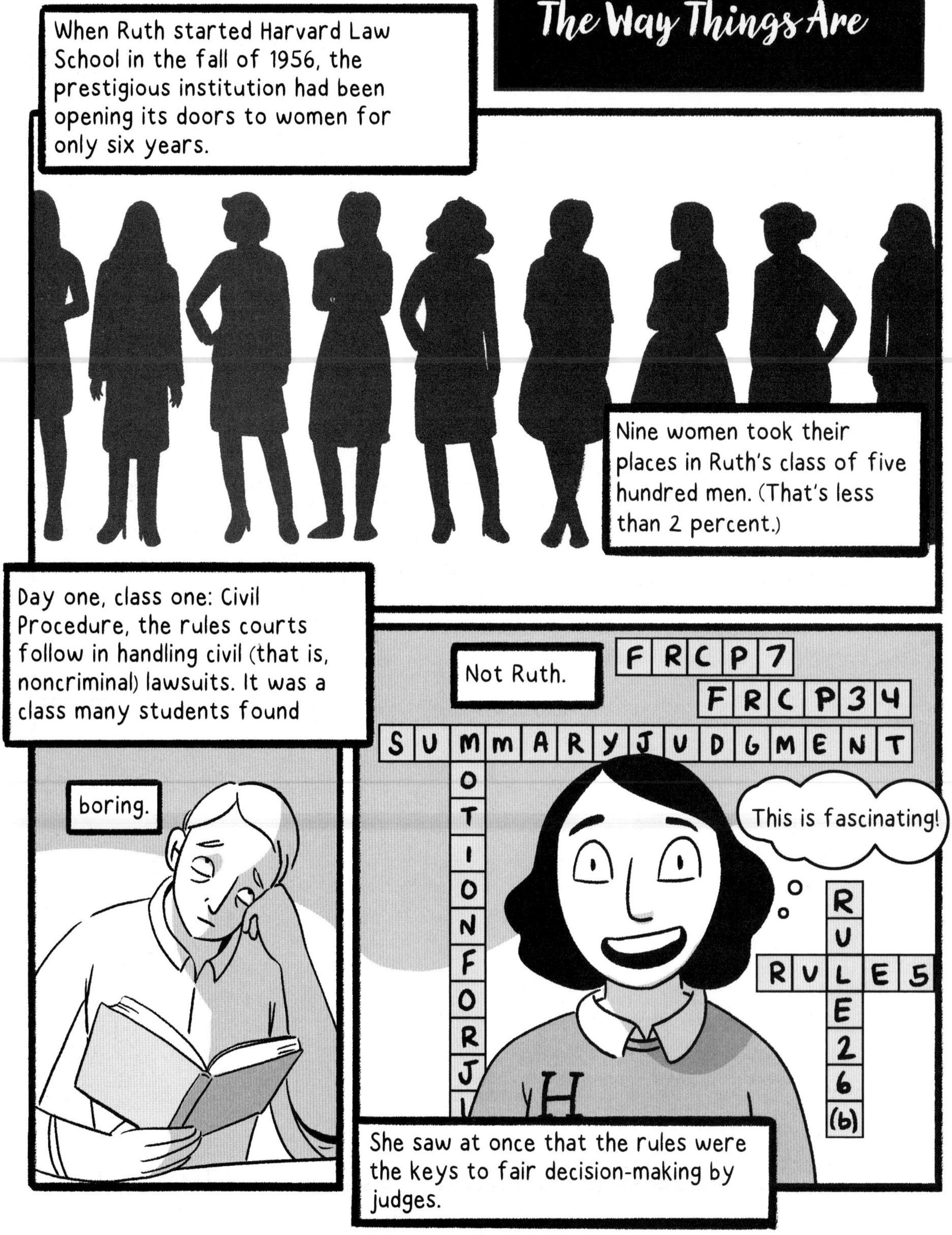
When Ruth started Harvard Law School in the fall of 1956, the prestigious institution had been opening its doors to women for only six years.
Nine women took their places in Ruth's class of five hundred men. (That's less than 2 percent.)
Day one, class one: Civil Procedure, the rules courts follow in handling civil (that is, noncriminal) lawsuits. It was a class many students found
boring.
Not Ruth.
FRCP7
FRCP34
SUMMARYJUDGMENT
MOTIONFORJ
This is fascinating!
RULE5
RULE26(b)
H
She saw at once that the rules were the keys to fair decision-making by judges.

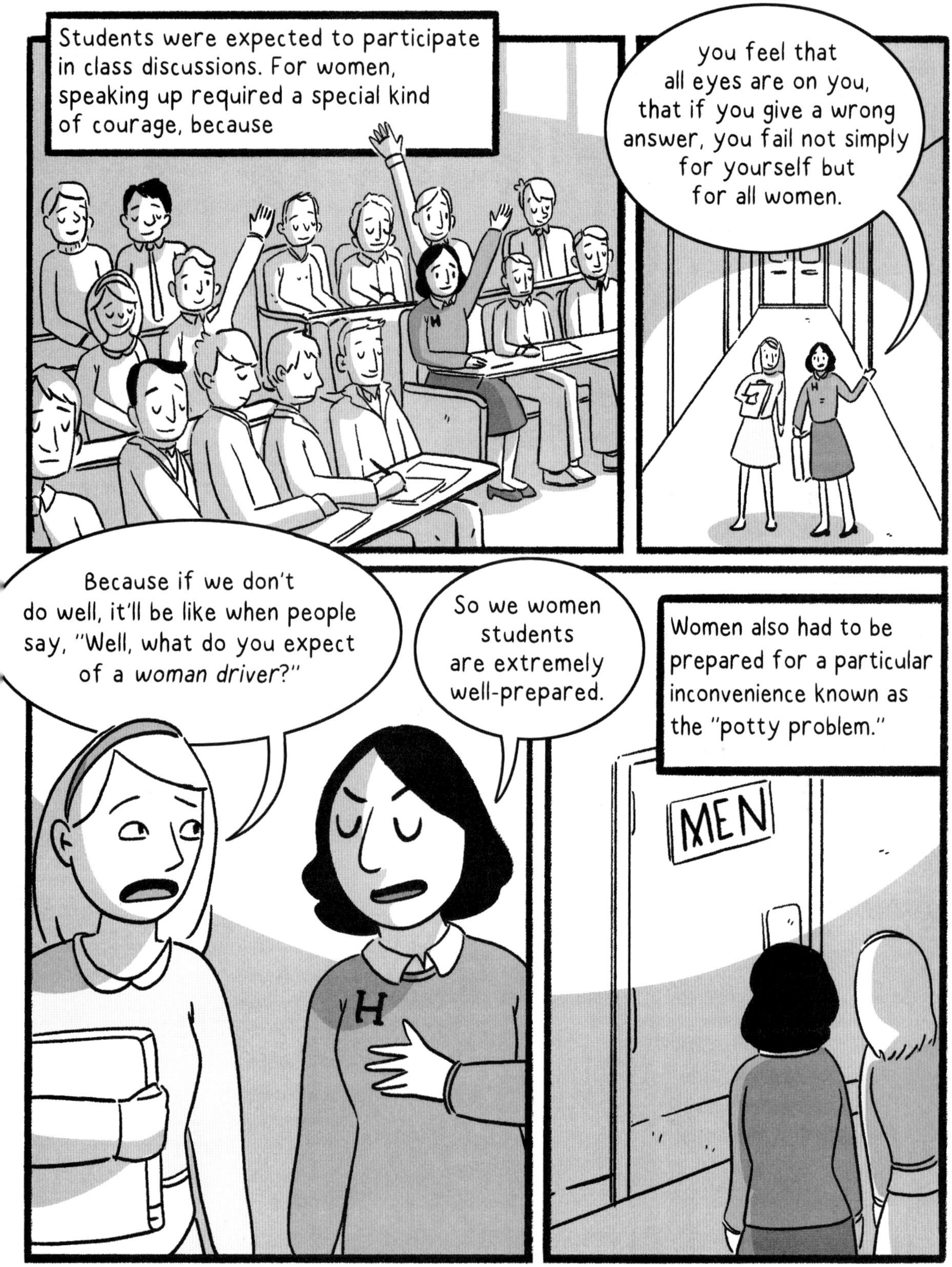
Students were expected to participate in class discussions. For women, speaking up required a special kind of courage, because
you feel that all eyes are on you, that if you give a wrong answer, you fail not simply for yourself but for all women.
Because if we don't do well, it'll be like when people say, "Well, what do you expect of a *woman driver*?"
So we women students are extremely well-prepared.
Women also had to be prepared for a particular inconvenience known as the "potty problem."
MEN

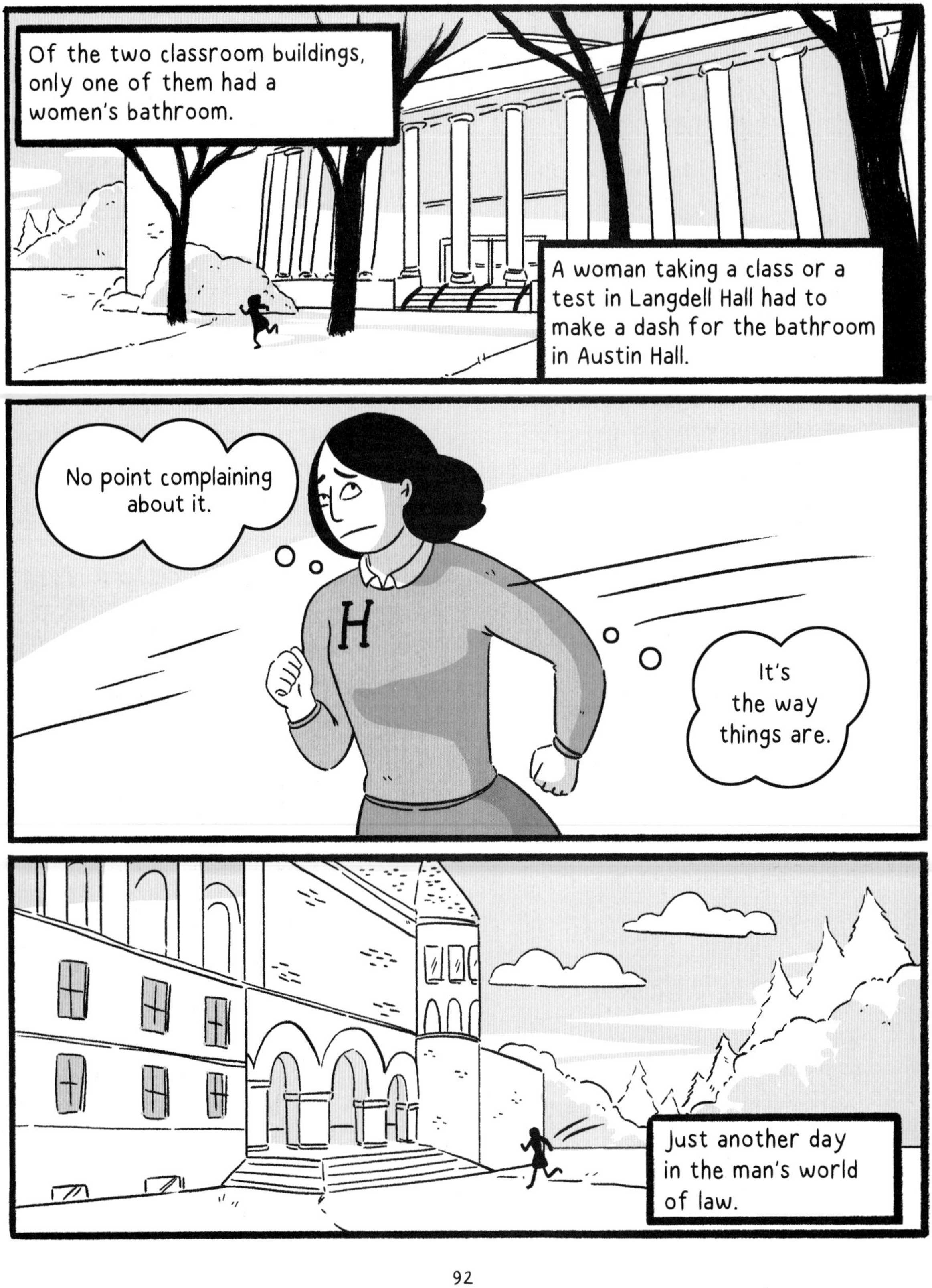
Of the two classroom buildings, only one of them had a women's bathroom.
A woman taking a class or a test in Langdell Hall had to make a dash for the bathroom in Austin Hall.
No point complaining about it.
It's the way things are.
Just another day in the man's world of law.

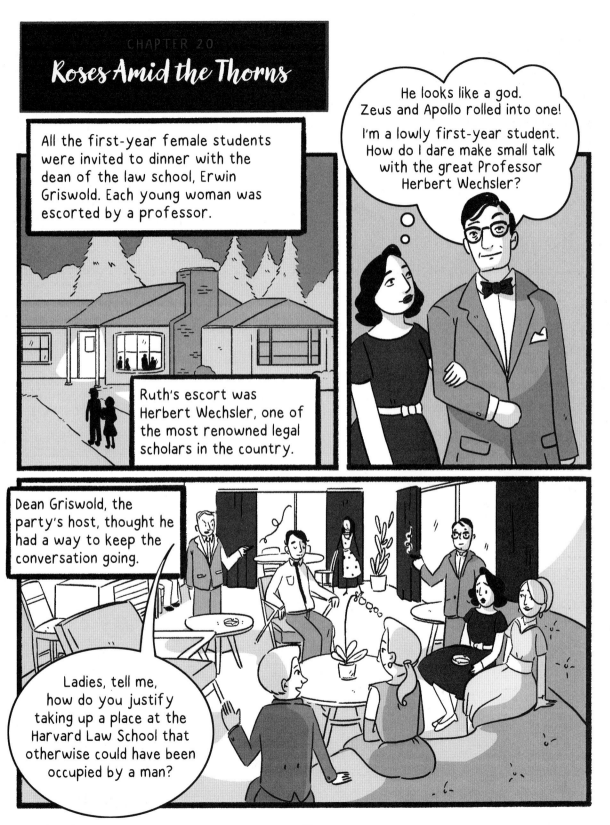

CHAPTER 20

Roses Amid the Thorns

All the first-year female students were invited to dinner with the dean of the law school, Erwin Griswold. Each young woman was escorted by a professor.

Ruth's escort was Herbert Wechsler, one of the most renowned legal scholars in the country.

He looks like a god. Zeus and Apollo rolled into one!

I'm a lowly first-year student. How do I dare make small talk with the great Professor Herbert Wechsler?

Dean Griswold, the party's host, thought he had a way to keep the conversation going.

Ladies, tell me, how do you justify taking up a place at the Harvard Law School that otherwise could have been occupied by a man?

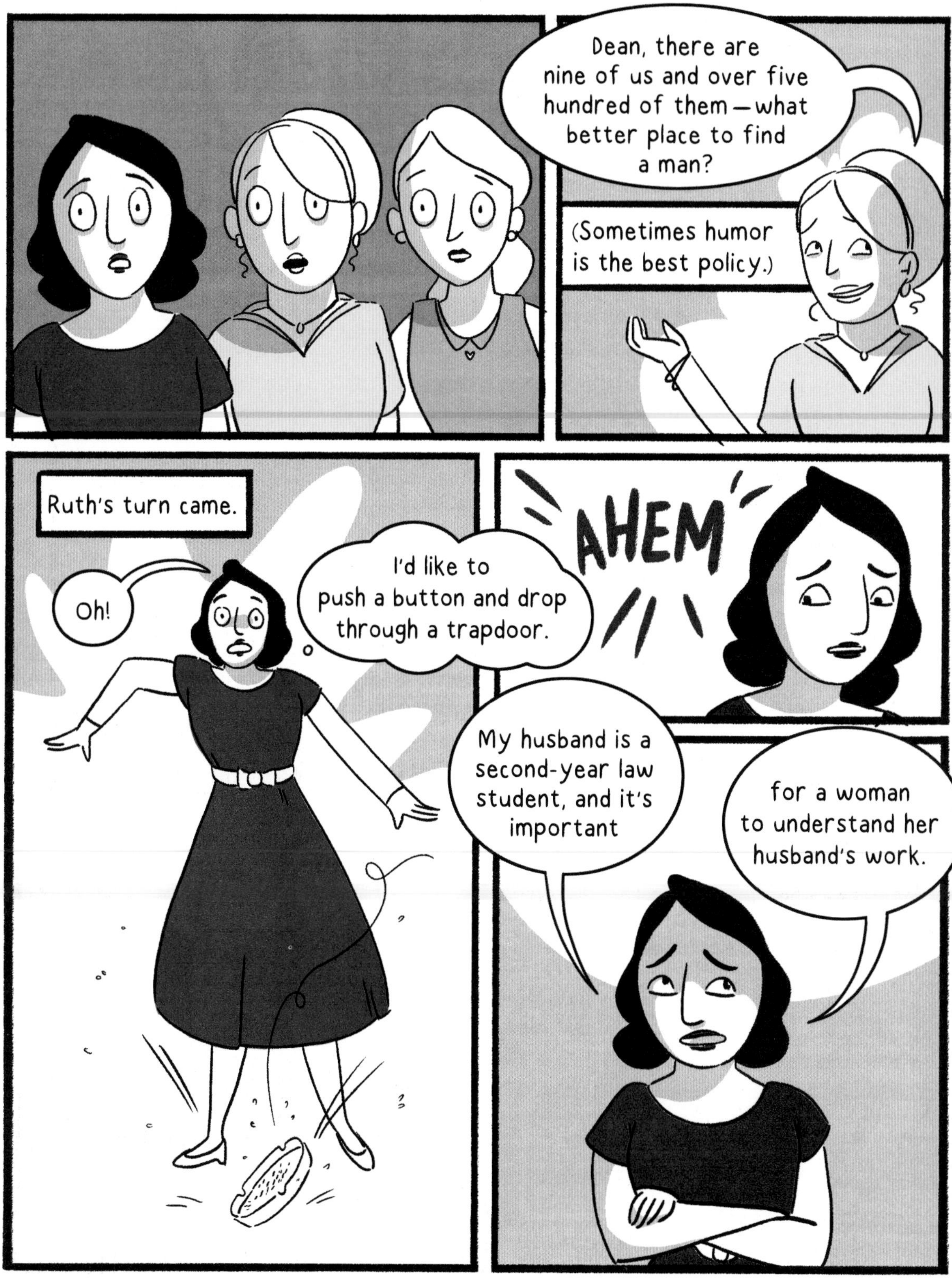
Dean, there are nine of us and over five hundred of them—what better place to find a man?
(Sometimes humor is the best policy.)
Ruth's turn came.
Oh!
I'd like to push a button and drop through a trapdoor.
AHEM
My husband is a second-year law student, and it's important
for a woman to understand her husband's work.

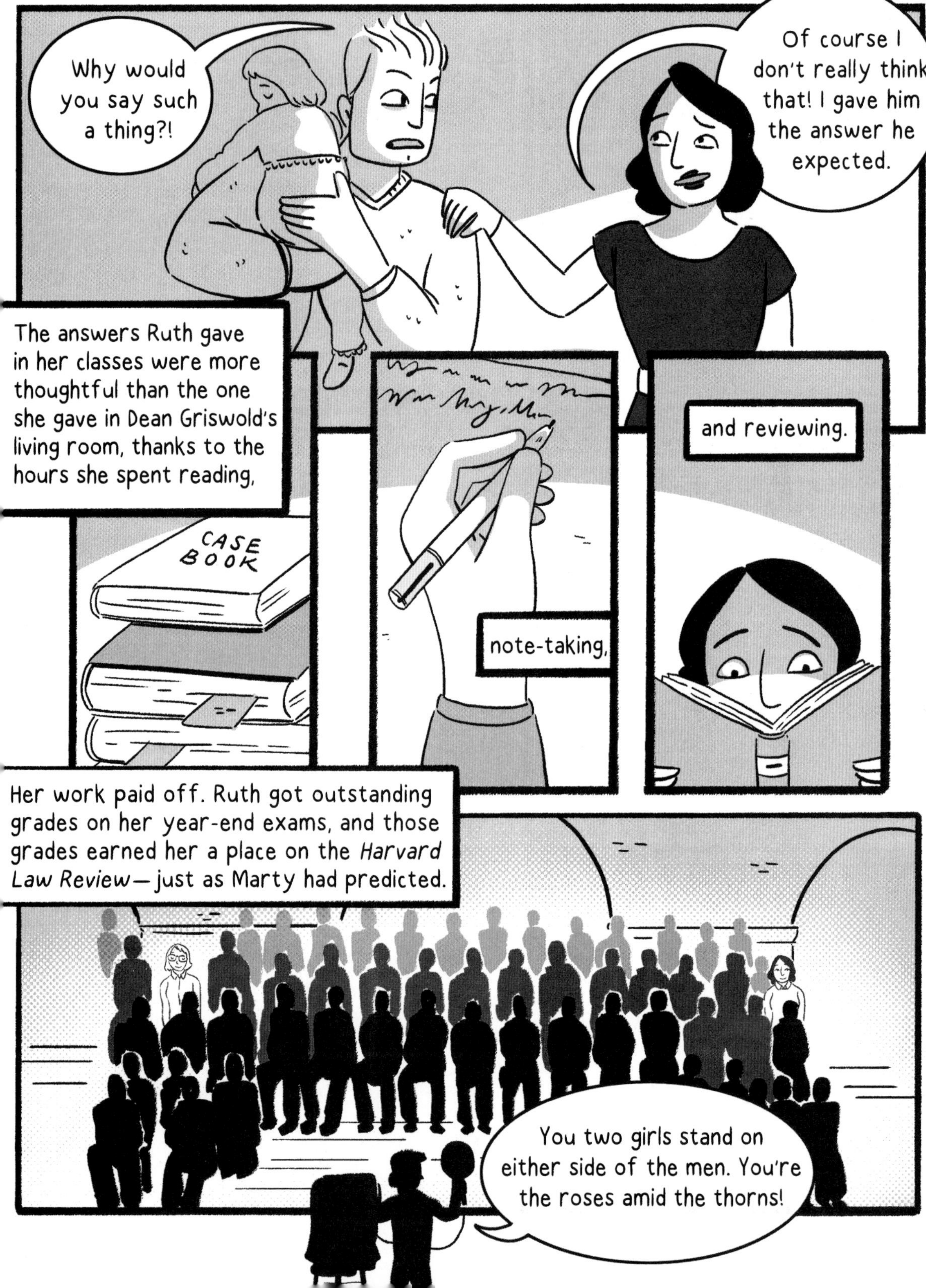
Why would you say such a thing?!
Of course I don't really think that! I gave him the answer he expected.
The answers Ruth gave in her classes were more thoughtful than the one she gave in Dean Griswold's living room, thanks to the hours she spent reading,
CASE BOOK
note-taking,
and reviewing.
Her work paid off. Ruth got outstanding grades on her year-end exams, and those grades earned her a place on the *Harvard Law Review*—just as Marty had predicted.
You two girls stand on either side of the men. You're the roses amid the thorns!

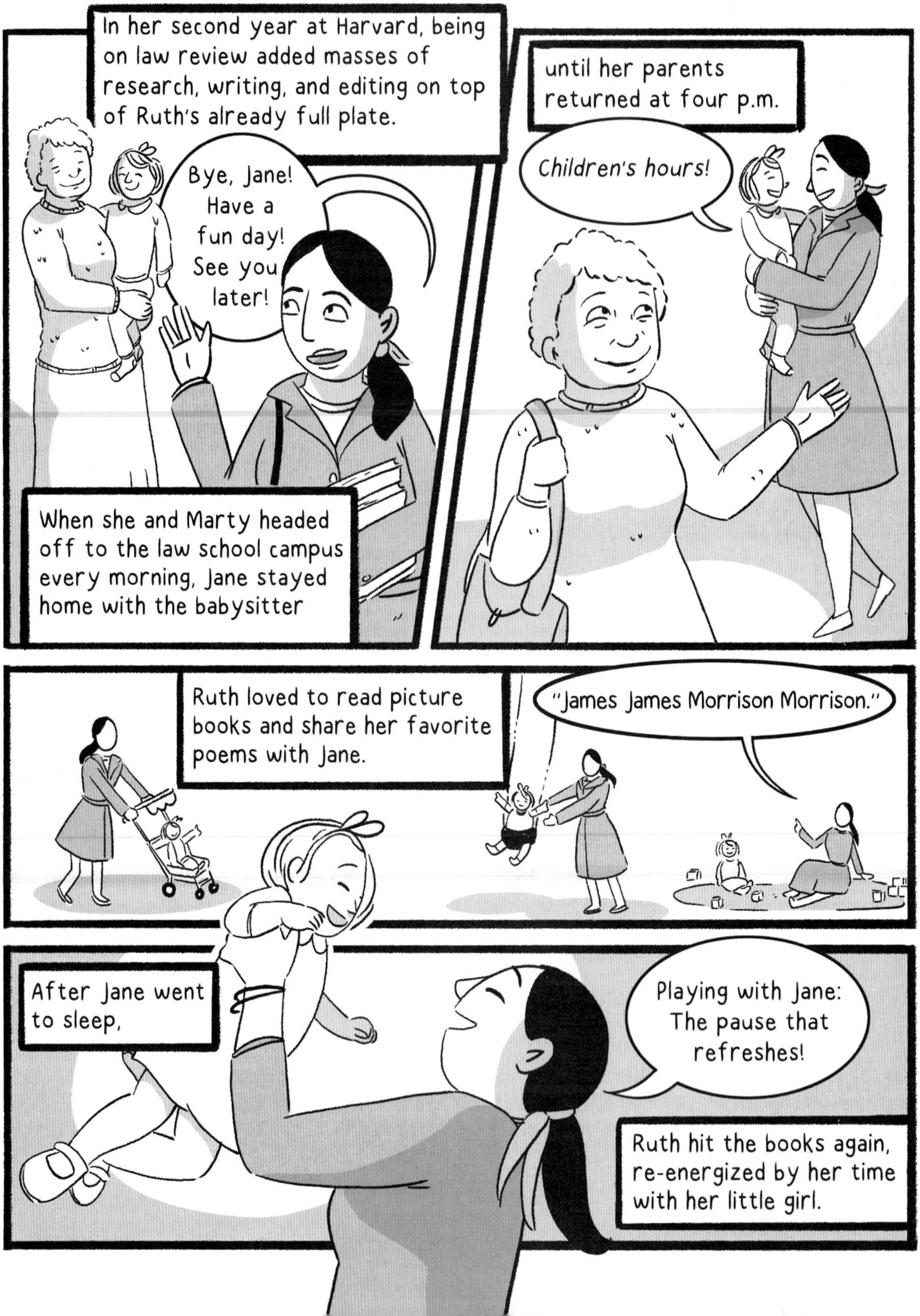
In her second year at Harvard, being on law review added masses of research, writing, and editing on top of Ruth's already full plate.
Bye, Jane! Have a fun day! See you later!
When she and Marty headed off to the law school campus every morning, Jane stayed home with the babysitter
until her parents returned at four p.m.
Children's hours!
Ruth loved to read picture books and share her favorite poems with Jane.
"James James Morrison Morrison."
After Jane went to sleep,
Playing with Jane: The pause that refreshes!
Ruth hit the books again, re-energized by her time with her little girl.

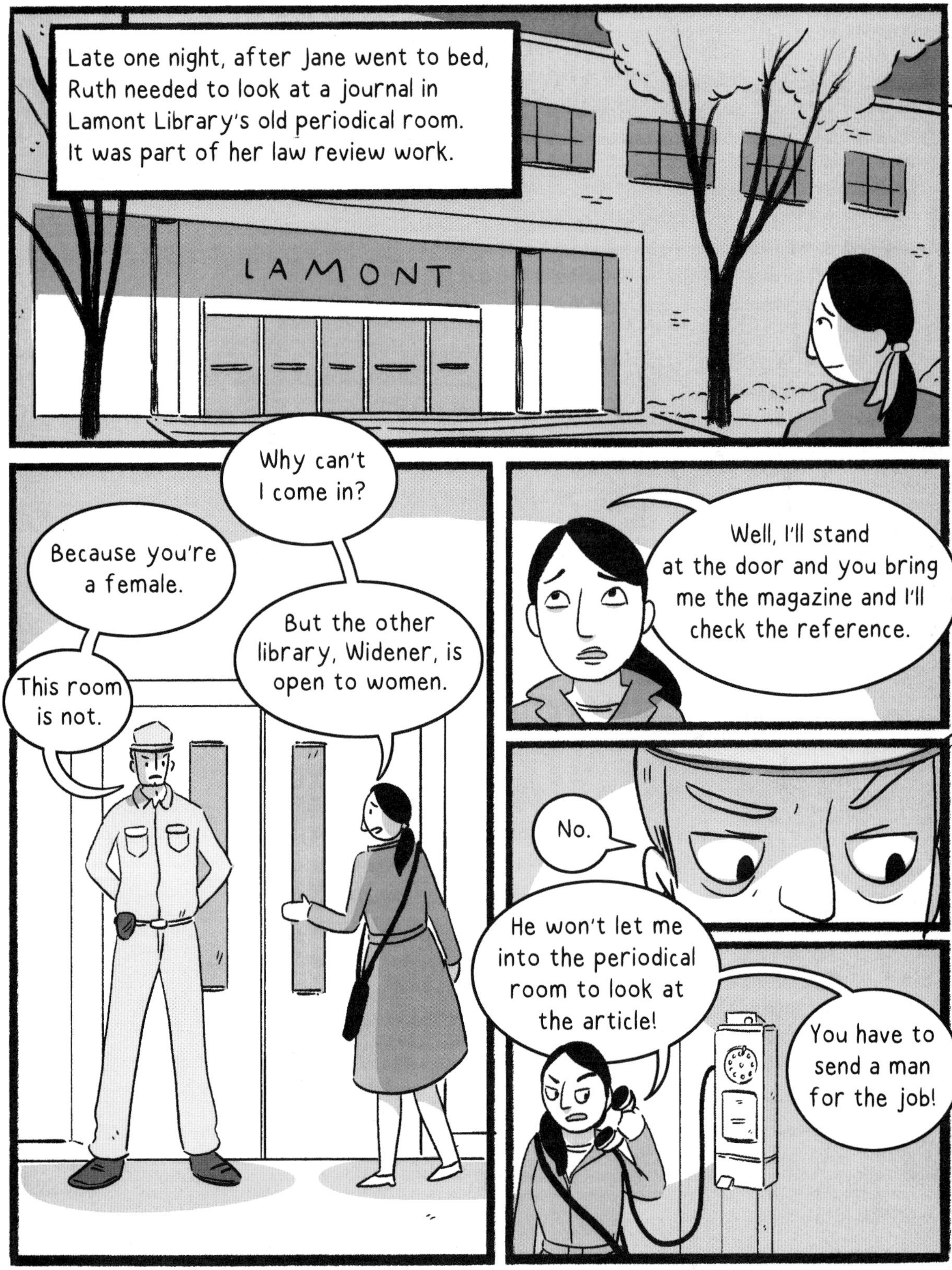
Late one night, after Jane went to bed, Ruth needed to look at a journal in Lamont Library's old periodical room. It was part of her law review work.
LAMONT
Why can't I come in?
Because you're a female.
This room is not.
But the other library, Widener, is open to women.
Well, I'll stand at the door and you bring me the magazine and I'll check the reference.
No.
He won't let me into the periodical room to look at the article!
You have to send a man for the job!

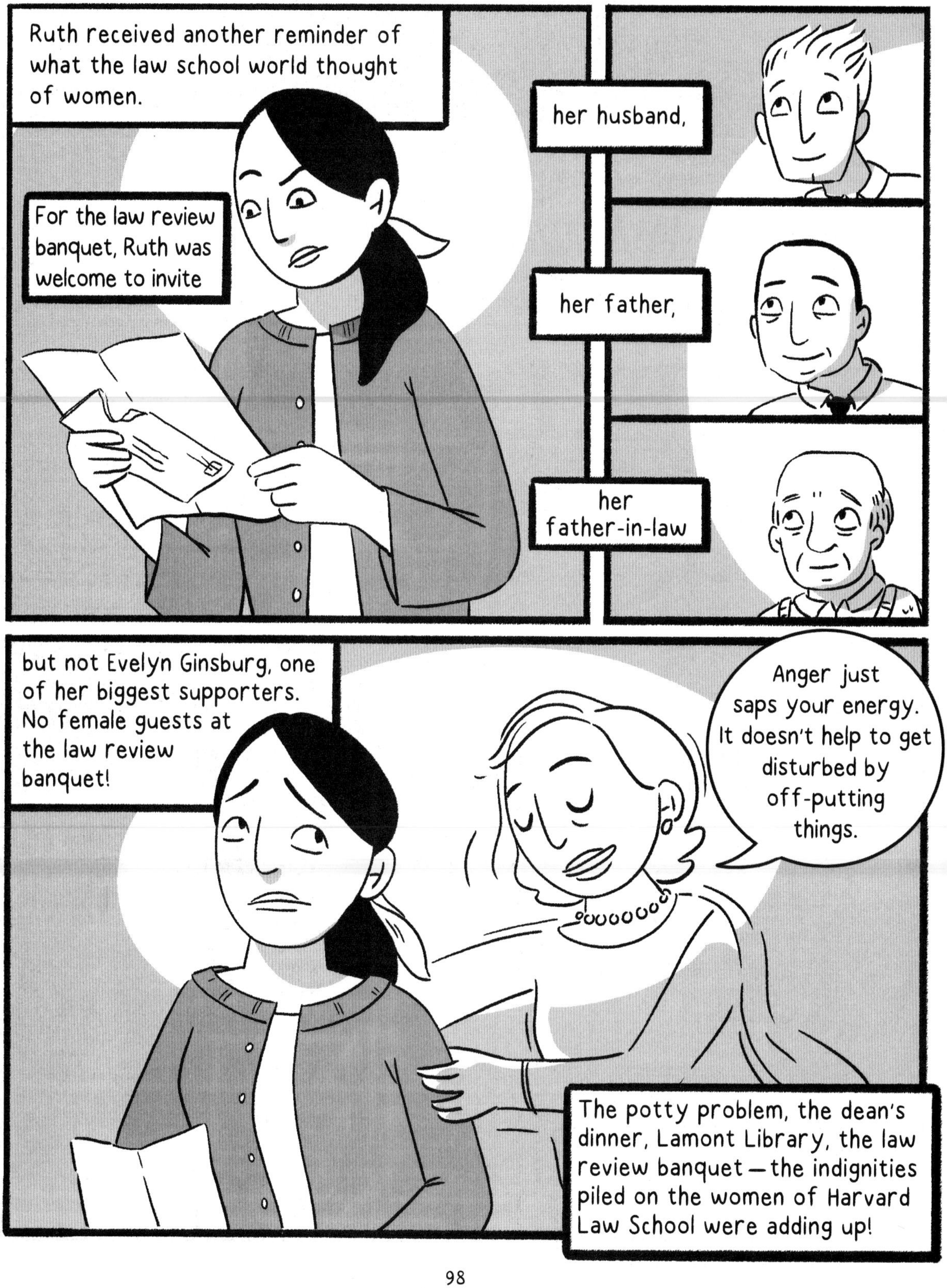
Ruth received another reminder of what the law school world thought of women.
For the law review banquet, Ruth was welcome to invite
her husband,
her father,
her father-in-law
but not Evelyn Ginsburg, one of her biggest supporters. No female guests at the law review banquet!
Anger just saps your energy. It doesn't help to get disturbed by off-putting things.
The potty problem, the dean's dinner, Lamont Library, the law review banquet—the indignities piled on the women of Harvard Law School were adding up!

CHAPTER 21

And Then Again

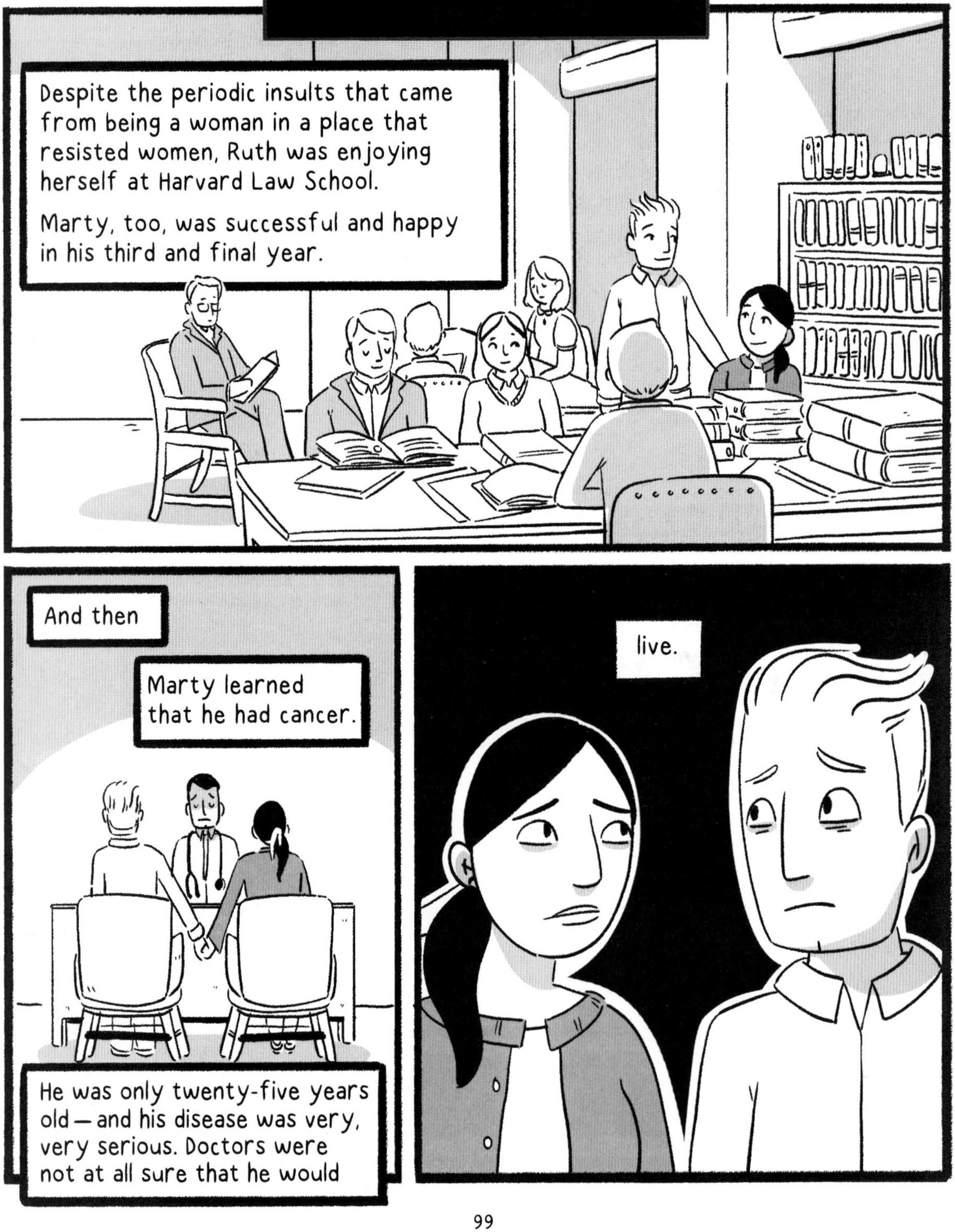
Despite the periodic insults that came from being a woman in a place that resisted women, Ruth was enjoying herself at Harvard Law School.
Marty, too, was successful and happy in his third and final year.
And then
Marty learned that he had cancer.
He was only twenty-five years old—and his disease was very, very serious. Doctors were not at all sure that he would
live.

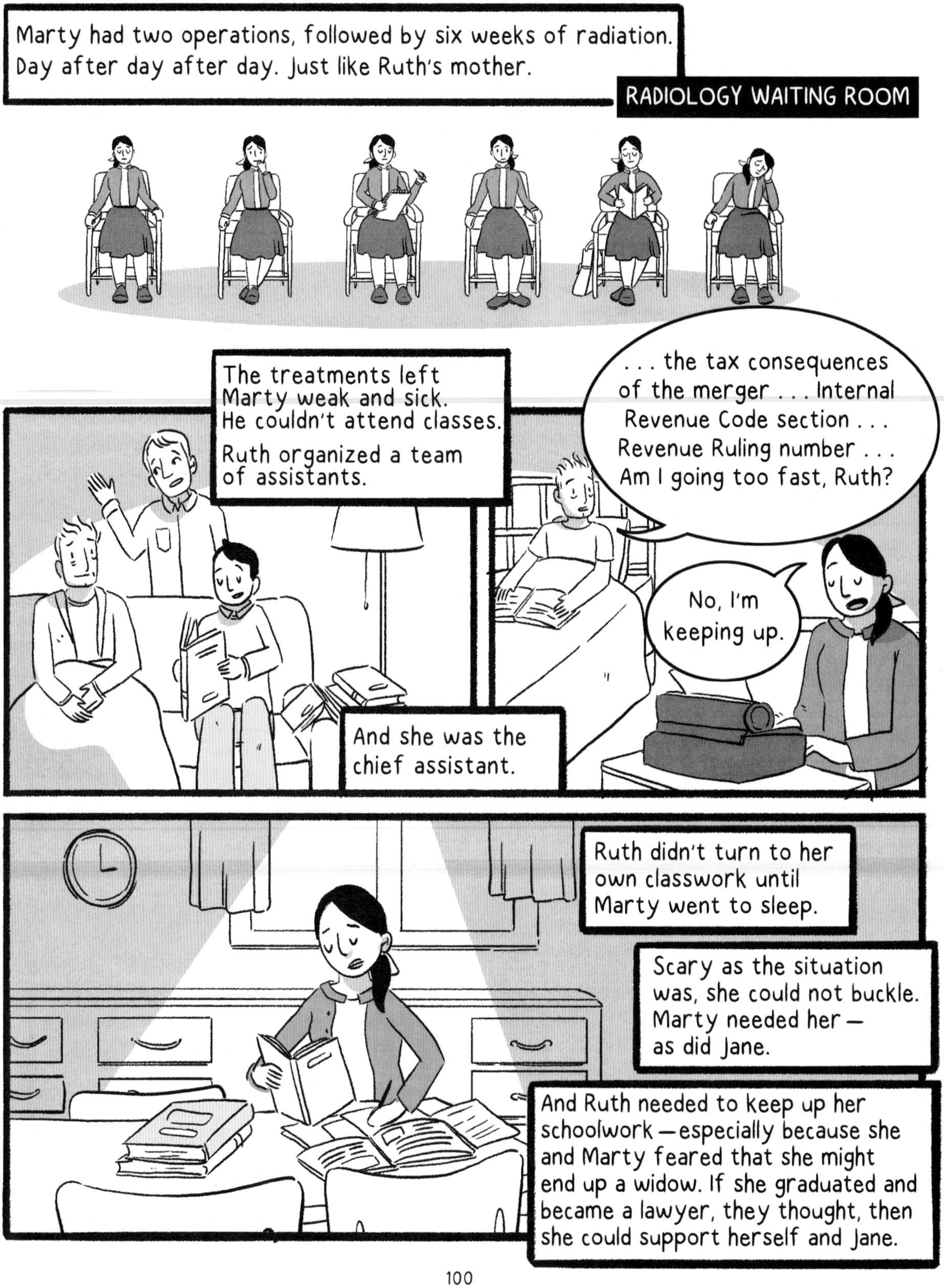
Marty had two operations, followed by six weeks of radiation. Day after day after day. Just like Ruth's mother.
RADIOLOGY WAITING ROOM
The treatments left Marty weak and sick. He couldn't attend classes.
Ruth organized a team of assistants.
And she was the chief assistant.
. . . the tax consequences of the merger . . . Internal Revenue Code section . . . Revenue Ruling number . . . Am I going too fast, Ruth?
No, I'm keeping up.
Ruth didn't turn to her own classwork until Marty went to sleep.
Scary as the situation was, she could not buckle. Marty needed her — as did Jane.
And Ruth needed to keep up her schoolwork — especially because she and Marty feared that she might end up a widow. If she graduated and became a lawyer, they thought, then she could support herself and Jane.

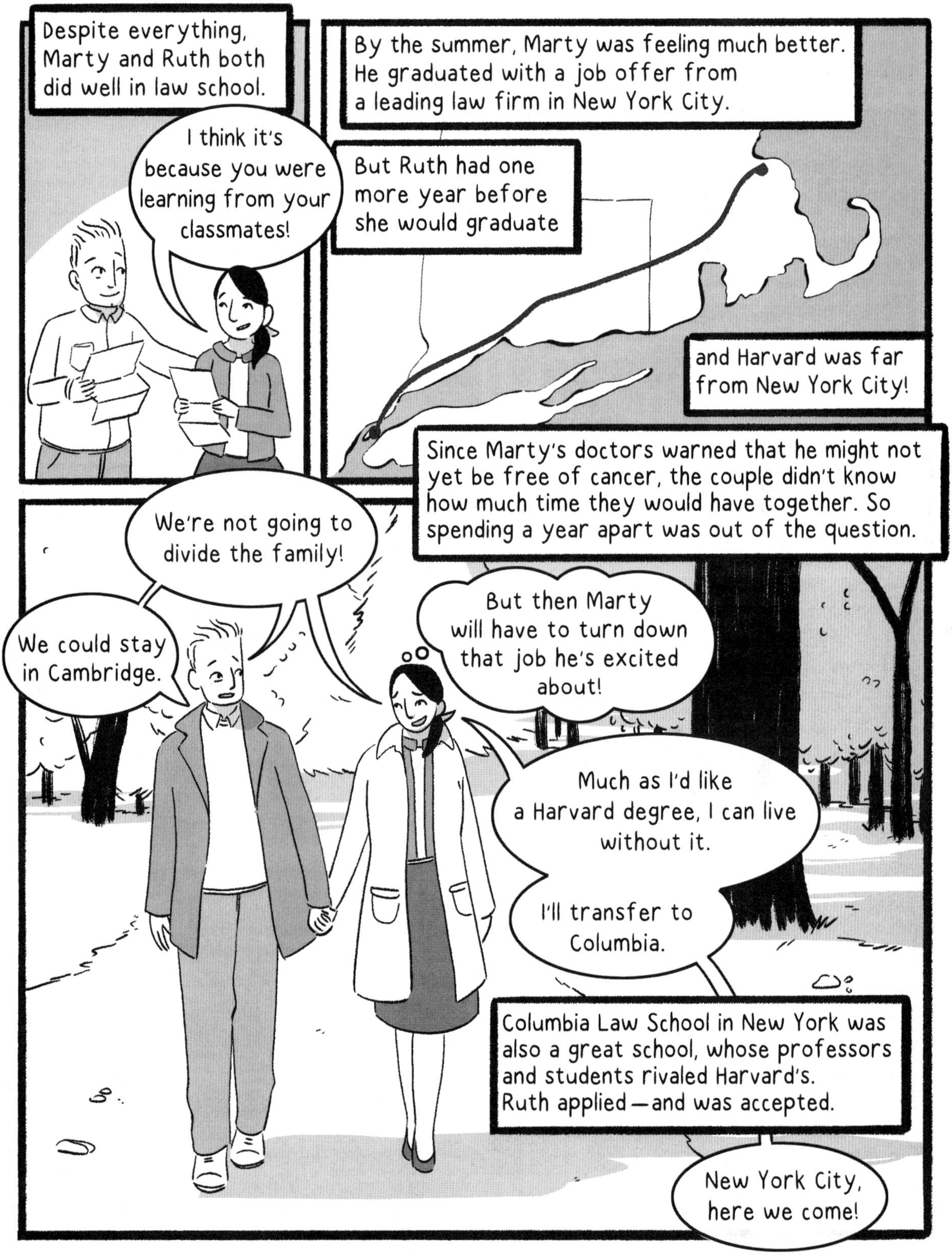

Despite everything, Marty and Ruth both did well in law school.
I think it's because you were learning from your classmates!
By the summer, Marty was feeling much better. He graduated with a job offer from a leading law firm in New York City.
But Ruth had one more year before she would graduate
and Harvard was far from New York City!
Since Marty's doctors warned that he might not yet be free of cancer, the couple didn't know how much time they would have together. So spending a year apart was out of the question.
We could stay in Cambridge.
We're not going to divide the family!
But then Marty will have to turn down that job he's excited about!
Much as I'd like a Harvard degree, I can live without it.
I'll transfer to Columbia.
Columbia Law School in New York was also a great school, whose professors and students rivaled Harvard's. Ruth applied—and was accepted.
New York City, here we come!

CHAPTER 22

What a Lawyer Looks Like

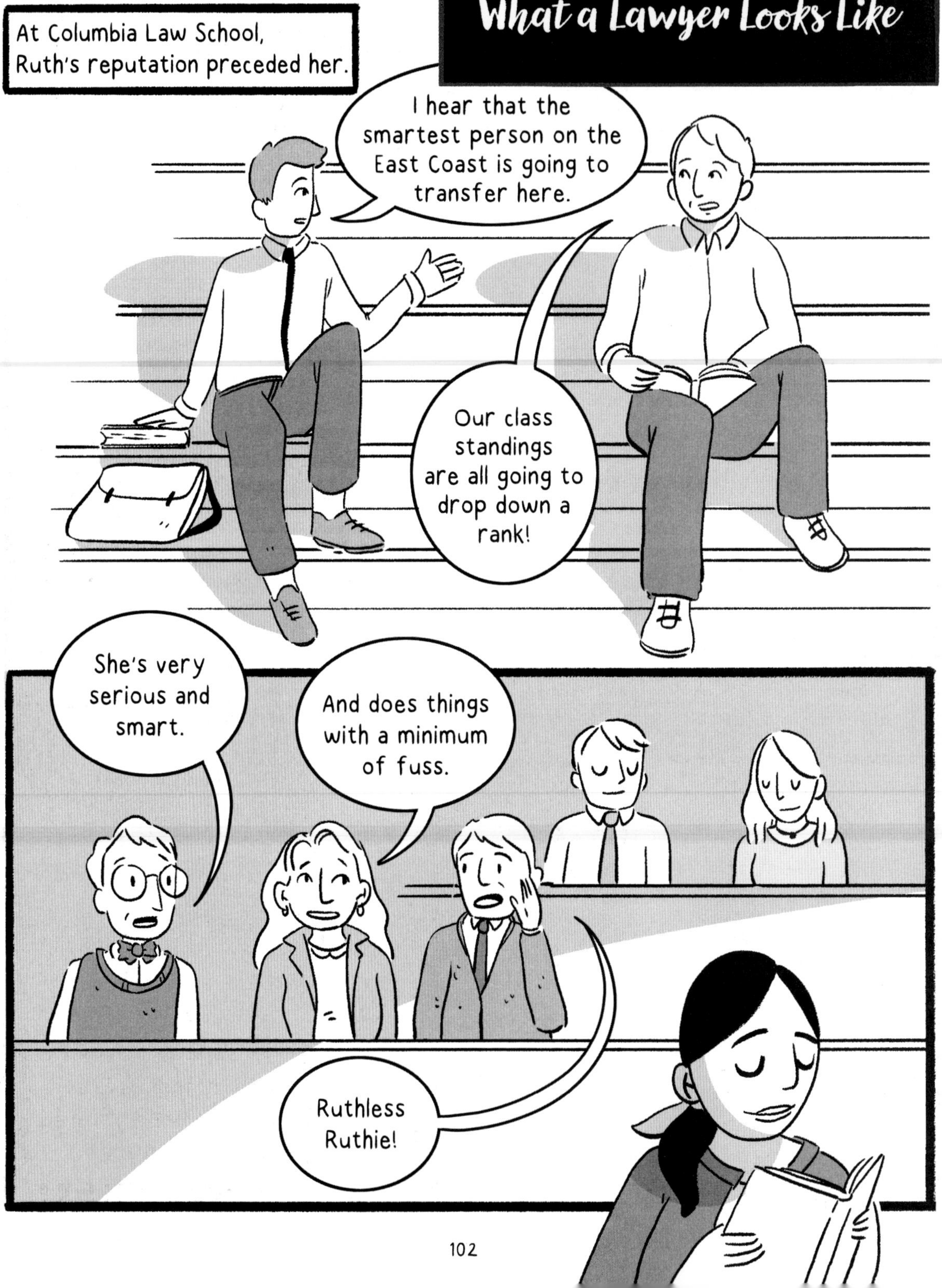
At Columbia Law School, Ruth's reputation preceded her.
I hear that the smartest person on the East Coast is going to transfer here.
Our class standings are all going to drop down a rank!
She's very serious and smart.
And does things with a minimum of fuss.
Ruthless Ruthie!

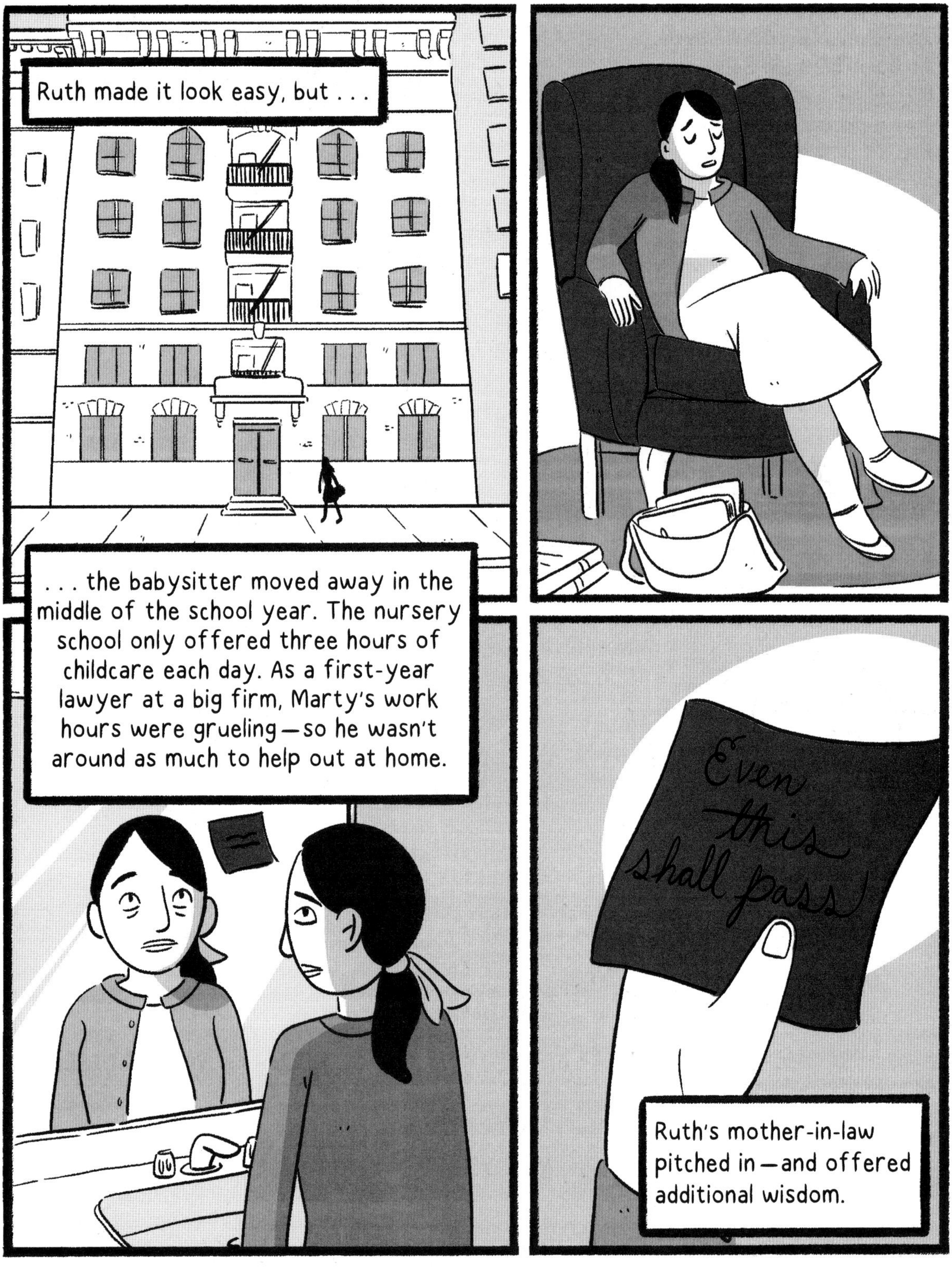
Ruth made it look easy, but . . .
. . . the babysitter moved away in the middle of the school year. The nursery school only offered three hours of childcare each day. As a first-year lawyer at a big firm, Marty's work hours were grueling—so he wasn't around as much to help out at home.
Even this shall pass
Ruth's mother-in-law pitched in—and offered additional wisdom.

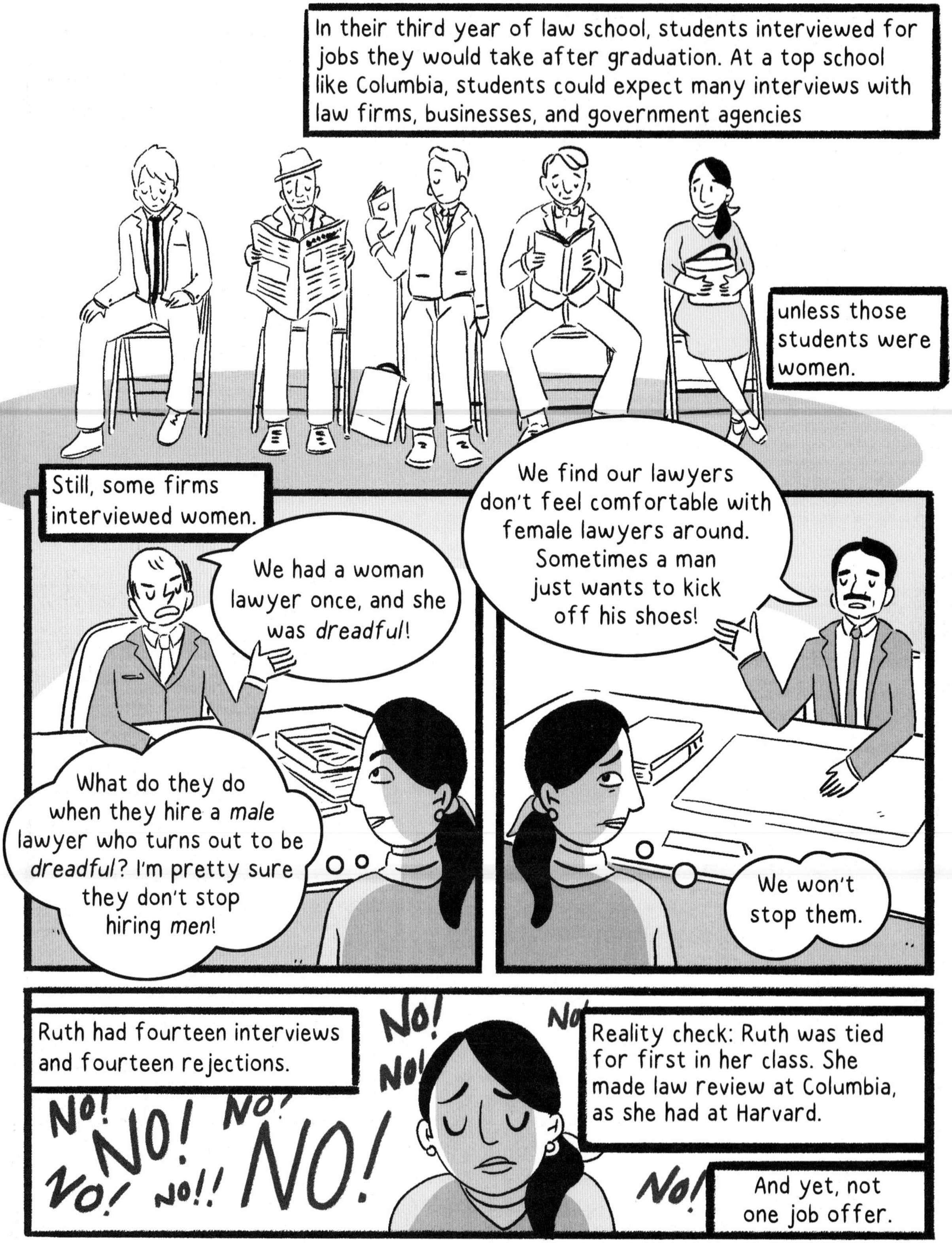
In their third year of law school, students interviewed for jobs they would take after graduation. At a top school like Columbia, students could expect many interviews with law firms, businesses, and government agencies
unless those students were women.
Still, some firms interviewed women.
We had a woman lawyer once, and she was *dreadful*!
What do they do when they hire a *male* lawyer who turns out to be *dreadful*? I'm pretty sure they don't stop hiring *men*!
We find our lawyers don't feel comfortable with female lawyers around. Sometimes a man just wants to kick off his shoes!
We won't stop them.
Ruth had fourteen interviews and fourteen rejections.
No! No! No! NO! No! No! No!! NO! No! No!
Reality check: Ruth was tied for first in her class. She made law review at Columbia, as she had at Harvard.
And yet, not one job offer.

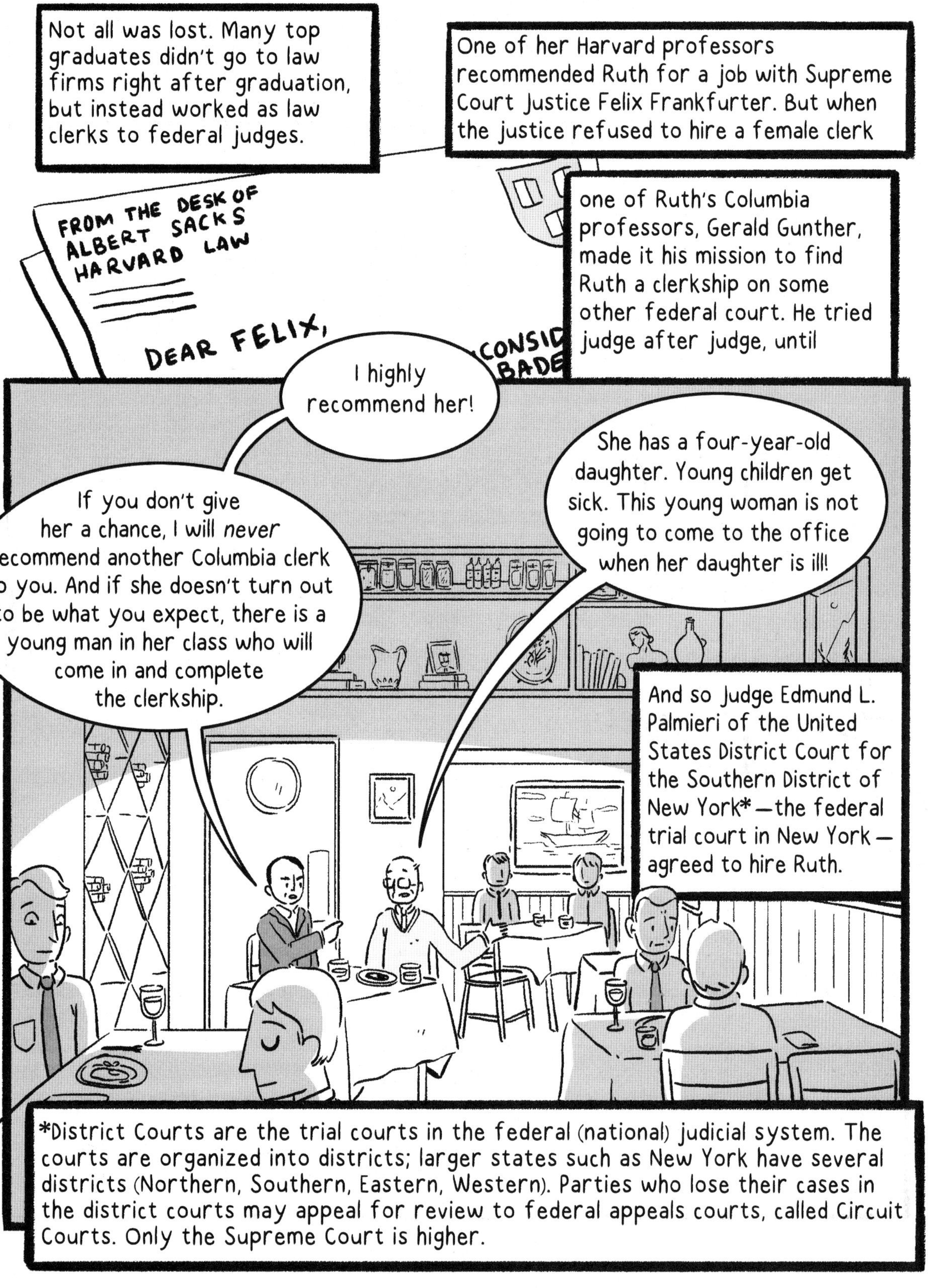
Not all was lost. Many top graduates didn't go to law firms right after graduation, but instead worked as law clerks to federal judges.
One of her Harvard professors recommended Ruth for a job with Supreme Court Justice Felix Frankfurter. But when the justice refused to hire a female clerk
FROM THE DESK OF ALBERT SACKS HARVARD LAW
DEAR FELIX,
one of Ruth's Columbia professors, Gerald Gunther, made it his mission to find Ruth a clerkship on some other federal court. He tried judge after judge, until
I highly recommend her!
If you don't give her a chance, I will *never* recommend another Columbia clerk to you. And if she doesn't turn out to be what you expect, there is a young man in her class who will come in and complete the clerkship.
She has a four-year-old daughter. Young children get sick. This young woman is not going to come to the office when her daughter is ill!
And so Judge Edmund L. Palmieri of the United States District Court for the Southern District of New York*—the federal trial court in New York—agreed to hire Ruth.
*District Courts are the trial courts in the federal (national) judicial system. The courts are organized into districts; larger states such as New York have several districts (Northern, Southern, Eastern, Western). Parties who lose their cases in the district courts may appeal for review to federal appeals courts, called Circuit Courts. Only the Supreme Court is higher.

CHAPTER 23

Balancing Act

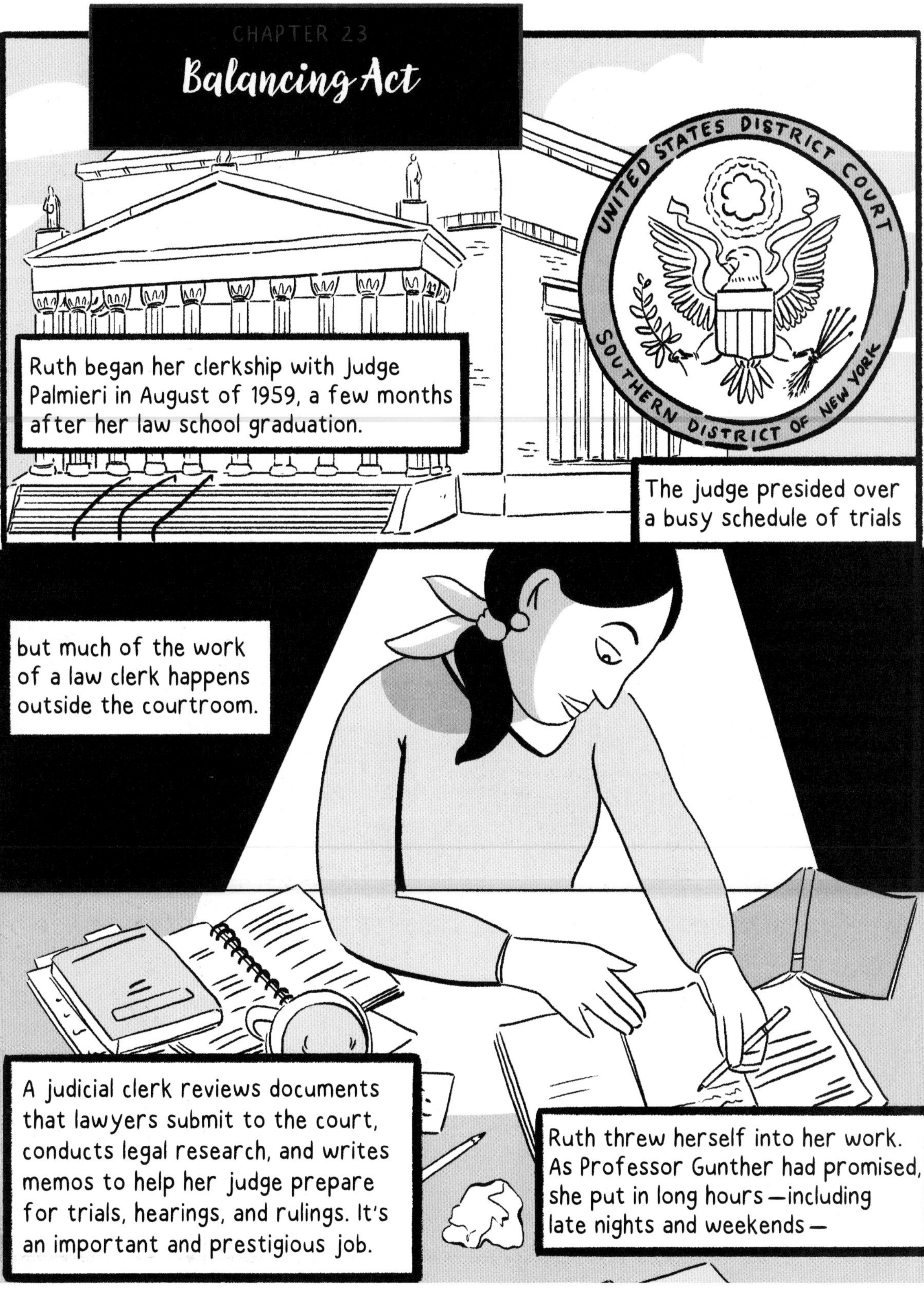
UNITED STATES DISTRICT COURT SOUTHERN DISTRICT OF NEW YORK
Ruth began her clerkship with Judge Palmieri in August of 1959, a few months after her law school graduation.
The judge presided over a busy schedule of trials
but much of the work of a law clerk happens outside the courtroom.
A judicial clerk reviews documents that lawyers submit to the court, conducts legal research, and writes memos to help her judge prepare for trials, hearings, and rulings. It's an important and prestigious job.
Ruth threw herself into her work. As Professor Gunther had promised, she put in long hours—including late nights and weekends—

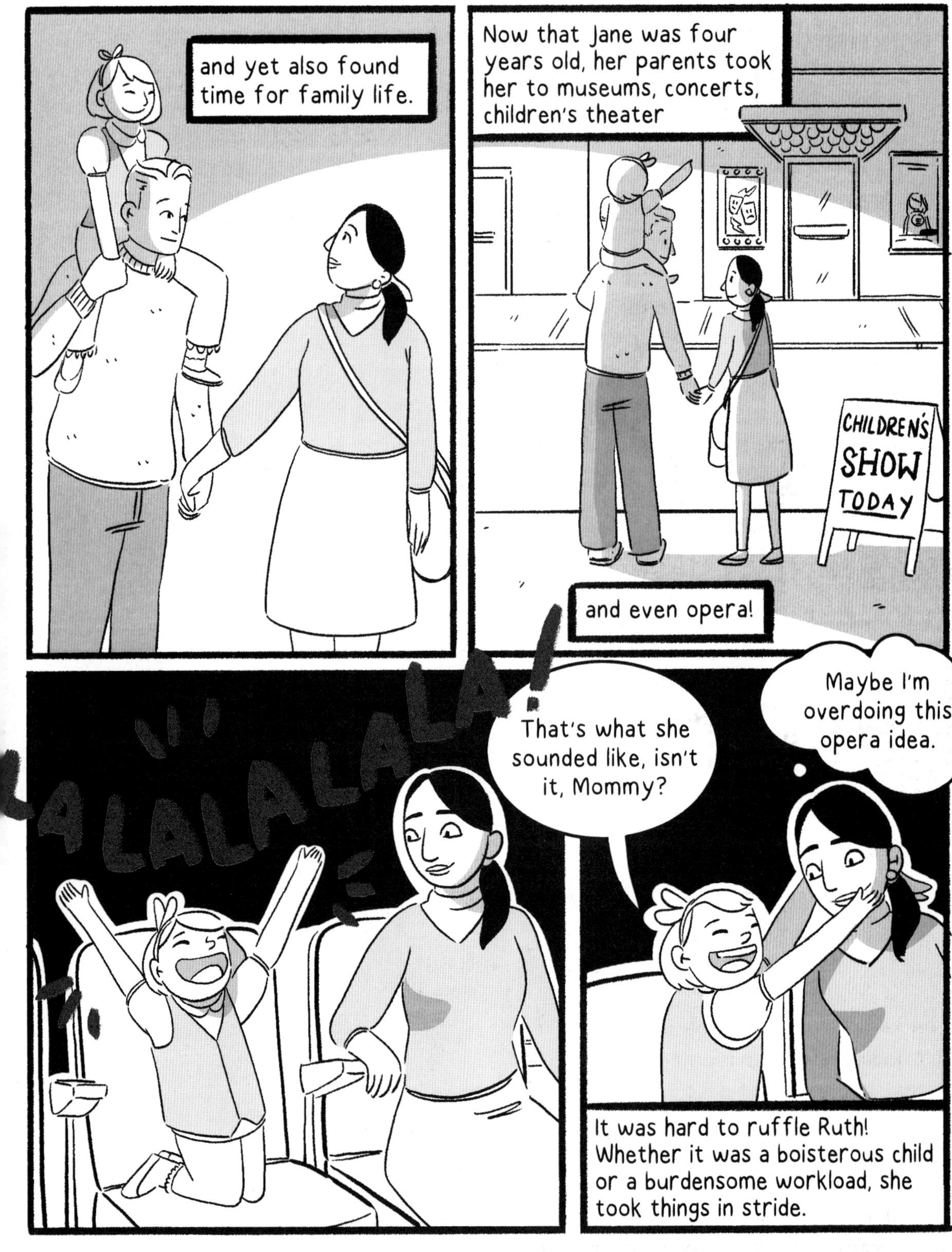
and yet also found time for family life.
Now that Jane was four years old, her parents took her to museums, concerts, children's theater
CHILDREN'S SHOW TODAY
and even opera!
LALALALALA!
That's what she sounded like, isn't it, Mommy?
Maybe I'm overdoing this opera idea.
It was hard to ruffle Ruth! Whether it was a boisterous child or a burdensome workload, she took things in stride.

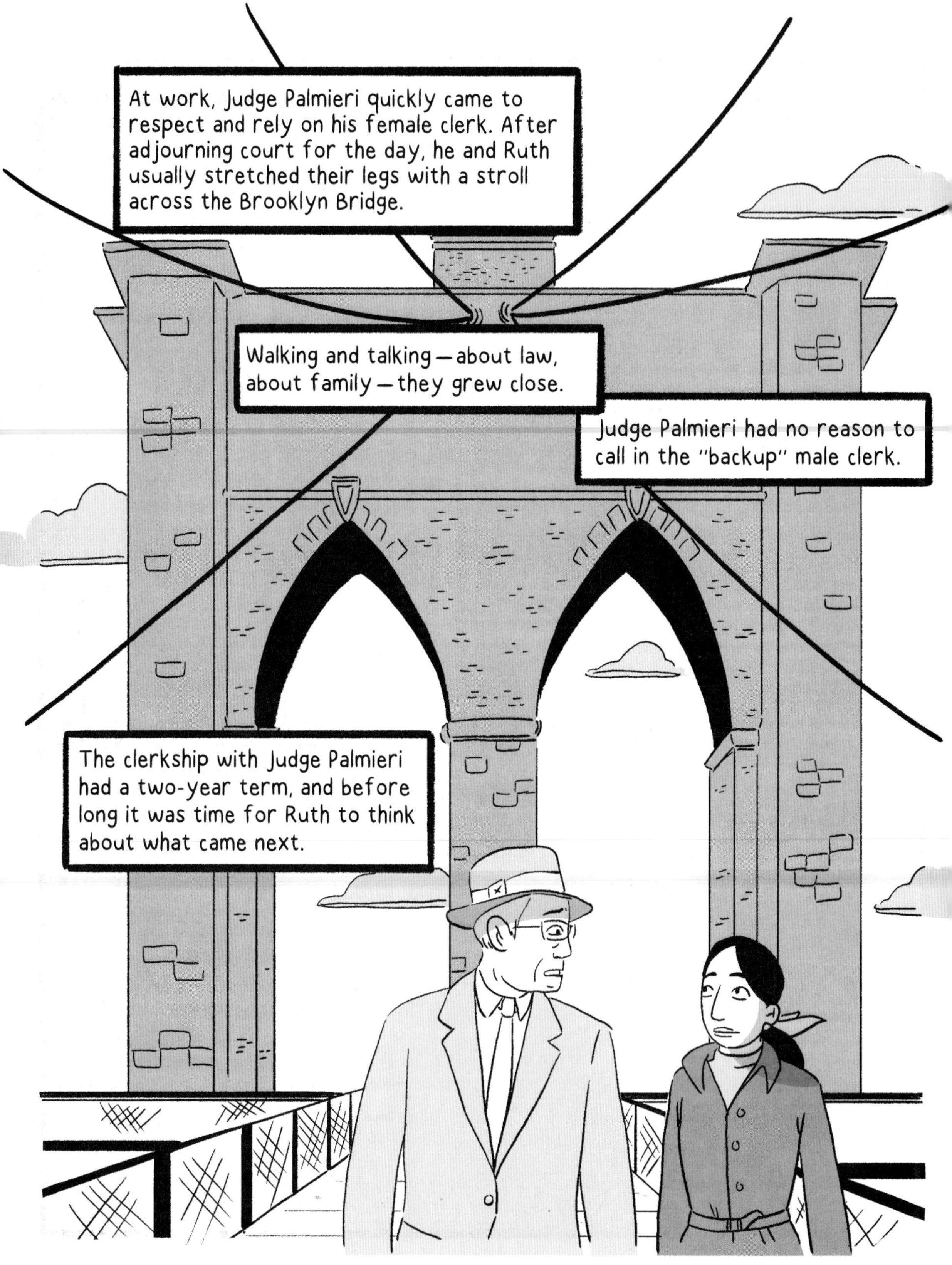
At work, Judge Palmieri quickly came to respect and rely on his female clerk. After adjourning court for the day, he and Ruth usually stretched their legs with a stroll across the Brooklyn Bridge.
Walking and talking—about law, about family—they grew close.
Judge Palmieri had no reason to call in the "backup" male clerk.
The clerkship with Judge Palmieri had a two-year term, and before long it was time for Ruth to think about what came next.

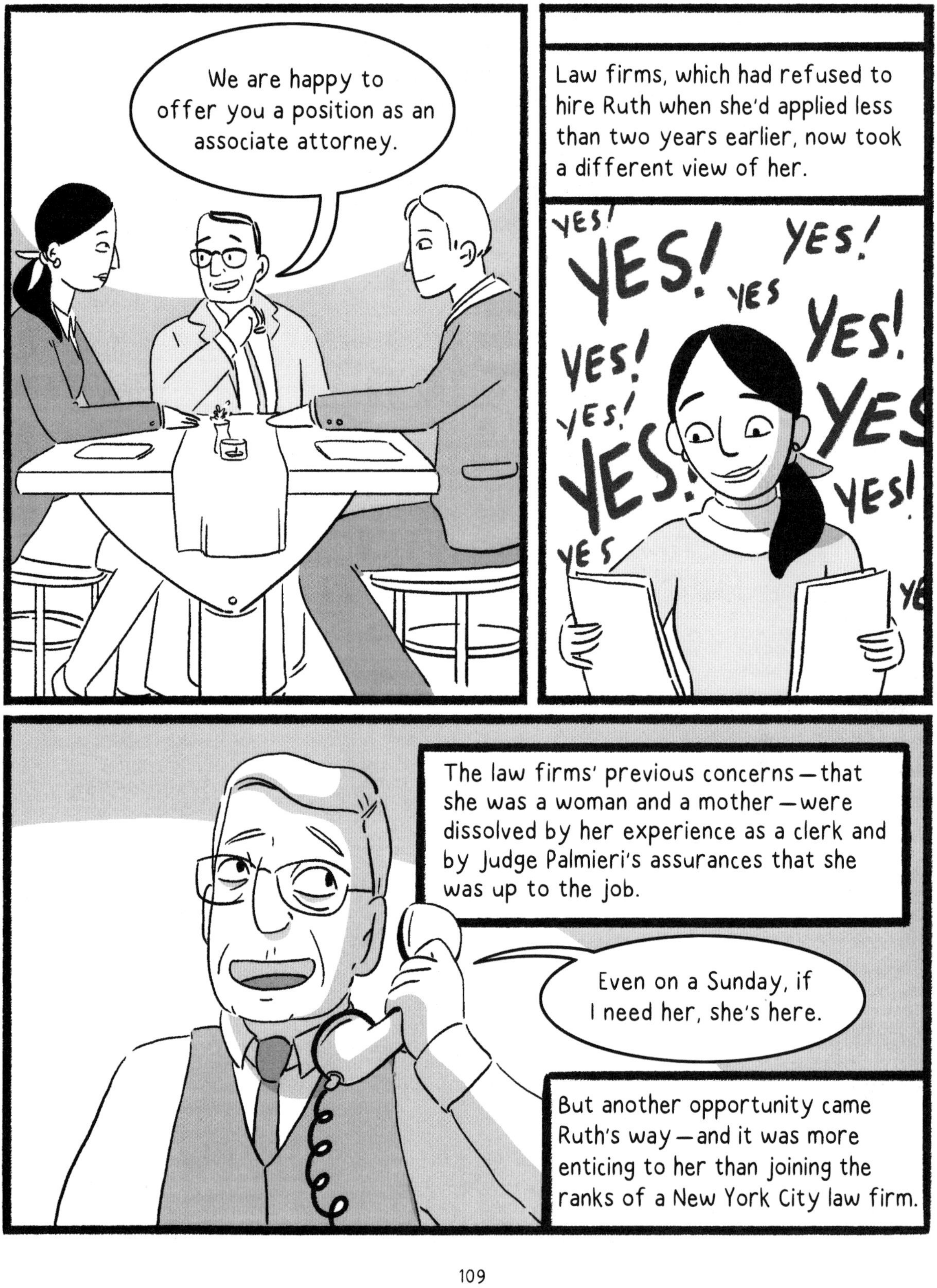
We are happy to offer you a position as an associate attorney.
Law firms, which had refused to hire Ruth when she'd applied less than two years earlier, now took a different view of her.
YES! YES! YES! YES YES! YES! YES! YES YES! YES! YES
The law firms' previous concerns—that she was a woman and a mother—were dissolved by her experience as a clerk and by Judge Palmieri's assurances that she was up to the job.
Even on a Sunday, if I need her, she's here.
But another opportunity came Ruth's way—and it was more enticing to her than joining the ranks of a New York City law firm.

CHAPTER 24

Across the Ocean

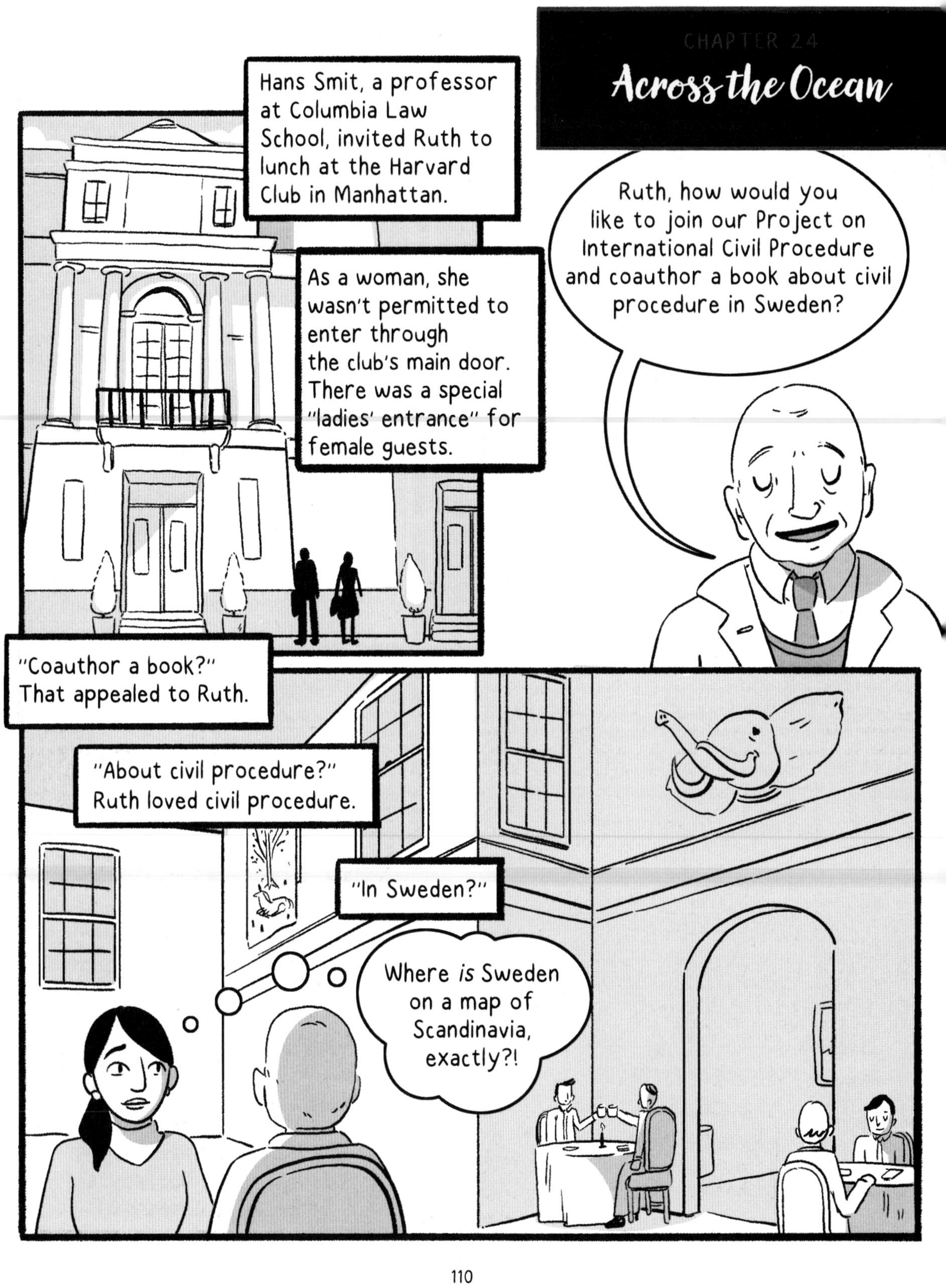

Hans Smit, a professor at Columbia Law School, invited Ruth to lunch at the Harvard Club in Manhattan.
As a woman, she wasn't permitted to enter through the club's main door. There was a special "ladies' entrance" for female guests.
Ruth, how would you like to join our Project on International Civil Procedure and coauthor a book about civil procedure in Sweden?
"Coauthor a book?" That appealed to Ruth.
"About civil procedure?" Ruth loved civil procedure.
"In Sweden?"
Where *is* Sweden on a map of Scandinavia, exactly?!

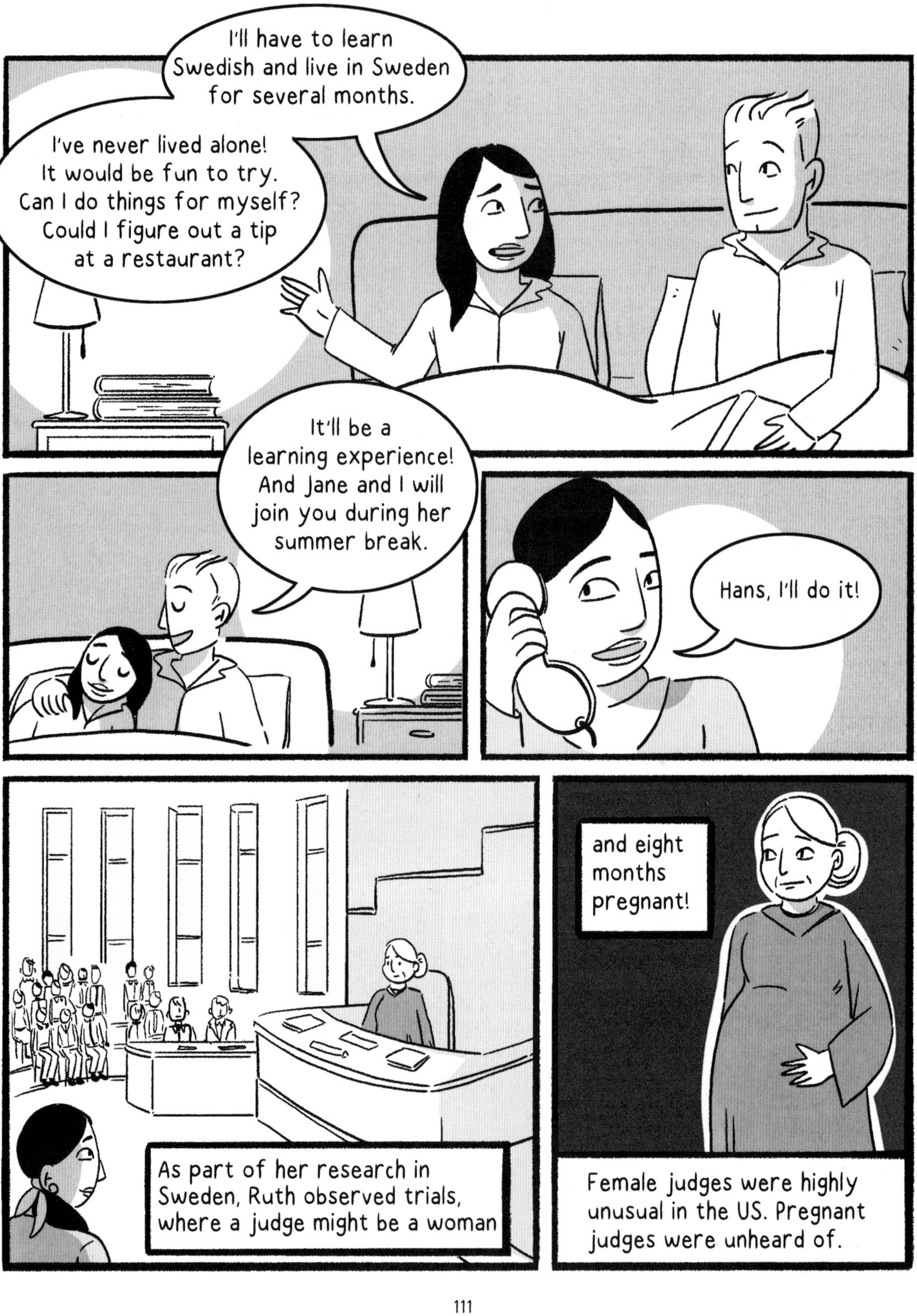
I'll have to learn Swedish and live in Sweden for several months.
I've never lived alone! It would be fun to try. Can I do things for myself? Could I figure out a tip at a restaurant?
It'll be a learning experience! And Jane and I will join you during her summer break.
Hans, I'll do it!
As part of her research in Sweden, Ruth observed trials, where a judge might be a woman
and eight months pregnant!
Female judges were highly unusual in the US. Pregnant judges were unheard of.

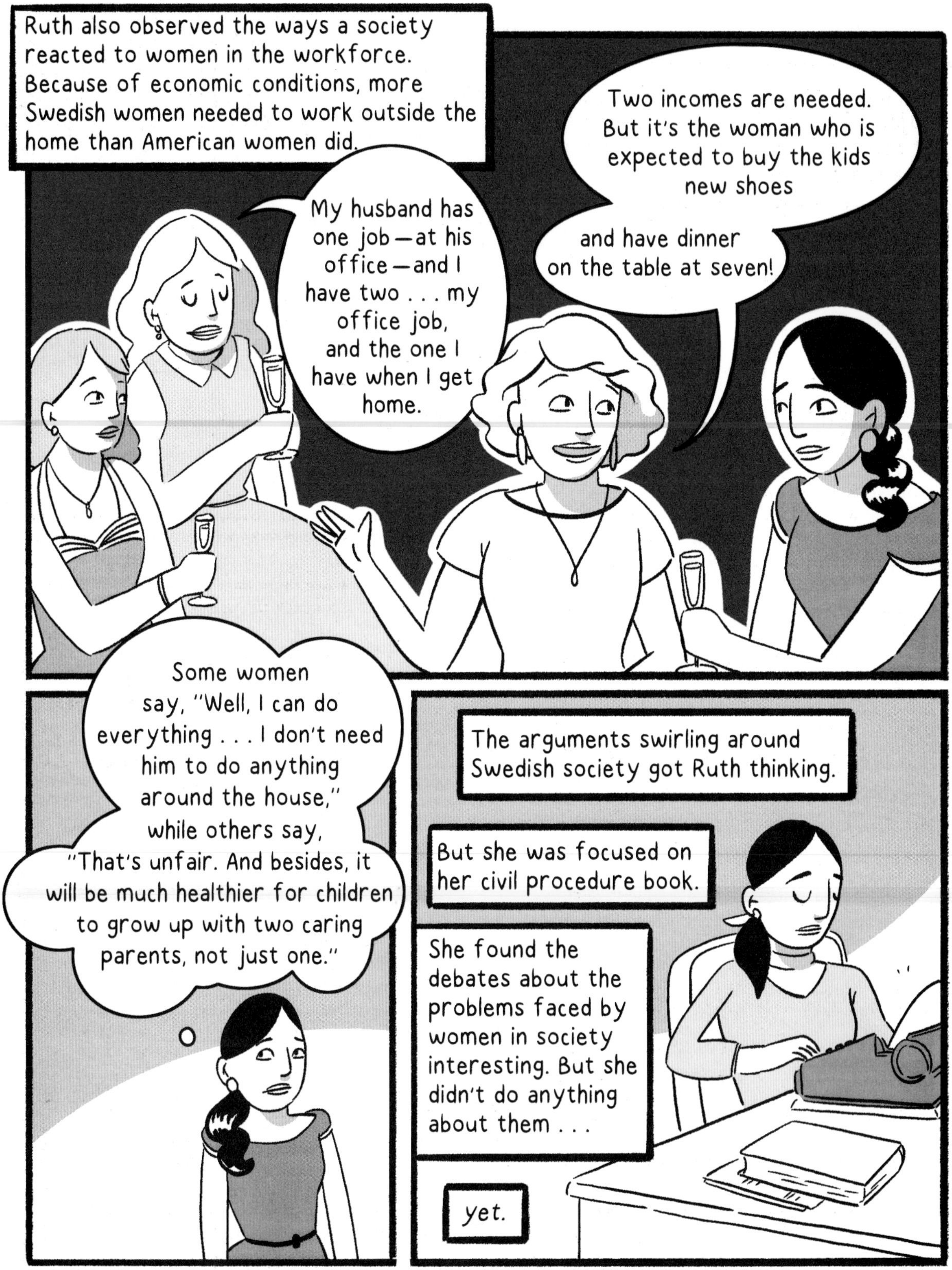
Ruth also observed the ways a society reacted to women in the workforce. Because of economic conditions, more Swedish women needed to work outside the home than American women did.
My husband has one job—at his office—and I have two . . . my office job, and the one I have when I get home.
Two incomes are needed. But it's the woman who is expected to buy the kids new shoes
and have dinner on the table at seven!
Some women say, "Well, I can do everything . . . I don't need him to do anything around the house," while others say, "That's unfair. And besides, it will be much healthier for children to grow up with two caring parents, not just one."
The arguments swirling around Swedish society got Ruth thinking.
But she was focused on her civil procedure book.
She found the debates about the problems faced by women in society interesting. But she didn't do anything about them . . .
yet.

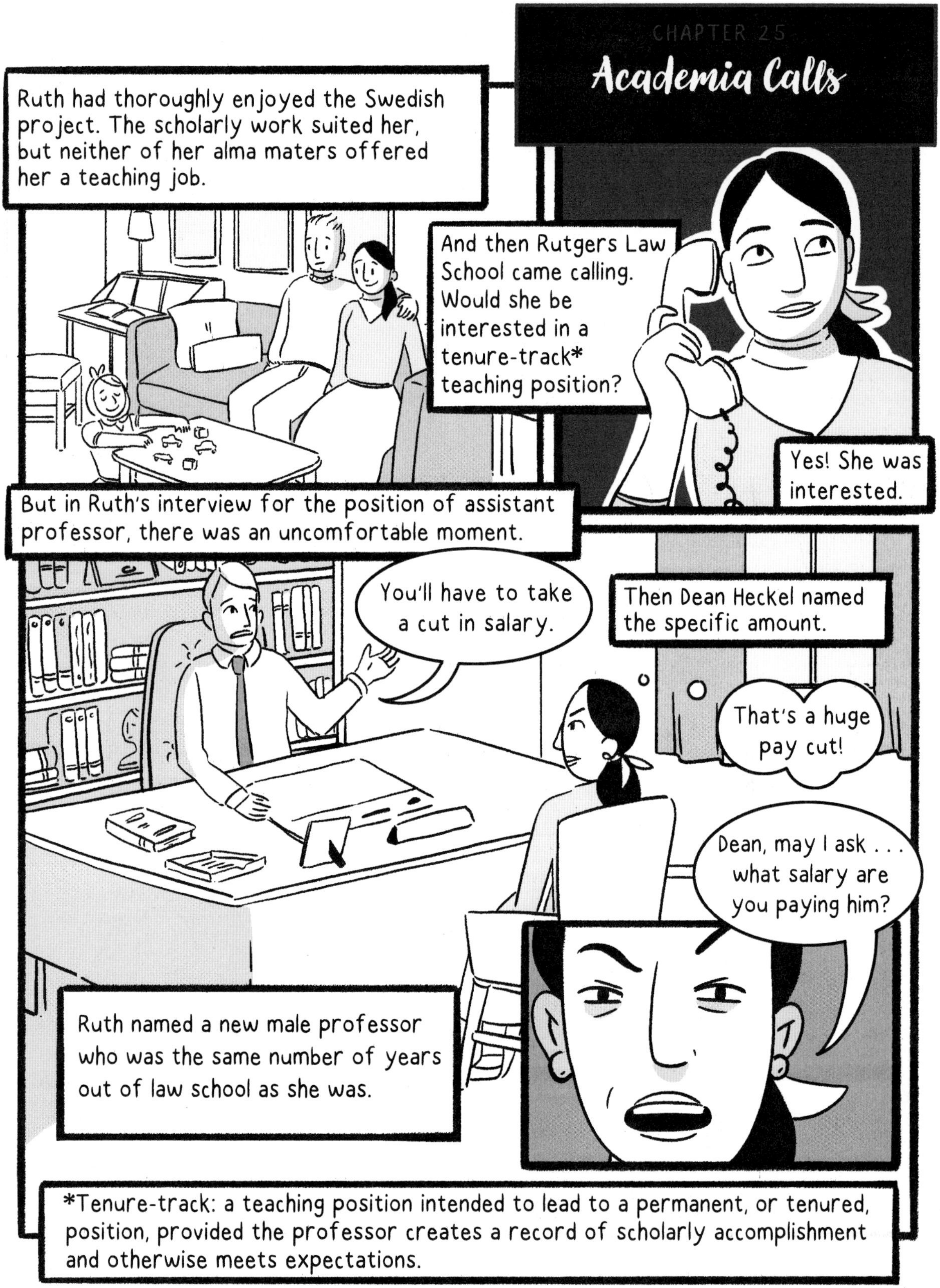
CHAPTER 25
Academia Calls
Ruth had thoroughly enjoyed the Swedish project. The scholarly work suited her, but neither of her alma maters offered her a teaching job.
And then Rutgers Law School came calling. Would she be interested in a tenure-track* teaching position?
Yes! She was interested.
But in Ruth's interview for the position of assistant professor, there was an uncomfortable moment.
You'll have to take a cut in salary.
Then Dean Heckel named the specific amount.
That's a huge pay cut!
Dean, may I ask . . . what salary are you paying him?
Ruth named a new male professor who was the same number of years out of law school as she was.
*Tenure-track: a teaching position intended to lead to a permanent, or tenured, position, provided the professor creates a record of scholarly accomplishment and otherwise meets expectations.

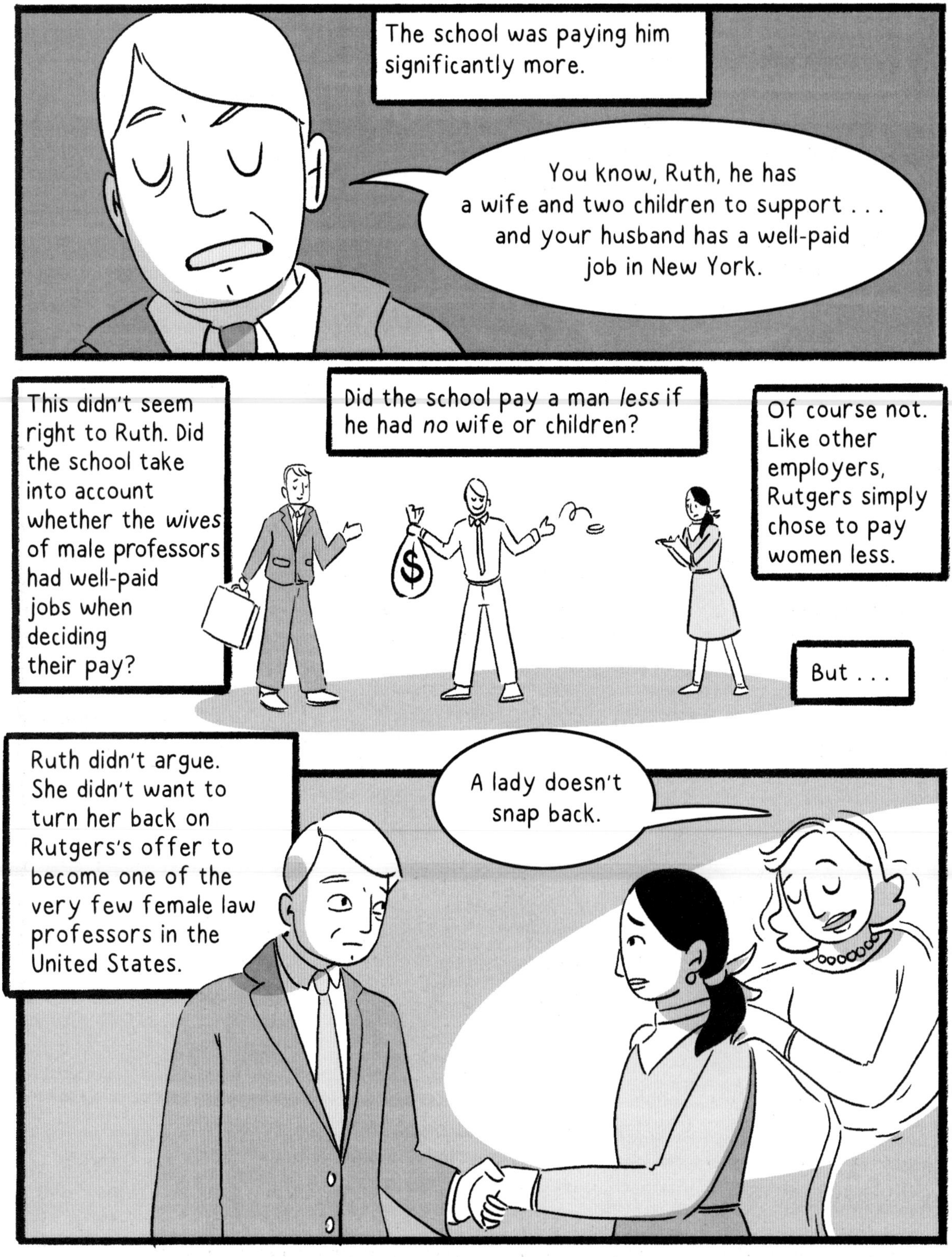
The school was paying him significantly more.
You know, Ruth, he has a wife and two children to support . . . and your husband has a well-paid job in New York.
This didn't seem right to Ruth. Did the school take into account whether the *wives* of male professors had well-paid jobs when deciding their pay?
Did the school pay a man *less* if he had *no* wife or children?
Of course not. Like other employers, Rutgers simply chose to pay women less.
But . . .
Ruth didn't argue. She didn't want to turn her back on Rutgers's offer to become one of the very few female law professors in the United States.
A lady doesn't snap back.

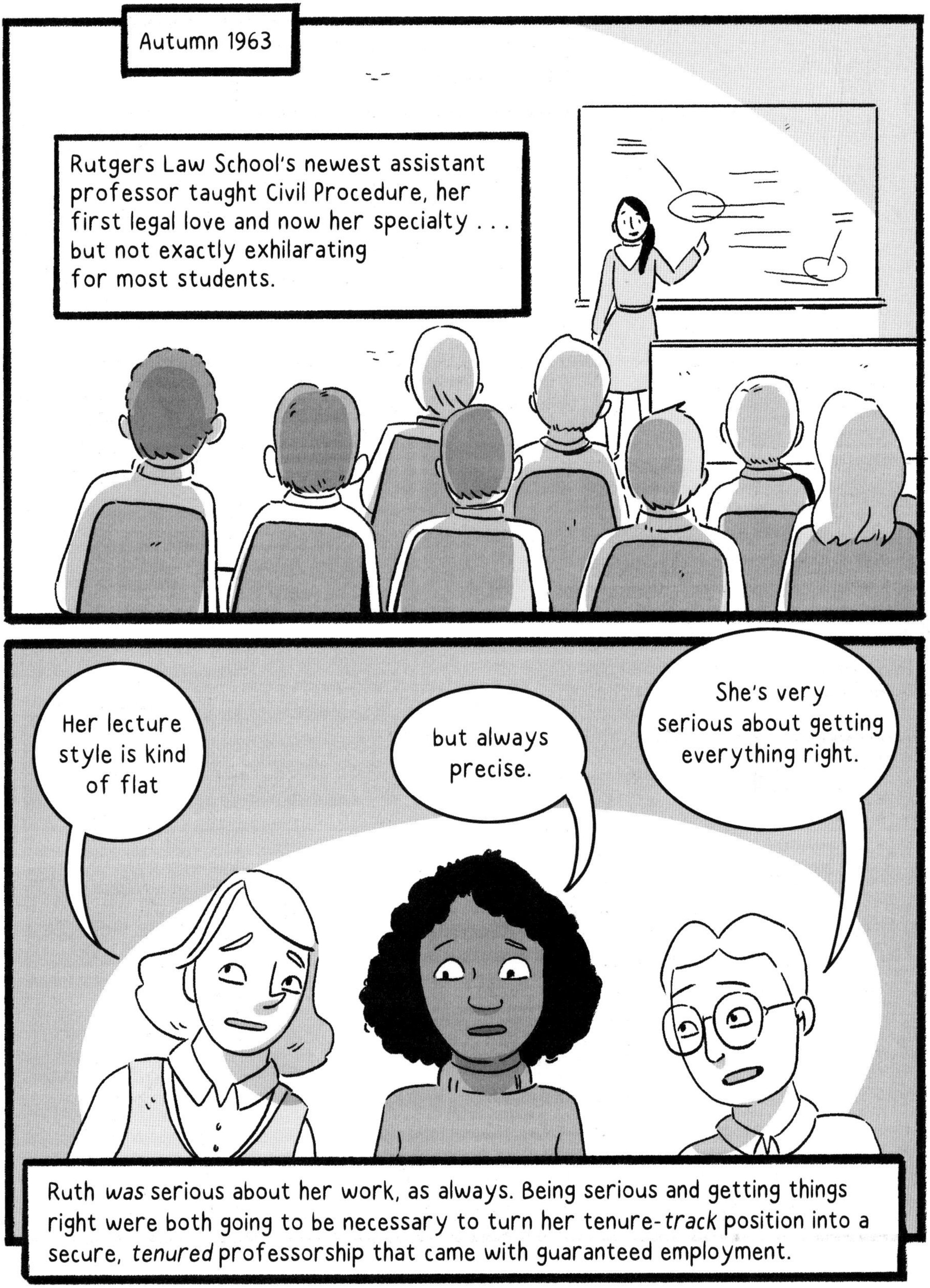
Autumn 1963
Rutgers Law School's newest assistant professor taught Civil Procedure, her first legal love and now her specialty . . . but not exactly exhilarating for most students.
Her lecture style is kind of flat
but always precise.
She's very serious about getting everything right.
Ruth *was* serious about her work, as always. Being serious and getting things right were both going to be necessary to turn her tenure-*track* position into a secure, *tenured* professorship that came with guaranteed employment.

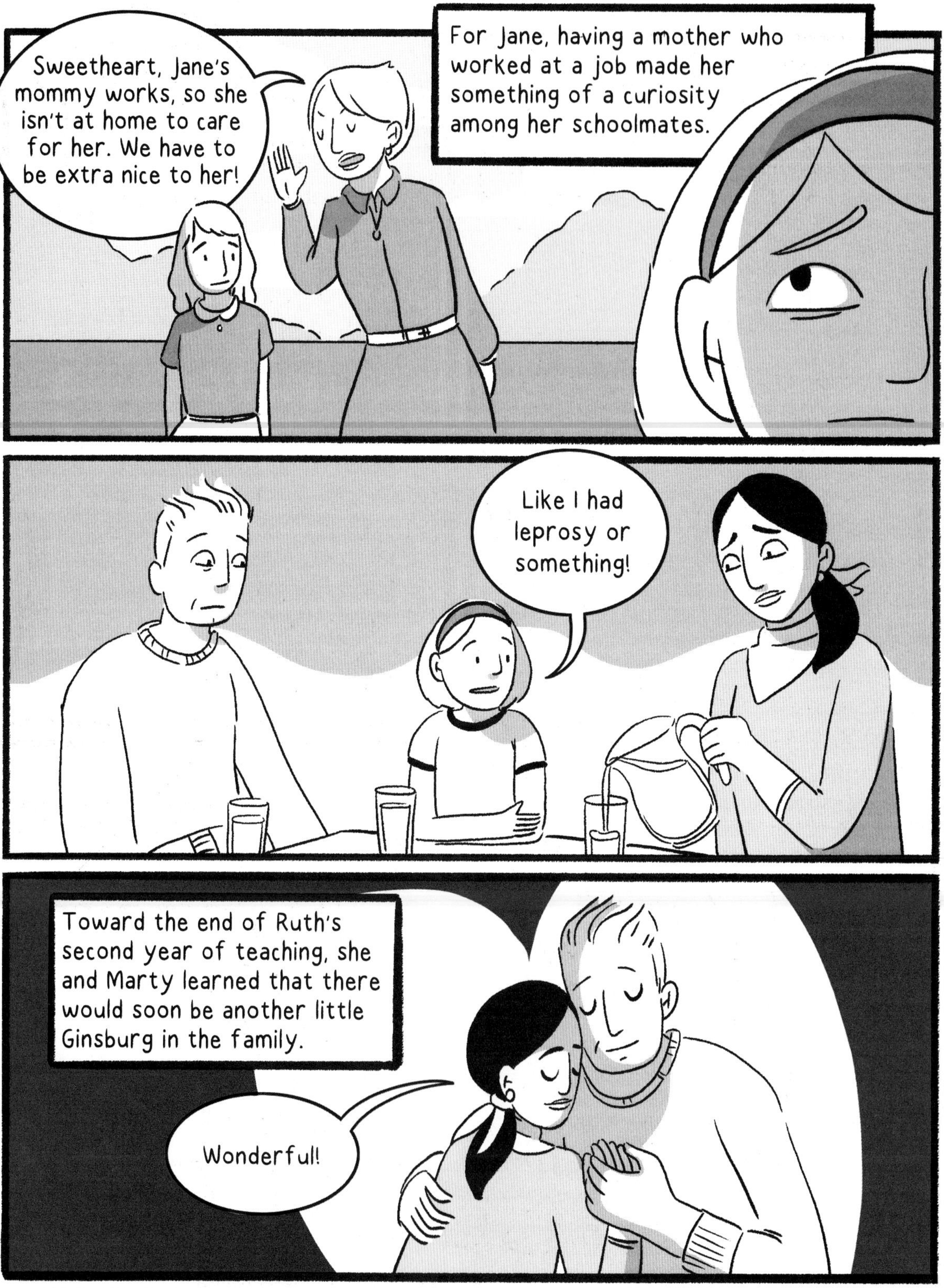
Sweetheart, Jane's mommy works, so she isn't at home to care for her. We have to be extra nice to her!
For Jane, having a mother who worked at a job made her something of a curiosity among her schoolmates.
Like I had leprosy or something!
Toward the end of Ruth's second year of teaching, she and Marty learned that there would soon be another little Ginsburg in the family.
Wonderful!

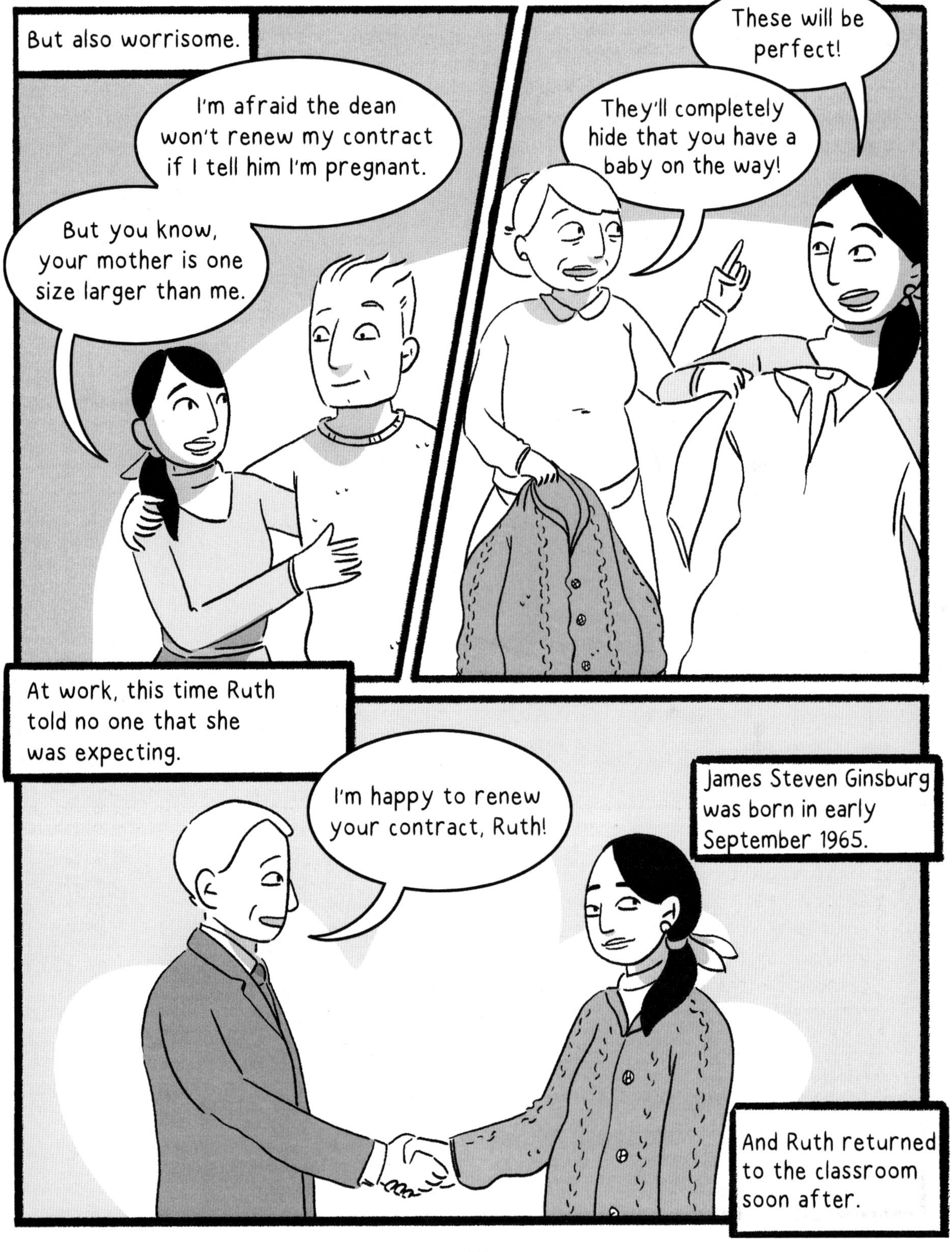

But also worrisome.
I'm afraid the dean won't renew my contract if I tell him I'm pregnant.
But you know, your mother is one size larger than me.
These will be perfect!
They'll completely hide that you have a baby on the way!
At work, this time Ruth told no one that she was expecting.
I'm happy to renew your contract, Ruth!
James Steven Ginsburg was born in early September 1965.
And Ruth returned to the classroom soon after.

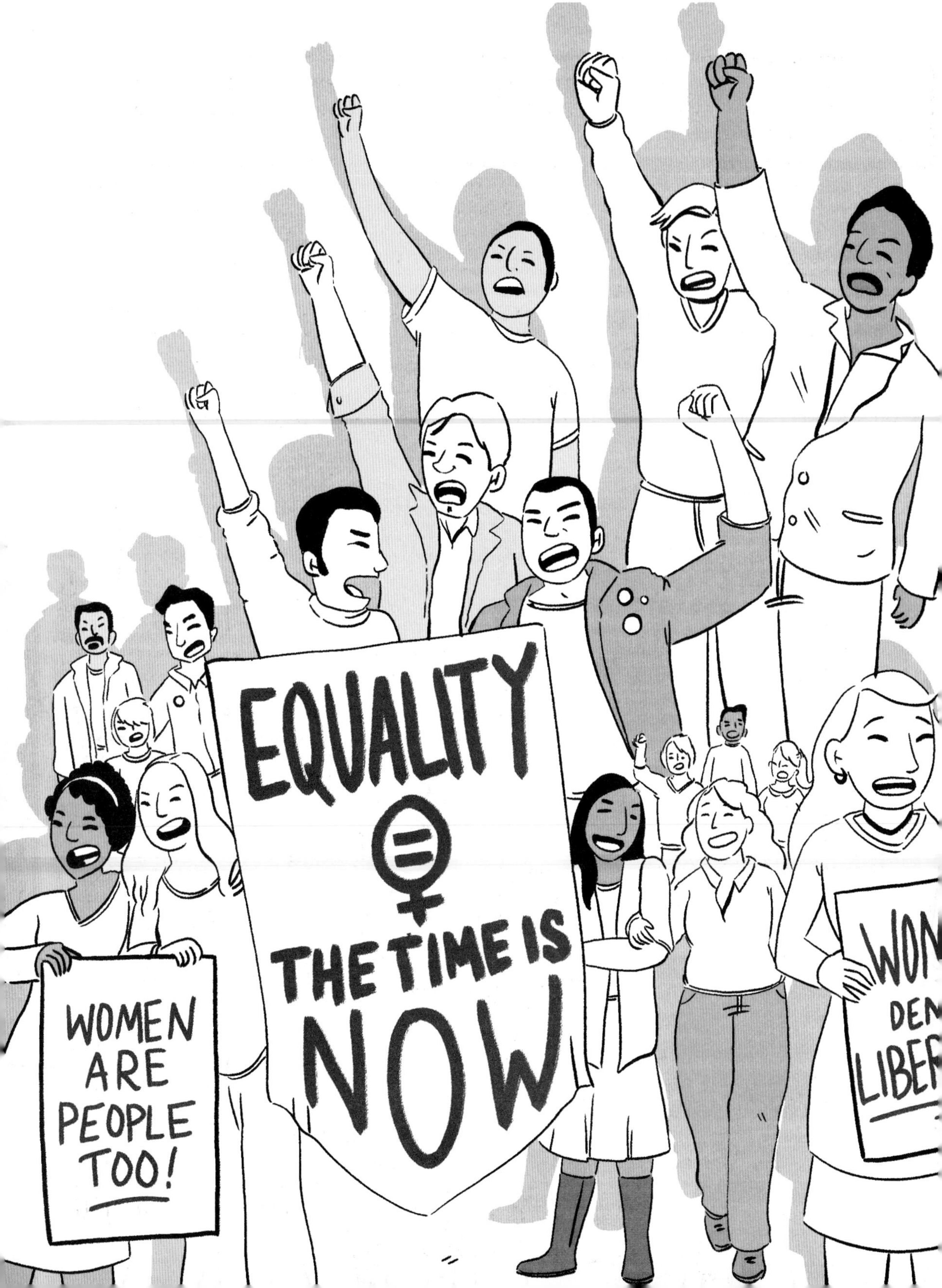
EQUALITY
THE TIME IS
NOW
WOMEN
ARE
PEOPLE
TOO!

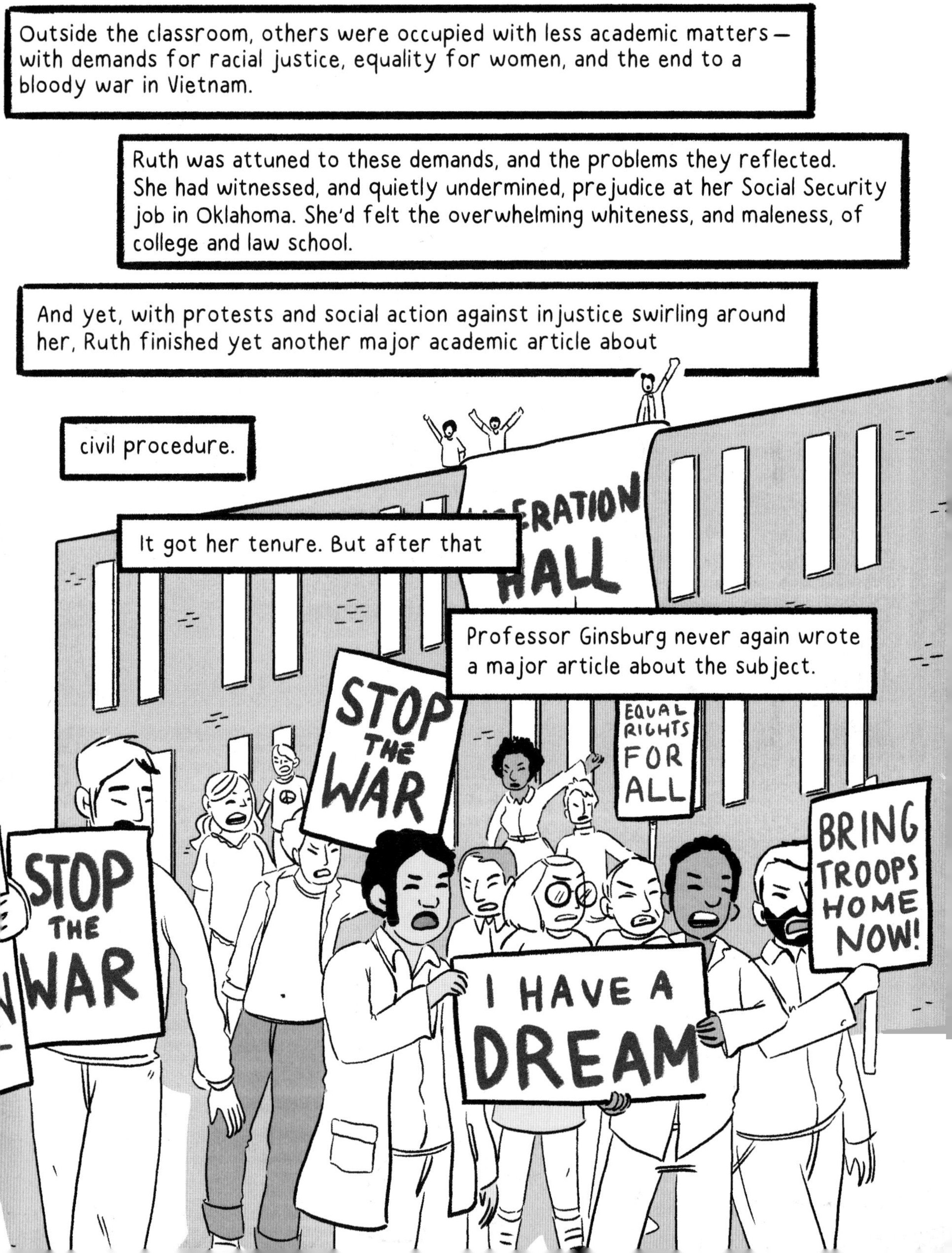
Outside the classroom, others were occupied with less academic matters—with demands for racial justice, equality for women, and the end to a bloody war in Vietnam.
Ruth was attuned to these demands, and the problems they reflected. She had witnessed, and quietly undermined, prejudice at her Social Security job in Oklahoma. She'd felt the overwhelming whiteness, and maleness, of college and law school.
And yet, with protests and social action against injustice swirling around her, Ruth finished yet another major academic article about
civil procedure.
It got her tenure. But after that
Professor Ginsburg never again wrote a major article about the subject.
STOP THE WAR
EQUAL RIGHTS FOR ALL
STOP THE WAR
BRING TROOPS HOME NOW!
I HAVE A DREAM

CHAPTER 26
Awakening

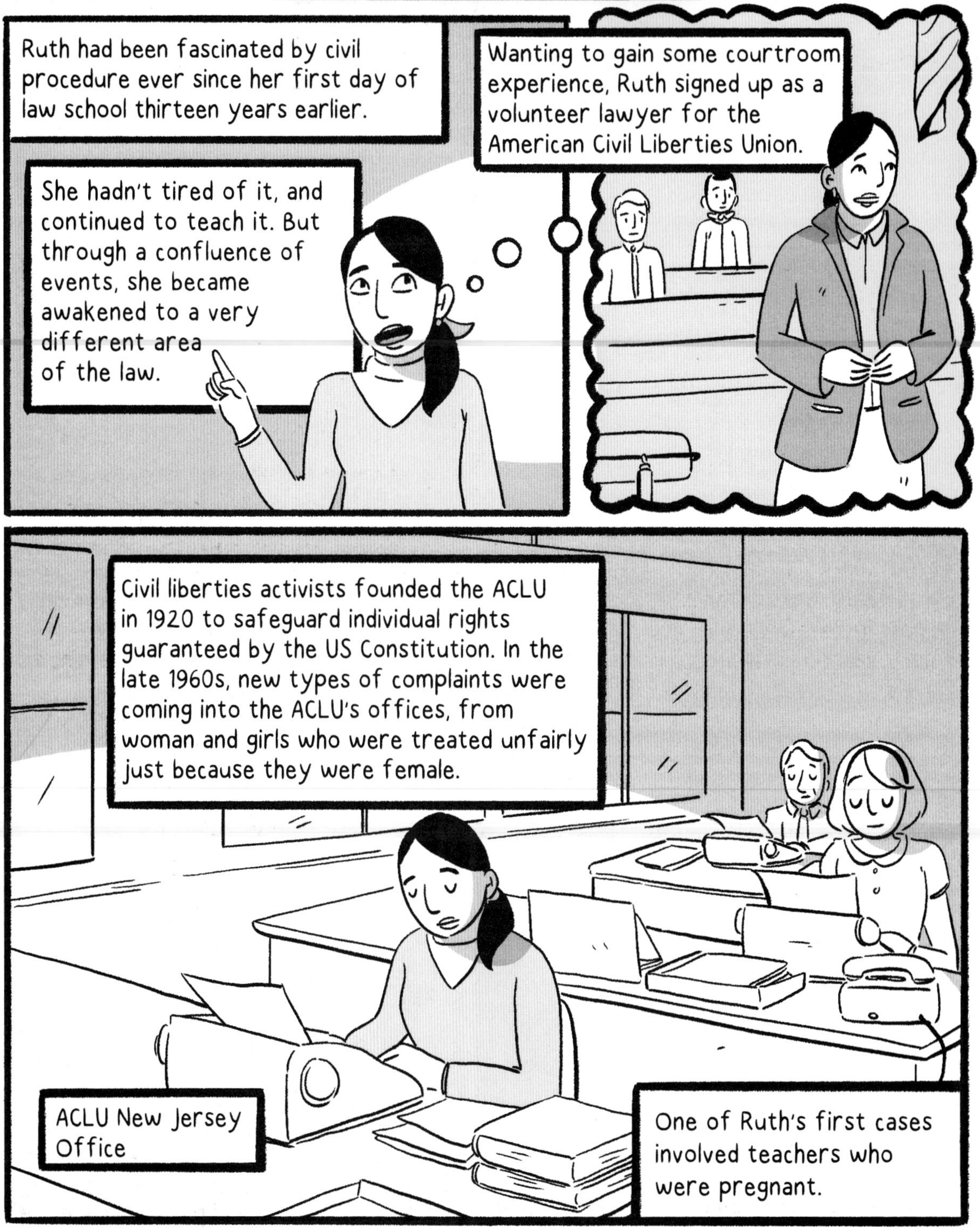
Ruth had been fascinated by civil procedure ever since her first day of law school thirteen years earlier.
She hadn't tired of it, and continued to teach it. But through a confluence of events, she became awakened to a very different area of the law.
Wanting to gain some courtroom experience, Ruth signed up as a volunteer lawyer for the American Civil Liberties Union.
Civil liberties activists founded the ACLU in 1920 to safeguard individual rights guaranteed by the US Constitution. In the late 1960s, new types of complaints were coming into the ACLU's offices, from woman and girls who were treated unfairly just because they were female.
ACLU New Jersey Office
One of Ruth's first cases involved teachers who were pregnant.

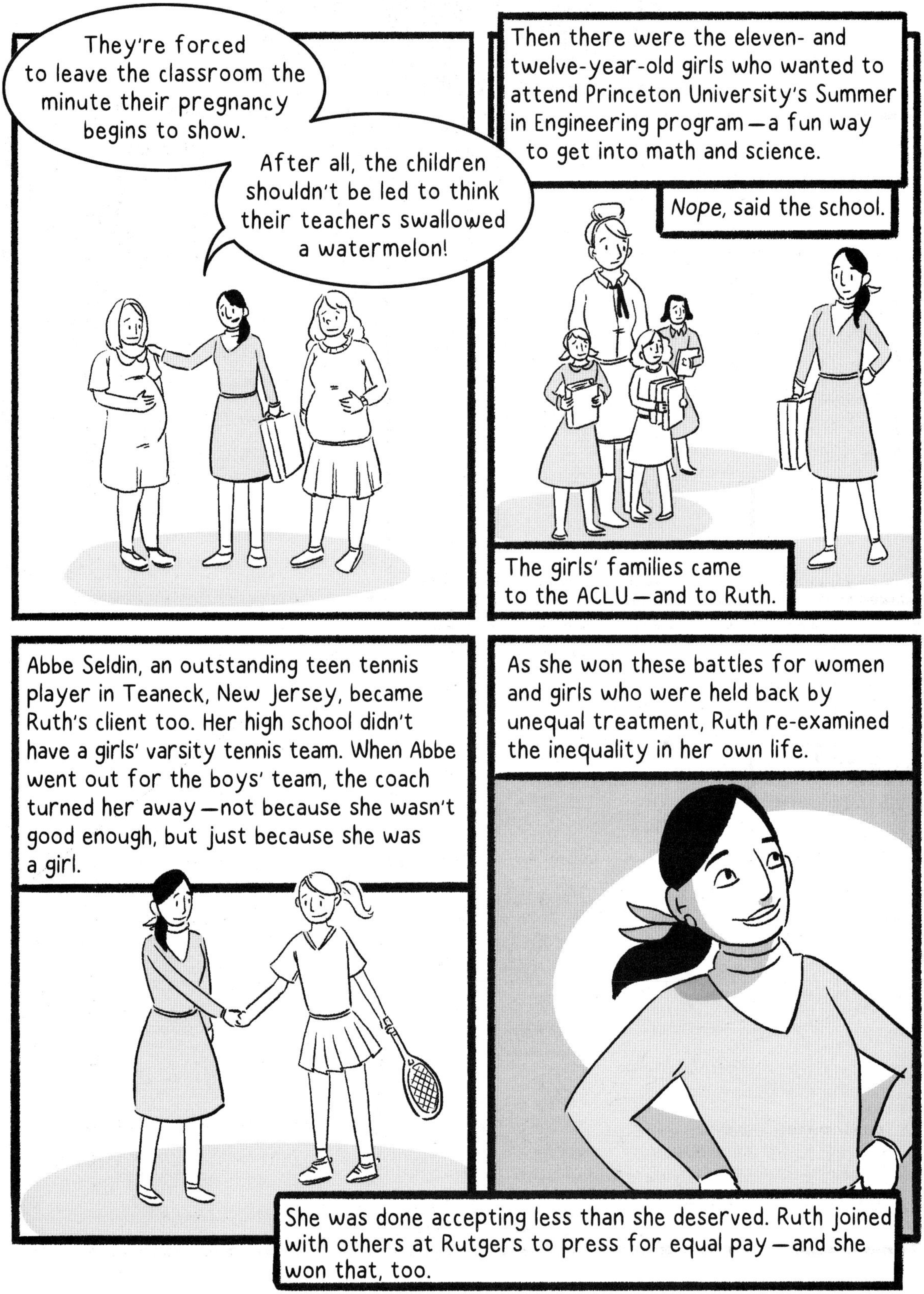
They're forced to leave the classroom the minute their pregnancy begins to show.
After all, the children shouldn't be led to think their teachers swallowed a watermelon!
Then there were the eleven- and twelve-year-old girls who wanted to attend Princeton University's Summer in Engineering program—a fun way to get into math and science.
Nope, said the school.
The girls' families came to the ACLU—and to Ruth.
Abbe Seldin, an outstanding teen tennis player in Teaneck, New Jersey, became Ruth's client too. Her high school didn't have a girls' varsity tennis team. When Abbe went out for the boys' team, the coach turned her away—not because she wasn't good enough, but just because she was a girl.
As she won these battles for women and girls who were held back by unequal treatment, Ruth re-examined the inequality in her own life.
She was done accepting less than she deserved. Ruth joined with others at Rutgers to press for equal pay—and she won that, too.

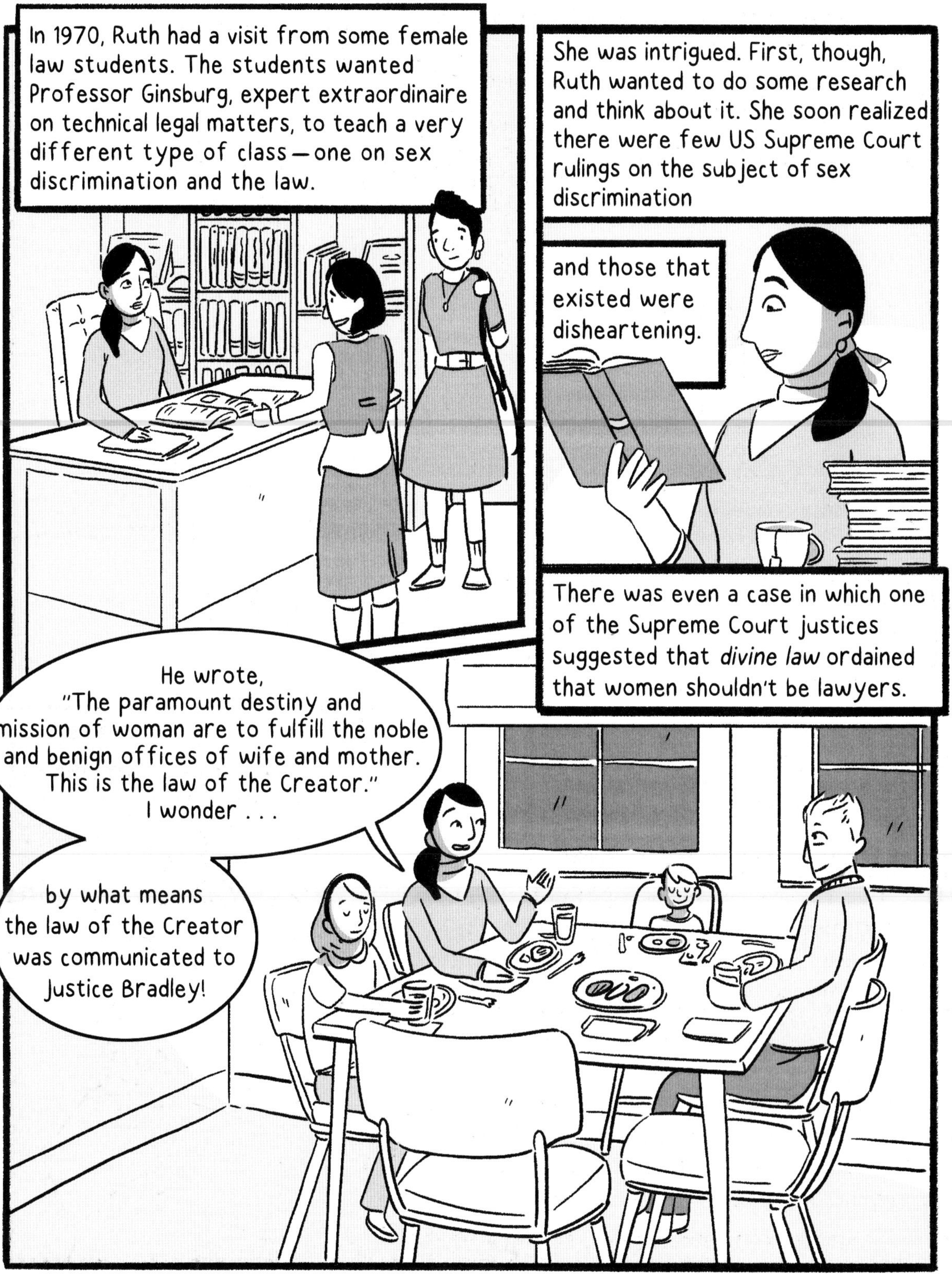
In 1970, Ruth had a visit from some female law students. The students wanted Professor Ginsburg, expert extraordinaire on technical legal matters, to teach a very different type of class—one on sex discrimination and the law.
She was intrigued. First, though, Ruth wanted to do some research and think about it. She soon realized there were few US Supreme Court rulings on the subject of sex discrimination
and those that existed were disheartening.
There was even a case in which one of the Supreme Court justices suggested that *divine law* ordained that women shouldn't be lawyers.
He wrote, "The paramount destiny and mission of woman are to fulfill the noble and benign offices of wife and mother. This is the law of the Creator." I wonder . . .
by what means the law of the Creator was communicated to Justice Bradley!

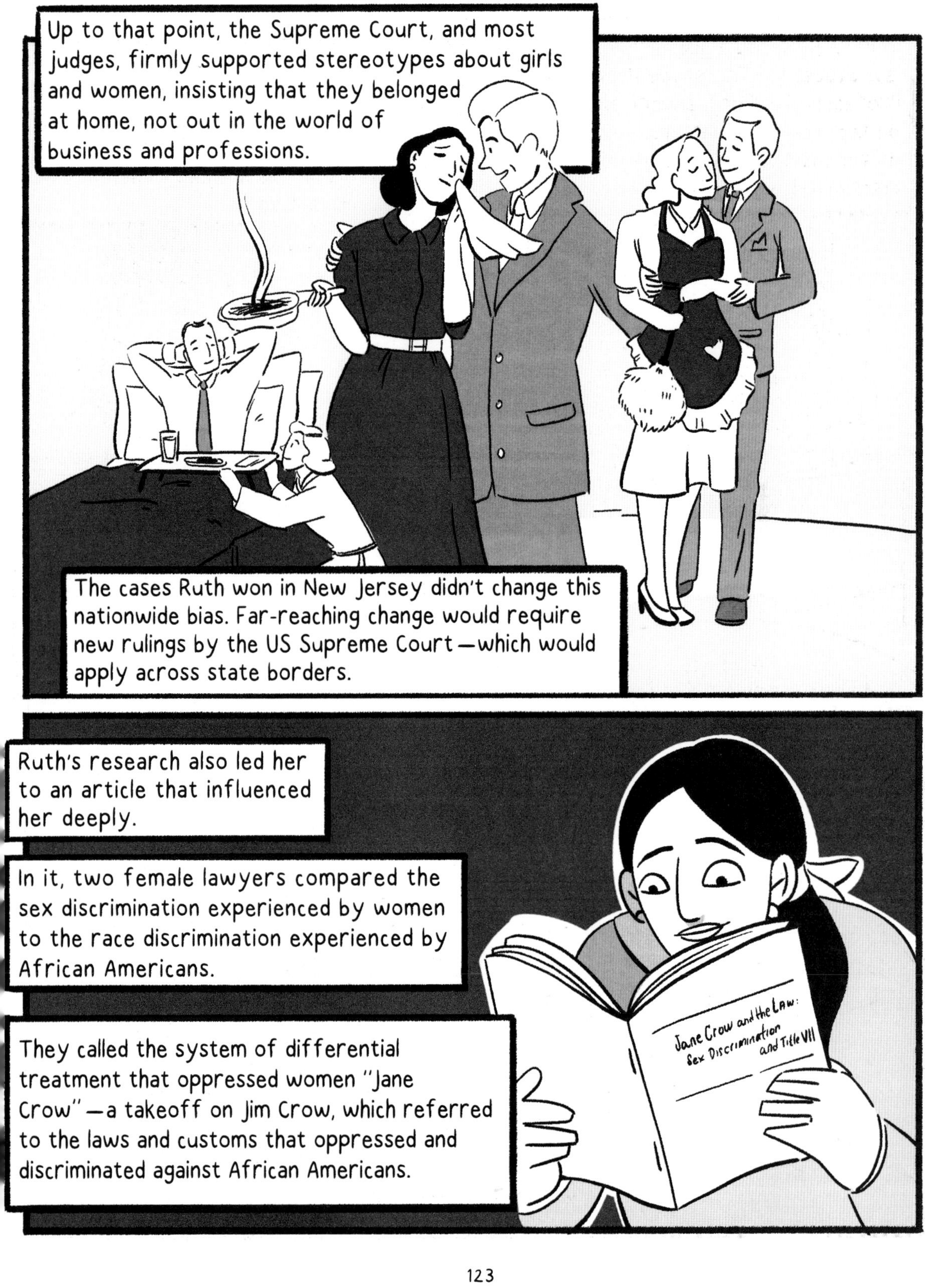
Up to that point, the Supreme Court, and most judges, firmly supported stereotypes about girls and women, insisting that they belonged at home, not out in the world of business and professions.
The cases Ruth won in New Jersey didn't change this nationwide bias. Far-reaching change would require new rulings by the US Supreme Court—which would apply across state borders.
Ruth's research also led her to an article that influenced her deeply.
In it, two female lawyers compared the sex discrimination experienced by women to the race discrimination experienced by African Americans.
They called the system of differential treatment that oppressed women "Jane Crow"—a takeoff on Jim Crow, which referred to the laws and customs that oppressed and discriminated against African Americans.
Jane Crow and the Law: Sex Discrimination and Title VII

"Land, like woman, was meant to be possessed."
—Curtis J. Berger, *Land Ownership and Use* (1968)

"Woman has always been dependent upon man."
—*Muller v. Oregon* (1908) (unanimous Supreme Court opinion)

How have people been putting up with such arbitrary distinctions?

How have *I* been putting up with them?

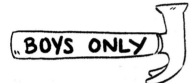
BOYS ONLY

"The natural and proper timidity and delicacy which belongs to the female sex evidently unfits it for many of the occupations of civil life."
—Supreme Court Justice Joseph P. Bradley, opinion in *Bradwell v. Illinois* (1873)

"The paramount destiny and mission of woman are to fulfill the noble and benign offices of wife and mother This is the law of the Creator."
—Justice Bradley in *Bradwell v. Illinois*

NO WOMEN

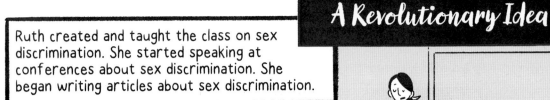

CHAPTER 27

A Revolutionary Idea

Ruth created and taught the class on sex discrimination. She started speaking at conferences about sex discrimination. She began writing articles about sex discrimination.

In all of this, she focused on the United States Constitution, and in particular the Constitution's Equal Protection Clause.

14th Amendment

Nor shall any State deprive any person of life, liberty, or property, without due process of law; nor deny to any person within its jurisdiction the equal protection of the laws.

The Equal Protection Clause is part of the Fourteenth Amendment, which was added to the Constitution after the Civil War. Its drafters intended to extend equal protection of the laws to people who used to be slaves, and to all African Americans. The men who adopted the Fourteenth Amendment in 1868 did not have equal rights for women and girls in mind.

But that didn't discourage Ruth.

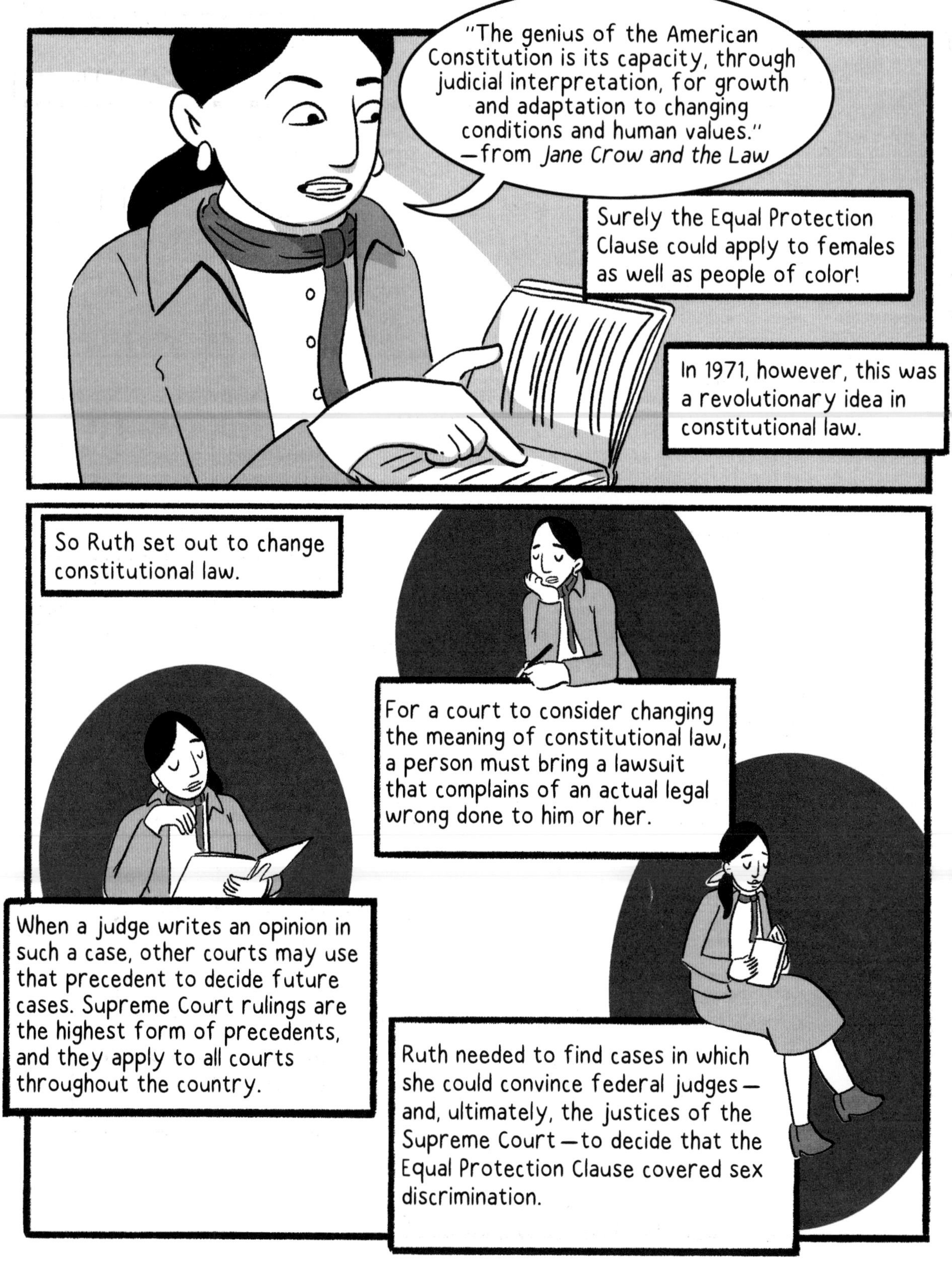
"The genius of the American Constitution is its capacity, through judicial interpretation, for growth and adaptation to changing conditions and human values."
—from *Jane Crow and the Law*
Surely the Equal Protection Clause could apply to females as well as people of color!
In 1971, however, this was a revolutionary idea in constitutional law.
So Ruth set out to change constitutional law.
For a court to consider changing the meaning of constitutional law, a person must bring a lawsuit that complains of an actual legal wrong done to him or her.
When a judge writes an opinion in such a case, other courts may use that precedent to decide future cases. Supreme Court rulings are the highest form of precedents, and they apply to all courts throughout the country.
Ruth needed to find cases in which she could convince federal judges—and, ultimately, the justices of the Supreme Court—to decide that the Equal Protection Clause covered sex discrimination.

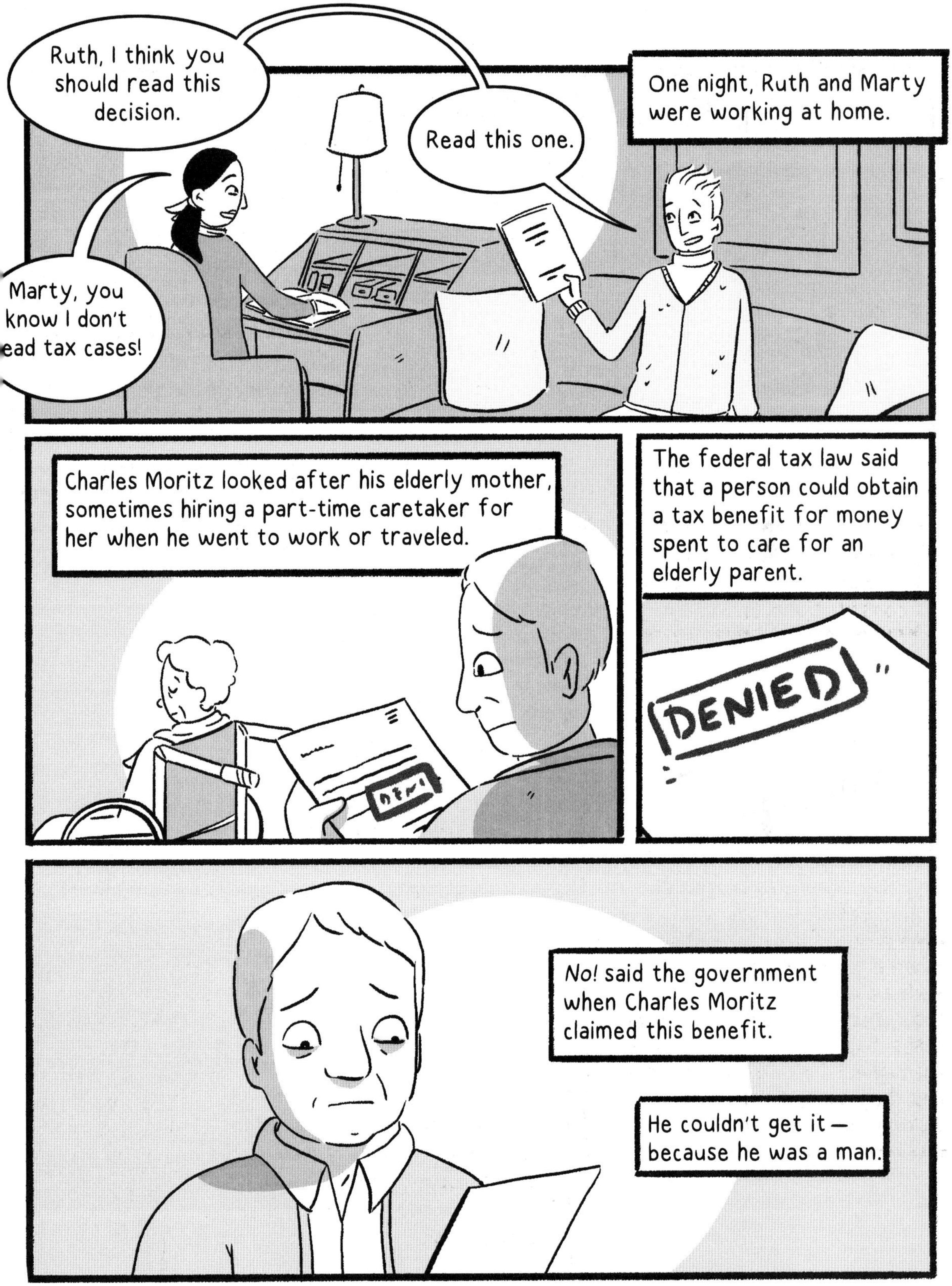
One night, Ruth and Marty were working at home.
Ruth, I think you should read this decision.
Read this one.
Marty, you know I don't ead tax cases!
Charles Moritz looked after his elderly mother, sometimes hiring a part-time caretaker for her when he went to work or traveled.
The federal tax law said that a person could obtain a tax benefit for money spent to care for an elderly parent.
DENIED
No! said the government when Charles Moritz claimed this benefit.
He couldn't get it— because he was a man.

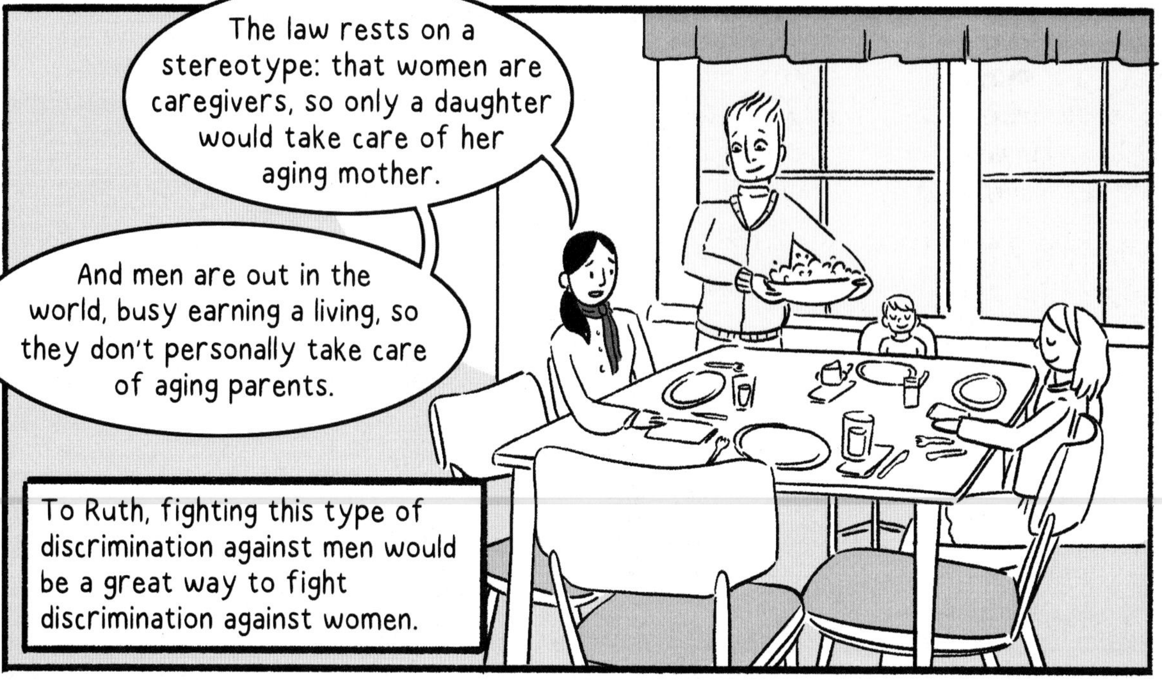
The law rests on a stereotype: that women are caregivers, so only a daughter would take care of her aging mother.
And men are out in the world, busy earning a living, so they don't personally take care of aging parents.
To Ruth, fighting this type of discrimination against men would be a great way to fight discrimination against women.

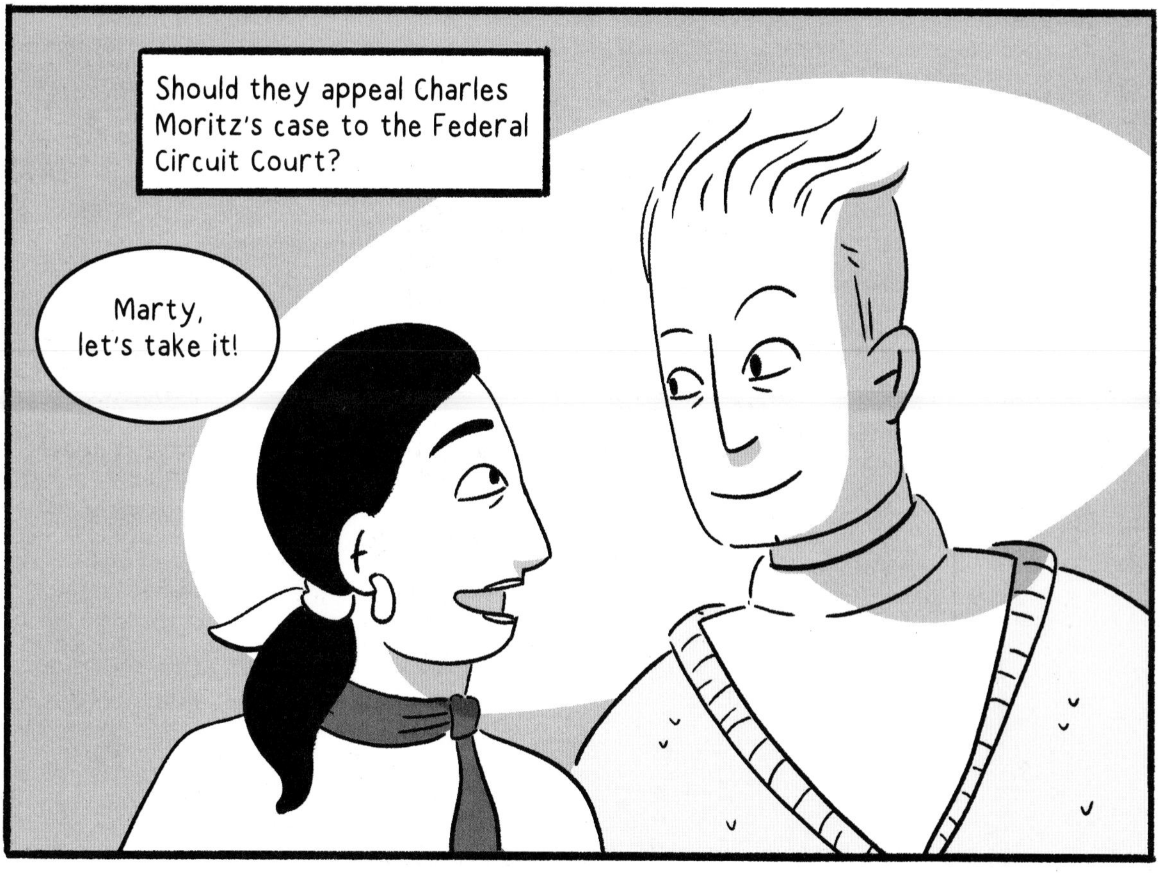
Should they appeal Charles Moritz's case to the Federal Circuit Court?
Marty, let's take it!

CHAPTER 28

A First

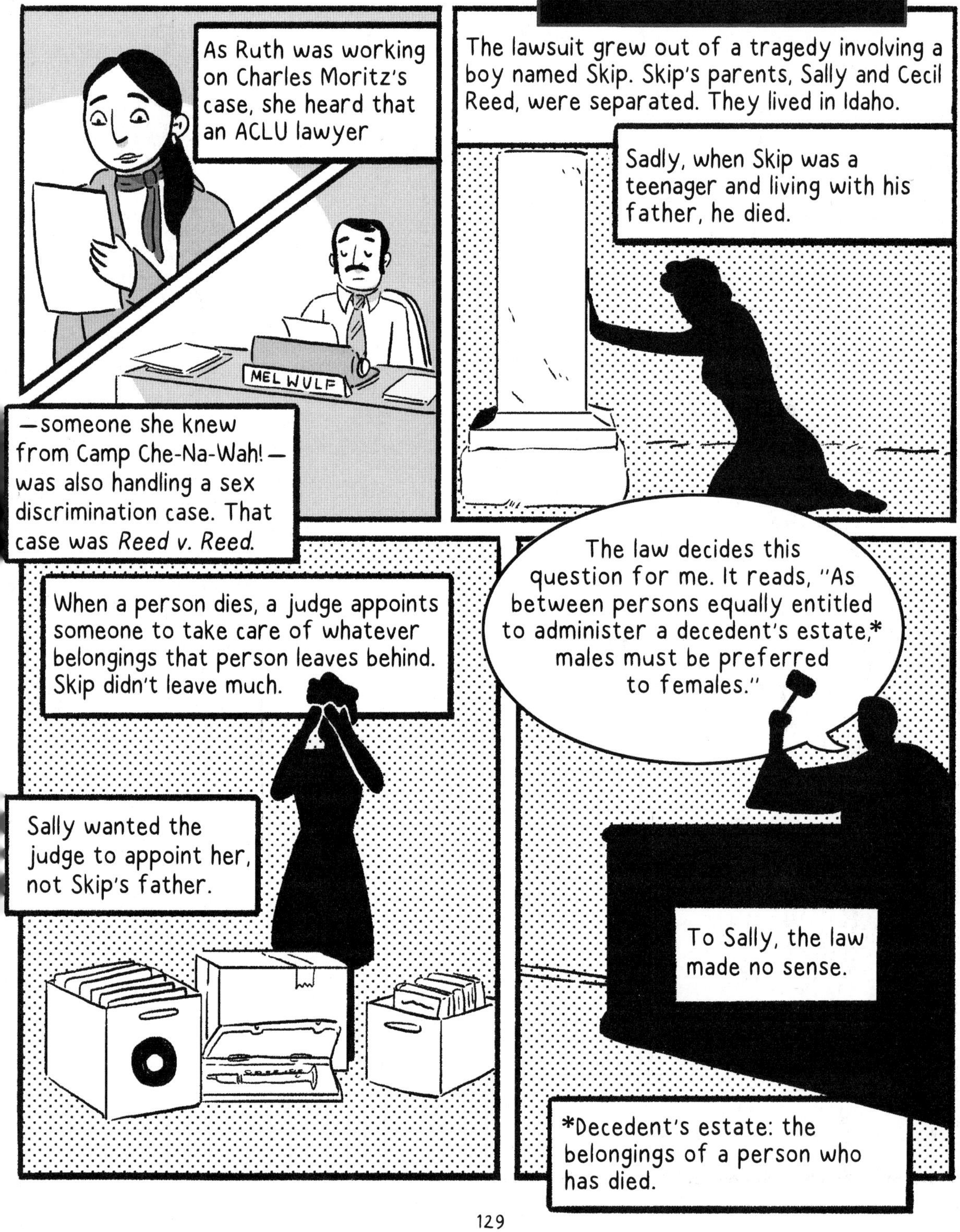
As Ruth was working on Charles Moritz's case, she heard that an ACLU lawyer
MEL WULF
—someone she knew from Camp Che-Na-Wah!—was also handling a sex discrimination case. That case was *Reed v. Reed*.
The lawsuit grew out of a tragedy involving a boy named Skip. Skip's parents, Sally and Cecil Reed, were separated. They lived in Idaho.
Sadly, when Skip was a teenager and living with his father, he died.
When a person dies, a judge appoints someone to take care of whatever belongings that person leaves behind. Skip didn't leave much.
Sally wanted the judge to appoint her, not Skip's father.
The law decides this question for me. It reads, "As between persons equally entitled to administer a decedent's estate,* males must be preferred to females."
To Sally, the law made no sense.
*Decedent's estate: the belongings of a person who has died.

To Ruth, Sally Reed's case and Charles Moritz's case created a valuable pair, showing that sex discrimination was not only irrational

When she and Marty finished their brief for the *Moritz* case, Ruth sent it to the lawyer handling Sally Reed's case.

Dear Mel:
Some of this should be useful for Reed v. Reed. Have you thought about whether it would be appropriate to have a woman co-counsel in that case???
Best regards,
RBG

but also hurt both men and women.

Ruth was not in the habit of asking for special consideration because she was a woman, but she really wanted to be part of the *Reed* team. The *Reed* case had already reached the US Supreme Court, so its impact on the law could be significant.

Ruth was invited to participate in *Reed*, and assembled a team of law students.

Their final brief was sixty-eight pages long.

Ruth needed all those pages. She wanted the Supreme Court justices to see that the Idaho law was part of a widespread pattern, across the nation

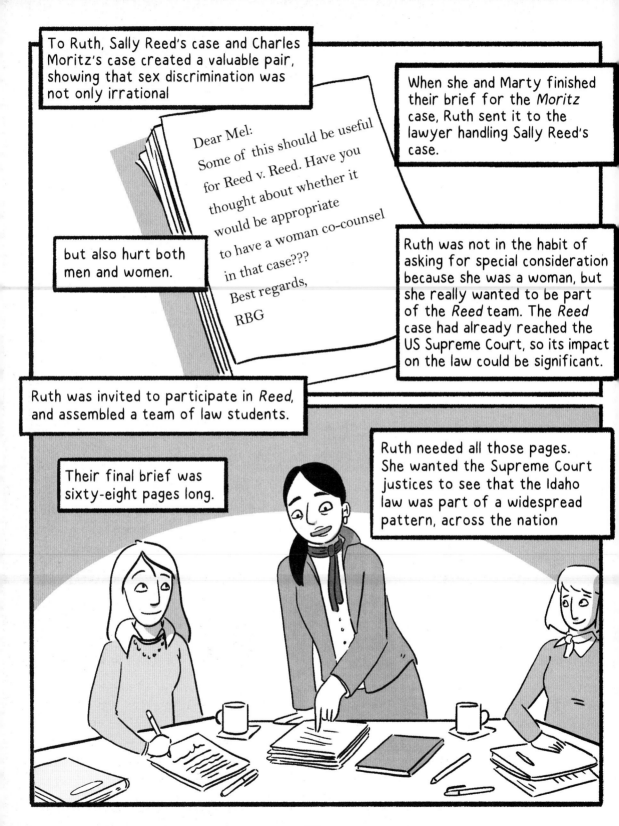

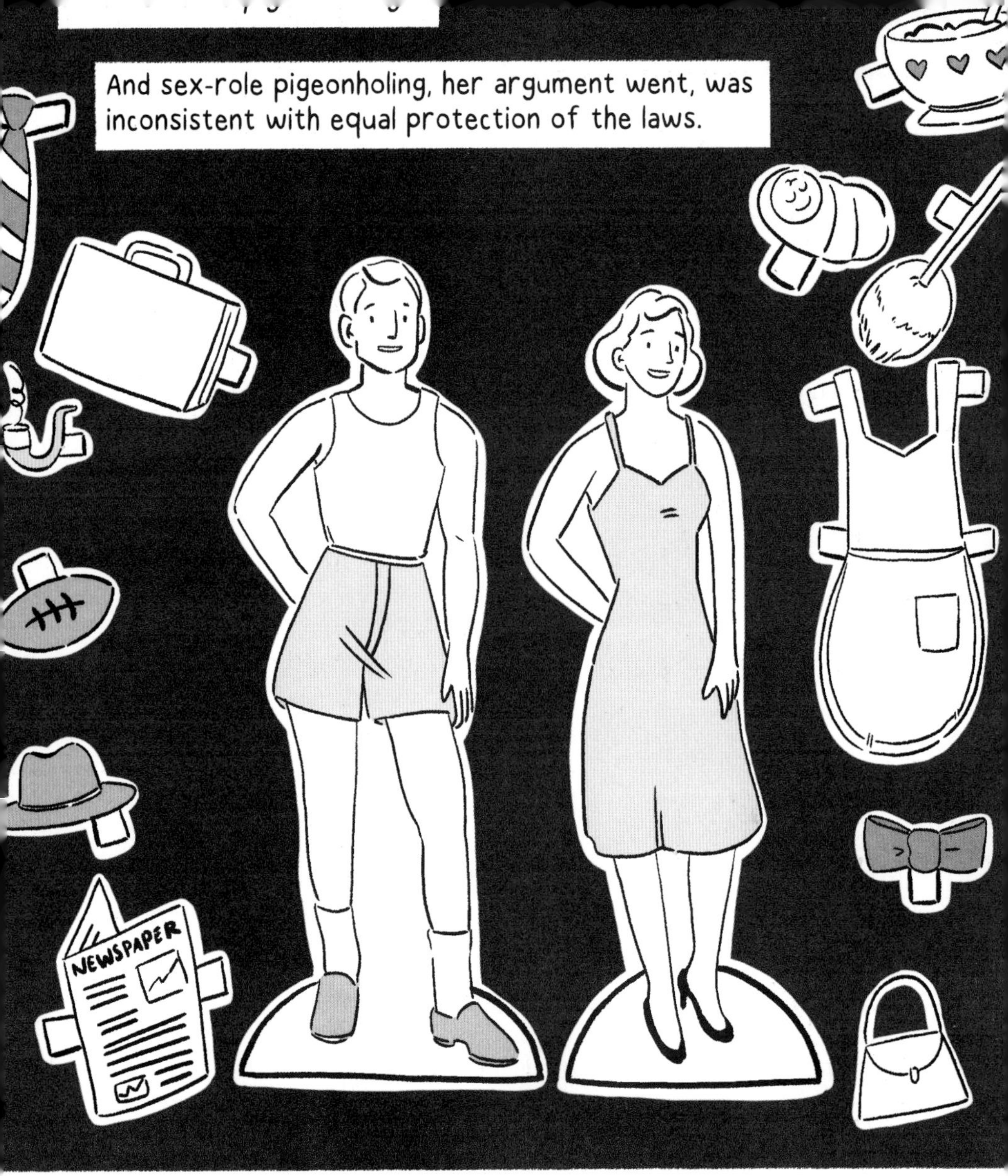
And sex-role pigeonholing, her argument went, was inconsistent with equal protection of the laws.
NEWSPAPER

The brief pointed out laws in various states that gave husbands the sole right to decide where a family lived, allowed girls to marry at a younger age than boys (which encouraged boys, but not girls, to pursue their education and careers), and discouraged men from working as childcare providers. There was even a state law that made it a crime to use "indecent" language in the presence of women—but cursing in front of men was perfectly legal.

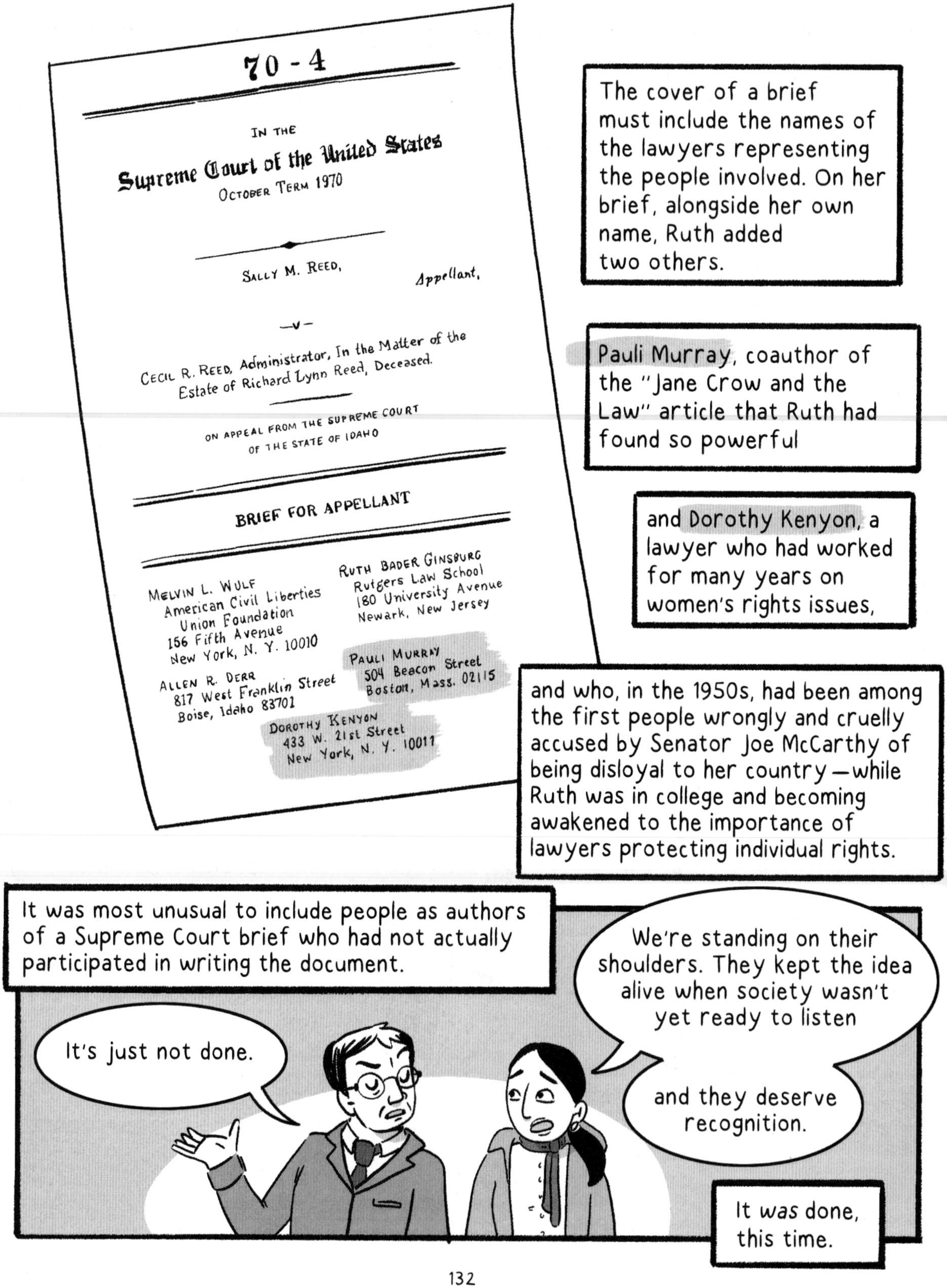
70 - 4
In the
Supreme Court of the United States
October Term 1970
Sally M. Reed,
Appellant,
—v—
Cecil R. Reed, Administrator, In the Matter of the Estate of Richard Lynn Reed, Deceased.
On appeal from the Supreme Court of the State of Idaho
BRIEF FOR APPELLANT
Melvin L. Wulf
American Civil Liberties Union Foundation
156 Fifth Avenue
New York, N. Y. 10010
Ruth Bader Ginsburg
Rutgers Law School
180 University Avenue
Newark, New Jersey
Allen R. Derr
817 West Franklin Street
Boise, Idaho 83701
Pauli Murray
504 Beacon Street
Boston, Mass. 02115
Dorothy Kenyon
433 W. 21st Street
New York, N. Y. 10011
The cover of a brief must include the names of the lawyers representing the people involved. On her brief, alongside her own name, Ruth added two others.
Pauli Murray, coauthor of the "Jane Crow and the Law" article that Ruth had found so powerful
and Dorothy Kenyon, a lawyer who had worked for many years on women's rights issues,
and who, in the 1950s, had been among the first people wrongly and cruelly accused by Senator Joe McCarthy of being disloyal to her country—while Ruth was in college and becoming awakened to the importance of lawyers protecting individual rights.
It was most unusual to include people as authors of a Supreme Court brief who had not actually participated in writing the document.
It's just not done.
We're standing on their shoulders. They kept the idea alive when society wasn't yet ready to listen
and they deserve recognition.
It *was* done, this time.

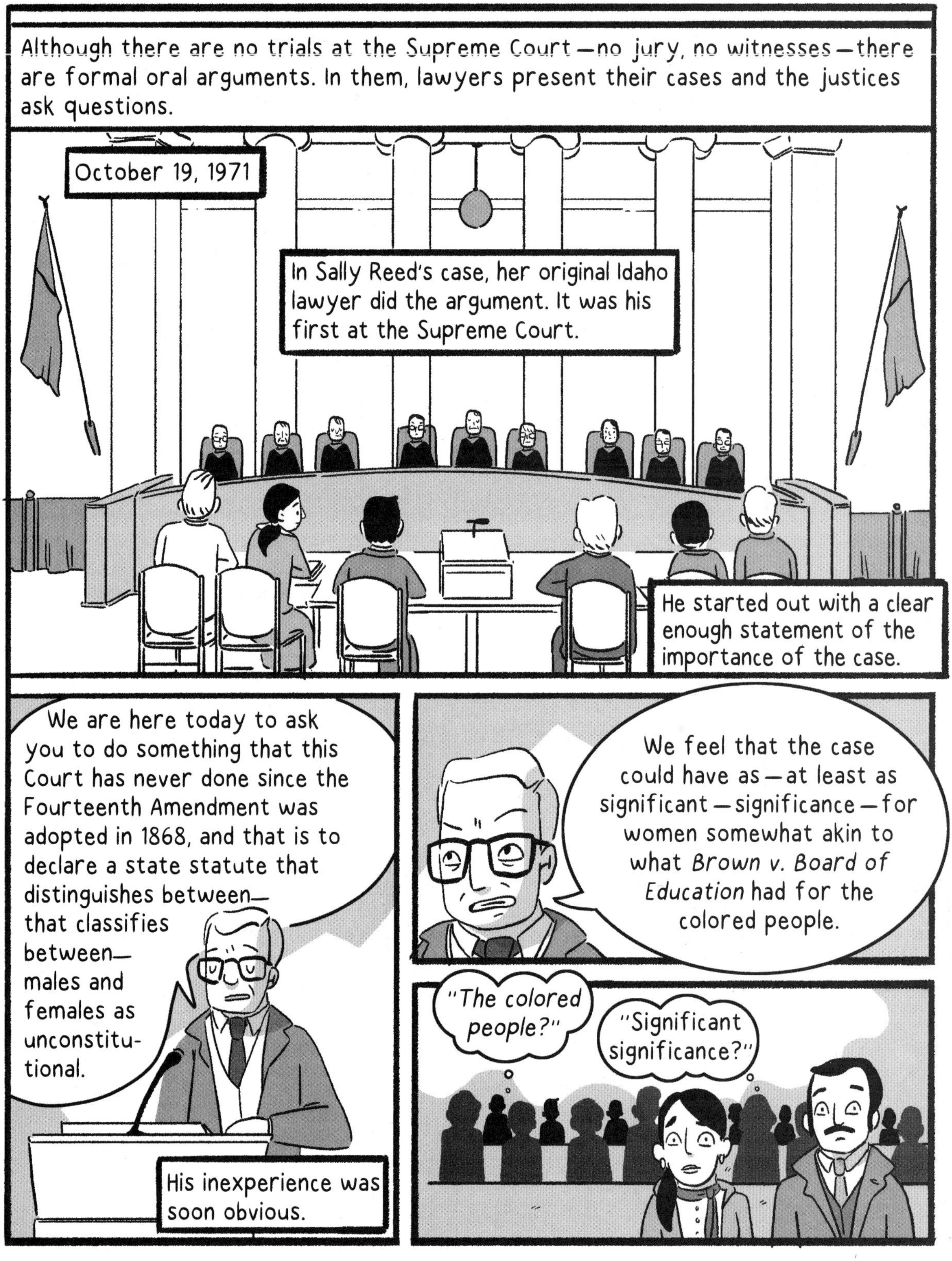
Although there are no trials at the Supreme Court—no jury, no witnesses—there are formal oral arguments. In them, lawyers present their cases and the justices ask questions.
October 19, 1971
In Sally Reed's case, her original Idaho lawyer did the argument. It was his first at the Supreme Court.
He started out with a clear enough statement of the importance of the case.
We are here today to ask you to do something that this Court has never done since the Fourteenth Amendment was adopted in 1868, and that is to declare a state statute that distinguishes between—that classifies between—males and females as unconstitutional.
His inexperience was soon obvious.
We feel that the case could have as—at least as significant—significance—for women somewhat akin to what *Brown v. Board of Education* had for the colored people.
"The colored people?"
"Significant significance?"

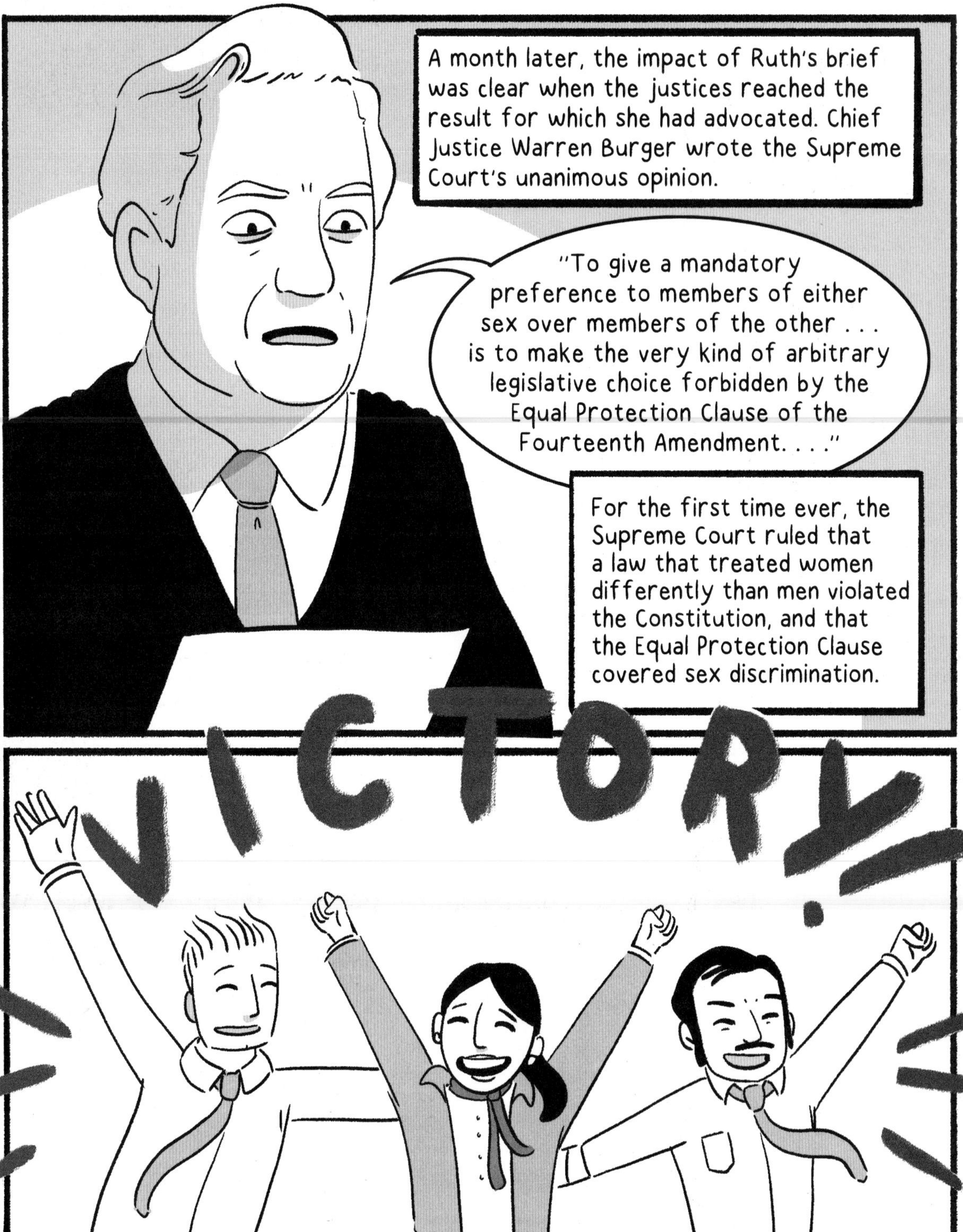

A month later, the impact of Ruth's brief was clear when the justices reached the result for which she had advocated. Chief Justice Warren Burger wrote the Supreme Court's unanimous opinion.
"To give a mandatory preference to members of either sex over members of the other . . . is to make the very kind of arbitrary legislative choice forbidden by the Equal Protection Clause of the Fourteenth Amendment. . . ."
For the first time ever, the Supreme Court ruled that a law that treated women differently than men violated the Constitution, and that the Equal Protection Clause covered sex discrimination.
VICTORY!

CHAPTER 29

Onward

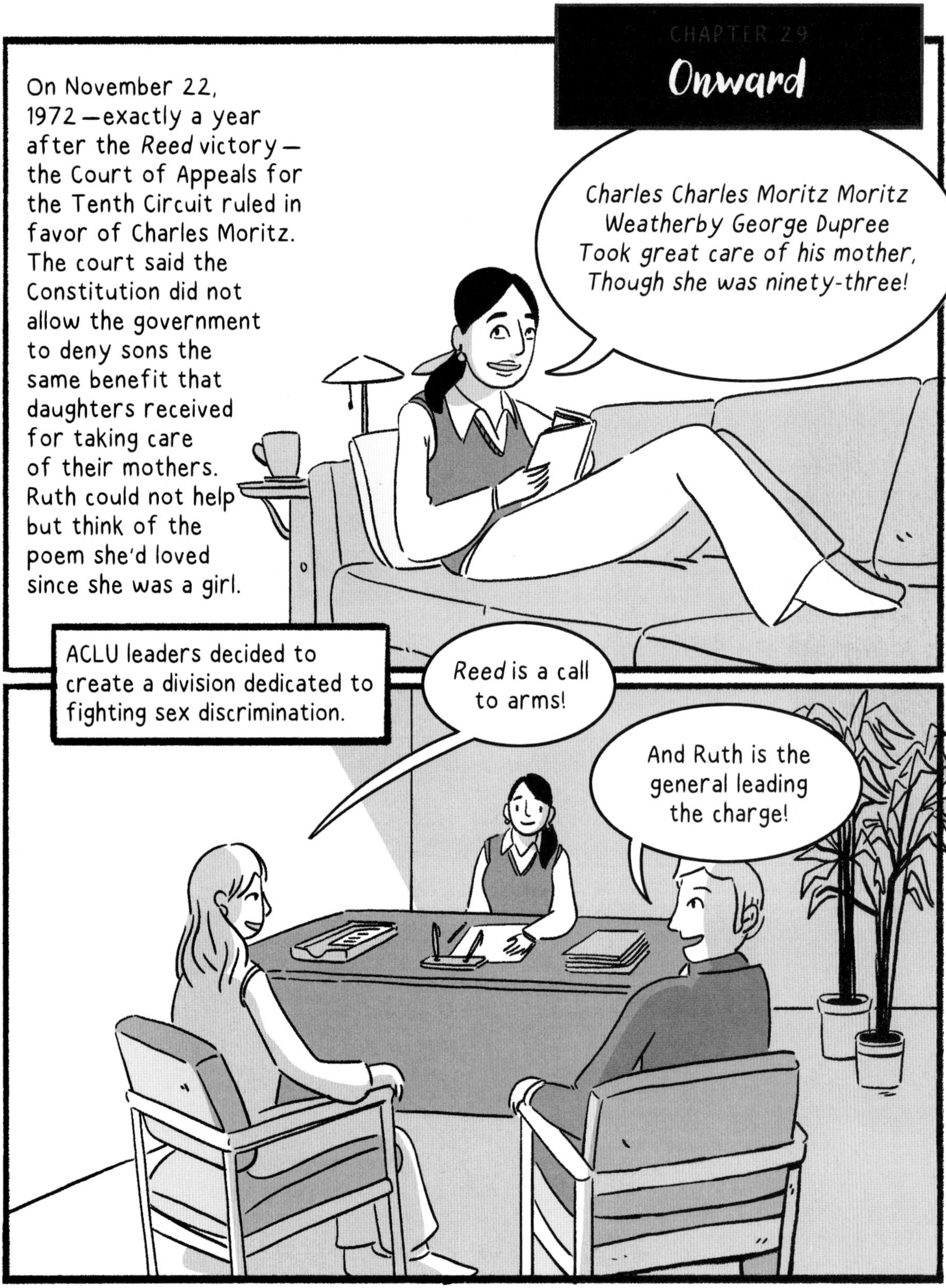
On November 22, 1972—exactly a year after the *Reed* victory—the Court of Appeals for the Tenth Circuit ruled in favor of Charles Moritz. The court said the Constitution did not allow the government to deny sons the same benefit that daughters received for taking care of their mothers. Ruth could not help but think of the poem she'd loved since she was a girl.
Charles Charles Moritz Moritz Weatherby George Dupree Took great care of his mother, Though she was ninety-three!
ACLU leaders decided to create a division dedicated to fighting sex discrimination.
Reed is a call to arms!
And Ruth is the general leading the charge!

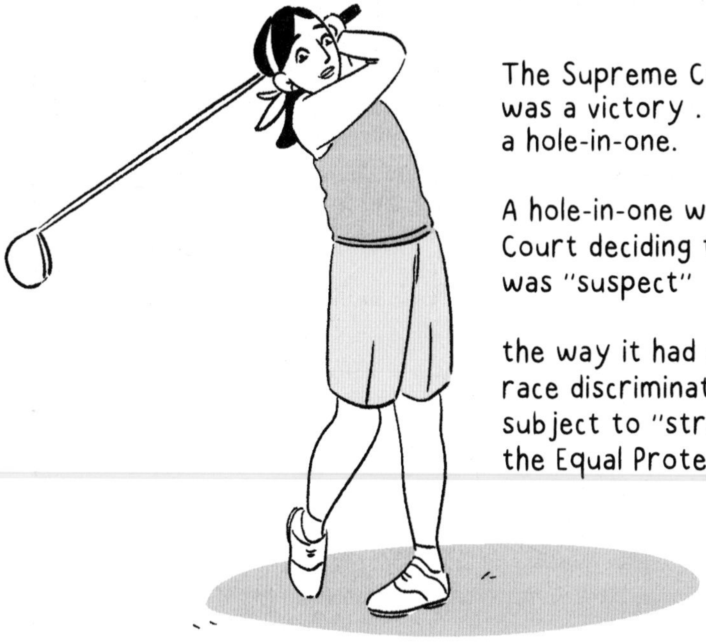

The Supreme Court's ruling in *Reed* was a victory . . . but not a hole-in-one.

A hole-in-one would be the Supreme Court deciding that sex discrimination was "suspect"

the way it had already decided that race discrimination was "suspect" and subject to "strict scrutiny" under the Equal Protection Clause,

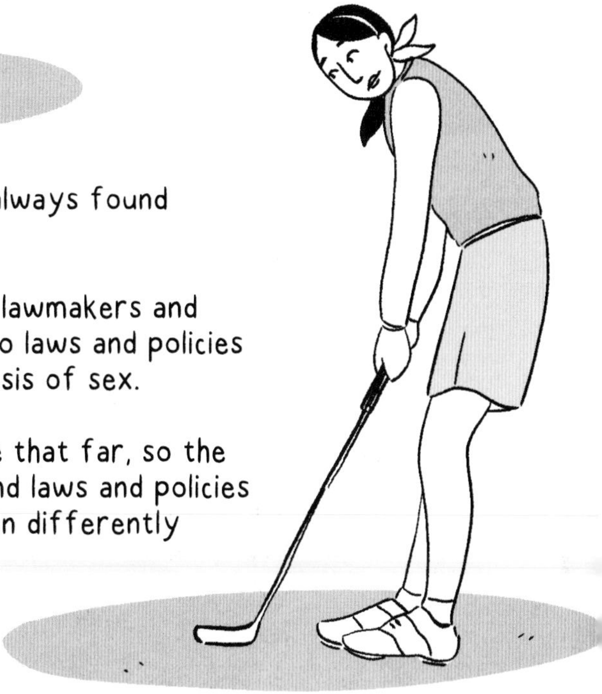

which meant it was almost always found unconstitutional.

That would be the guidance lawmakers and lower courts needed to undo laws and policies that discriminated on the basis of sex.

But the justices hadn't gone that far, so the government could still defend laws and policies that treated men and women differently

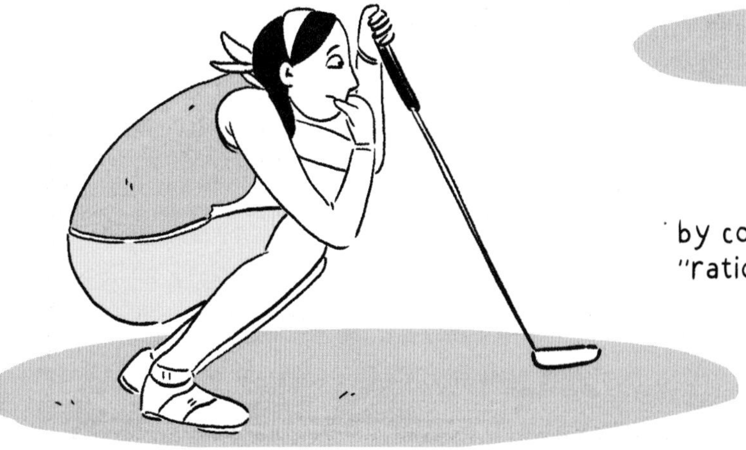

by coming up with some sort of "rational" explanation for them.

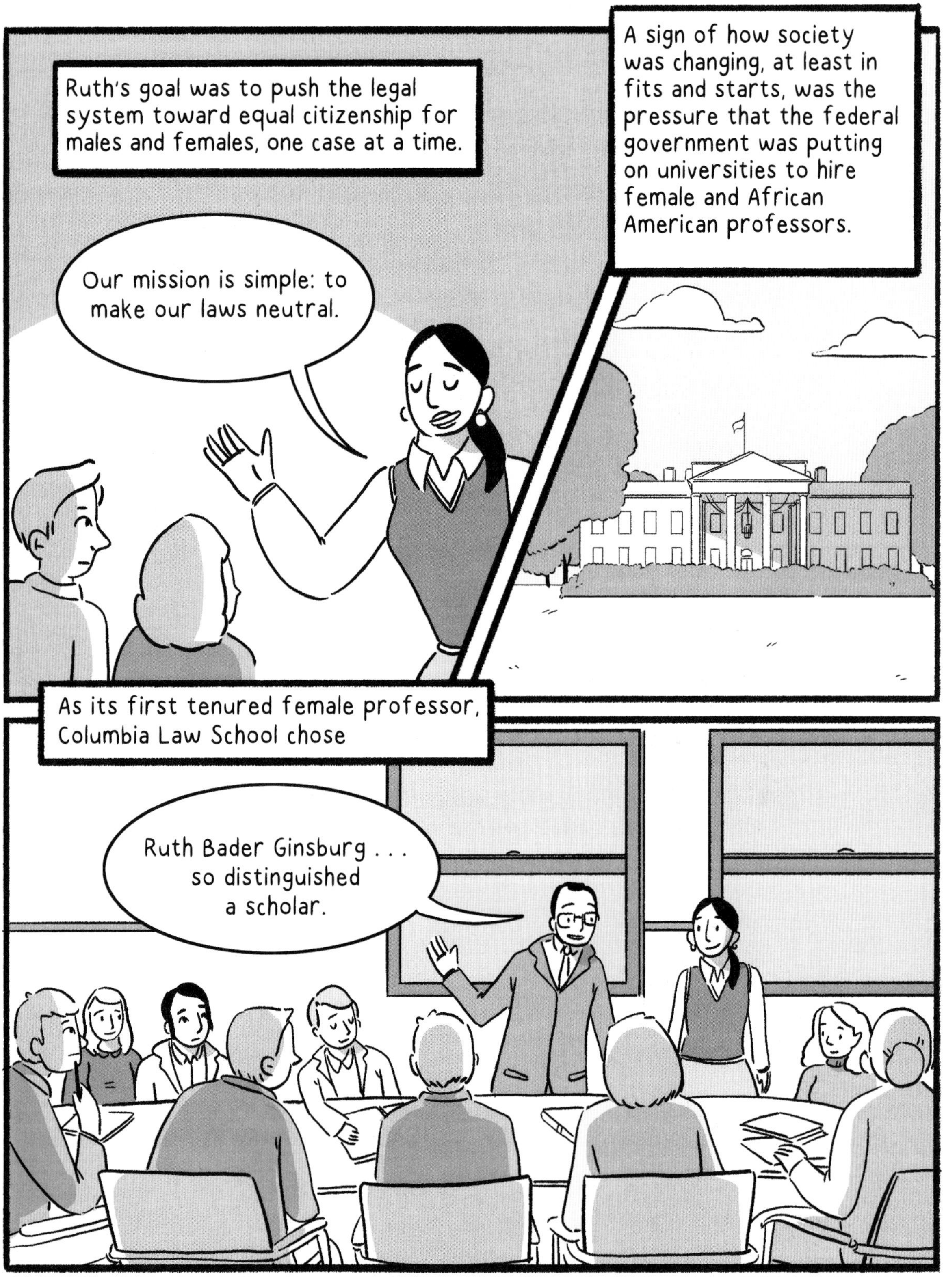
Ruth's goal was to push the legal system toward equal citizenship for males and females, one case at a time.
Our mission is simple: to make our laws neutral.
A sign of how society was changing, at least in fits and starts, was the pressure that the federal government was putting on universities to hire female and African American professors.
As its first tenured female professor, Columbia Law School chose
Ruth Bader Ginsburg . . . so distinguished a scholar.

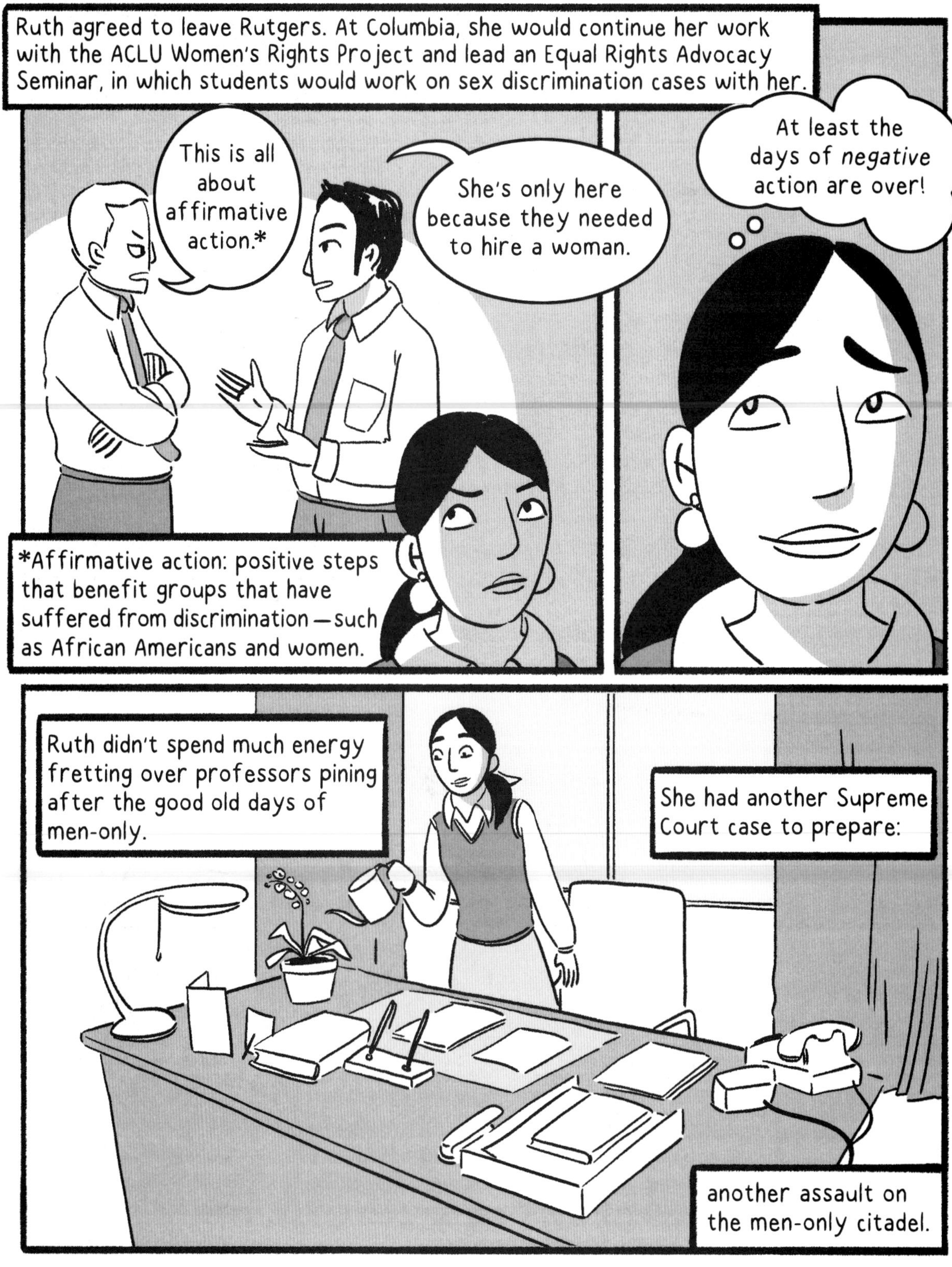
Ruth agreed to leave Rutgers. At Columbia, she would continue her work with the ACLU Women's Rights Project and lead an Equal Rights Advocacy Seminar, in which students would work on sex discrimination cases with her.
This is all about affirmative action.*
She's only here because they needed to hire a woman.
*Affirmative action: positive steps that benefit groups that have suffered from discrimination—such as African Americans and women.
At least the days of *negative* action are over!
Ruth didn't spend much energy fretting over professors pining after the good old days of men-only.
She had another Supreme Court case to prepare:
another assault on the men-only citadel.

CHAPTER 30
"I Ask No Favor"

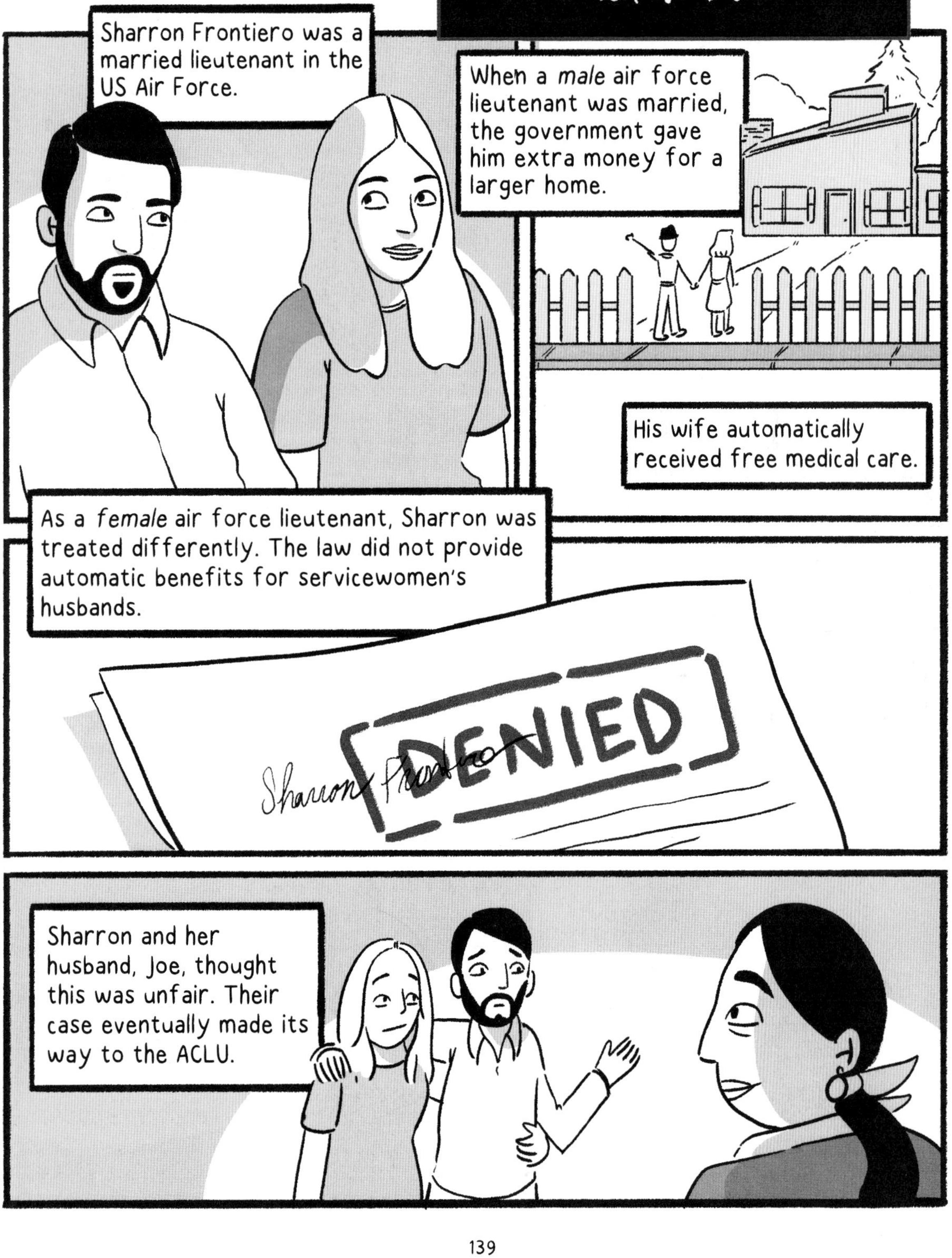
Sharron Frontiero was a married lieutenant in the US Air Force.
When a *male* air force lieutenant was married, the government gave him extra money for a larger home.
His wife automatically received free medical care.
As a *female* air force lieutenant, Sharron was treated differently. The law did not provide automatic benefits for servicewomen's husbands.
DENIED
Sharron and her husband, Joe, thought this was unfair. Their case eventually made its way to the ACLU.

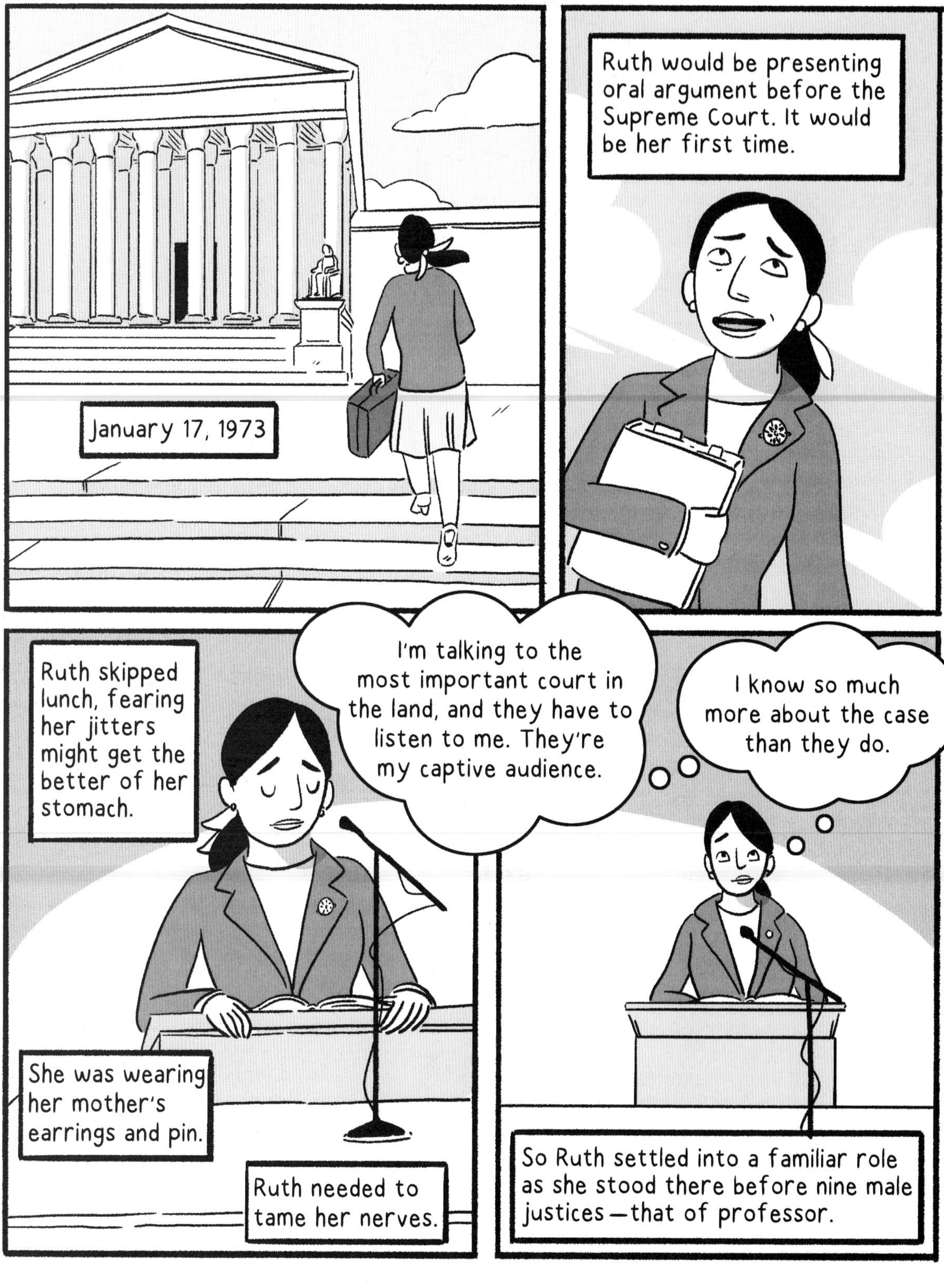
January 17, 1973
Ruth would be presenting oral argument before the Supreme Court. It would be her first time.
Ruth skipped lunch, fearing her jitters might get the better of her stomach.
I'm talking to the most important court in the land, and they have to listen to me. They're my captive audience.
She was wearing her mother's earrings and pin.
Ruth needed to tame her nerves.
I know so much more about the case than they do.
So Ruth settled into a familiar role as she stood there before nine male justices—that of professor.

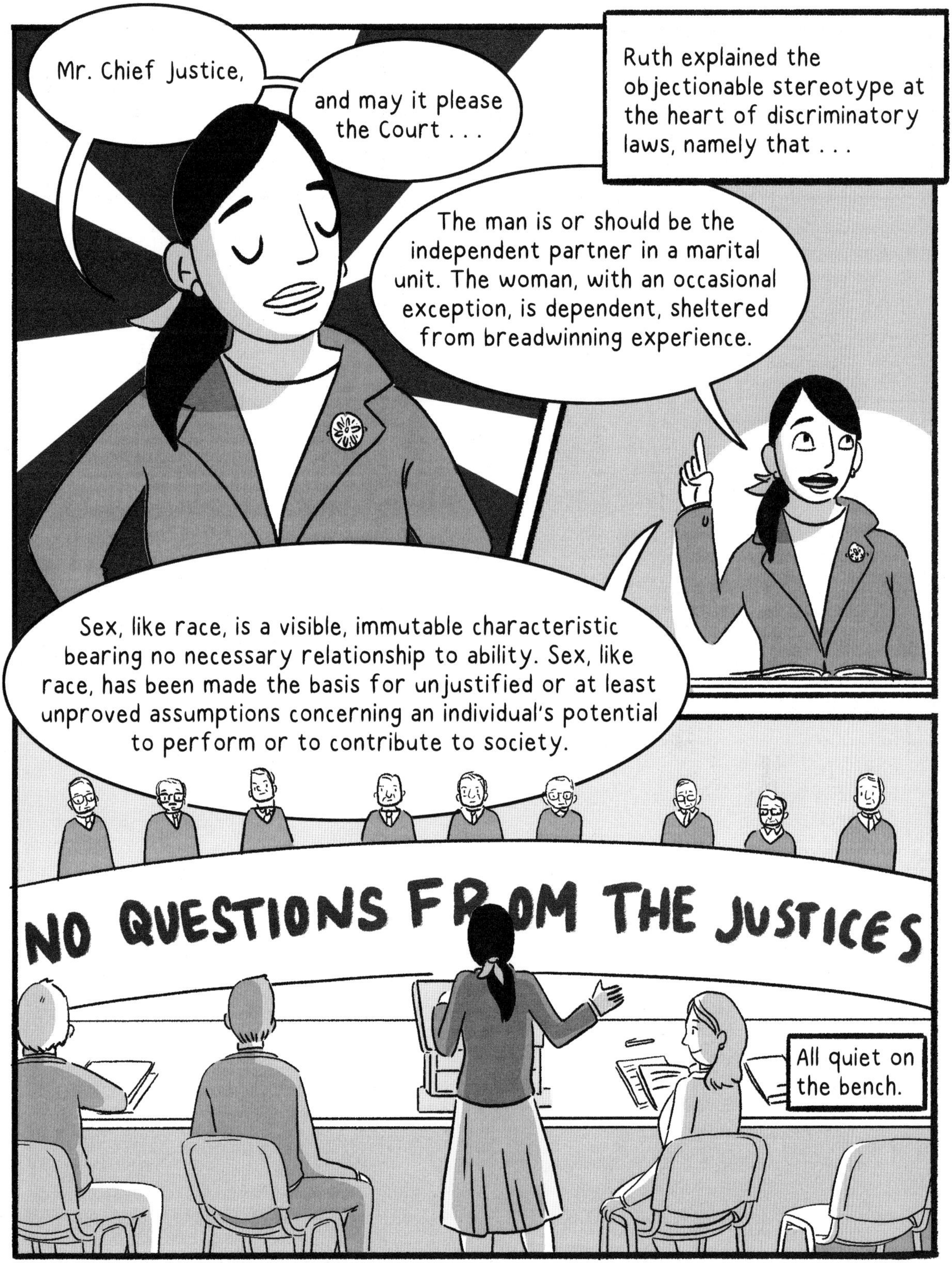
Mr. Chief Justice,
and may it please the Court . . .
Ruth explained the objectionable stereotype at the heart of discriminatory laws, namely that . . .
The man is or should be the independent partner in a marital unit. The woman, with an occasional exception, is dependent, sheltered from breadwinning experience.
Sex, like race, is a visible, immutable characteristic bearing no necessary relationship to ability. Sex, like race, has been made the basis for unjustified or at least unproved assumptions concerning an individual's potential to perform or to contribute to society.
NO QUESTIONS FROM THE JUSTICES
All quiet on the bench.

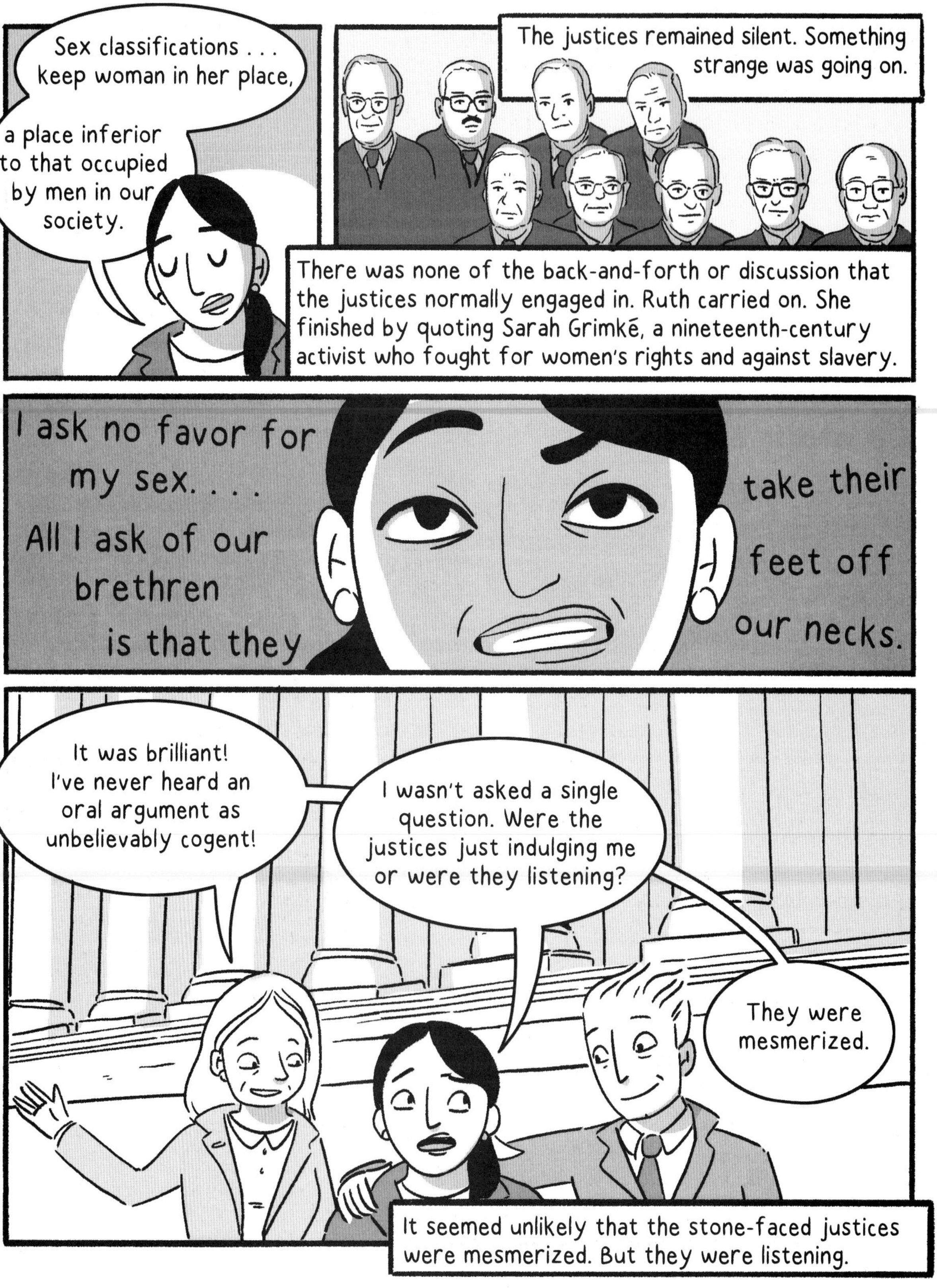
Sex classifications . . . keep woman in her place,
a place inferior to that occupied by men in our society.
The justices remained silent. Something strange was going on.
There was none of the back-and-forth or discussion that the justices normally engaged in. Ruth carried on. She finished by quoting Sarah Grimké, a nineteenth-century activist who fought for women's rights and against slavery.
I ask no favor for my sex. . . . All I ask of our brethren is that they take their feet off our necks.
It was brilliant! I've never heard an oral argument as unbelievably cogent!
I wasn't asked a single question. Were the justices just indulging me or were they listening?
They were mesmerized.
It seemed unlikely that the stone-faced justices were mesmerized. But they were listening.

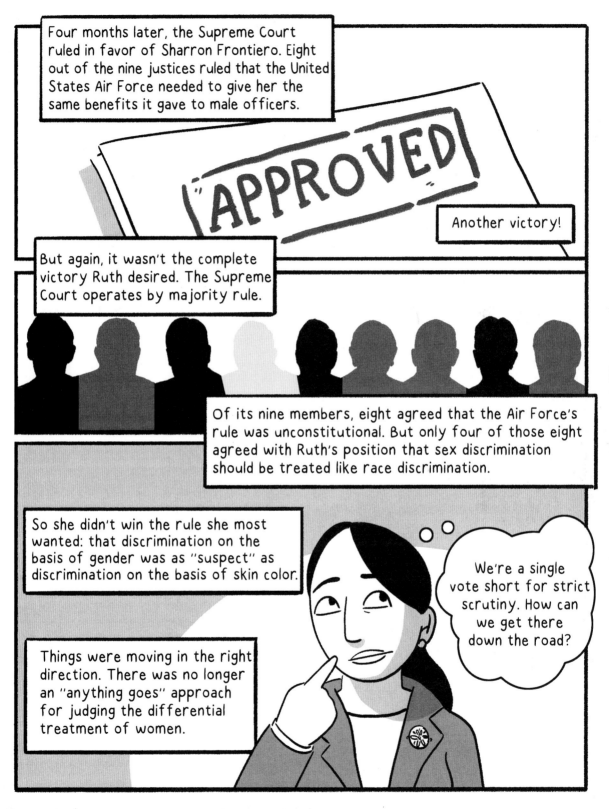

Four months later, the Supreme Court ruled in favor of Sharron Frontiero. Eight out of the nine justices ruled that the United States Air Force needed to give her the same benefits it gave to male officers.

Another victory!

But again, it wasn't the complete victory Ruth desired. The Supreme Court operates by majority rule.

Of its nine members, eight agreed that the Air Force's rule was unconstitutional. But only four of those eight agreed with Ruth's position that sex discrimination should be treated like race discrimination.

So she didn't win the rule she most wanted: that discrimination on the basis of gender was as "suspect" as discrimination on the basis of skin color.

We're a single vote short for strict scrutiny. How can we get there down the road?

Things were moving in the right direction. There was no longer an "anything goes" approach for judging the differential treatment of women.

CHAPTER 31

No Nonsense

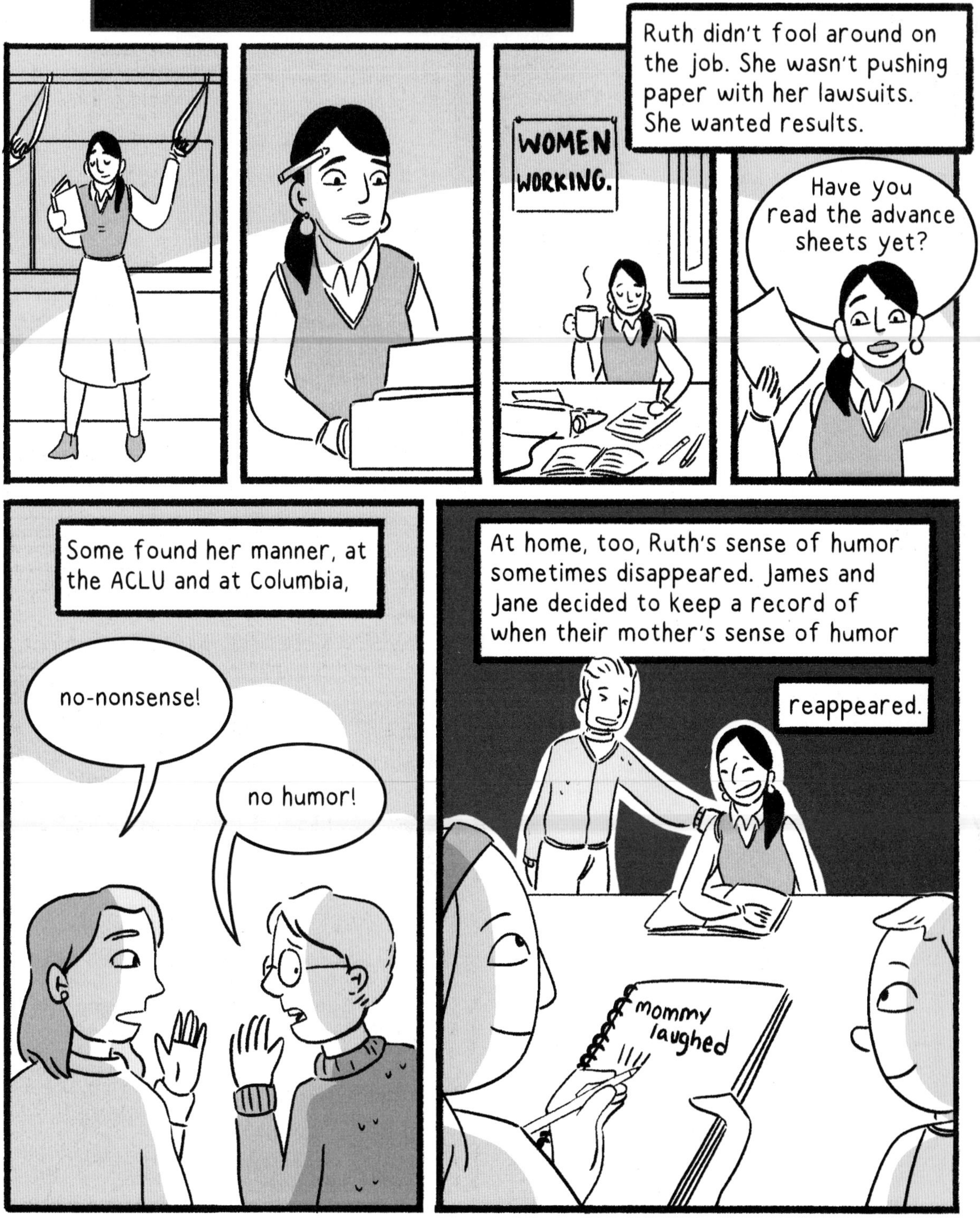
Ruth didn't fool around on the job. She wasn't pushing paper with her lawsuits. She wanted results.
WOMEN WORKING.
Have you read the advance sheets yet?
Some found her manner, at the ACLU and at Columbia,
no-nonsense!
no humor!
At home, too, Ruth's sense of humor sometimes disappeared. James and Jane decided to keep a record of when their mother's sense of humor
reappeared.
mommy laughed

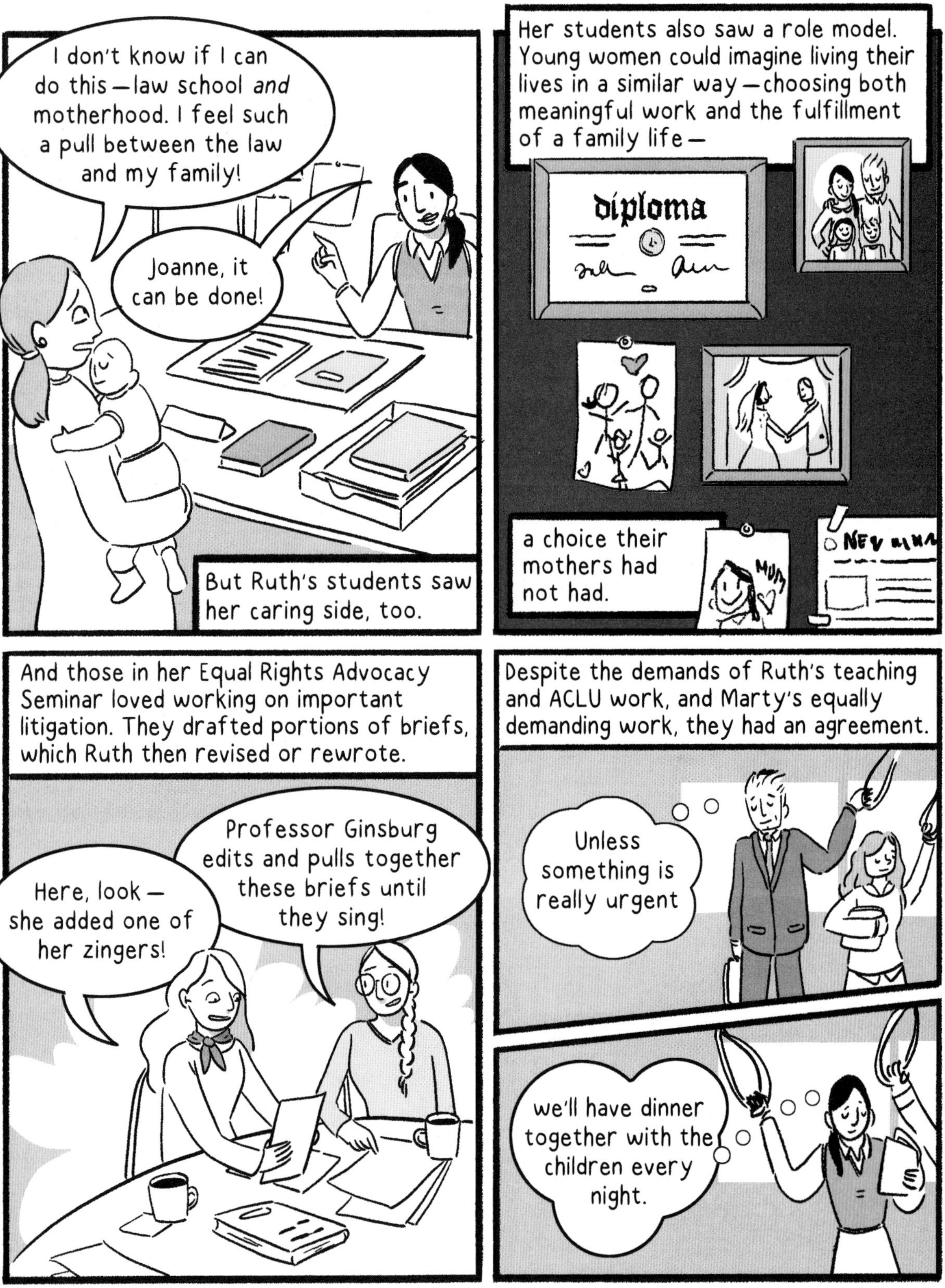
I don't know if I can do this—law school *and* motherhood. I feel such a pull between the law and my family!
Joanne, it can be done!
But Ruth's students saw her caring side, too.
Her students also saw a role model. Young women could imagine living their lives in a similar way—choosing both meaningful work and the fulfillment of a family life—
diploma
a choice their mothers had not had.
MUM
And those in her Equal Rights Advocacy Seminar loved working on important litigation. They drafted portions of briefs, which Ruth then revised or rewrote.
Here, look—she added one of her zingers!
Professor Ginsburg edits and pulls together these briefs until they sing!
Despite the demands of Ruth's teaching and ACLU work, and Marty's equally demanding work, they had an agreement.
Unless something is really urgent
we'll have dinner together with the children every night.

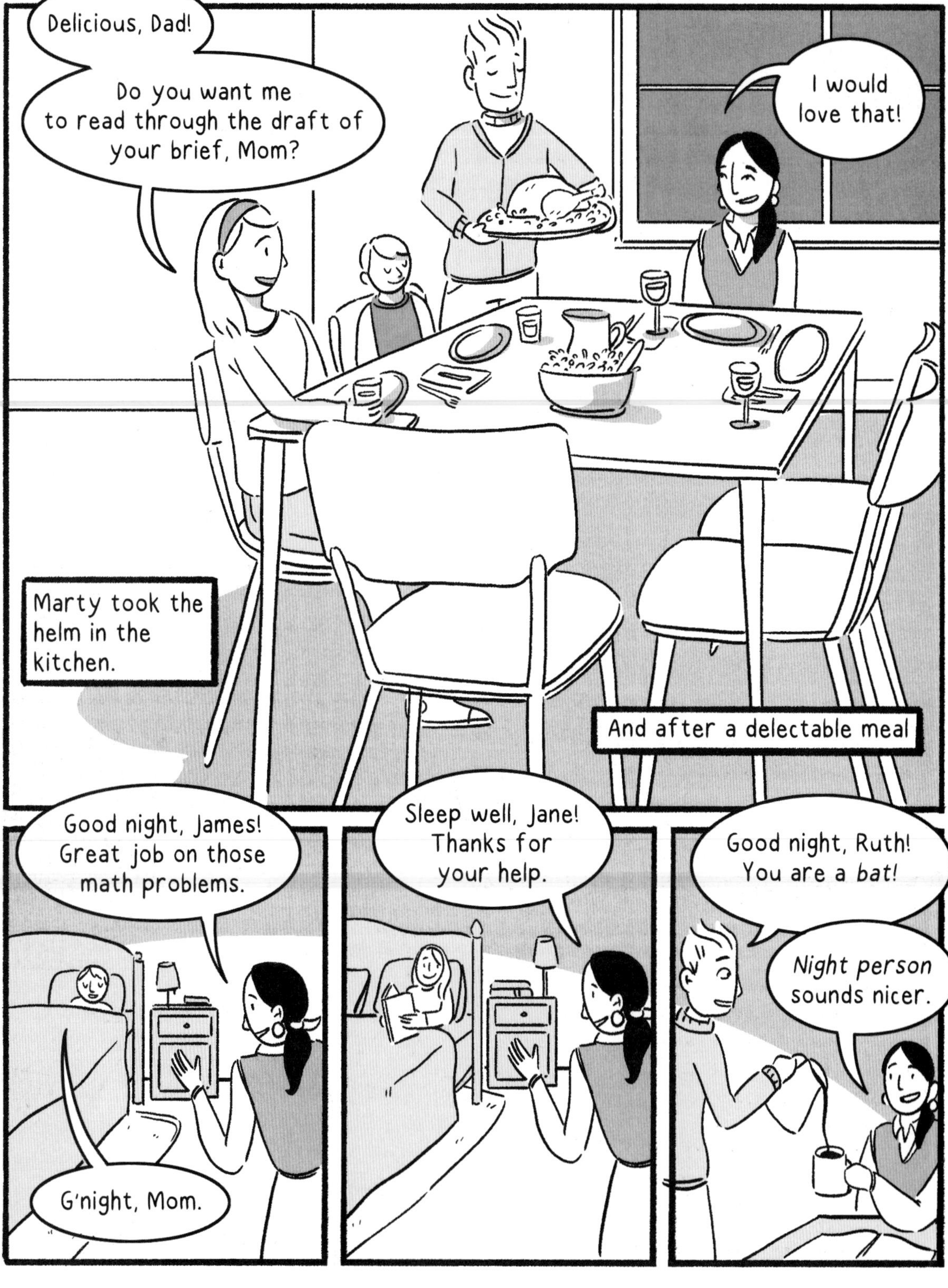
Delicious, Dad!
Do you want me to read through the draft of your brief, Mom?
I would love that!
Marty took the helm in the kitchen.
And after a delectable meal
Good night, James! Great job on those math problems.
G'night, Mom.
Sleep well, Jane! Thanks for your help.
Good night, Ruth! You are a *bat*!
Night person sounds nicer.

Step by Step

What kept Ruth so busy?

1. Prepare for seminar.
2. Prepare lecture.
3. Review Conflict of Laws syllabus.
4. Draft Court of Appeals brief.
5. Edit Supreme Court brief.
6. Research law review article.
7. Consult with Herma Hill Kay on our new casebook on sex discrimination law.
8. Meet with student editors of Women's Rights Law Reporter.
9. Prepare ERA article.
10. Edit law review article on gender in the Supreme Court.
11. Prepare for ACLU board meeting.
12. Correspondence with cocounsel.

WOMEN ON JURIES: STAY HOME!

WOMEN NEED NOT APPLY!

PREGNANT WOMEN AT WORK, GO HOME!

NO FEMALE POLICE OFFICERS

NO MEN IN NURSING SCHOOL

Identifying and removing the barriers that restricted what women could do, and that also restricted what men could do, took a lot of work.

And the work required a strategy. Otherwise time and effort might be wasted on cases that were unlikely to produce significant change.

Ruth's strategy was not to drive a bulldozer into all sex-based barriers

but to focus on those that seemed most important and vulnerable

and take them down systematically.

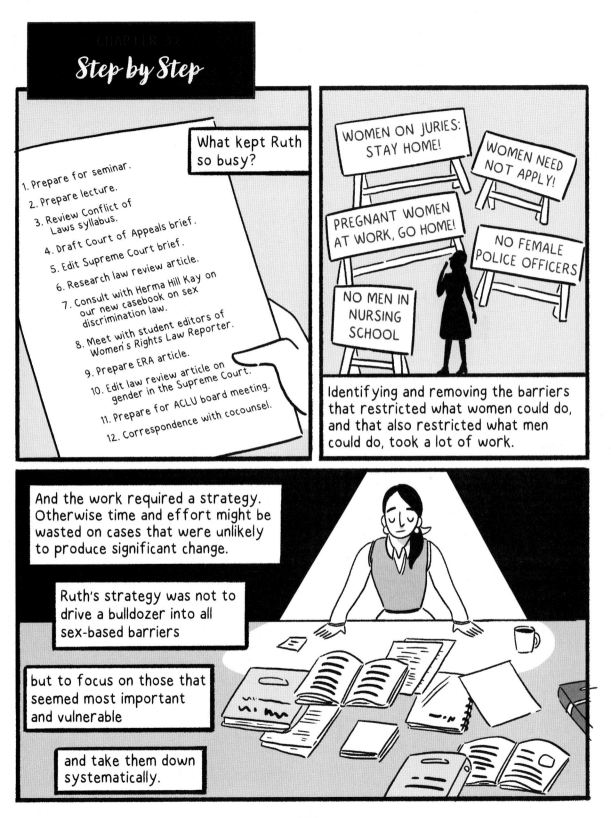

There could have been an alternative to Ruth's gradual approach—and that was the Equal Rights Amendment to the Constitution. Unlike the rest of the Constitution, the proposed ERA said it plainly: No discrimination on the basis of sex.

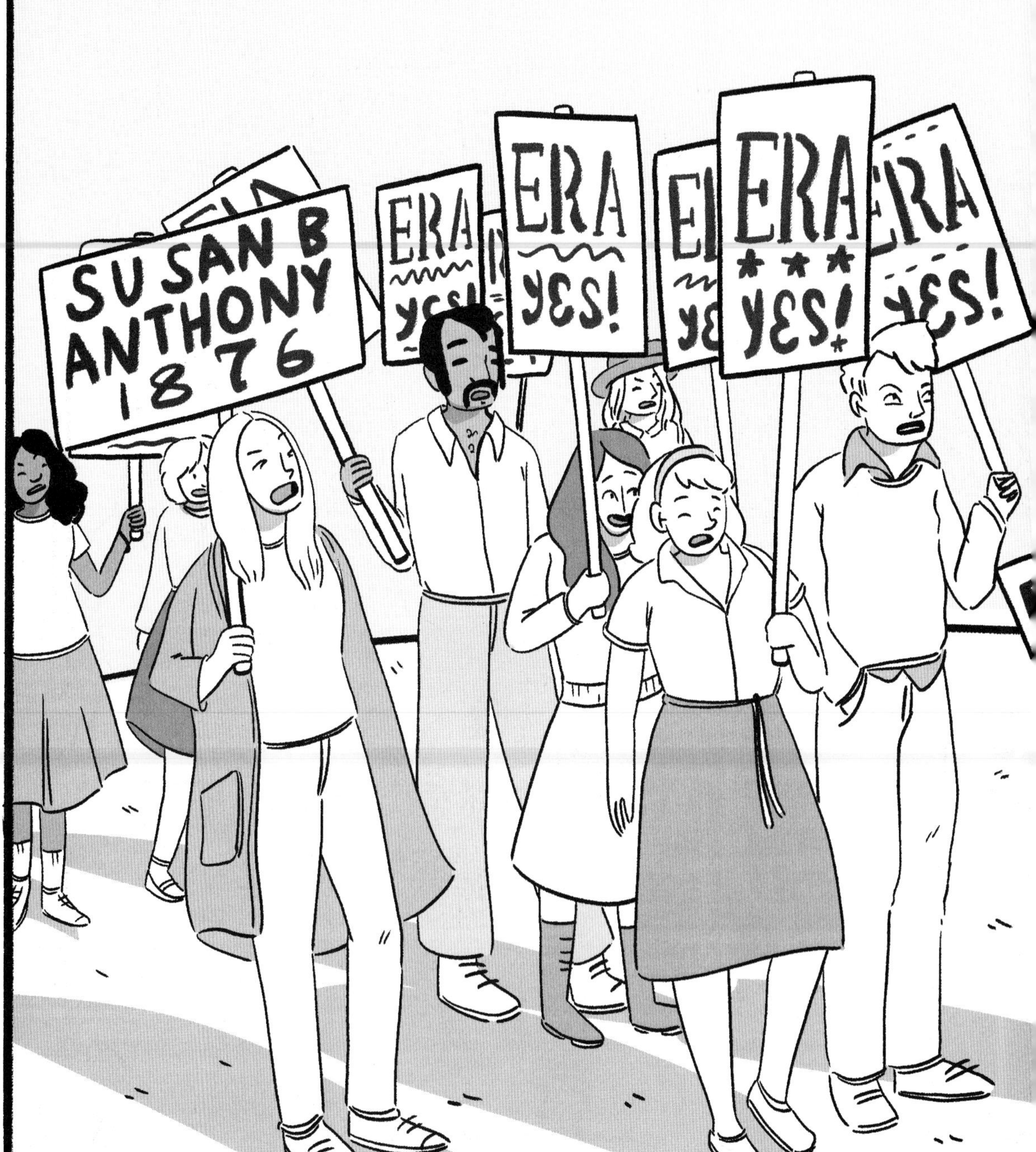

SUSAN B ANTHONY 1876
ERA YES!
ERA YES!
ERA YES!
ERA YES!

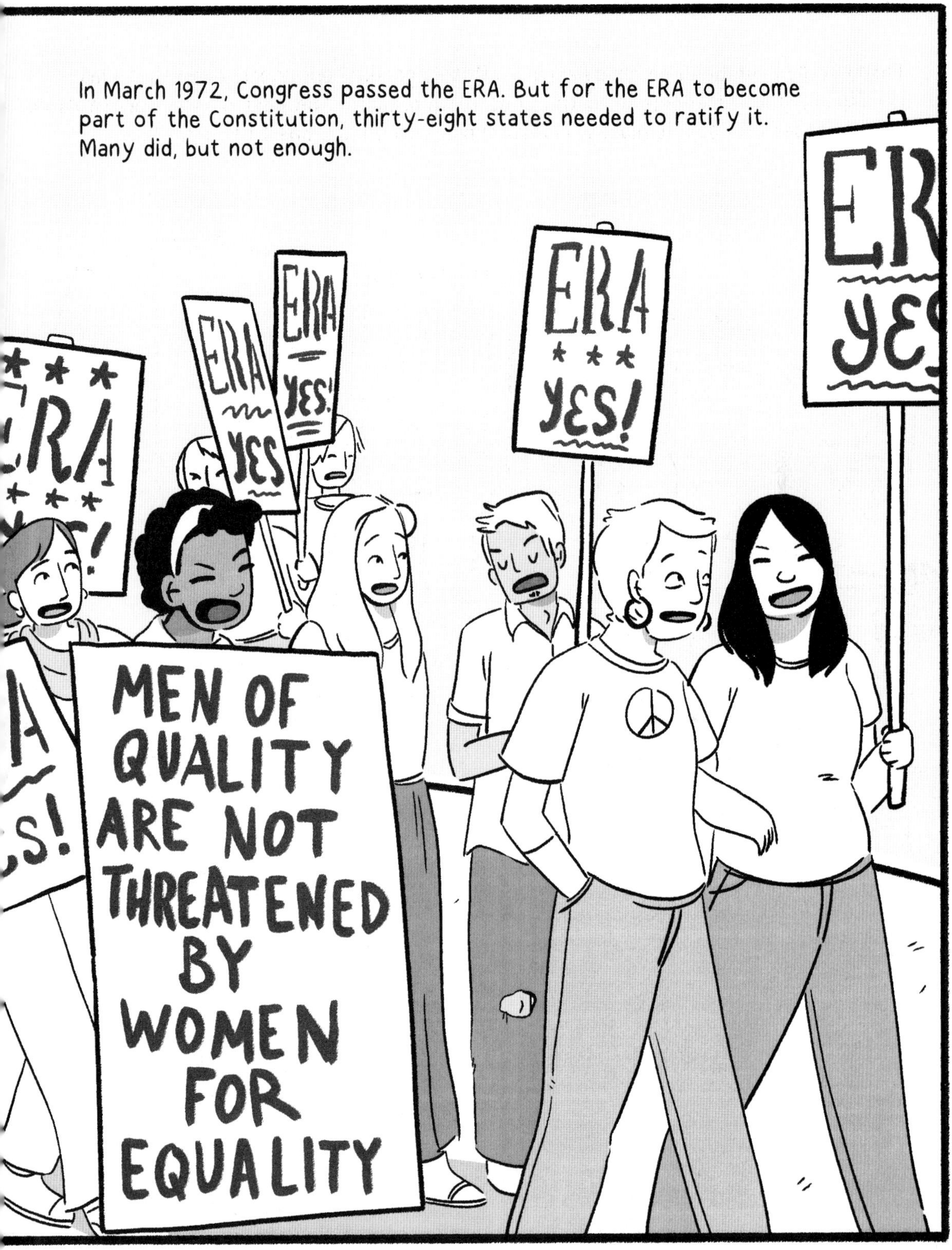
In March 1972, Congress passed the ERA. But for the ERA to become part of the Constitution, thirty-eight states needed to ratify it. Many did, but not enough.
ERA YES
ERA YES!
ERA *** YES!
MEN OF QUALITY ARE NOT THREATENED BY WOMEN FOR EQUALITY

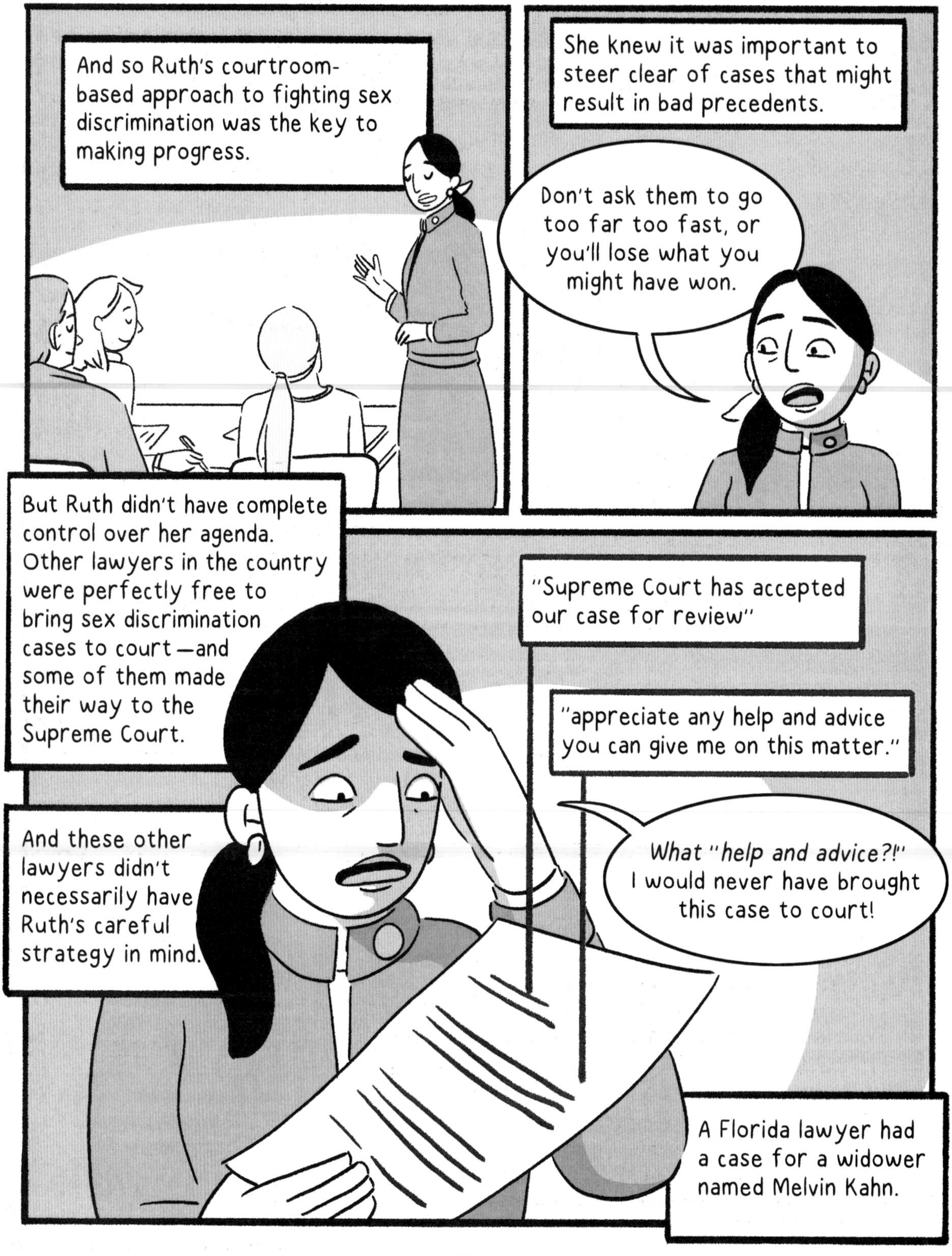

And so Ruth's courtroom-based approach to fighting sex discrimination was the key to making progress.
She knew it was important to steer clear of cases that might result in bad precedents.
Don't ask them to go too far too fast, or you'll lose what you might have won.
But Ruth didn't have complete control over her agenda. Other lawyers in the country were perfectly free to bring sex discrimination cases to court—and some of them made their way to the Supreme Court.
And these other lawyers didn't necessarily have Ruth's careful strategy in mind.
"Supreme Court has accepted our case for review"
"appreciate any help and advice you can give me on this matter."
What "help and advice?!" I would never have brought this case to court!
A Florida lawyer had a case for a widower named Melvin Kahn.

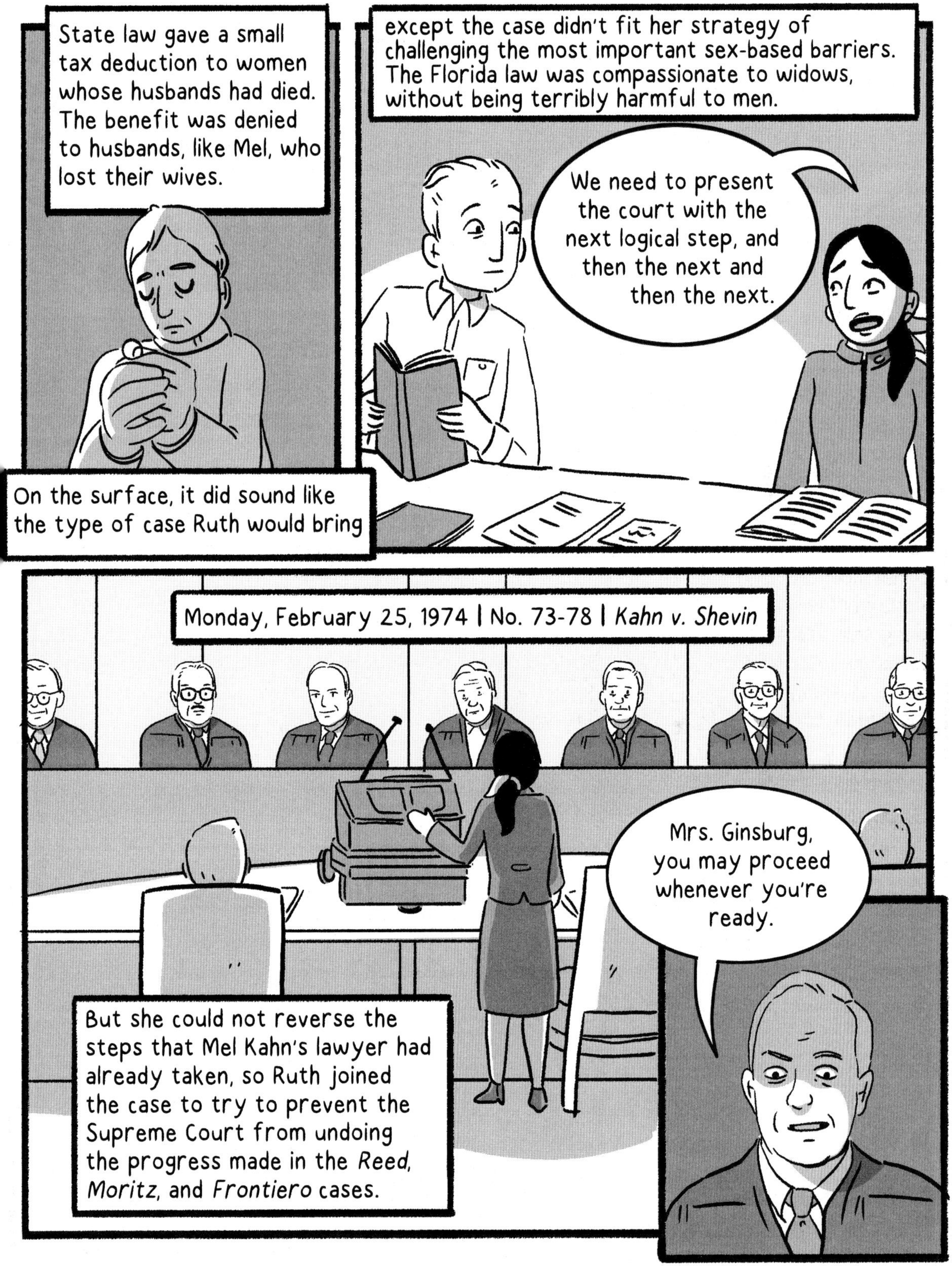
State law gave a small tax deduction to women whose husbands had died. The benefit was denied to husbands, like Mel, who lost their wives.
On the surface, it did sound like the type of case Ruth would bring
except the case didn't fit her strategy of challenging the most important sex-based barriers. The Florida law was compassionate to widows, without being terribly harmful to men.
We need to present the court with the next logical step, and then the next and then the next.
Monday, February 25, 1974 | No. 73-78 | *Kahn v. Shevin*
Mrs. Ginsburg, you may proceed whenever you're ready.
But she could not reverse the steps that Mel Kahn's lawyer had already taken, so Ruth joined the case to try to prevent the Supreme Court from undoing the progress made in the *Reed*, *Moritz*, and *Frontiero* cases.

It wasn't an easy afternoon in court—even the lectern seemed to be fighting Ruth!

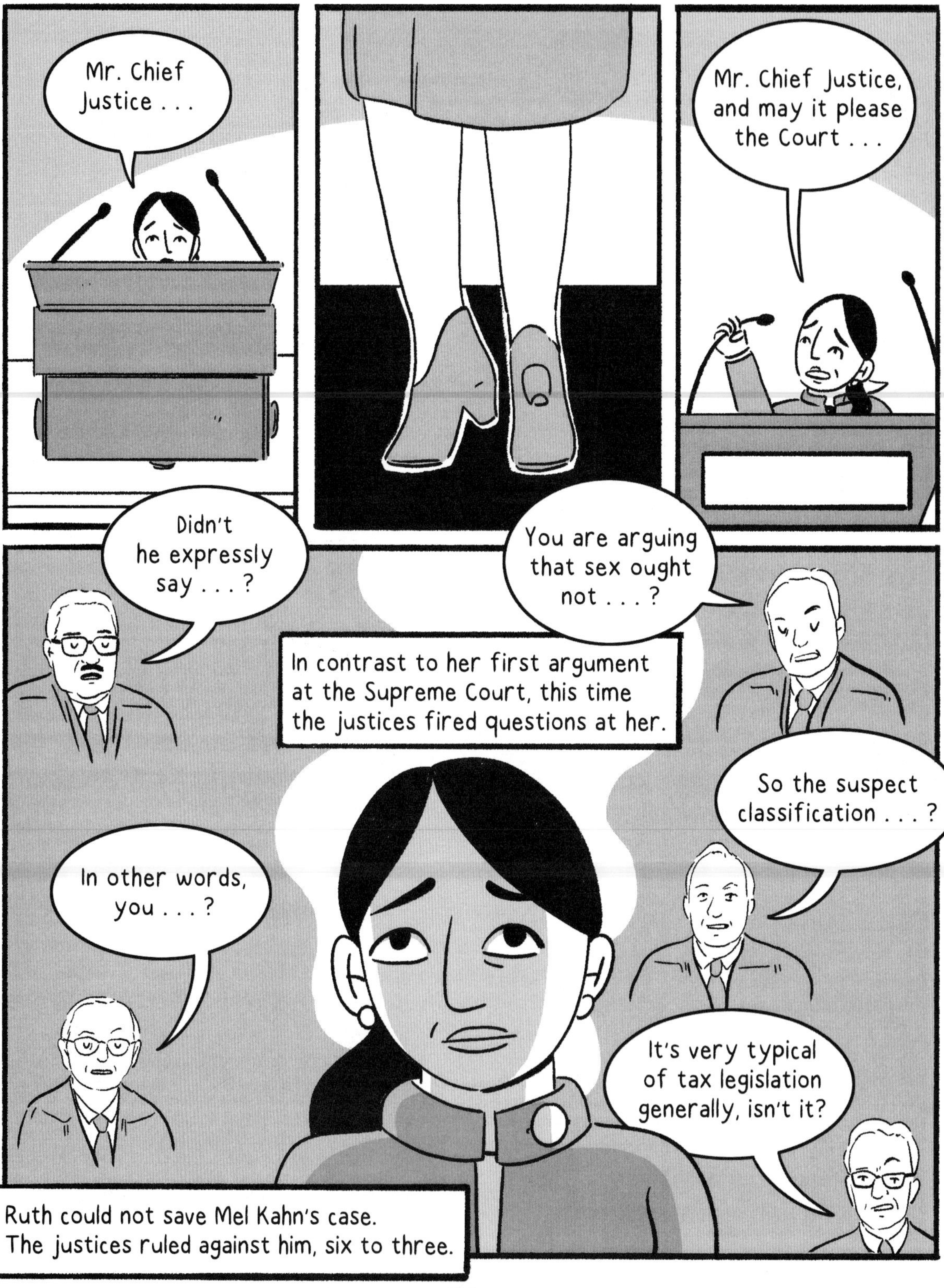

Mr. Chief Justice . . .
Mr. Chief Justice, and may it please the Court . . .
Didn't he expressly say . . . ?
You are arguing that sex ought not . . . ?
In contrast to her first argument at the Supreme Court, this time the justices fired questions at her.
So the suspect classification . . . ?
In other words, you . . . ?
It's very typical of tax legislation generally, isn't it?
Ruth could not save Mel Kahn's case. The justices ruled against him, six to three.

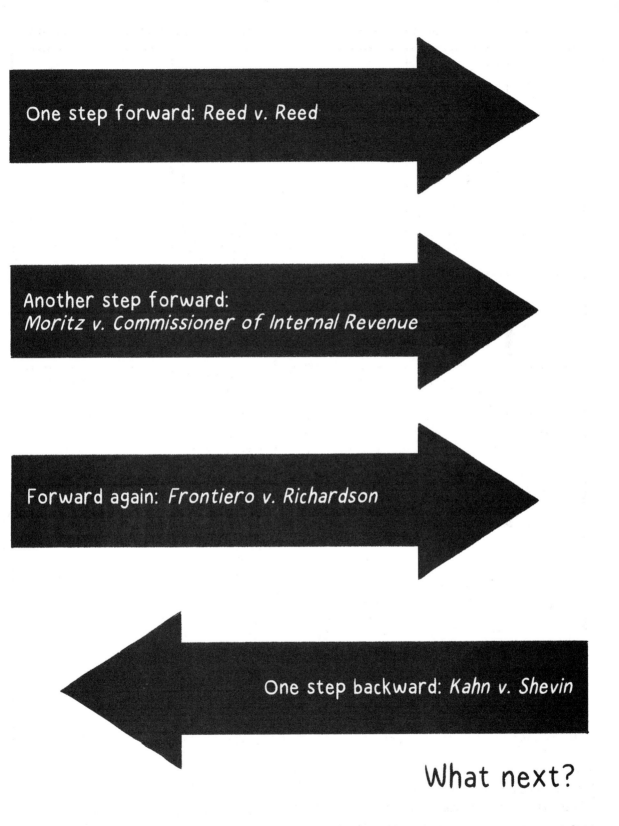

One step forward: *Reed v. Reed*

Another step forward:
Moritz v. Commissioner of Internal Revenue

Forward again: *Frontiero v. Richardson*

One step backward: *Kahn v. Shevin*

What next?

CHAPTER 33

That Double-Edged Sword

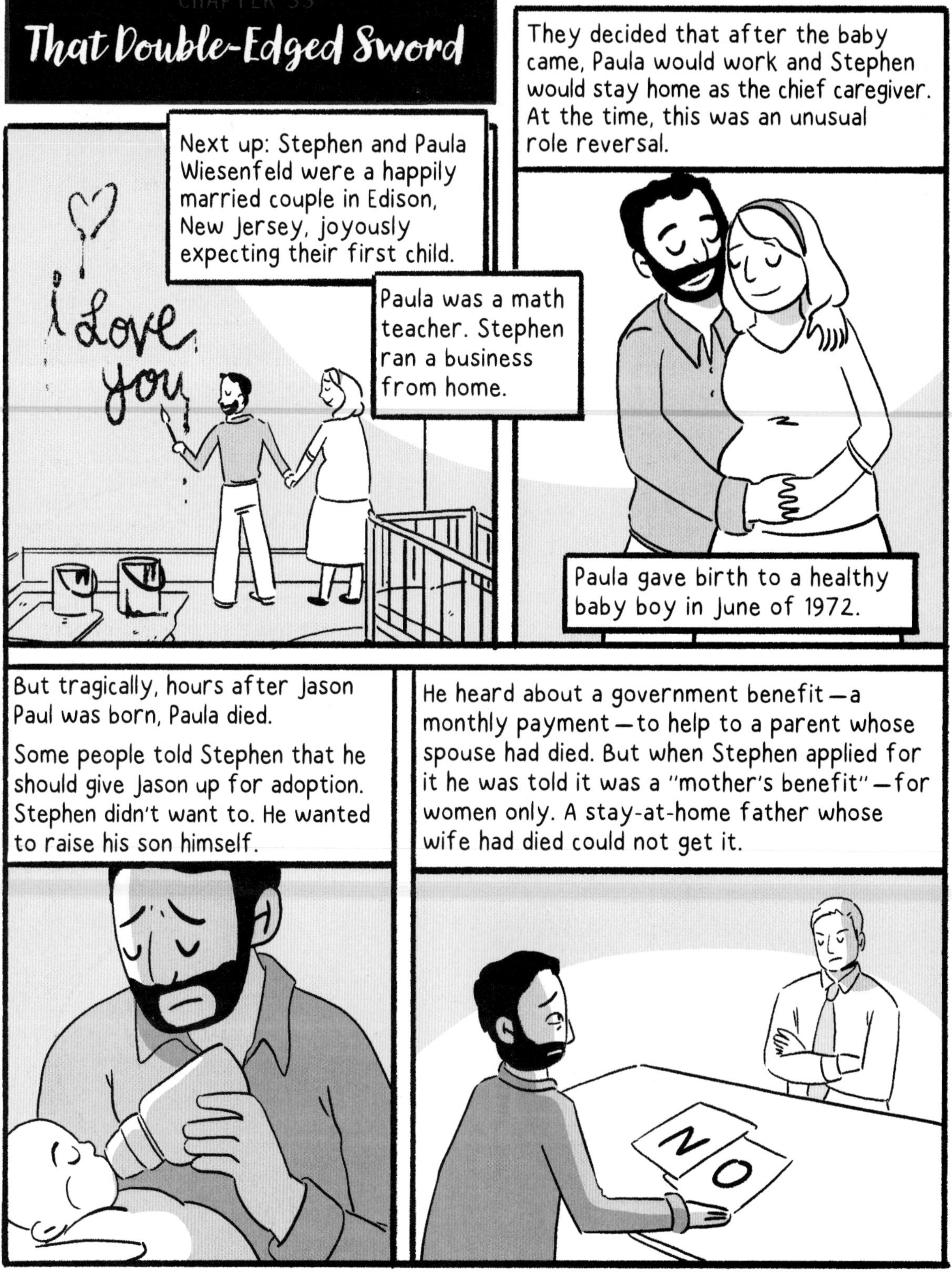
Next up: Stephen and Paula Wiesenfeld were a happily married couple in Edison, New Jersey, joyously expecting their first child.
i Love you
Paula was a math teacher. Stephen ran a business from home.
They decided that after the baby came, Paula would work and Stephen would stay home as the chief caregiver. At the time, this was an unusual role reversal.
Paula gave birth to a healthy baby boy in June of 1972.
But tragically, hours after Jason Paul was born, Paula died.
Some people told Stephen that he should give Jason up for adoption. Stephen didn't want to. He wanted to raise his son himself.
He heard about a government benefit—a monthly payment—to help to a parent whose spouse had died. But when Stephen applied for it he was told it was a "mother's benefit"—for women only. A stay-at-home father whose wife had died could not get it.
NO

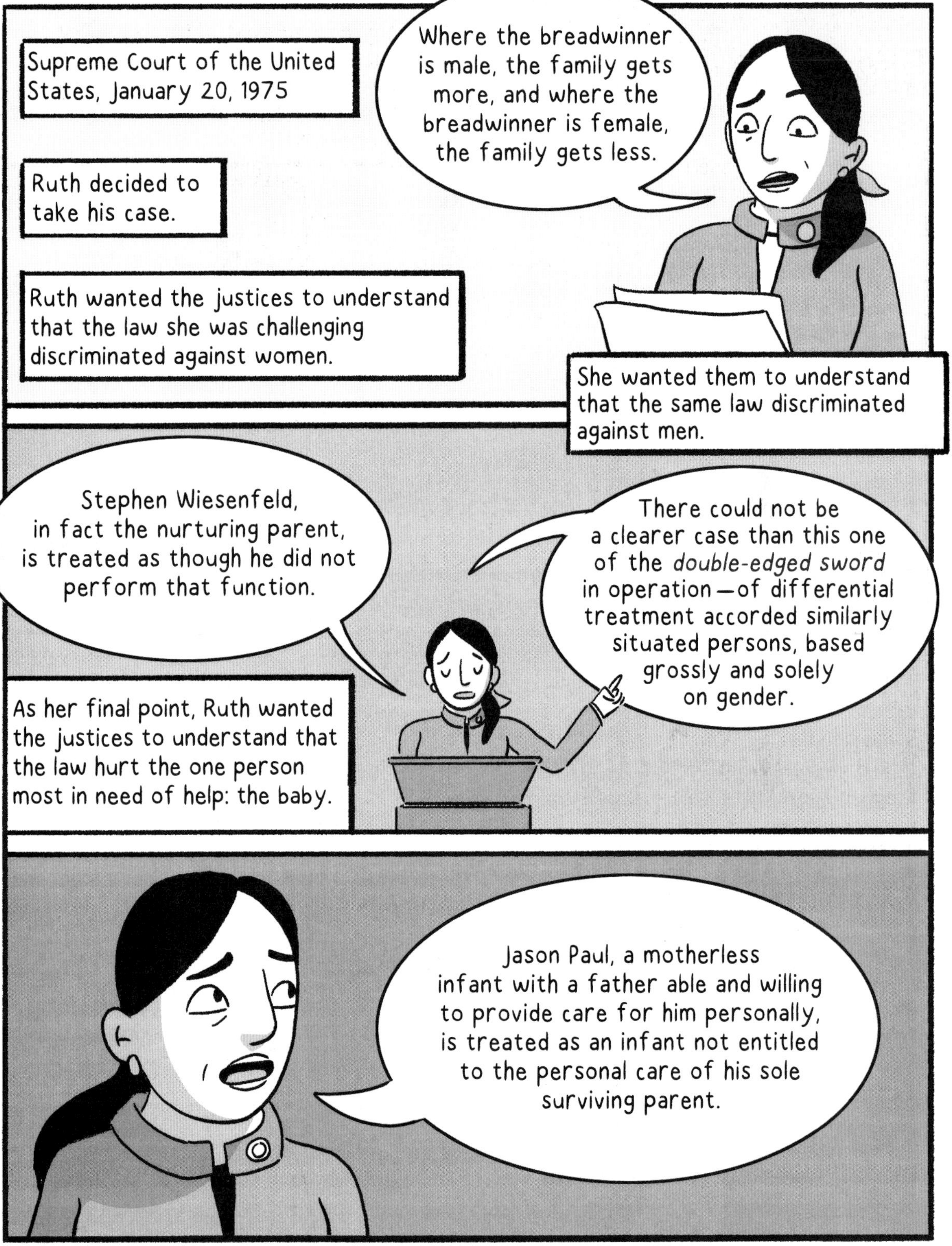

Supreme Court of the United States, January 20, 1975
Where the breadwinner is male, the family gets more, and where the breadwinner is female, the family gets less.
Ruth decided to take his case.
Ruth wanted the justices to understand that the law she was challenging discriminated against women.
She wanted them to understand that the same law discriminated against men.
Stephen Wiesenfeld, in fact the nurturing parent, is treated as though he did not perform that function.
There could not be a clearer case than this one of the *double-edged sword* in operation—of differential treatment accorded similarly situated persons, based grossly and solely on gender.
As her final point, Ruth wanted the justices to understand that the law hurt the one person most in need of help: the baby.
Jason Paul, a motherless infant with a father able and willing to provide care for him personally, is treated as an infant not entitled to the personal care of his sole surviving parent.

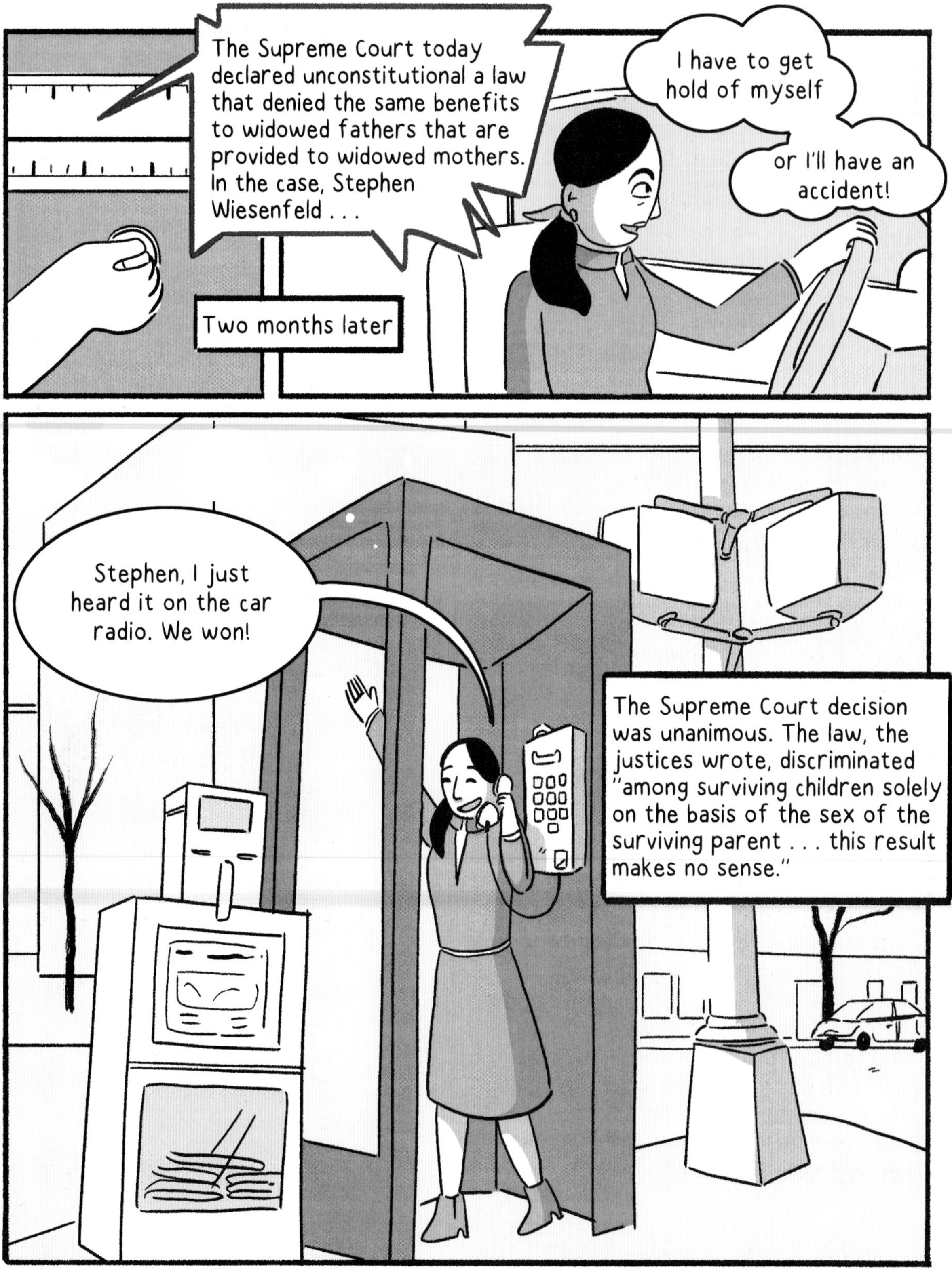

The Supreme Court today declared unconstitutional a law that denied the same benefits to widowed fathers that are provided to widowed mothers. In the case, Stephen Wiesenfeld . . .
I have to get hold of myself
or I'll have an accident!
Two months later
Stephen, I just heard it on the car radio. We won!
The Supreme Court decision was unanimous. The law, the justices wrote, discriminated "among surviving children solely on the basis of the sex of the surviving parent . . . this result makes no sense."

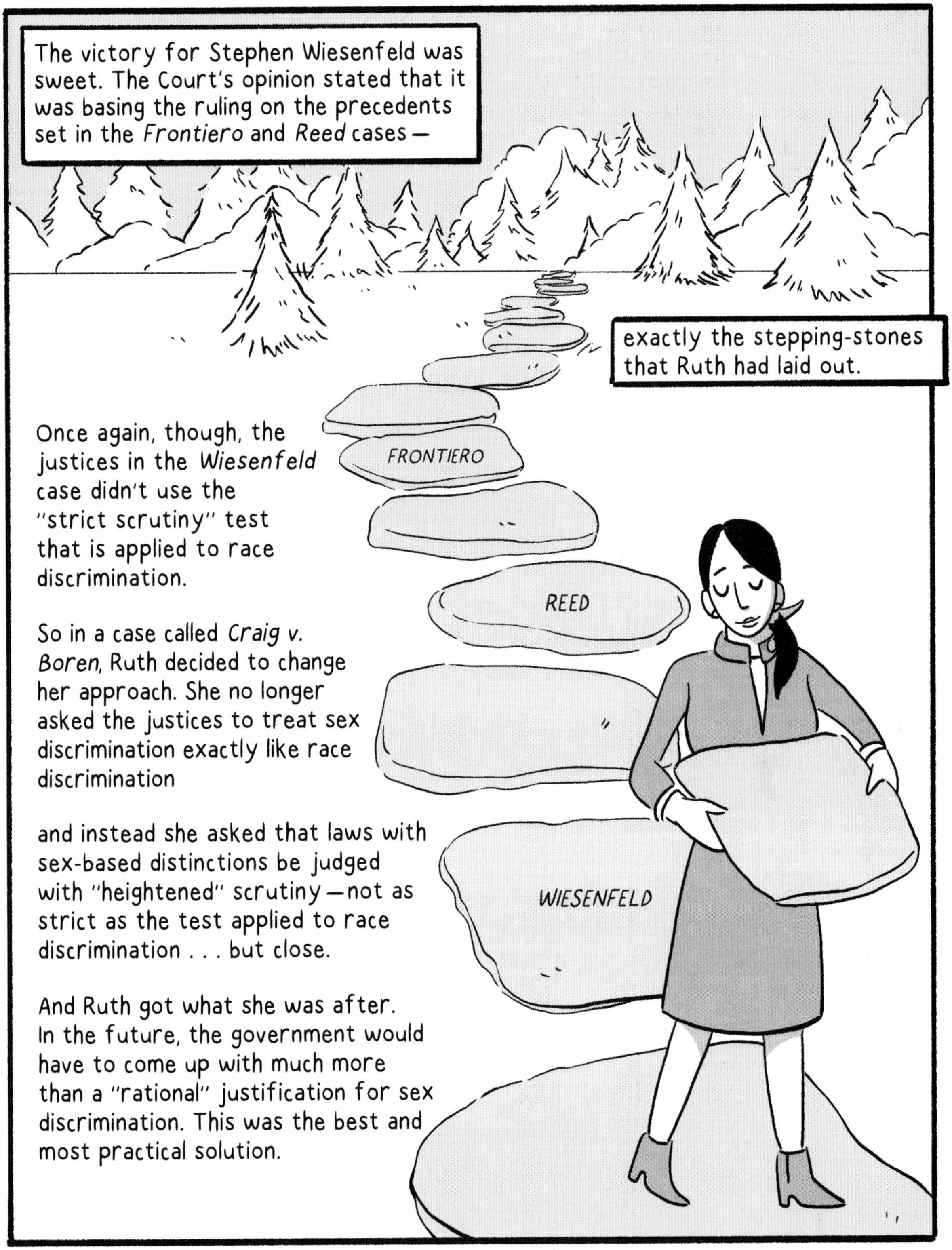
The victory for Stephen Wiesenfeld was sweet. The Court's opinion stated that it was basing the ruling on the precedents set in the *Frontiero* and *Reed* cases—
exactly the stepping-stones that Ruth had laid out.
FRONTIERO
REED
WIESENFELD
Once again, though, the justices in the *Wiesenfeld* case didn't use the "strict scrutiny" test that is applied to race discrimination.
So in a case called *Craig v. Boren*, Ruth decided to change her approach. She no longer asked the justices to treat sex discrimination exactly like race discrimination
and instead she asked that laws with sex-based distinctions be judged with "heightened" scrutiny—not as strict as the test applied to race discrimination . . . but close.
And Ruth got what she was after. In the future, the government would have to come up with much more than a "rational" justification for sex discrimination. This was the best and most practical solution.

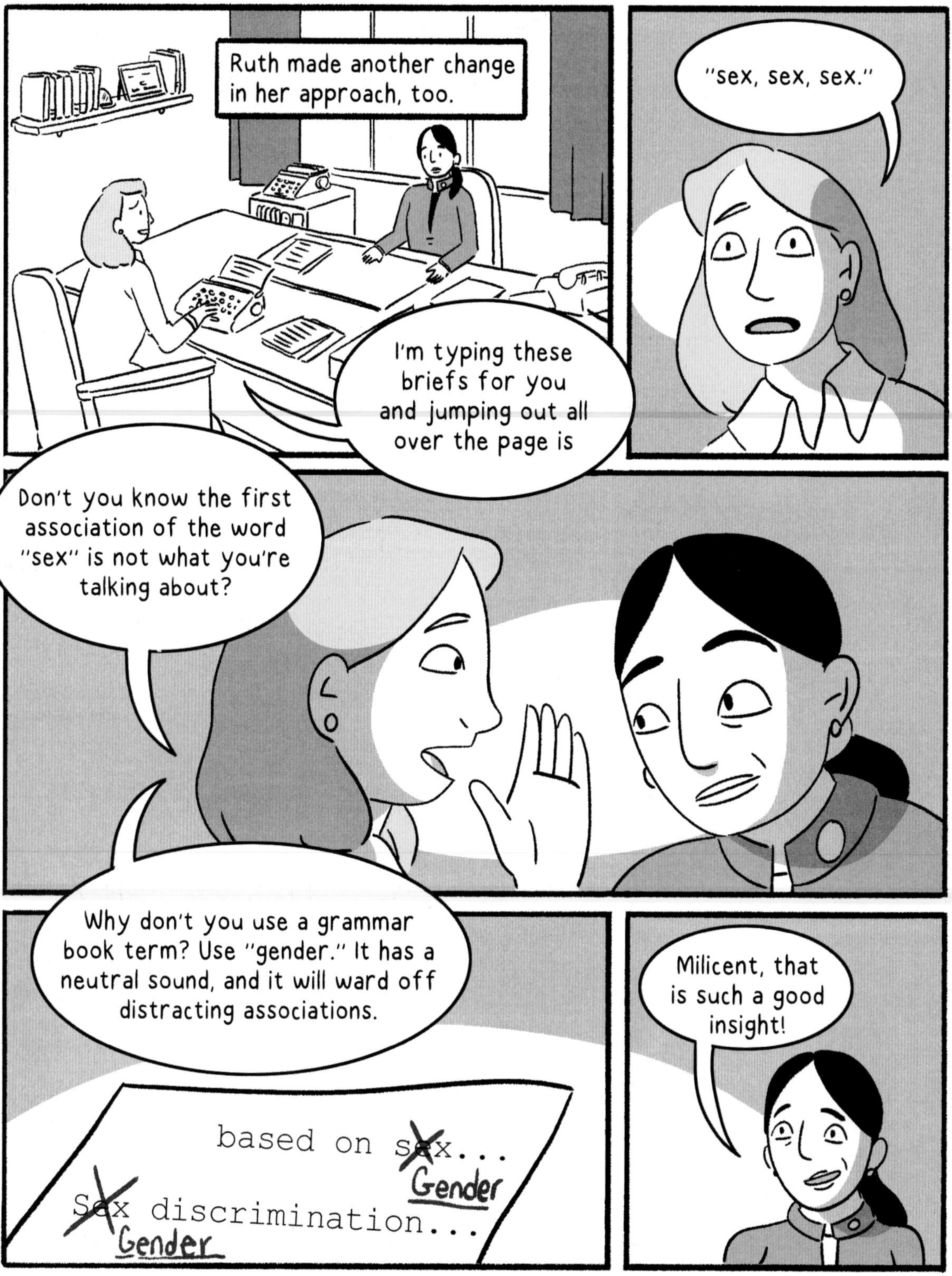

Ruth made another change in her approach, too.
I'm typing these briefs for you and jumping out all over the page is
"sex, sex, sex."
Don't you know the first association of the word "sex" is not what you're talking about?
Why don't you use a grammar book term? Use "gender." It has a neutral sound, and it will ward off distracting associations.
based on sex...
Gender
Sex discrimination...
Gender
Milicent, that is such a good insight!

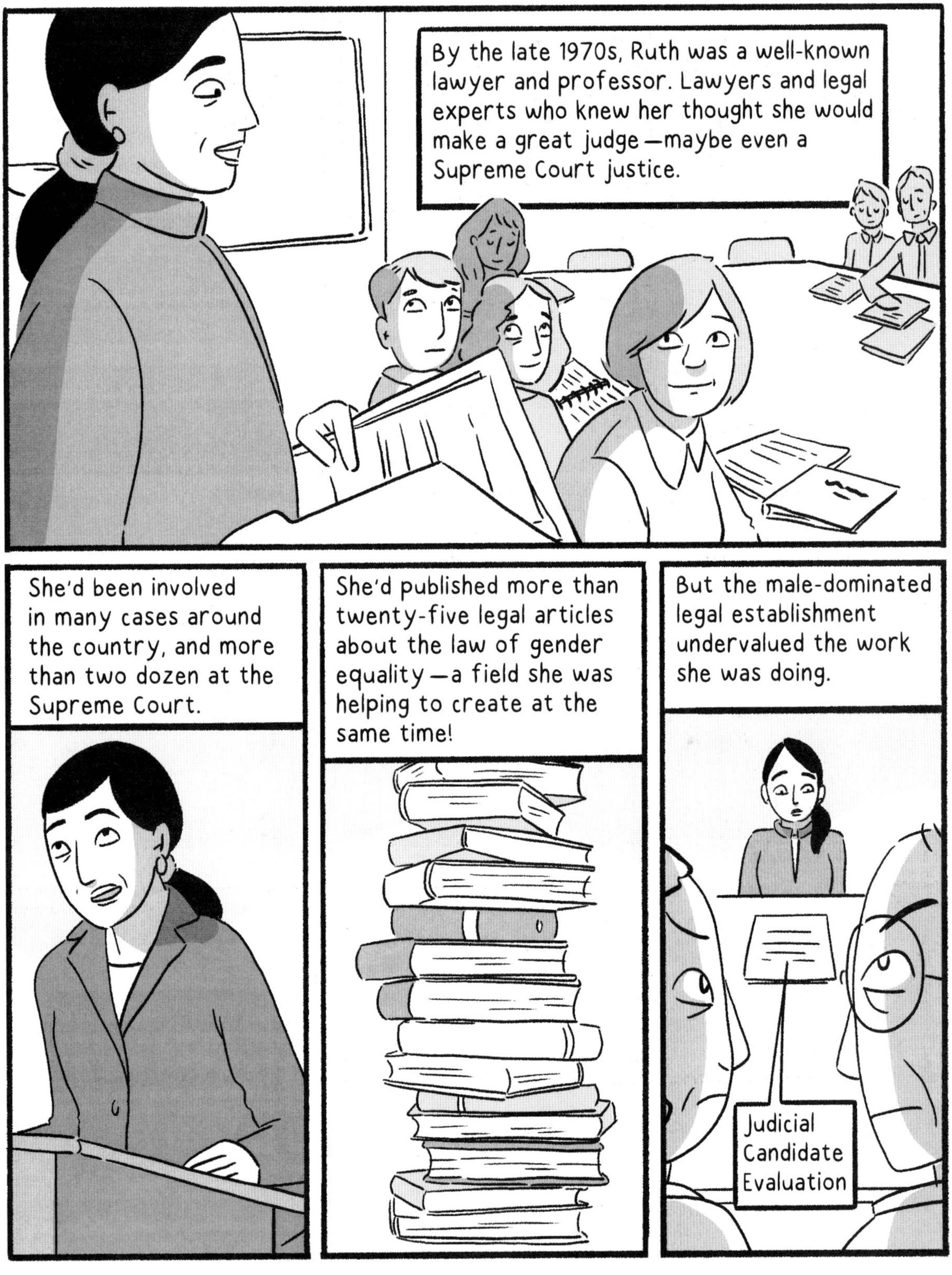

By the late 1970s, Ruth was a well-known lawyer and professor. Lawyers and legal experts who knew her thought she would make a great judge—maybe even a Supreme Court justice.
She'd been involved in many cases around the country, and more than two dozen at the Supreme Court.
She'd published more than twenty-five legal articles about the law of gender equality—a field she was helping to create at the same time!
But the male-dominated legal establishment undervalued the work she was doing.
Judicial Candidate Evaluation

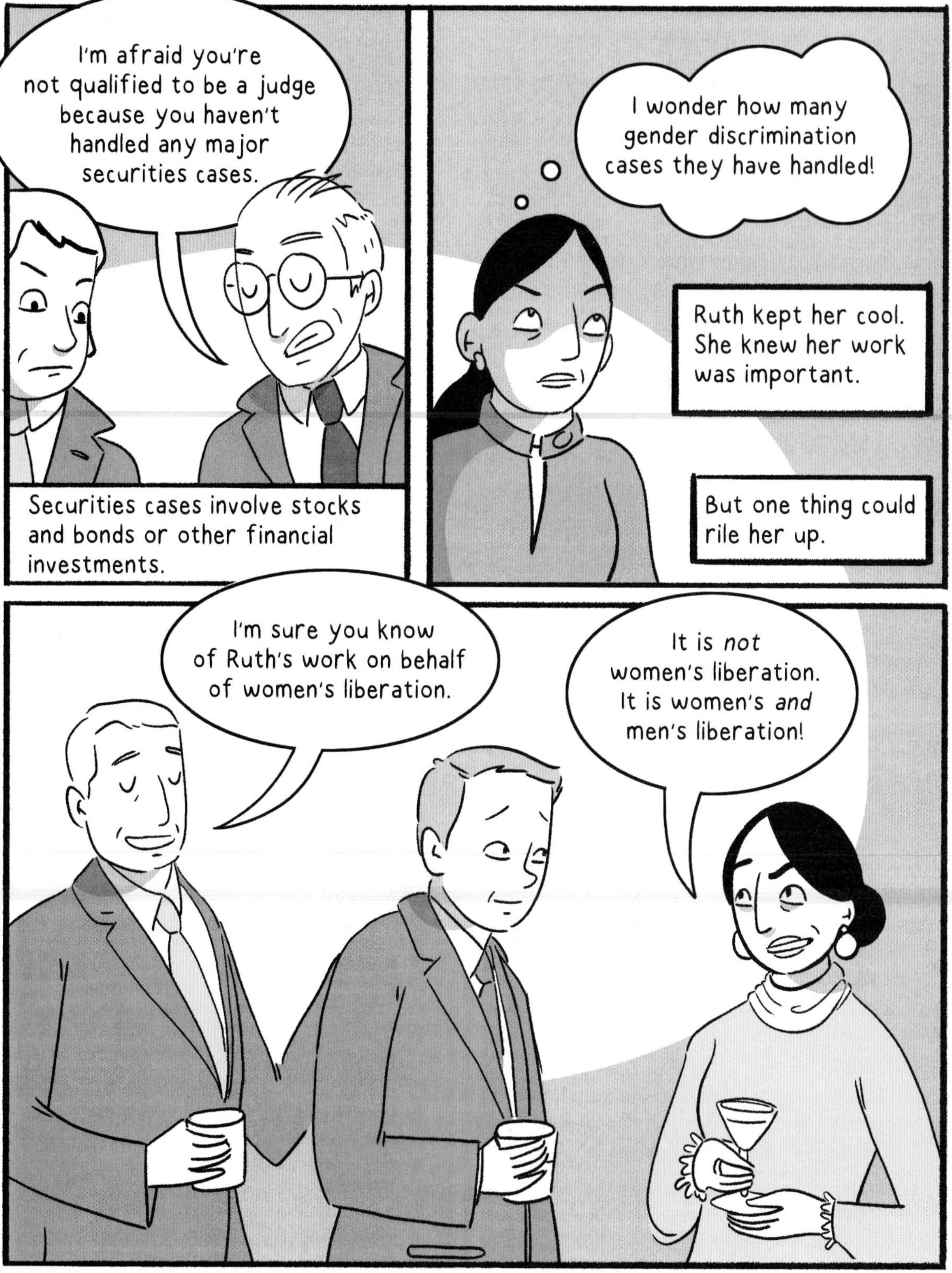
I'm afraid you're not qualified to be a judge because you haven't handled any major securities cases.
Securities cases involve stocks and bonds or other financial investments.
I wonder how many gender discrimination cases they have handled!
Ruth kept her cool. She knew her work was important.
But one thing could rile her up.
I'm sure you know of Ruth's work on behalf of women's liberation.
It is *not* women's liberation. It is women's *and* men's liberation!

No Tokens

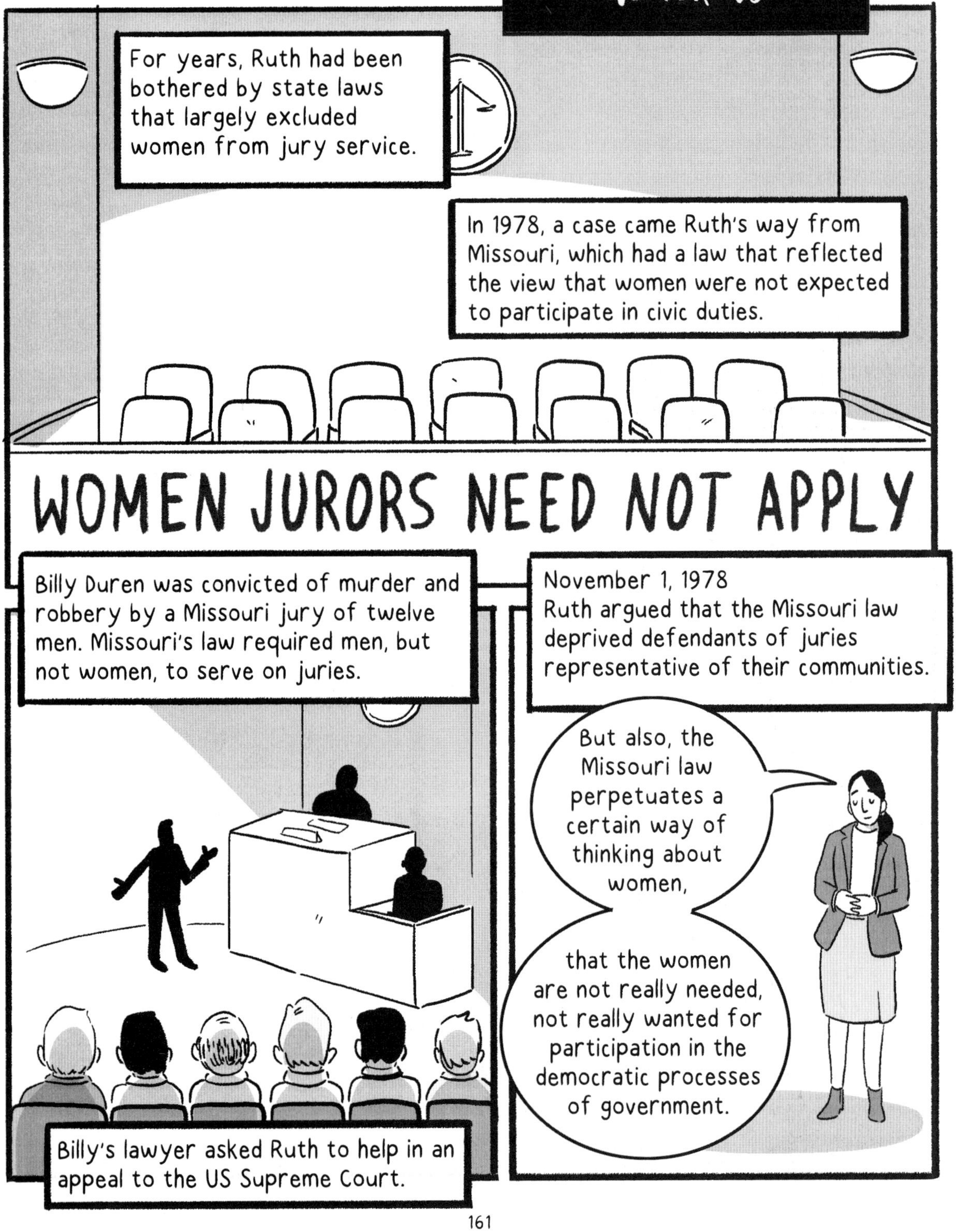
For years, Ruth had been bothered by state laws that largely excluded women from jury service.
In 1978, a case came Ruth's way from Missouri, which had a law that reflected the view that women were not expected to participate in civic duties.
WOMEN JURORS NEED NOT APPLY
Billy Duren was convicted of murder and robbery by a Missouri jury of twelve men. Missouri's law required men, but not women, to serve on juries.
Billy's lawyer asked Ruth to help in an appeal to the US Supreme Court.
November 1, 1978
Ruth argued that the Missouri law deprived defendants of juries representative of their communities.
But also, the Missouri law perpetuates a certain way of thinking about women,
that the women are not really needed, not really wanted for participation in the democratic processes of government.

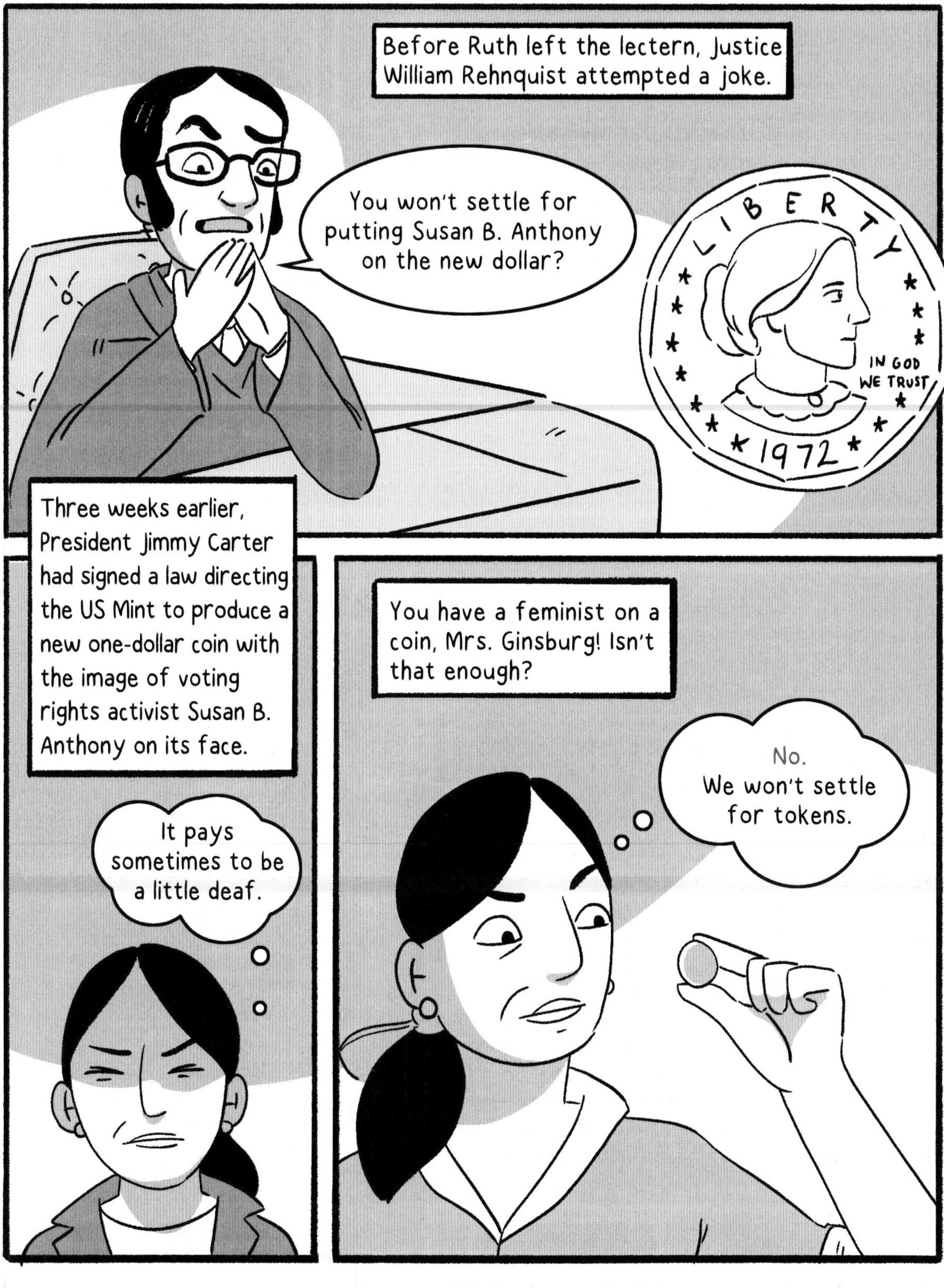
Before Ruth left the lectern, Justice William Rehnquist attempted a joke.
You won't settle for putting Susan B. Anthony on the new dollar?
LIBERTY
IN GOD WE TRUST
1972
Three weeks earlier, President Jimmy Carter had signed a law directing the US Mint to produce a new one-dollar coin with the image of voting rights activist Susan B. Anthony on its face.
It pays sometimes to be a little deaf.
You have a feminist on a coin, Mrs. Ginsburg! Isn't that enough?
No.
We won't settle for tokens.

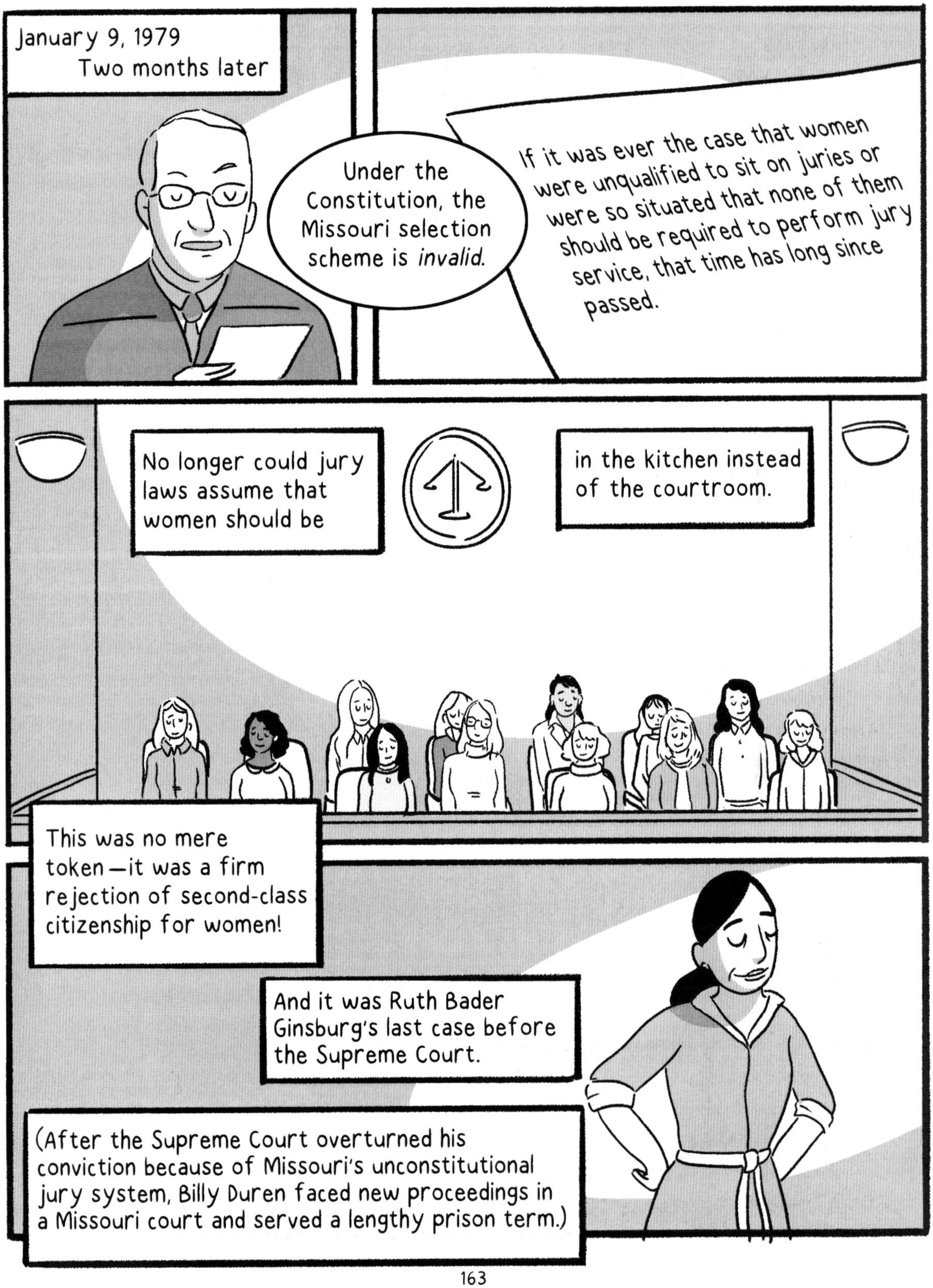
January 9, 1979
Two months later
Under the Constitution, the Missouri selection scheme is *invalid.*
If it was ever the case that women were unqualified to sit on juries or were so situated that none of them should be required to perform jury service, that time has long since passed.
No longer could jury laws assume that women should be
in the kitchen instead of the courtroom.
This was no mere token—it was a firm rejection of second-class citizenship for women!
And it was Ruth Bader Ginsburg's last case before the Supreme Court.
(After the Supreme Court overturned his conviction because of Missouri's unconstitutional jury system, Billy Duren faced new proceedings in a Missouri court and served a lengthy prison term.)

Be the Change

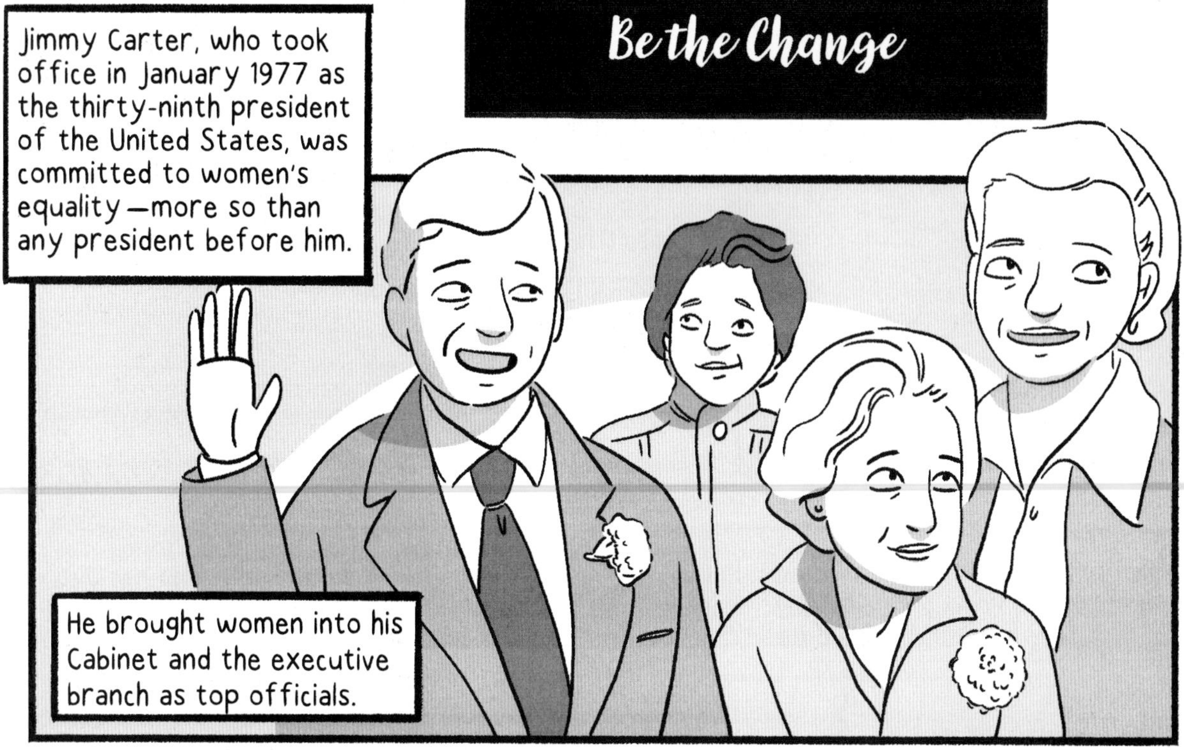
Jimmy Carter, who took office in January 1977 as the thirty-ninth president of the United States, was committed to women's equality—more so than any president before him.
He brought women into his Cabinet and the executive branch as top officials.

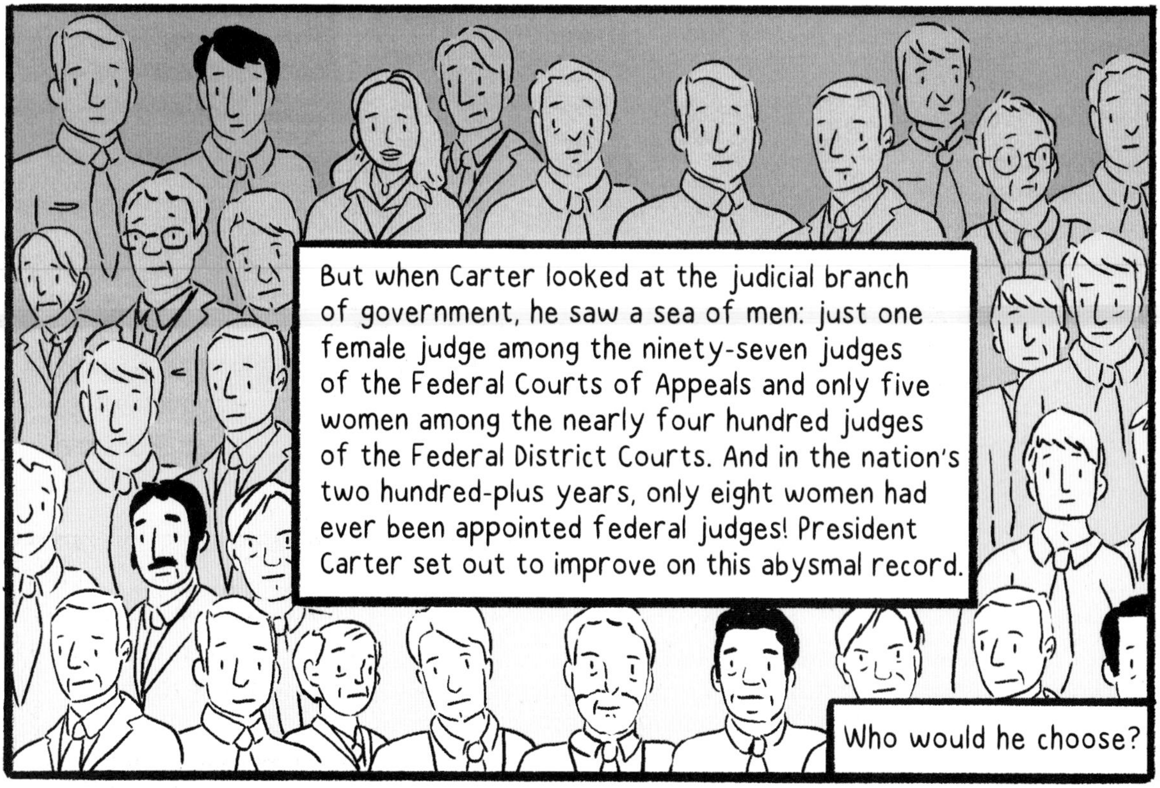
But when Carter looked at the judicial branch of government, he saw a sea of men: just one female judge among the ninety-seven judges of the Federal Courts of Appeals and only five women among the nearly four hundred judges of the Federal District Courts. And in the nation's two hundred-plus years, only eight women had ever been appointed federal judges! President Carter set out to improve on this abysmal record.
Who would he choose?

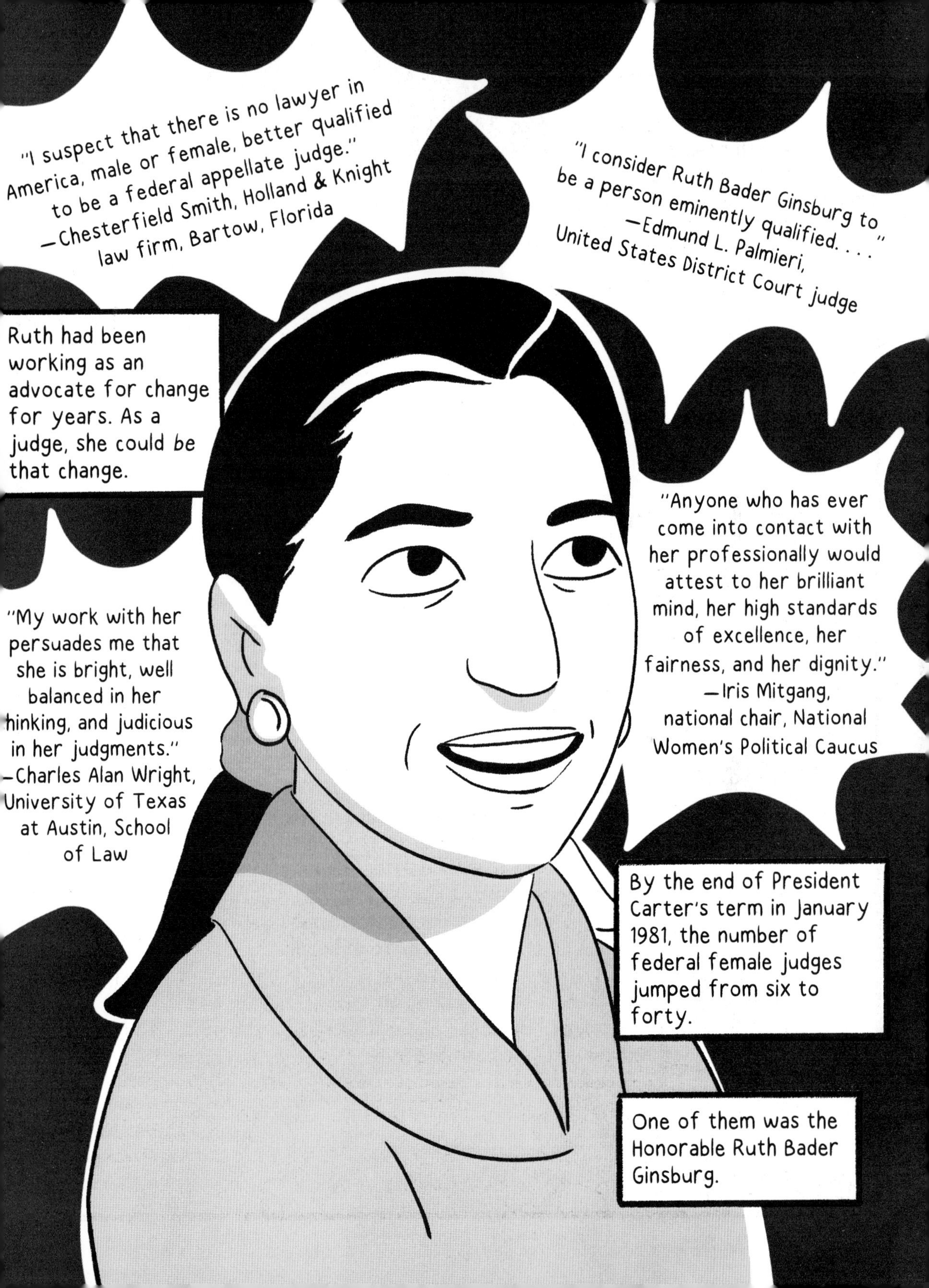
"I suspect that there is no lawyer in America, male or female, better qualified to be a federal appellate judge." —Chesterfield Smith, Holland & Knight law firm, Bartow, Florida
"I consider Ruth Bader Ginsburg to be a person eminently qualified. . . ." —Edmund L. Palmieri, United States District Court judge
Ruth had been working as an advocate for change for years. As a judge, she could *be* that change.
"My work with her persuades me that she is bright, well balanced in her hinking, and judicious in her judgments." —Charles Alan Wright, University of Texas at Austin, School of Law
"Anyone who has ever come into contact with her professionally would attest to her brilliant mind, her high standards of excellence, her fairness, and her dignity." —Iris Mitgang, national chair, National Women's Political Caucus
By the end of President Carter's term in January 1981, the number of federal female judges jumped from six to forty.
One of them was the Honorable Ruth Bader Ginsburg.

CHAPTER 36

Judge Ginsburg

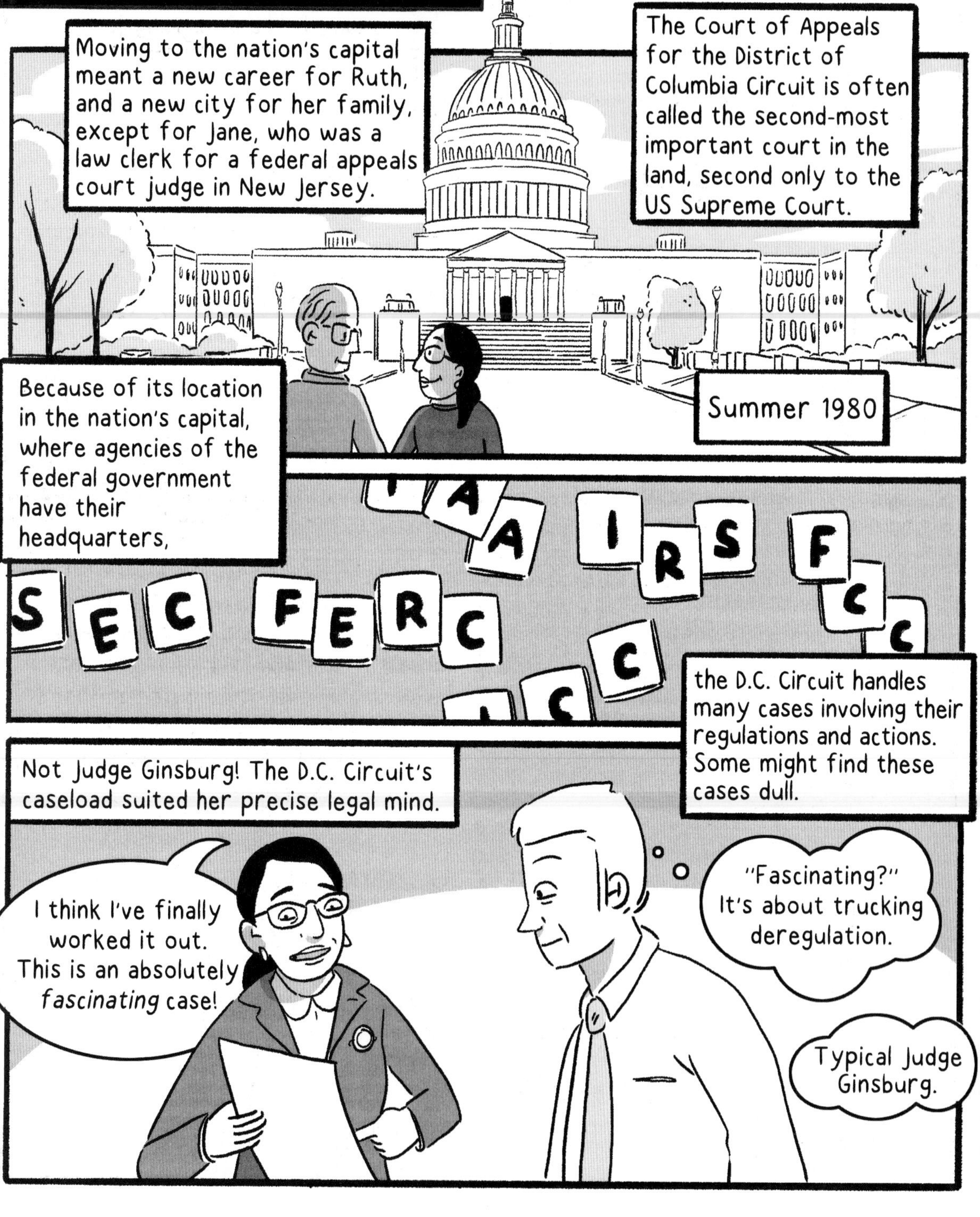

Moving to the nation's capital meant a new career for Ruth, and a new city for her family, except for Jane, who was a law clerk for a federal appeals court judge in New Jersey.
The Court of Appeals for the District of Columbia Circuit is often called the second-most important court in the land, second only to the US Supreme Court.
Because of its location in the nation's capital, where agencies of the federal government have their headquarters,
Summer 1980
SEC
FERC
IRS
FCC
the D.C. Circuit handles many cases involving their regulations and actions. Some might find these cases dull.
Not Judge Ginsburg! The D.C. Circuit's caseload suited her precise legal mind.
I think I've finally worked it out. This is an absolutely *fascinating* case!
"Fascinating?" It's about trucking deregulation.
Typical Judge Ginsburg.

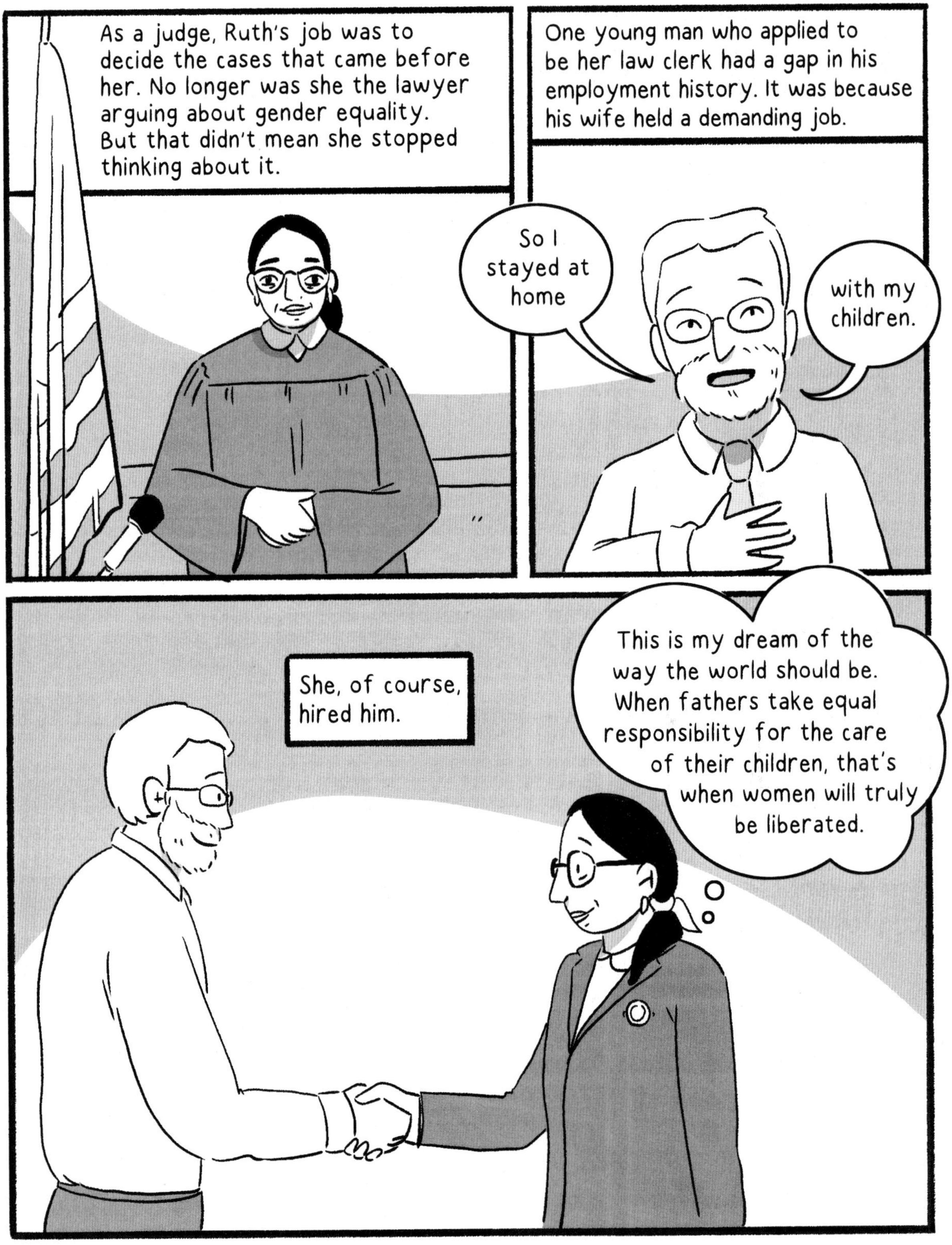
As a judge, Ruth's job was to decide the cases that came before her. No longer was she the lawyer arguing about gender equality. But that didn't mean she stopped thinking about it.
One young man who applied to be her law clerk had a gap in his employment history. It was because his wife held a demanding job.
So I stayed at home
with my children.
She, of course, hired him.
This is my dream of the way the world should be. When fathers take equal responsibility for the care of their children, that's when women will truly be liberated.

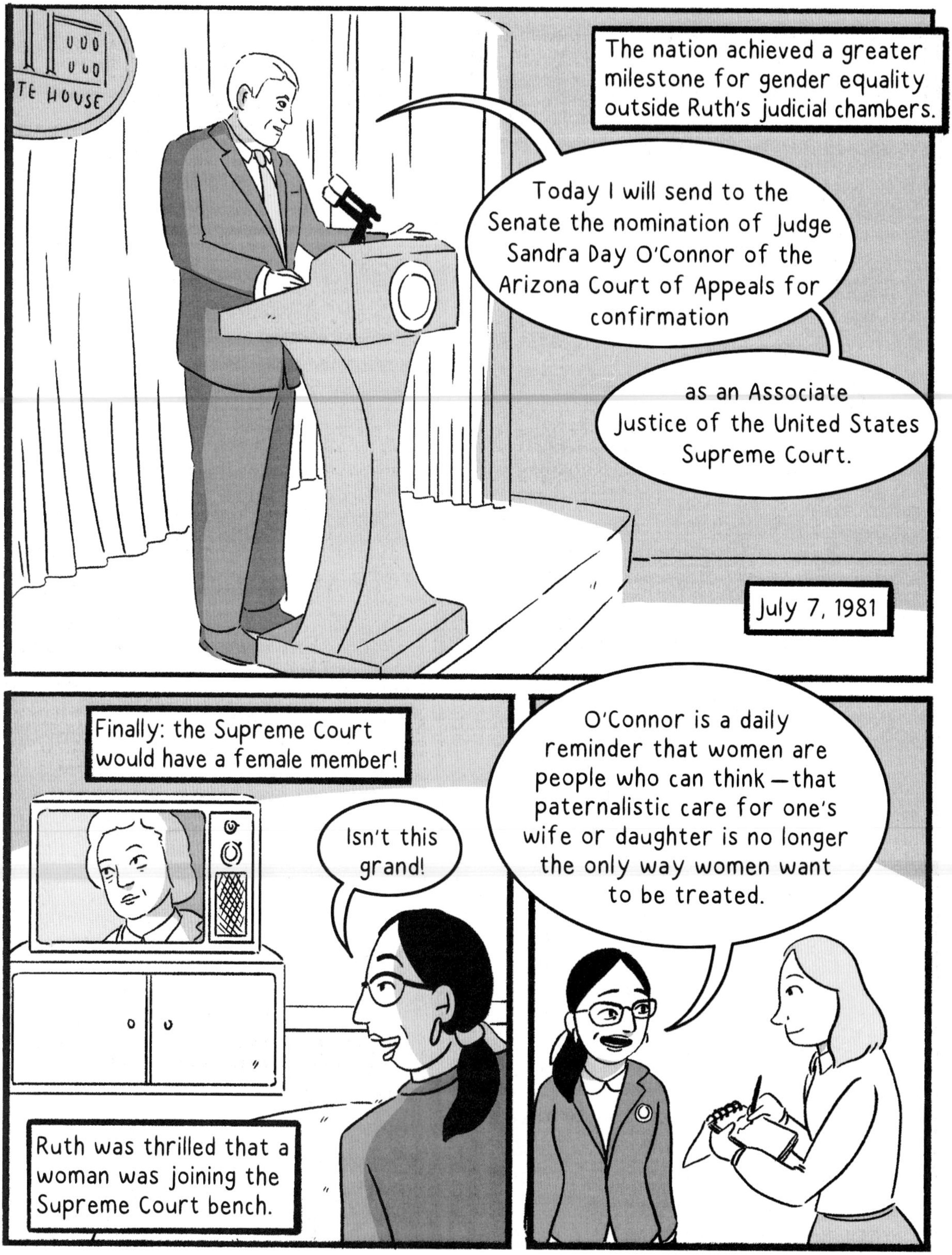
TE HOUSE
The nation achieved a greater milestone for gender equality outside Ruth's judicial chambers.
Today I will send to the Senate the nomination of Judge Sandra Day O'Connor of the Arizona Court of Appeals for confirmation
as an Associate Justice of the United States Supreme Court.
July 7, 1981
Finally: the Supreme Court would have a female member!
Isn't this grand!
Ruth was thrilled that a woman was joining the Supreme Court bench.
O'Connor is a daily reminder that women are people who can think—that paternalistic care for one's wife or daughter is no longer the only way women want to be treated.

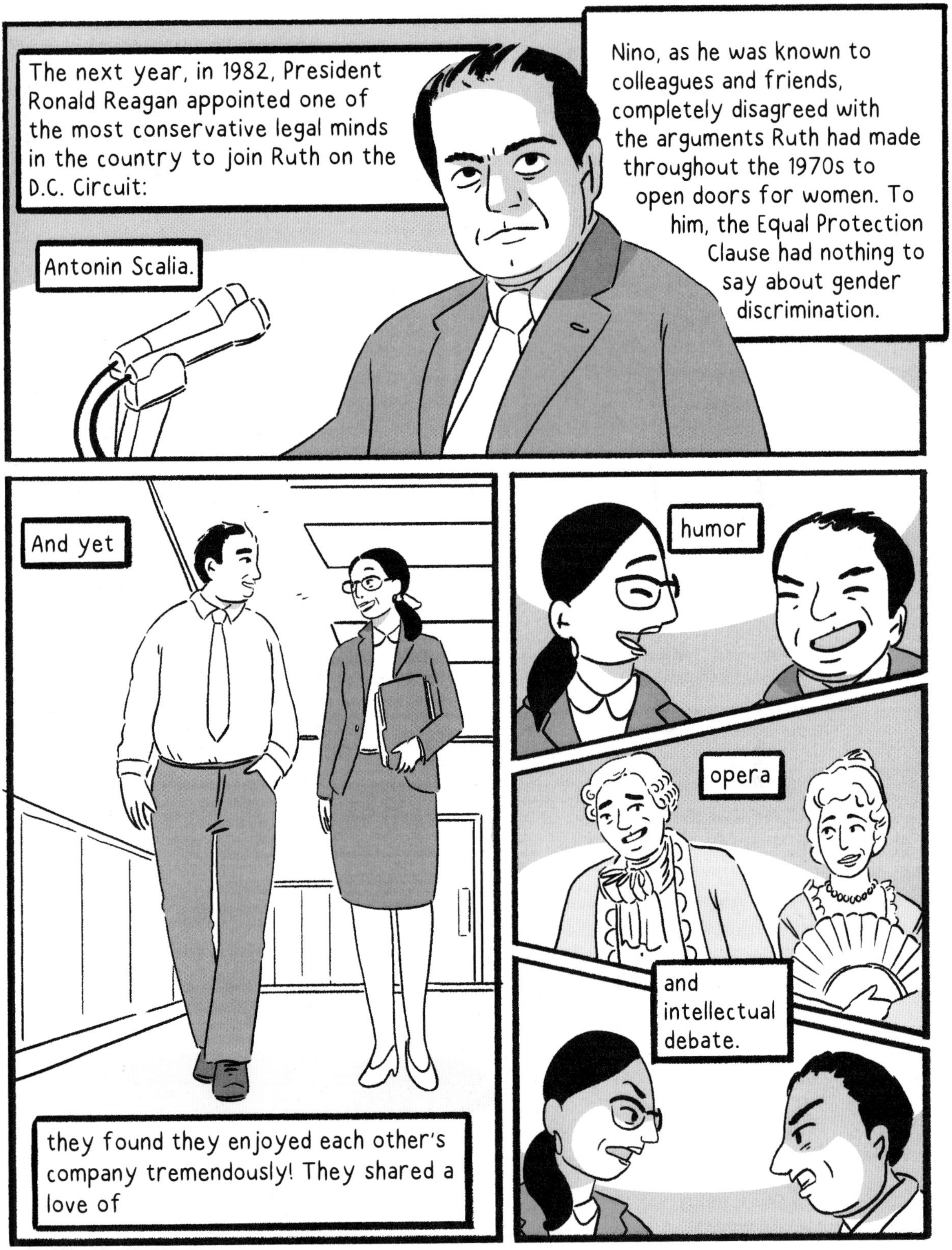
The next year, in 1982, President Ronald Reagan appointed one of the most conservative legal minds in the country to join Ruth on the D.C. Circuit:
Antonin Scalia.
Nino, as he was known to colleagues and friends, completely disagreed with the arguments Ruth had made throughout the 1970s to open doors for women. To him, the Equal Protection Clause had nothing to say about gender discrimination.
And yet
they found they enjoyed each other's company tremendously! They shared a love of
humor
opera
and intellectual debate.

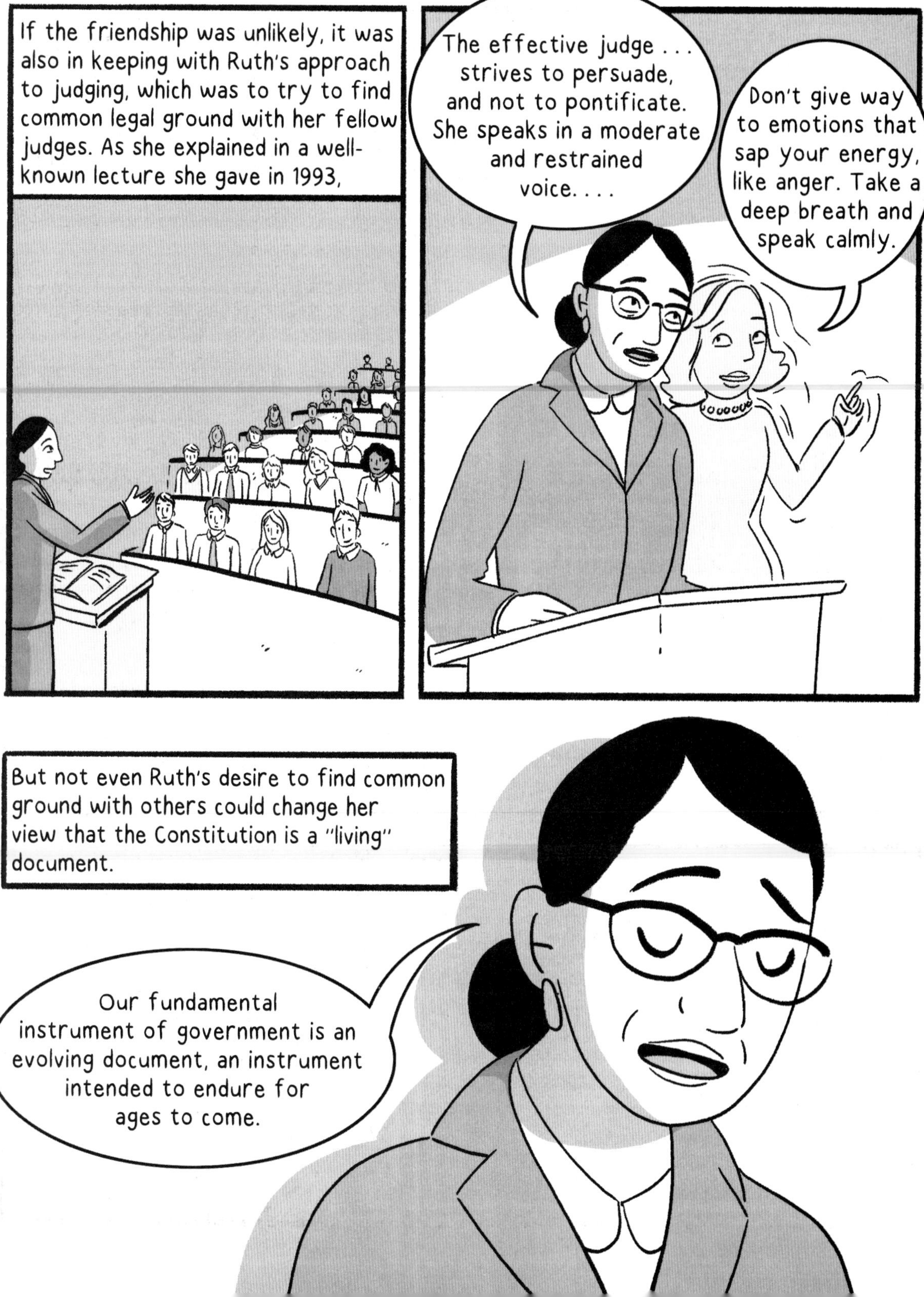

If the friendship was unlikely, it was also in keeping with Ruth's approach to judging, which was to try to find common legal ground with her fellow judges. As she explained in a well-known lecture she gave in 1993,
The effective judge . . . strives to persuade, and not to pontificate. She speaks in a moderate and restrained voice. . . .
Don't give way to emotions that sap your energy, like anger. Take a deep breath and speak calmly.
But not even Ruth's desire to find common ground with others could change her view that the Constitution is a "living" document.
Our fundamental instrument of government is an evolving document, an instrument intended to endure for ages to come.

Most important to Ruth was for judges always to remember that the law affected real people. It wasn't an academic exercise.

She took her clerks on outings to underscore the point that court rulings determined the fate of the mentally ill . . . the poor . . . the dispossessed . . . the disadvantaged.

The equal dignity of individuals

is part of our constitutional legacy.

The CONSTITUTION of the United States

We The People of the United States

The Declaration of Indep

CHAPTER 37

Journey to Justice

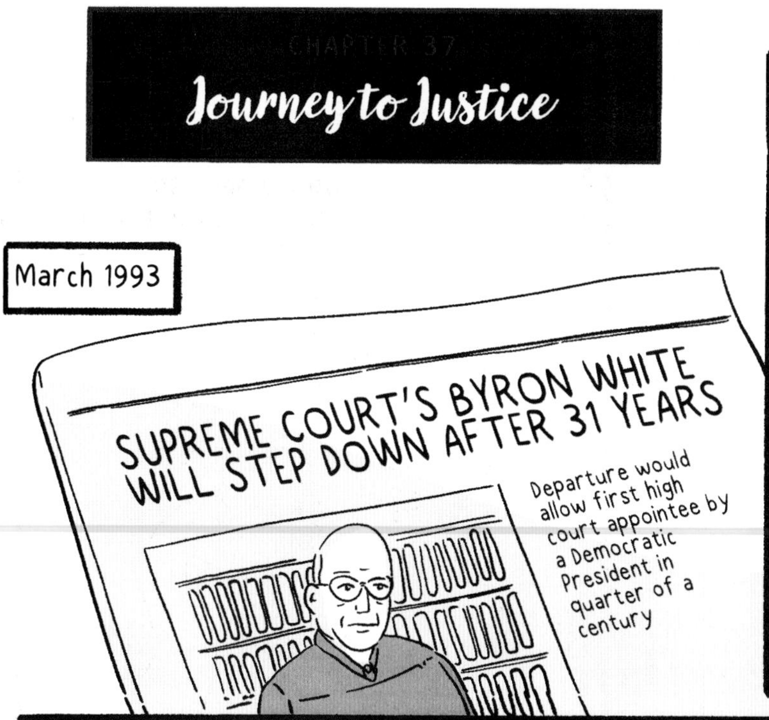
March 1993
SUPREME COURT'S BYRON WHITE WILL STEP DOWN AFTER 31 YEARS
Departure would allow first high court appointee by a Democratic President in quarter of a century

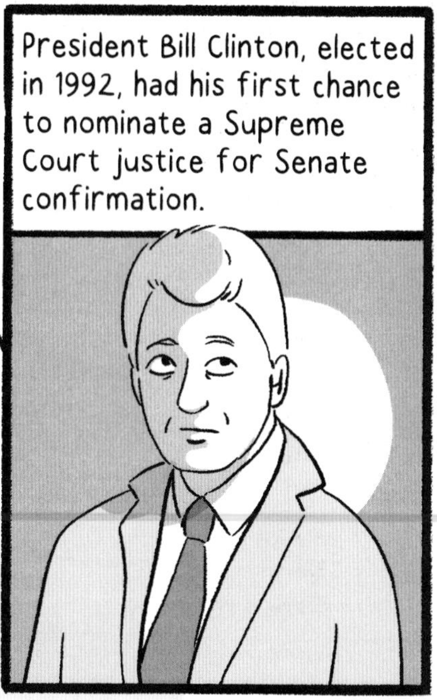
President Bill Clinton, elected in 1992, had his first chance to nominate a Supreme Court justice for Senate confirmation.

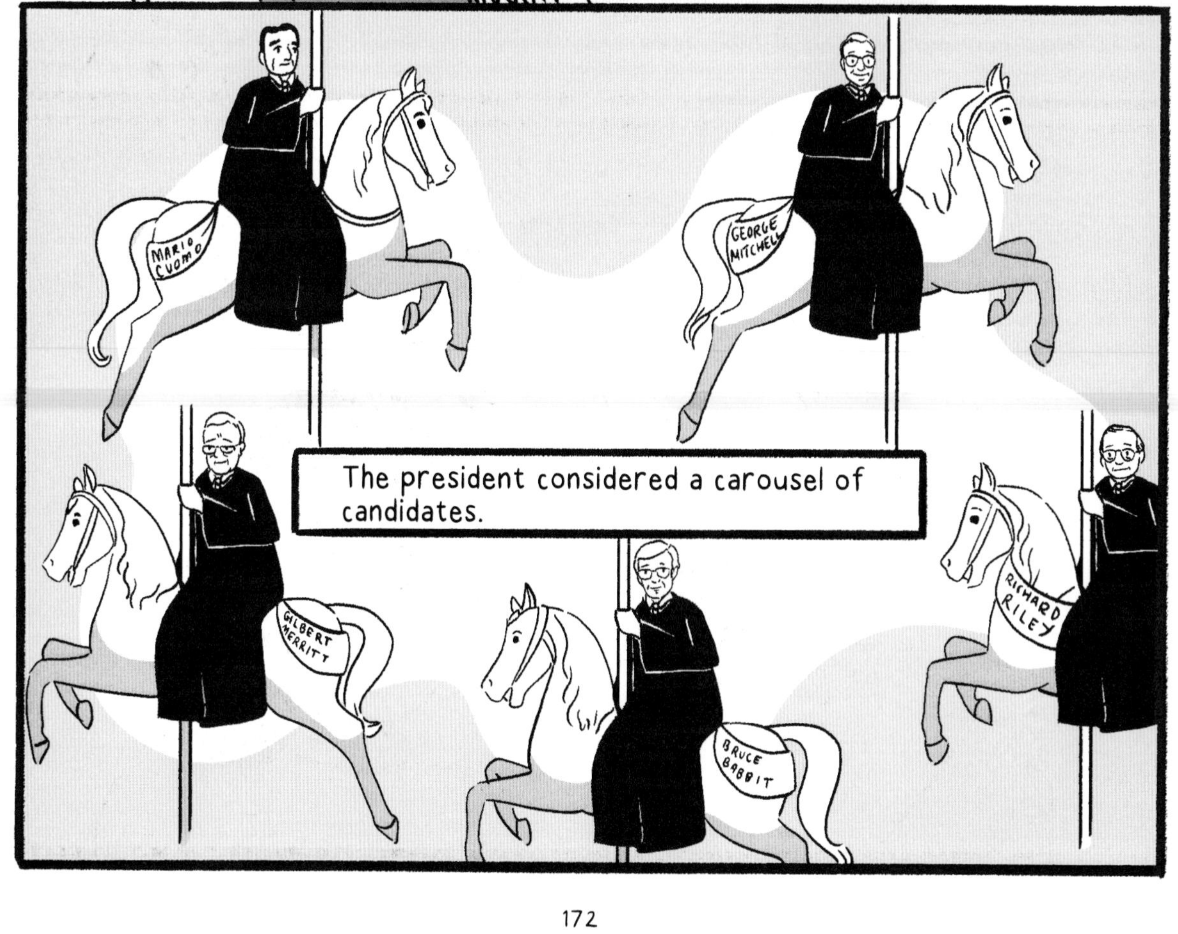
MARIO CUOMO
GEORGE MITCHELL
The president considered a carousel of candidates.
GILBERT MERRITT
BRUCE BABBIT
RICHARD RILEY

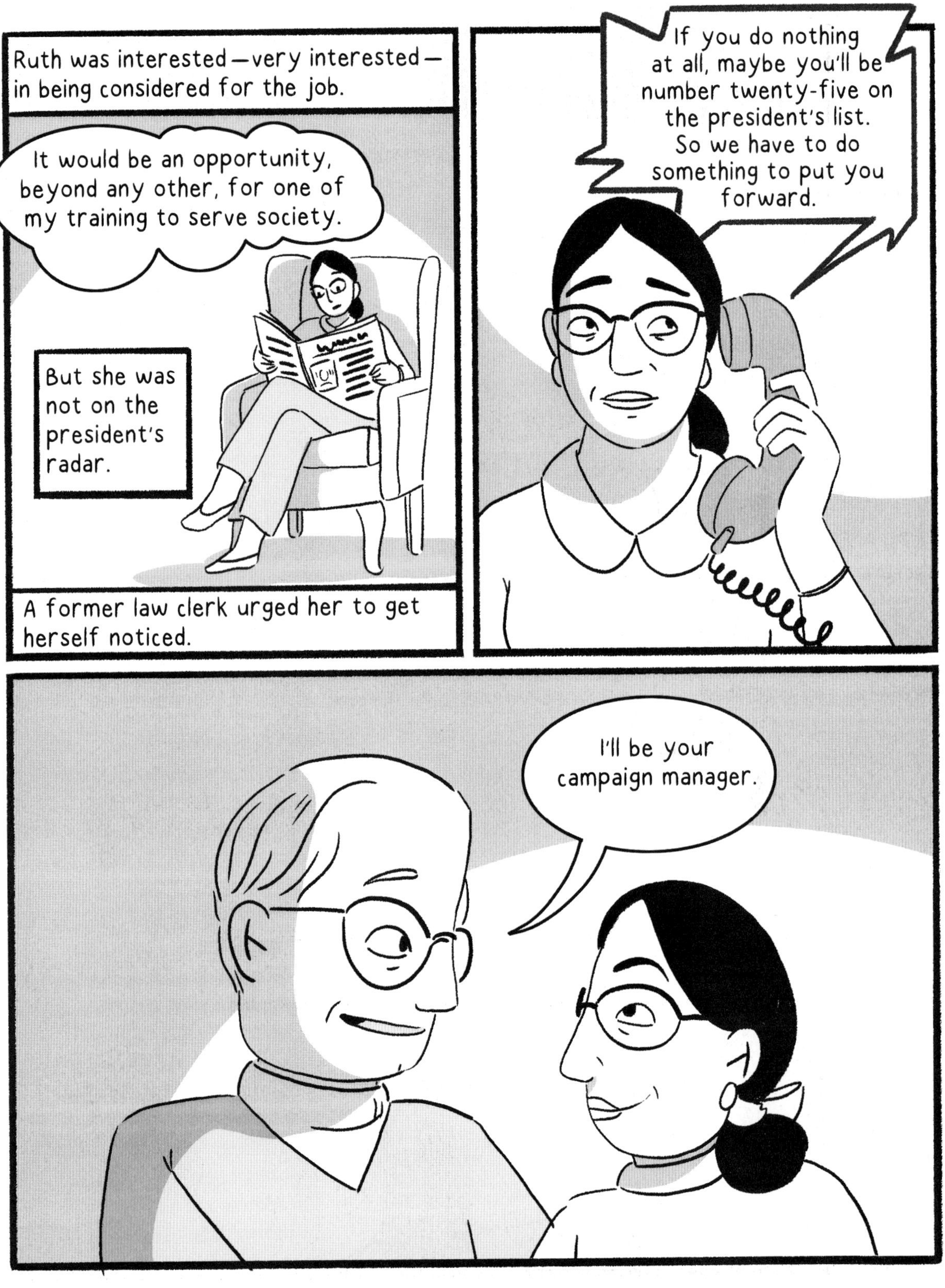
Ruth was interested—very interested—in being considered for the job.
It would be an opportunity, beyond any other, for one of my training to serve society.
But she was not on the president's radar.
A former law clerk urged her to get herself noticed.
If you do nothing at all, maybe you'll be number twenty-five on the president's list. So we have to do something to put you forward.
I'll be your campaign manager.

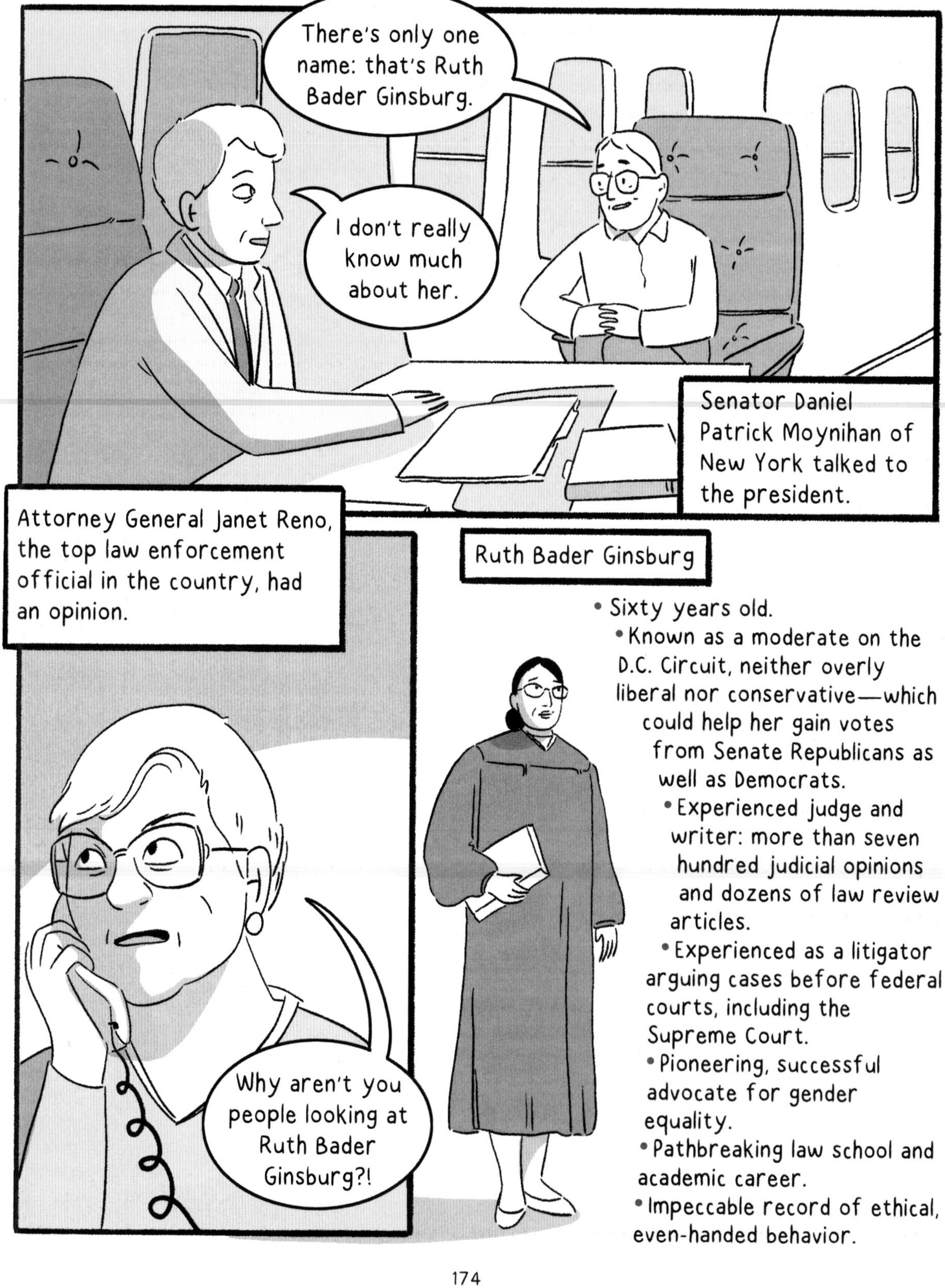
There's only one name: that's Ruth Bader Ginsburg.
I don't really know much about her.
Senator Daniel Patrick Moynihan of New York talked to the president.
Attorney General Janet Reno, the top law enforcement official in the country, had an opinion.
Why aren't you people looking at Ruth Bader Ginsburg?!
Ruth Bader Ginsburg
• Sixty years old.
• Known as a moderate on the D.C. Circuit, neither overly liberal nor conservative—which could help her gain votes from Senate Republicans as well as Democrats.
• Experienced judge and writer: more than seven hundred judicial opinions and dozens of law review articles.
• Experienced as a litigator arguing cases before federal courts, including the Supreme Court.
• Pioneering, successful advocate for gender equality.
• Pathbreaking law school and academic career.
• Impeccable record of ethical, even-handed behavior.

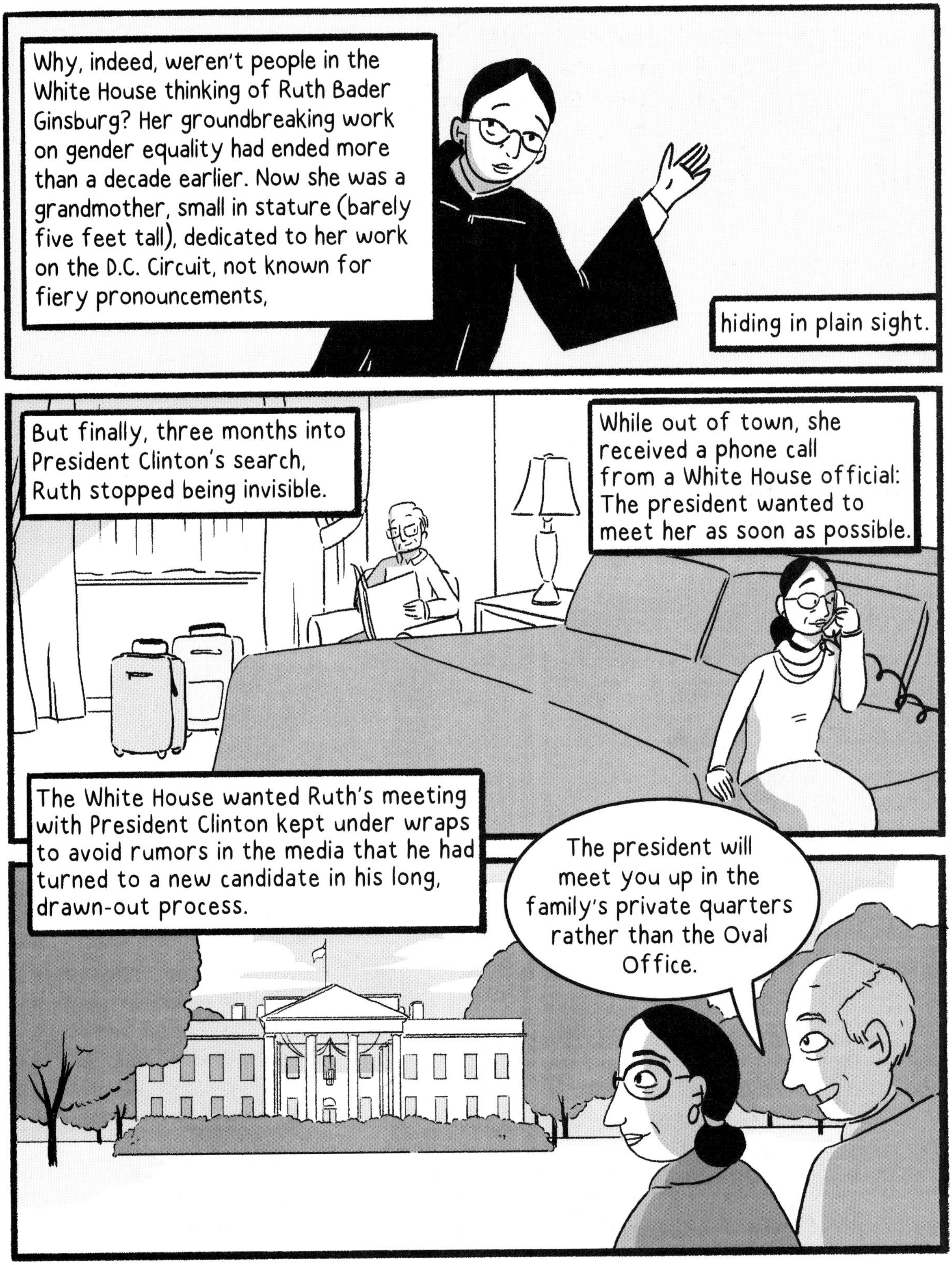

Why, indeed, weren't people in the White House thinking of Ruth Bader Ginsburg? Her groundbreaking work on gender equality had ended more than a decade earlier. Now she was a grandmother, small in stature (barely five feet tall), dedicated to her work on the D.C. Circuit, not known for fiery pronouncements,
hiding in plain sight.
But finally, three months into President Clinton's search, Ruth stopped being invisible.
While out of town, she received a phone call from a White House official: The president wanted to meet her as soon as possible.
The White House wanted Ruth's meeting with President Clinton kept under wraps to avoid rumors in the media that he had turned to a new candidate in his long, drawn-out process.
The president will meet you up in the family's private quarters rather than the Oval Office.

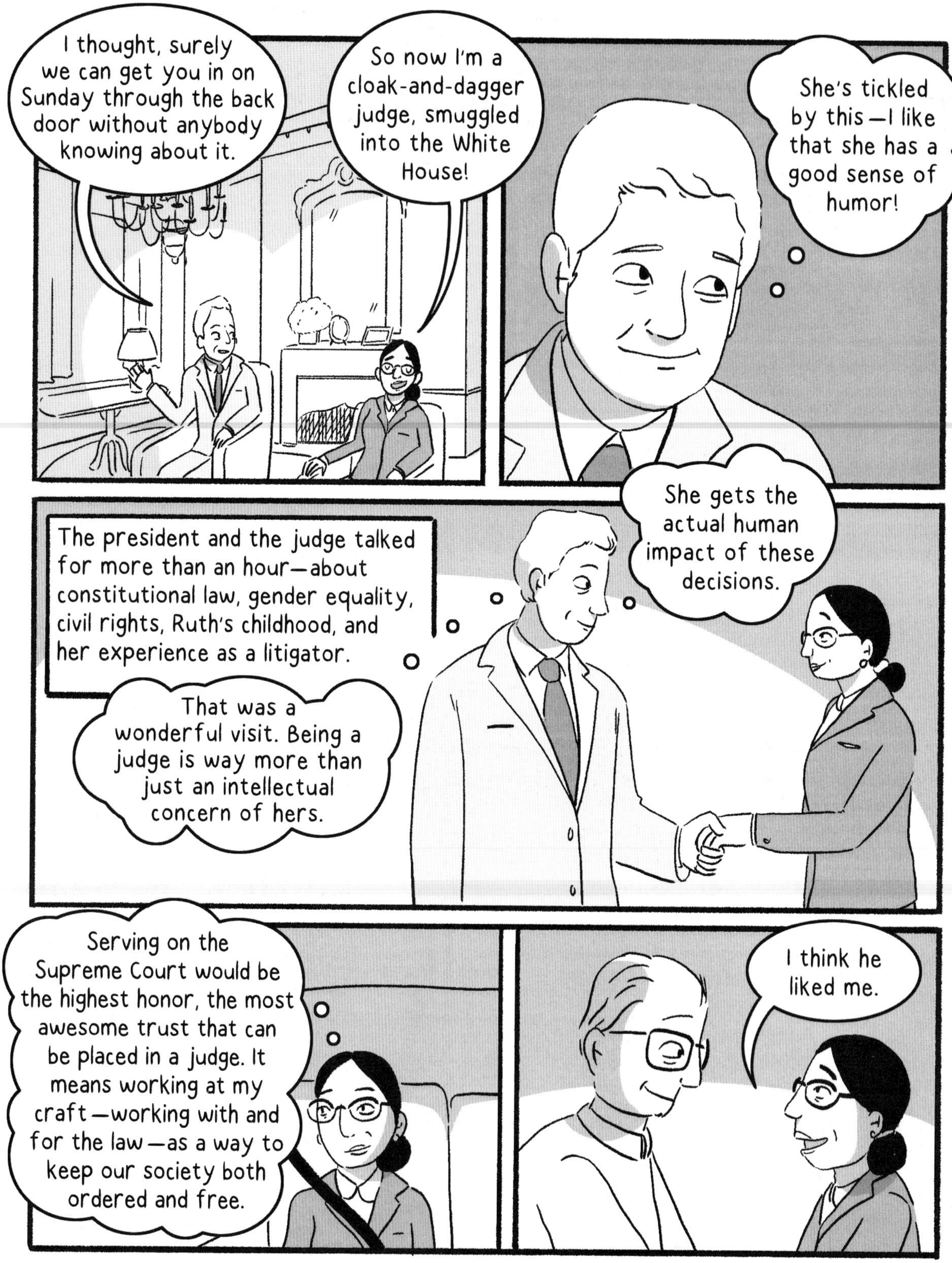
I thought, surely we can get you in on Sunday through the back door without anybody knowing about it.
So now I'm a cloak-and-dagger judge, smuggled into the White House!
She's tickled by this—I like that she has a good sense of humor!
The president and the judge talked for more than an hour—about constitutional law, gender equality, civil rights, Ruth's childhood, and her experience as a litigator.
She gets the actual human impact of these decisions.
That was a wonderful visit. Being a judge is way more than just an intellectual concern of hers.
Serving on the Supreme Court would be the highest honor, the most awesome trust that can be placed in a judge. It means working at my craft—working with and for the law—as a way to keep our society both ordered and free.
I think he liked me.

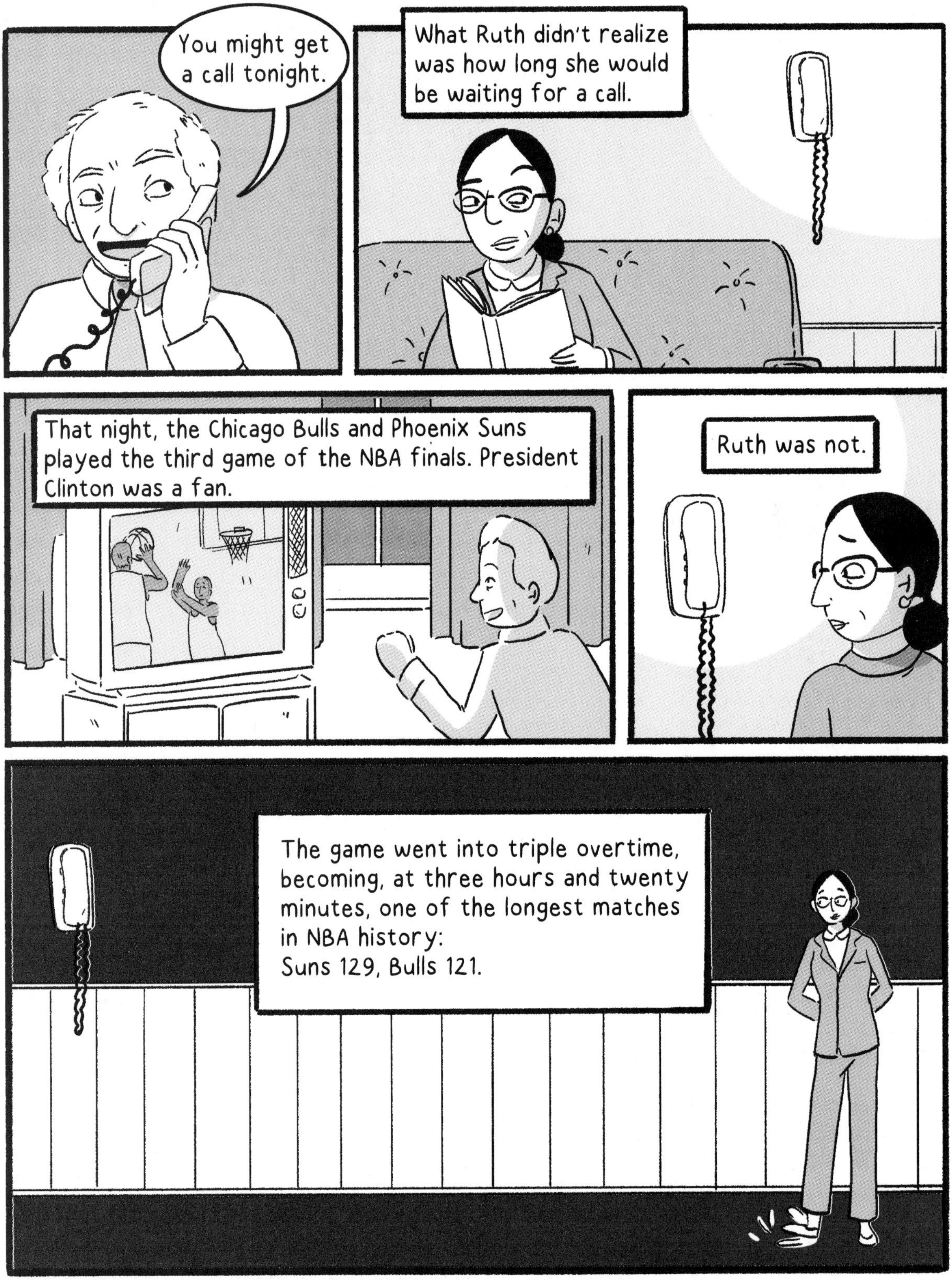
You might get a call tonight.
What Ruth didn't realize was how long she would be waiting for a call.
That night, the Chicago Bulls and Phoenix Suns played the third game of the NBA finals. President Clinton was a fan.
Ruth was not.
The game went into triple overtime, becoming, at three hours and twenty minutes, one of the longest matches in NBA history:
Suns 129, Bulls 121.

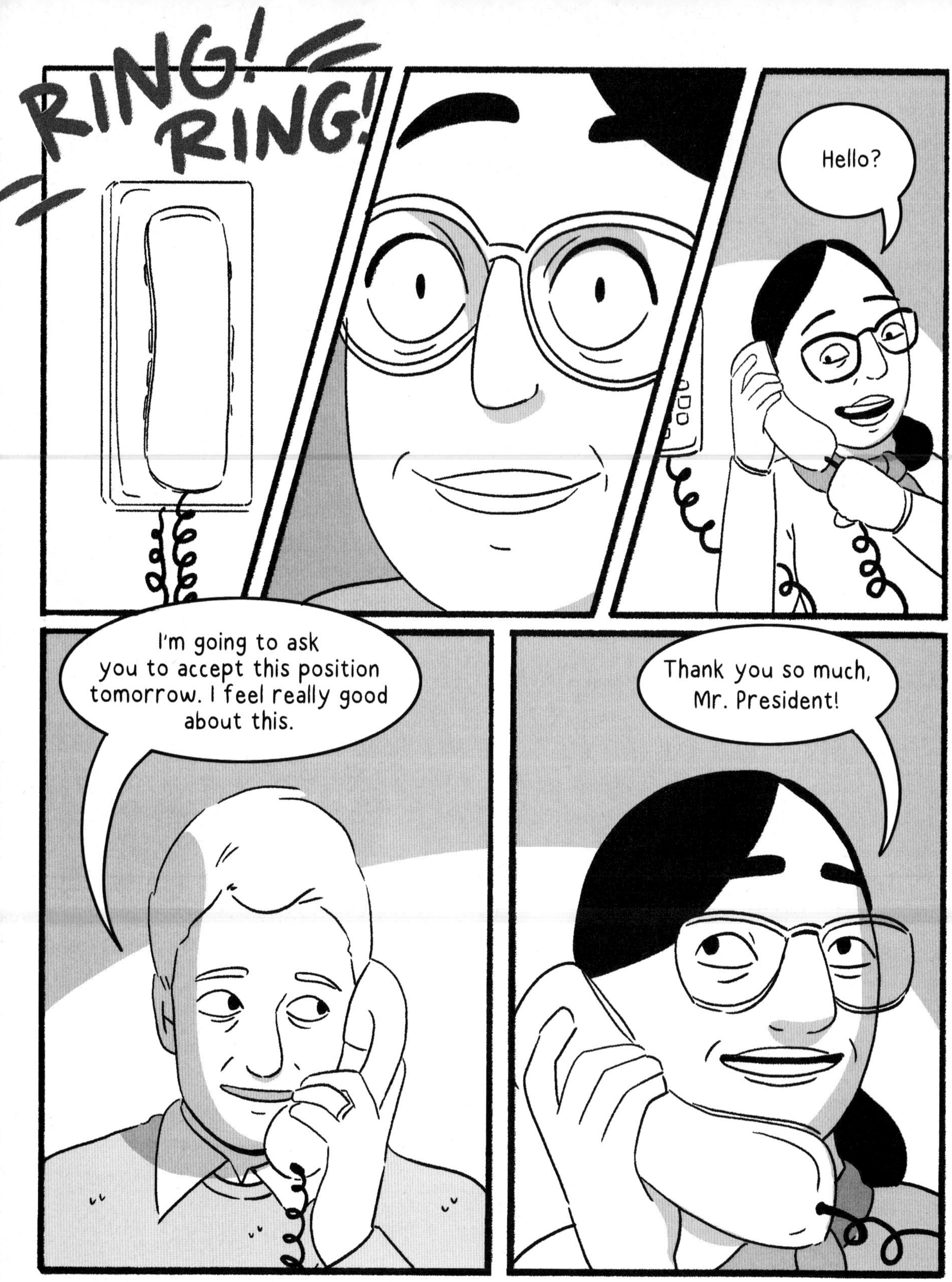
RING! RING!
Hello?
I'm going to ask you to accept this position tomorrow. I feel really good about this.
Thank you so much, Mr. President!

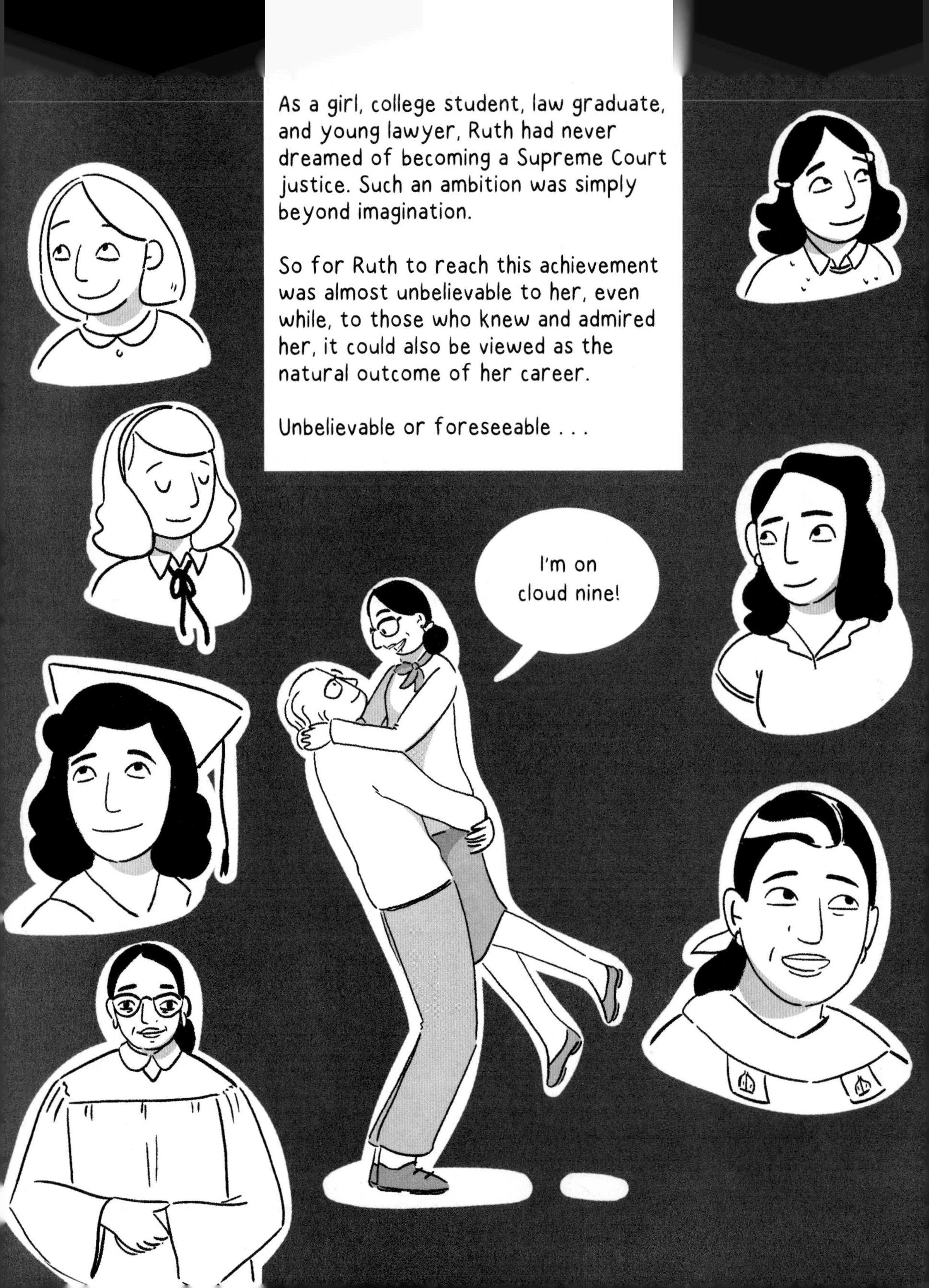
As a girl, college student, law graduate, and young lawyer, Ruth had never dreamed of becoming a Supreme Court justice. Such an ambition was simply beyond imagination.
So for Ruth to reach this achievement was almost unbelievable to her, even while, to those who knew and admired her, it could also be viewed as the natural outcome of her career.
Unbelievable or foreseeable . . .
I'm on cloud nine!

June 14, 1993, White House Rose Garden
I am proud to nominate for Associate Justice of the Supreme Court Ruth Bader Ginsburg!
Throughout her life, she has repeatedly stood for the individual, the person less well off, the outsider in society, and has given those people greater hope by telling them that they have a place in our legal system
by giving them a sense that the Constitution and the laws protect all the American people, not simply the powerful.
Mr. President, I am grateful beyond measure for the confidence you have placed in me and I will strive with all that I have to live up to your expectations in making this appointment. The announcement the president just made . . . contributes to the end of the days when women, at least half the talent pool in our society, appear in high places only as one-at-a-time performers.
My daughter Jane reminded me . . . in her high school yearbook on her graduation in 1973, the listing for Jane Ginsburg under "ambition" was "to see her mother appointed to the Supreme Court."
The next line read, "If necessary, Jane will appoint her." Jane is so pleased, Mr. President, that you did it instead—and her brother, James, is too.

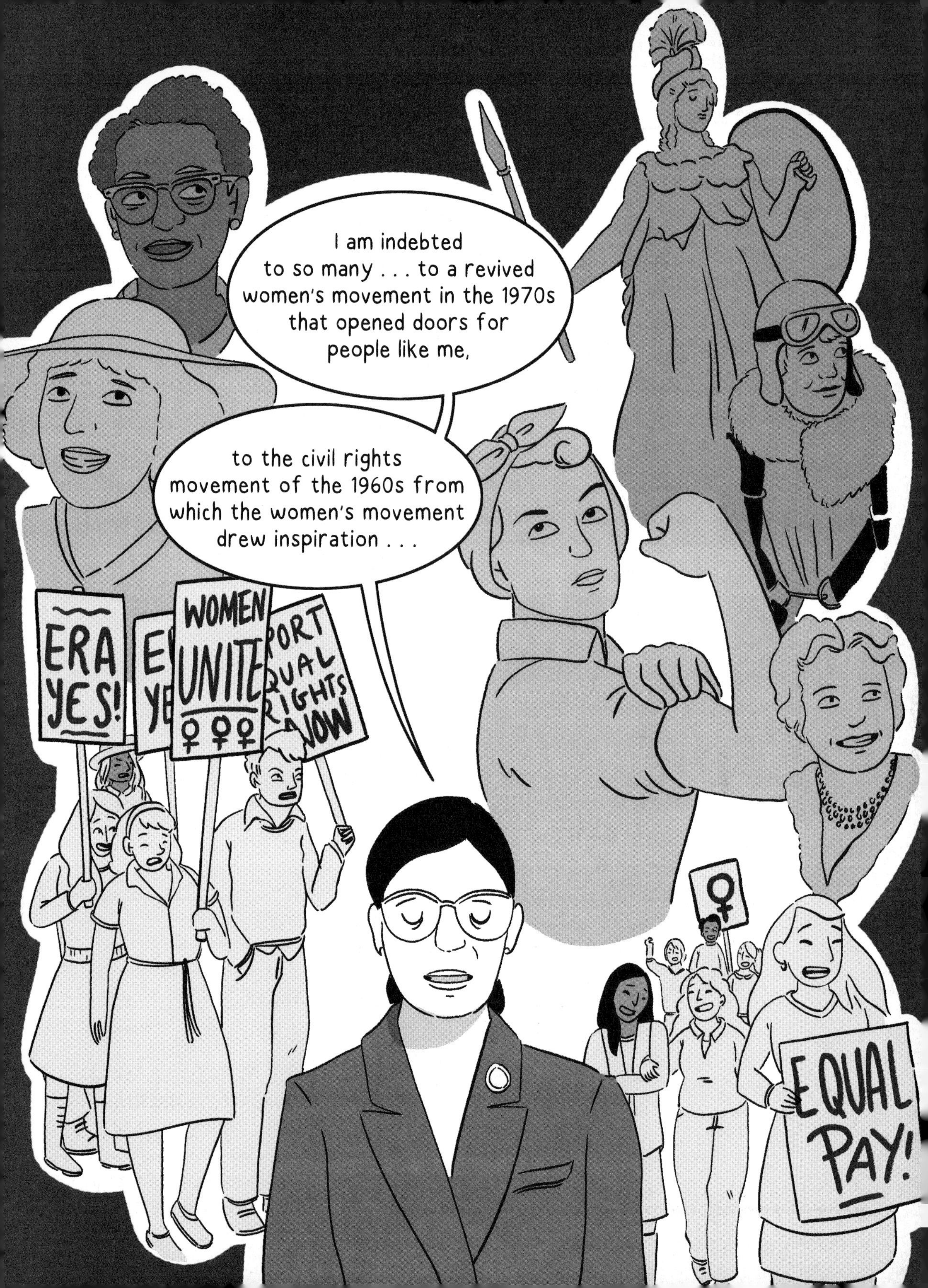
I am indebted to so many . . . to a revived women's movement in the 1970s that opened doors for people like me,
to the civil rights movement of the 1960s from which the women's movement drew inspiration . . .
ERA YES!
WOMEN UNITE ♀♀♀
EQUAL PAY!

It is to my mother, Celia Amster Bader, the bravest and strongest person I have known, who was taken from me much too soon. I pray that I may be all that she would have been

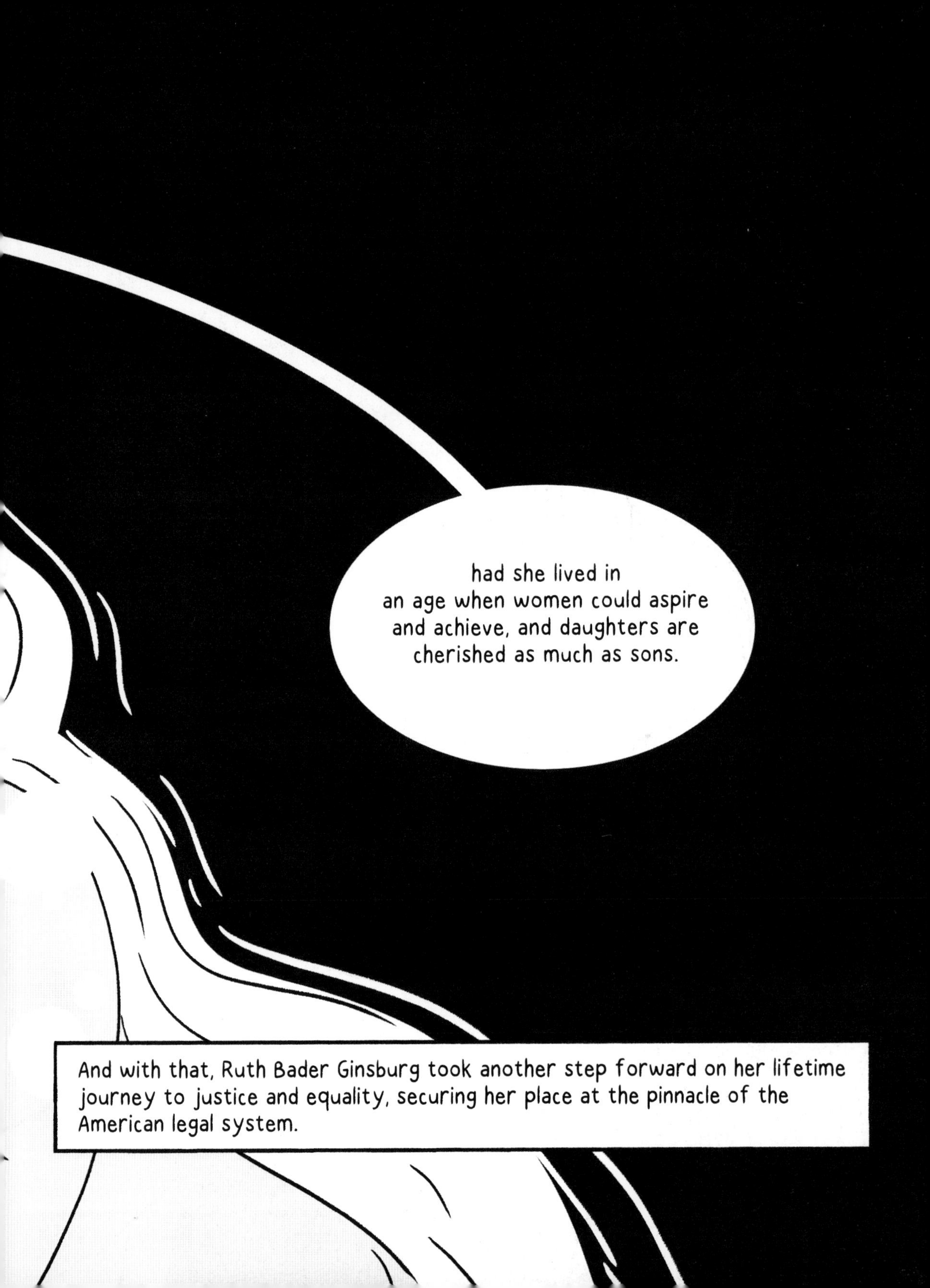
had she lived in an age when women could aspire and achieve, and daughters are cherished as much as sons.
And with that, Ruth Bader Ginsburg took another step forward on her lifetime journey to justice and equality, securing her place at the pinnacle of the American legal system.

EPILOGUE

Becoming RBG

On Monday, October 4, 1993, for the first time in history, two female justices settled into their chairs on the raised mahogany bench of the US Supreme Court. Sandra Day O'Connor had been appointed twelve years earlier by President Ronald Reagan. Ruth Bader Ginsburg became the second female justice. Though appointed by presidents from different political parties, the two women quickly forged a bond. "Justice O'Connor is the most helpful big sister anyone could have," Justice Ginsburg said.

Justice Ginsburg also became the first Jewish female justice. "My heritage as a Jew and my occupation as a judge fit together symmetrically," she said. "The demand for justice runs through the entirety of Jewish history and Jewish tradition. I take pride in and draw strength from my heritage."

Justice Ginsburg joined her friend Justice Antonin Scalia, whom President Reagan had appointed in 1986, on the high court. The two continued to be at loggerheads on important questions of constitutional interpretation—yet their friendship only deepened. "Call us the odd couple," Justice Scalia said in an interview. "She likes opera, and she's a very nice person. What's not to like? Except her views on the law." As for Justice Ginsburg's take on Scalia: "What I like about him is that he's very funny and very smart." Something both justices cherished was an exquisite perk that came with their jobs—being invited to take the stage with the Washington National Opera.

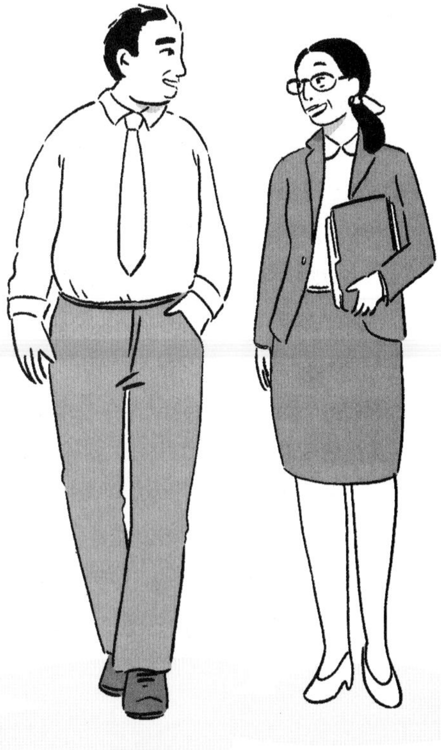

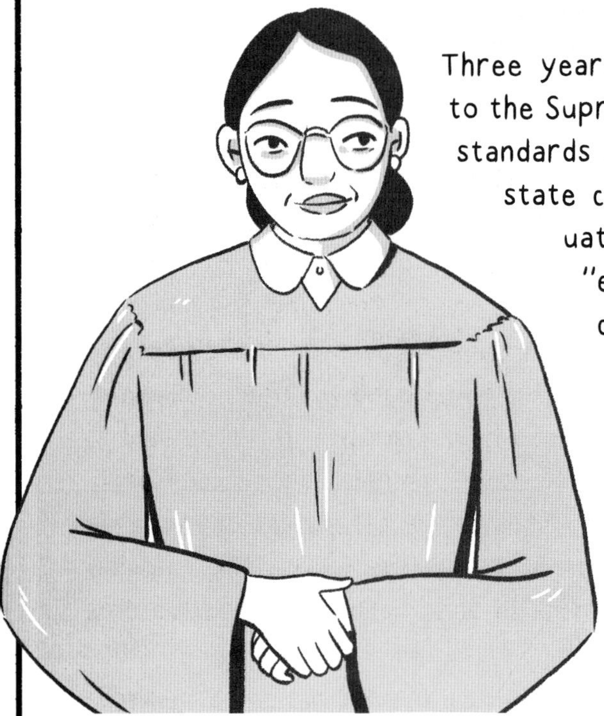

Three years on the job, in 1996, a case came to the Supreme Court challenging the admission standards at the Virginia Military Institute, a state college. VMI was dedicated to graduating, as its mission statement said, "educated and honorable men . . . confident in the functions and attitudes of leadership." High school boys were welcome to apply for admission to VMI. High school girls were not.

Seven members of the Supreme Court—including both female justices—voted to strike VMI's exclusionary rule as a violation of the Equal Protection Clause. The job of writing the majority opinion was given to Justice O'Connor, but . . . "This should be Ruth's," she said generously, knowing how hard her sister justice had worked as a lawyer to advance the law of gender equality.

Justice Ginsburg's opinion for the majority stated that only an "exceedingly persuasive justification" could be a defense against gender-based distinctions. She cited as precedents the Court's rulings in the Sally Reed, Sharron Frontiero, and Stephen Wiesenfeld cases—all of which bore her own thumbprint from when she argued them decades before. It was as if all of Ruth's efforts as a litigator—when she stood at the same podium she now faced from her perch up on the bench—had led to her ruling as Justice Ginsburg in the VMI case.

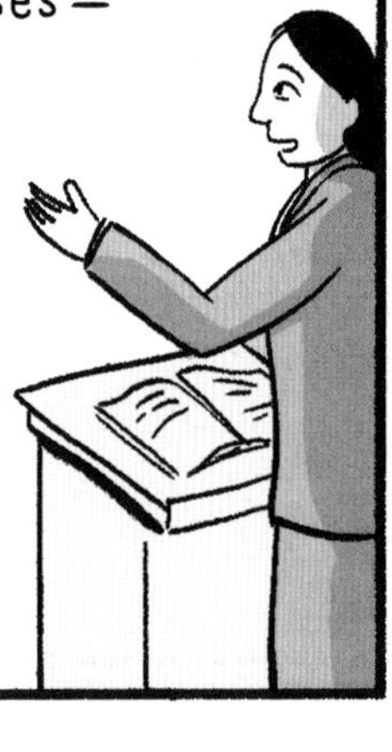

Not every day was a victory, on the bench or off. Ruth was diagnosed with colon cancer in 1999. But she scheduled her chemotherapy treatments for Fridays, so she could recover from the unpleasant effects over the weekend. Ruth never missed an oral argument. And her bout with cancer led to a beneficial change in her life. . . .

At the age of sixty-six, Ruth became a gym rat. She wanted to stay strong.

After Justice O'Connor retired in 2006 to take care of her ailing husband, Justice Ginsburg was the sole woman on the Supreme Court for three years. (President George W. Bush nominated a man, Samuel Alito, to replace O'Connor.) "It's lonely for me," she admitted in an interview. As important, she thought having only one woman on the Court gave the public the wrong impression in the twenty-first century. "It's almost like being back in law school in 1956, when there were nine of us in a class of over five hundred," she told a newspaper reporter. "Every time you went to answer a question, you were answering for your entire sex. . . . You were different and the object of curiosity."

But Justice Ginsburg carried on, bringing her unique perspective to cases. In 2007, she was on the losing side of a ruling in a significant gender discrimination case. Lilly Ledbetter, a manager at a Goodyear tire plant in Alabama, learned through an anonymous note that for years the company had been paying her, the sole female area manager, much less than it paid men. A majority of justices ruled that she couldn't sue for discrimination that had occurred years earlier—even though Goodyear had intentionally kept Lilly in the dark about the unequal pay for all those years.

Justice Ginsburg disagreed deeply with the Court's ruling. The male justices, she felt, really didn't understand the bias women could encounter at work. She not only wrote a dissent—which is not so unusual—but announced it from the bench. And that *was* unusual. She said that the law "was meant to govern real-world employment practices and that world is what the Court ignores today." She concluded with a pointed observation: "Today, the ball lies . . . in Congress's court." In other words, Congress could pass a law that adopted her dissent and transform a defeat into a victory—and that is exactly what happened. When Barack Obama became the forty-fourth president of the United States in 2009, the first law he signed was the Lilly Ledbetter Fair Pay Act.

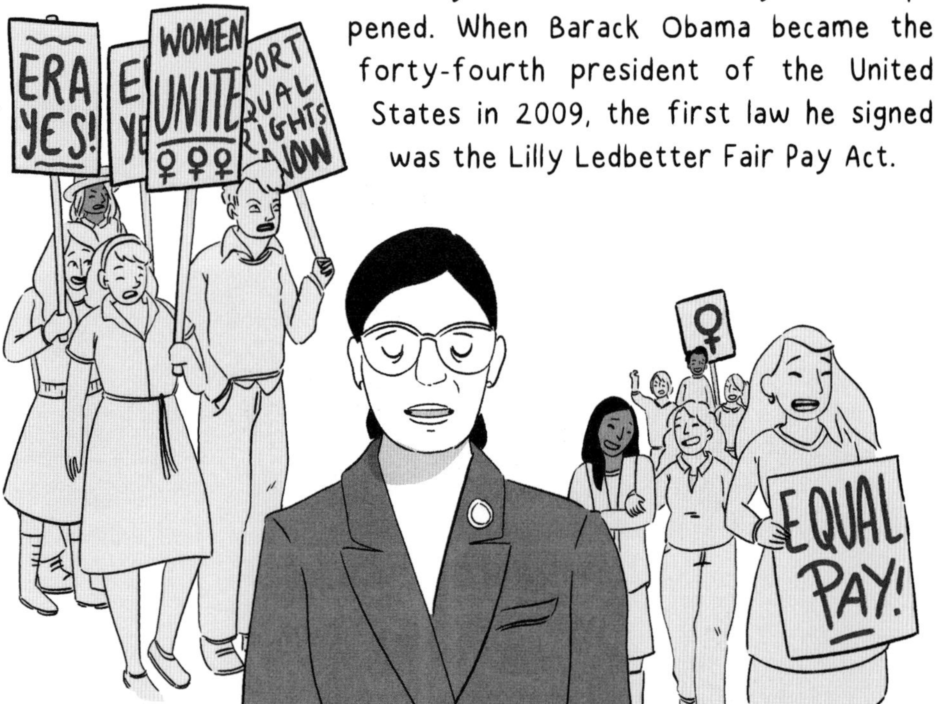
ERA YES!
WOMEN UNITE
EQUAL PAY!

In 2009, President Obama had the opportunity to appoint a new justice to the Supreme Court when Justice David Souter retired. He chose Sonia Sotomayor.

And in 2010, President Obama selected Elena Kagan for the Court after Justice John Paul Stevens retired.

Three women justices—one-third of the Supreme Court! Back in 1993, at the Senate confirmation hearings on her nomination to the Court, then-Judge Ginsburg had told the assembled senators, "Indeed, in my lifetime, I expect to see three, four, perhaps even more women on the High Court bench, women not shaped from the same mold, but of different complexions." At the time, people smiled. Now this prediction was a reality.

But if Ruth no longer experienced that loneliness that came from being the only woman on the Supreme Court, she suffered a far deeper loneliness. On June 27, 2010, her dear Marty died of cancer. He was seventy-eight years old. Marty left behind Ruth; his children, Jane and James, now grown—Jane a professor at Columbia Law School, James a classical music producer—grandchildren; and countless friends and admirers.

Despite the pain of losing the man she called her life partner, Justice Ginsburg did not crumble. She could not; she needed to keep her spirit strong, because on a Supreme Court that had become dominated by conservative justices appointed by Presidents Reagan, George H.W. Bush, and George W. Bush, she found herself taking on the role of *dissenter*. From opposing a decision that permitted vast sums of corporate money to influence elections (*Citizens United v. Federal Election Commission*), to disagreeing with the majority in cases involving racial and other discrimination in the workplace (*Vance v. Ball State University*; *University of Texas Southwest Medical Center v. Nassar*), Justice Ginsburg made her views known.

Court-watchers grew accustomed to seeing Justice Ginsburg on the bench wearing her special jabot — a type of collar with which she dressed up her plain judicial robe — that signified she was dissenting. She also had a particular jabot for when she announced the majority opinion — and a closetful of others that she wore as the spirit moved her.

And when, in the case of *Shelby County v. Holder*, the majority struck down an important part of the Voting Rights Act, a law designed to prevent discrimination against minority voters, Justice Ginsburg dissented again. Her voice from the bench on that day, June 25, 2013, was calm and low as usual. But it carried far beyond the courtroom. Her passionate dissent energized people who saw a Supreme Court that they feared was ignoring the realities of discrimination in the United States.

People started talking and writing about Justice Ginsburg—on blogs, in newspapers and magazines, in books, on television, across the dinner table. They drank their coffee out of mugs emblazoned with Justice Ginsburg's face. They wore RBG-themed T-shirts and jewelry and Halloween costumes. They sent RBG-inspired greeting cards.

RBG, the shorthand with which Justice Ginsburg had signed her notes, memos, and correspondence for years, became a byword for dissenting—for disagreeing in service of hewing to important principles of fairness and equality.

Even when dissenting in case after case, Justice Ginsburg maintained her optimism about the possibility of creating positive change through the law, step by step. Her optimism had deep roots—roots that reach into the Preamble to the Constitution, a pocket-size copy of which she carried with her always.

"My explanation of the genius of this Constitution," she said: "It begins 'We, the people of the United States.' What people? In 1787, white property-owning men. But the Preamble next says, 'in order to form a more perfect Union.' The union has become more perfect as it has become more embracive, so that we the people today includes people left out at the beginning. Not only people who were held in human bondage, but Native Americans and half the population—women. The Preamble is my favorite part of the original Constitution."

For many people, explanations like this made RBG *their* favorite part of the Supreme Court. Others did not concur. Like Justice Scalia (who died in 2016), they did not view the Constitution as a living document subject to evolving interpretation over changing times. But if one thing is clear in this debate, it is this: Listening to one another across this divide and engaging with opposing ideas are necessary steps for "We, the people" to keep and protect that "more perfect Union" that Ruth Bader Ginsburg worked so hard to achieve.

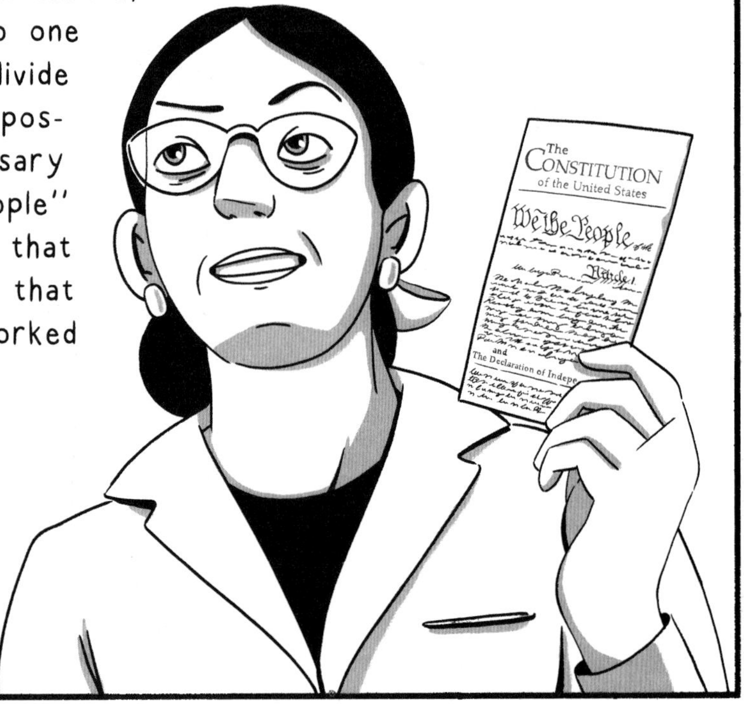
The
CONSTITUTION
of the United States
We the People
and
The Declaration of

TIMELINE

March 15, 1933 - Joan Ruth Bader is born to Nathan Bader and Celia Amster Bader at Beth Moses Hospital, Brooklyn, New York.

1934 - Ruth's older sister, Marilyn, dies of meningitis.

1938 - Ruth starts kindergarten at P.S. 238 in Brooklyn.

1946 - Graduation from P.S. 238. In the fall, Ruth starts James Madison High School in Brooklyn. Her mother is diagnosed with cancer.

June 1950 - Celia Bader dies of cancer. Ruth graduates from high school, but does not attend her graduation because of her mother's death.

1950 - Ruth enters Cornell University in Ithaca, New York. She meets Martin (Marty) D. Ginsburg.

1953 - Marty, who is a year ahead of Ruth in school, leaves Ithaca to attend Harvard Law School in Cambridge, Massachusetts.

June 1954 - Ruth graduates from Cornell. She and Marty get married a week later.

1954 - Ruth and Marty move to Fort Sill, Oklahoma, where Marty serves in the US Army and Ruth works at various jobs, including in the Lawton, Oklahoma, Social Security Administration office.

July 1955 - Ruth and Marty's daughter, Jane, is born.

1956 - The family moves to Cambridge, Massachusetts, where Marty enters his second year of Harvard Law School and Ruth begins her first year. By her second year, Ruth makes the *Harvard Law Review*.

1958 - The family moves to New York City so Marty can take a job at a law firm. Ruth enters Columbia Law School in New York City for her last year of law school. She makes *Columbia Law Review*, too.

1959 - Ruth graduates from Columbia Law School, tied for first in her class.

1959–1961 - Ruth works as a judicial clerk for Judge Edmund L. Palmieri of the US District Court of the Southern District of New York.

1961–1963 - Ruth works as a research associate, and then as associate director, for the Columbia Law School Project on International Procedure. For this job, she spends time in Sweden.

1963 - Ruth joins the faculty of the Rutgers School of Law in Newark, New Jersey, where she is a professor until 1972.

1965 - Ruth and Marty's second child, James, is born.

1971 - Ruth begins teaching a seminar about sex discrimination and the law. She and Marty agree to represent Charles Moritz, and in that case she writes her first major brief arguing that sex discrimination violates the US Constitution's guarantee of equal protection under the law. Ruth also coauthors her first brief for the Supreme Court of the United States in *Reed v. Reed*. After the Supreme Court rules favorably in *Reed*, Ruth helps the American Civil Liberties Union launch its Women's Rights Project.

1972 - Columbia Law School hires Ruth as its first tenured female professor. She begins teaching at Columbia while also maintaining her position as leader of the ACLU Women's Rights Project. The US Court of Appeals for the Tenth Circuit decides the *Moritz* case in favor of Ruth's client.

1973 - In January, Ruth argues her first case at the Supreme Court in *Frontiero v. Richardson*. In May, the Supreme Court rules in favor of Ruth's client, Sharron Frontiero.

1974 - Ruth argues *Kahn v. Shevin* before the Supreme Court, a case she loses.

1975 - Ruth argues Stephen Wiesenfeld's case before the Supreme Court in January. In March, the Supreme Court issues its decision in Stephen's favor in *Weinberger v. Wiesenfeld*.

1976 - Ruth files a brief for the ACLU in *Craig v. Boren*. The Supreme Court's decision in the case largely adopts the new approach she urged the justices to take in ruling in sex discrimination cases.

1978 - Ruth argues *Duren v. Missouri* before the Supreme Court.

1979 - The Supreme Court rules in the *Duren* case, invalidating Missouri's system of excusing women from jury service.

1980 - President Jimmy Carter appoints Ruth to the US Court of Appeals for the District of Columbia Circuit. Judge Ruth Bader Ginsburg and her family move to Washington, D.C.

1993 - President Bill Clinton appoints Judge Ginsburg to the Supreme Court. On August 10, Justice Ruth Bader Ginsburg takes the oath of office and becomes the second woman to serve on the US Supreme Court.

1996 - Justice Ginsburg writes the Supreme Court's majority opinion in *United States v. Virginia* (the Virginia Military Institute case).

1999 - Justice Ginsburg undergoes surgery and other treatments for colon cancer, but does not miss a day in court.

2007 - Justice Ginsburg announces her strong dissent in *Ledbetter v. Goodyear Tire & Rubber*.

2009 - President Barack Obama signs the Lilly Ledbetter Fair Pay Act, which essentially adopts Justice Ginsburg's approach in her *Ledbetter* dissent and makes it the law. Shortly afterward, Justice Ginsburg has surgery for pancreatic cancer. Again, she does not miss any court sessions.

2010 - Marty Ginsburg dies of cancer.

2013–2014 - Justice Ginsburg writes notable dissents from Supreme Court rulings in *Fisher v. University of Texas* (2013), *Vance v. Ball State University* (2013), *University of Texas Southwest Medical Center v. Nassar* (2013), *Shelby County v. Holder* (2013), and *Burwell v. Hobby Lobby Stores* (2014).

2018 - In December, Justice Ginsburg has surgery to treat lung cancer. She misses some oral arguments at the Court, but reads the transcripts, works from home, and returns to the bench in February 2019.

SELECTED BIBLIOGRAPHY

Books

Bayer, Linda. *Ruth Bader Ginsburg*. Philadelphia: Chelsea House Publishers, 2000.

Carmon, Irin, and Shana Knizhnik. *Notorious RBG: The Life and Times of Ruth Bader Ginsburg*. New York: Dey St., 2015.

DeHart, Jane Sherron. *Ruth Bader Ginsburg: A Life*. New York: Alfred A. Knopf, 2018.

Dodson, Scott, ed. *The Legacy of Ruth Bader Ginsburg*. New York: Cambridge University Press, 2015.

Gilbert, Lynn, and Gaylen Moore. *Particular Passions: Ruth Bader Ginsburg*, 1981. http://www.particular passions.com/ruth-bader-ginsburg/.

Ginsburg, Ruth Bader, with Mary Hartnett and Wendy W. Williams. *My Own Words*. New York: Simon & Schuster, 2016.

Strebeigh, Fred. *Equal: Women Reshape American Law*. New York: W.W. Norton, 2009.

Toobin, Jeffrey. *The Nine: Inside the Secret World of the Supreme Court*. New York: Anchor Books, 2008.

Articles, Papers, Reports, and Interviews

American Civil Liberties Union. "Timeline of Major Supreme Court Decisions on Women's Rights." n.d. https://www.aclu.org/sites/default/files/field_document/lib16-wrptimeline-v04.pdf.

———. *Tribute: The Legacy of Ruth Bader Ginsburg and the WRP Staff*. n.d. https://www.aclu.org/other /tribute-legacy-ruth-bader-ginsburg-and-wrp-staff.

"At the U.S. Supreme Court: A Conversation With Justice Ruth Bader Ginsburg." *Stanford Lawyer*, November 11, 2013.

Barnes, Robert. "The Question Facing Ruth Bader Ginsburg: Stay or Go?" *Washington Post*, October 4, 2013.

Bazelon, Emily. "The Place of Women on the Court." *New York Times*, July 7, 2009.

Berke, Richard L. "Clinton Names Ruth Ginsburg, Advocate for Women, to Court." *New York Times*, June 15, 1993.

Biskupic, Joan. "Looking at Human Problems, With Judicial Restraint." *Washington Post*, July 20, 1993.

Bowman, Cynthia Grant. "Women in the Legal Profession." *Maine Law Review* (2009).

Chira, Susan. "Career Trailblazers Recall Era of Overt Discrimination." *Chicago Tribune*, August 15, 1993.

Epstein, Nadine. "Ruth Bader Ginsburg: 'The Notorious RBG.'" *Moment Magazine*, May 4, 2015.

Franklin, Cary. "The Anti-Stereotyping Principles in Constitutional Sex Discrimination Law." *New York University Law Review* (April 2010).

Fritz, Sara. "Without Great Expectations, Ginsburg Found Her Way to Top." *Los Angeles Times*, July 21, 1993.

Galanes, Philip. "Ruth Bader Ginsburg and Gloria Steinem on the Unending Fight for Women's Rights." *New York Times*, November 14, 2015.

Garner, Bryan. "Interviews with United States Supreme Court Justices." *The Scribes Journal of Legal Writing* (2010). https://legaltimes.typepad.com/files/garner-transcripts-1.pdf.

Ginsburg, Ruth Bader. "The Changing Complexion of Harvard Law School." *Harvard Women's Law Journal* (2004).

———. "Litigating for Gender Equality in the 1970s." *Wilson Center*, May 21, 2002. https://www.wilsoncenter
    .org/event/presentation-litigating-for-gender-equality-the-1970s.

———. "Remarks on Women's Progress at the Bar and on the Bench." *Harvard Journal of Law and Gender* (2007).

———. "Speaking in a Judicial Voice." *New York Law Review* (1992).

Ruth Bader Ginsburg, interview by Debbie Levy at the Supreme Court of the United States, Washington, D.C., August 18, 2017 (on file with author).

Ruth Bader Ginsburg Papers, 1897–2005. Library of Congress, Washington, D.C.

Gluck, Abbe R. "A Conversation with Justice Ruth Bader Ginsburg." *Columbia Journal of Gender and Law* (2013).

Greenhouse, Linda. "In dissent, Ginsburg finds her voice at Supreme Court," *New York Times*, May 31, 2007.

———. "Introduction: Learning to Listen to Ruth Bader Ginsburg." *City University of New York Law Review* (2004).

———. "Word for Word: A Talk with Ginsburg on Life and the Court." *New York Times*, January 7, 1994.

Gugliotta, Guy, and Eleanor Randolph. "A Mentor, Role Model and Heroine of Feminist Lawyers." *Washington Post*, June 15, 1993.

Kagan, Elena, and Ruth Bader Ginsburg. "Remarks Commemorating Celebration 55: The Women's Leadership Summit." *Harvard Journal of Law and Gender* (2009).

Margolick, David. "Trial by Adversity Shapes Jurist's Outlook." *New York Times*, June 25, 1993.

Merritt, Deborah Jones, and David M. Lieberman. "Ruth Bader Ginsburg's Jurisprudence of Opportunity and Equality." *Columbia Law Review* (2004).

"Reed v. Reed at 40: Equal Protection and Women's Rights." *Journal of Gender, Social Policy & the Law* (2011).

Rosen, Jeffrey. "The Book of Ruth." *New Republic*, August 2, 1993.

———. "The New Look of Liberalism on the Court." *New York Times*, October 5, 1997.

Saulnier, Beth. "Justice Prevails." *Cornell Alumni Magazine*, November/December 2013.

Schwarz, John. "Between the Lines of the Voting Rights Opinion." *New York Times*, June 25, 2013.

Showalter, Elaine. "Fighting Words." *New Republic*, October 3, 2016.

Stein, Robert A. "A Conversation Between Justice Ruth Bader Ginsburg and Professor Robert A. Stein." *Minnesota Law Review* (2014).

Toobin, Jeffrey. "Heavyweight: How Ruth Bader Ginsburg Has Moved the Supreme Court." *The New Yorker*, March 11, 2015.

"Transcript of Interview of U.S. Supreme Court Associate Justice Ruth Bader Ginsburg." *Ohio State Law Journal* (2009).

University of Michigan Law School. "A Conversation with Ruth Bader Ginsburg, Associate Justice of the Supreme Court of the United States." *The Tanner Lectures on Human Values*, February 6, 2015 (on file with author).

U.S. Congress, Senate. Committee on the Judiciary. *Nomination of Ruth Bader Ginsburg, to Be Associate Justice of the Supreme Court of the United States, Hearings before the Committee on the Judiciary*. 103rd Cong., 1st sess. July 20, 21, 22, and 23, 1993.

Von Drehle, David. "Conventional Roles Hid a Revolutionary Intellect." *Washington Post*, July 18 1993.

———. "Redefining Fair With a Careful Simple Assault." *Washington Post*, July 19, 1993.

Walsh, Amy. "Ruth Bader Ginsburg: Extending the Constitution." *John Marshall Law Review* (1998).

Ward, Stephanie Frances. "Family Ties." *ABA Journal*, October 1, 2010.

Weisberg, Jessica. "Supreme Court Justice Ruth Bader Ginsburg: I'm Not Going Anywhere." *Elle*, September 23, 2014.

Williams, Wendy Webster. "Ruth Bader Ginsburg's Equal Protection Clause: 1970-80." *Columbia Journal of Gender and Law* (2013).

Video

Academy of Achievement. "Ruth Bader Ginsburg: Interview," August 17, 2010 and July 14, 2016. http://www.achievement.org/achiever/ruth-bader-ginsburg/#interview.

Cornell University. "From Brooklyn to the Bench: A Conversation with Ruth Bader Ginsburg," September 23, 2014. https://www.youtube.com/watch?v=htJXKesFpE8.

C-SPAN. "A Conversation with Justice Ginsburg," April 10, 2009. https://www.c-span.org/video/?285214-1/conversation-justice-ruth-bader-ginsburg&start=3283.

———. "Conversation with Justice Ginsburg," September 15, 2011. https://www.c-span.org/video/?301560-1/conversation-justice-ginsburg.

———. "Conversation with Justice Ruth Bader Ginsburg," June 13, 2015. Interview with California Supreme Court justice Goodwin Liu. https://www.c-span.org/video/?326578-1/conversation-supreme-court-justice-ruth-bader-ginsburg.

———. "Justice Ginsburg Grade School Tour," June 3, 1994. http://www.c-span.org/video/?57503-1/justice-ginsburg-grade-school-tour.

———. "Justice Ginsburg on a Meaningful Life," February 6, 2017. The Rathbun Lecture. https://www.c-span.org/video/?423329-1/justice-ruth-bader-ginsburg-delivers-rathbun-lecture-meaningful-life.

———. "Justice Profile: Ruth Bader Ginsburg," May 2, 2001. https://www.c-span.org/video/?164025-1/justice-profile-ruth-bader-ginsburg.

———. "Justice Ruth Bader Ginsburg Remarks," February 4, 2015. https://www.c-span.org/video/?324177-1/discussion-supreme-court-justice-ruth-bader-ginsburg.

———. "Justice Ruth Bader Ginsburg Remarks at Georgetown Law," September 20, 2017. https://www.c-span.org/video/?434298-1/justice-ruth-bader-ginsburg-addresses-georgetown-law-students.

———. "Supreme Court Justice Ginsburg," July 1, 2009. https://www.c-span.org/video/?286075-1/supreme-court-justice-ginsburg.

Harvard Law School. "A conversation with Ruth Bader Ginsburg at HLS," February 7, 2013. https://www.youtube.com/watch?v=umvkXhtbbpk.

Library of Congress. "Justice Ginsburg at the Young Readers Center," March 16, 2017. https://www.loc.gov/today/cyberlc/feature_wdesc.php?rec=7822.

MSNBC. "Full Interview with Supreme Court Justice Ruth Bader Ginsburg, February 17, 2015. http://www.msnbc.com/msnbc/watch/meet-justice-ruth-bader-ginsburg-400410691740?v=railb&.

Washington & Lee Law School. "A Q&A With The Honorable Ruth Bader Ginsburg," February 1, 2017. https://vimeo.com/202439401.

Websites

Oyez. https://www.oyez.org/. Various dates. Read and hear oral arguments, opinion announcements, and opinions of the Supreme Court of the United States.

Supreme Court of the United States—Speeches. Various dates. https://www.supremecourt.gov/publicinfo/speeches/speeches.aspx. Speeches by Justice Ginsburg, as well as the other justices, are posted here.

QUOTATION SOURCES

This book is a graphic novel–style biography. As biography, it is a true narrative of Ruth Bader Ginsburg's life. As a graphic book, it includes dialogue. These notes document the sources for all dialogue and quotations that come from books, articles, transcripts, video, audio, and other materials; and from interviews in which participants recalled what was said or thought in the scenes shown in the book. Some dialogue is invented—rooted in what is known about the speakers and events, but not traceable to a particular source.

Chapter 1: Fun and Games, Family and Sorrow

Page 13. Anecdote about D in penmanship. C-SPAN, "Justice Ginsburg Grade School Tour."

Chapter 2: Its Ugly Head

Page 17. "Why . . . other nights." Ginsburg, Hartnett, and Williams, *My Own Words*, 14.

Page 18. JEWS! flyer. http://www.alamy.com/stock-photo-anti-semitic-and-anti-communist-pamphlet-issued -by-the-nazi-organisation-48400877.html.

Page 18. "Christ killers." Ginsburg, interview by Debbie Levy. ("Sweet boys, but they were not allowed to come into our houses because the women who took care of them said Jews are Christ killers.")

Page 19. "No dogs or Jews allowed." U.S. Congress, Senate, *Nomination of Ruth Bader Ginsburg*, 139.

Chapter 3: We Do Not Allow Intolerance

Page 20. "We interrupt . . . received." C-SPAN, "How Americans First Learned of Pearl Harbor," December 7, 2011. https://www.c-span.org/video/?303099-1/americans-learned-pearl-harbor.

Page 22. "It is . . . human beings." *Fireside Chats of Franklin D. Roosevelt*, "On Progress of War and Plans for Peace," July 28, 1943, http://docs.fdrlibrary.marist.edu/072843.html.

Page 23. "I thought . . . indulges in it." Eleanor Roosevelt, "My Day," April 14, 1943, https://www2.gwu .edu/~erpapers/myday/displaydoc.cfm?_y=1943&_f=md056470.

Chapter 4: What a Lady Is

Page 27. "Anger, resentment . . . anyplace." Epstein, "Ruth Bader Ginsburg."

Page 26–27. "a lady." Harvard Law School, "A conversation." (To be a "lady" meant "not to be haughty. A lady doesn't get disturbed by things that may be off-putting, she reacts calmly, without anger, and she has nothing to do with . . . jealousy.")

Page 27. "independent." Galanes, "Ruth Bader Ginsburg and Gloria Steinem." ("She wanted me to be independent. And what she meant was becoming a high school history teacher because she never dreamed there would be other opportunities.")

Chapter 5: If Not a Robin

Page 30. "mouth the words." Stein, "A Conversation."

Chapter 6: Out of the Kitchen

Page 35. Chocolate pudding story. Library of Congress, "Justice Ginsburg at the Young Readers Center."

Page 36. "Once again . . . Trent." Generic Radio Workshop Library, "The Romance of Helen Trent," n. d., http://m.genericradio.com/show.php?id=1e2a657824f4ee61.

Page 36. "Even when . . . beyond." Ginsburg, interview by Debbie Levy.

Chapter 7: A Double Edge

Page 38. "Si . . . different." Ginsburg, interview by Debbie Levy. ("I noticed Si was different as soon as he came home.")

Chapter 8: That Painful Trouble

Page 41–42. "four great documents . . . everlasting peace." Ginsburg, Hartnett, and Williams, *My Own Words*, 10–11.

Page 44. "We must . . . thinking." Ginsburg, Hartnett, and Williams, 17.

Chapter 9: And Then

Page 46. "strong . . . never cries." Ginsburg, interview by Debbie Levy. ("And when we left the doctor's office, she was crying. My mother was a very strong person. She didn't cry. That's when I figured she knew she was dying.")

Page 47. "C." Ginsburg, Hartnett, and Williams, *My Own Words*, 18.

Page 48. "What would . . . dying?" Ginsburg, interview by Debbie Levy.

Chapter 10: Gone

Page 53. "Maybe . . . to Barnard?" Ginsburg, interview by Debbie Levy. ("But then she thought, well, maybe I should stay with my father and go to Barnard.")

Page 58. "this really hurts." Epstein, "Ruth Bader Ginsburg." ("One of the searing memories of my youth was when my mother died and there was a minyan every day, and I couldn't be part of it. That really hurt me.")

Page 58. "I can't . . . good for me." Ginsburg, interview by Debbie Levy. ("I wasn't going to do much good for him and it certainly wasn't going to be good for me.")

Chapter 11: Finding Her Place

Page 59. "comfortable or." Cornell University, "From Brooklyn to the Bench."

Page 60. "The most important . . . M.R.S." American Civil Liberties Union, *Tribute*. ("For most girls growing up in the '40s, the most important degree was not your B.A., but your M.R.S.")

Page 61. "Four guys . . . hopeless." Lindsey Nair, "W&L, VMI Host Supreme Court Justice Ruth Bader Ginsburg," *The Columns*, February 2, 2017, https://columns.wlu.edu/wl-vmi-host-supreme-court-justice -ruth-bader-ginsburg/. Also, Galanes, "Ruth Bader Ginsburg and Gloria Steinem."

Page 61. "ever so much smarter than men." Saulnier, "Justice Prevails." ("Women in my class were ever so much smarter than the men.")

Page 61. "suppress how smart they are." Cornell University, "From Brooklyn to the Bench."

Page 61. "brainier." Weisberg, "Supreme Court Justice Ruth Bader Ginsburg." ("They tried to make the man feel that he was brainier.")

Page 62. "not supposed to study." Ginsburg, interview by Debbie Levy.

Chapter 12: Friends at First Sight

Page 64. "very sure of himself." Ginsburg, interview by Debbie Levy.

Chapter 12: She Has a Brain!

Page 66. "everything . . . can't be." Ginsburg, interview by Debbie Levy. ("I was given a lesson plan for the Spanish-American War and everything the United States did was right. And I knew that couldn't be.")

Page 66. "I . . . don't like." Ginsburg, interview by Debbie Levy. ("I didn't like it [teaching history].")

Page 66. "He is . . . had a brain." Weisberg, "Supreme Court Justice Ruth Bader Ginsburg." ("He was the only boy I had ever met who cared that I had a brain.")

Chapter 14: Deep Impressions

Page 68. "He is magnetic." Simon Lesser, "We Spoke to Ruth Bader Ginsburg About Nabokov and Legal Writing," *The Culture Trip*, December 1, 2016, https://theculturetrip.com/north-america/usa/articles/justice-ruth-bader-ginsburg-on-how-nabokov-influenced-her-writing/. ("He was magnetically engaging. He stood alone, not comparable to any other lecturer.")

Page 68. "in love with the sound of words." Nina Totenberg, "Skip the Legalese and Keep It Short," NPR, June 13, 2011, http://www.npr.org/2011/06/13/137036622/skip-the-legalese-and-keep-it-short-justices-say.

Page 69. "Seek the right word . . . order." Ruth Bader Ginsburg, "Ruth Bader Ginsburg's Advice for Living," *New York Times*, October 1, 2016.

Page 69. "Make word pictures." Debra Bruno, "Balancing Act: Ruth Bader Ginsburg Remembers Her First Steps in the Law," *Legal Times*, November 12, 2007.

Page 71. "Our country . . . most basic values." "At the U.S. Supreme Court."

Page 71. "I really . . . become successful." Ginsburg, Hartnett, and Williams, *My Own Words*, 21.

Page 72. "Are you now . . . Party?" Patricia Bosworth, "Are You Now or Have You Ever?" *New York Times*, November 26, 2000.

Page 73. "You could be a lawyer . . . community." "At the U.S. Supreme Court."

Page 73. "Lawyers . . . self-incrimination." Academy of Achievement, "Ruth Bader Ginsburg: Interview." ("I saw that there were lawyers standing up for these people, reminding our Congress that we have a First Amendment, guaranteeing free speech, and we have a Fifth Amendment guarantee against self-incrimination.")

Chapter 15: Let Her Try

Page 74. "No woman . . . save her." Ginsburg, "Remarks on Women's Progress."

Page 74. "can't work as hard" and "afraid of emotional outbursts" and "responsibility is in the home." Bowman, "Women in the Legal Profession."

Page 75. "something to talk about . . . is doing." Jay Matthews, "The Spouse of Ruth: Marty Ginsburg, the Pre-Feminist Feminist," *Washington Post*, June 19, 1993.

Page 75. "sights set on Harvard." Gluck, "A Conversation."

Page 77. "If she wants . . . support her." University of Michigan Law School, "A Conversation with Ruth Bader Ginsburg."

Chapter 16: Advice

Page 79. "Of course . . . the disease." Ginsburg, Hartnett, and Williams, *My Own Words*, 22–23.

Page 80. "In every . . . deaf." T. Rees Shapiro, "Martin Ginsburg Dies at 78," *Washington Post*, June 28, 2010.

Chapter 17: Detour

Page 84. Social Security anecdotes. Ginsburg, interview by Debbie Levy.

Page 85. Jack's White Café anecdote. U.S. Congress, Senate, *Nomination of Ruth Bader Ginsburg*, 252.

Chapter 18: Parents

Page 87. "What is . . . casserole." Matthews, "The Spouse of Ruth."

Page 87. "I had . . . learn to cook." Nina Totenberg, "Martin Ginsburg's Legacy: Love of Justice (Ginsburg)," NPR, July 3, 2010, http://www.npr.org/templates/story/story.php?storyId=128249680.

Page 87. "It's . . . chemistry." Matthews, "The Spouse of Ruth."

Page 88. "How will . . . an infant." Saulnier, "Justice Prevails."

Page 89. "Ruth, if . . . a way." Saulnier.

Page 89. "Do I . . . enough?" Saulnier.

Chapter 19: The Way Things Are

Page 91. "all eyes . . . well-prepared." Gluck, "A Conversation."

Page 92. "mad dash" and "the way things." "At the U.S. Supreme Court."

Chapter 20: Roses Amid the Thorns

Page 93. "god, Zeus, Apollo." Ruth Bader Ginsburg, "In Memory of Herbert Wechsler," *Columbia Law Review*, 2000. Also, Galanes, "Ruth Bader Ginsburg and Gloria Steinem."

Page 93. "lowly first-year . . . Wechsler." Ginsburg, "In Memory of Herbert Wechsler."

Page 93. "Ladies . . . man?" Herma Hill Kay, "Ruth Bader Ginsburg, Law Professor Extraordinaire," in Dodson, ed., *The Legacy of Ruth Bader Ginsburg*. ("Dean Erwin Griswold . . . pointedly asked each woman why she occupied a place that would otherwise have gone to a man.")

Page 94. "what better . . . find a man." C-SPAN, "Justice Profile."

Page 94. "push a button . . . trapdoor." C-SPAN.

Page 94. "My husband . . . work." Galanes, "Ruth Bader Ginsburg and Gloria Steinem."

Page 95. "I gave him . . . expected." Galanes.

Page 95. "roses amid the thorns." Carmon and Knizhnik, *Notorious RBG*, 35.

Page 96. "Children's hours!" Sarah Ahmen, "Ruth Bader Ginsburg Says Being a Mother Is the Reason for Her Success," *Babble*, January, 2015, https://www.babble.com/entertainment/ruth-bader-ginsburg-credits -daughter-with-success/.

Page 96. "the pause that refreshes." Ward, "Family Ties."

Page 97. "Well, I'll stand . . . reference." Gilbert and Moore, *Particular Passions*.

Page 97. "You have to . . . job." Gilbert and Moore.

Chapter 21: And Then Again

Page 101. "learning . . . classmates." Harvard Law School, "A conversation."

Page 101. "We're not . . . family." Ginsburg, "The Changing Complexion."

Chapter 22: What a Lawyer Looks Like

Page 102. "the smartest person . . . down a rank." Margolick, "Trial by Adversity."

Page 102. "serious and smart . . . minimum of fuss." Margolick.

Page 102. "Ruthless Ruthie!" Gugliotta and Randolph, "A Mentor."

Page 104. "We had . . . she was dreadful." NYU Law News, "Justice Ruth Bader Ginsburg discusses *Roe v. Wade*, her legal career, and women on the Supreme Court," February 20, 2018, https://www.law.nyu.edu/news/Ruth-Bader-Ginsburg-Kenji-Yoshino-Center-for-Diversity-Inclusion-and-Belonging.

Page 105. "She has . . . daughter." "At the U.S. Supreme Court."

Page 105. "If you don't . . . complete the clerkship." "At the U.S. Supreme Court."

Chapter 23: Balancing Act

Page 107. "Maybe I'm . . . this." Marisa M. Kashino, "Stage Presence: Ruth Bader Ginsburg's Love of the Arts," *Washingtonian*, October 10, 2012.

Page 109. "Even on a Sunday." Harvard Law School, "A conversation."

Chapter 24: Across the Ocean

Page 110. "Where is Sweden . . . exactly?" David Von Drehle, "Conventional Roles." ("Ginsburg was not even sure where Sweden was relative to, say, Norway.")

Page 111. "never lived alone . . . for myself." C-SPAN, "Conversation with Justice Ginsburg," September 15, 2011.

Page 112. "Two incomes . . . at seven." Galanes, "Ruth Bader Ginsburg and Gloria Steinem."

Page 112. "Well, I . . . not just one." Franklin, "The Anti-Stereotyping Principles."

Chapter 25: Academia Calls

Page 113. "huge." C-SPAN, "Justice Ruth Bader Ginsburg Remarks," February 4, 2005.

Page 114. "You know . . . New York." "Transcript of Interview," *Ohio State Law Journal*.

Page 115. "flat . . . precise." Showalter, "Fighting Words." ("Her women students at Rutgers also described her speaking 'flatly, sometimes haltingly, but always precisely.'")

Page 115. "very serious . . . everything right." Von Drehle, "Conventional Roles."

Page 116. "Like I had . . . or something." Ward, "Family Ties."

Page 117. "I'm afraid . . . larger than me." Paraphrased from "Transcript of Interview," *Ohio State Law Journal*. Also, Saulnier, "Justice Prevails."

Chapter 26: Awakening

Page 121. "the minute . . . watermelon." Gluck, "A Conversation."

Page 122. "The paramount . . . Creator." Supreme Court Justice Joseph P. Bradley, concurring opinion in *Bradwell v. Illinois*, 83 U.S. 130 (1873).

Page 122. "by what means . . . communicated." "*Reed v. Reed* at 40."

Page 124. "Land . . . possessed." Ginsburg, "The Changing Complexion."

Page 124. "The natural . . . civil life." Bradley, concurring opinion.

Page 124. "Woman . . . man." *Muller v. Oregon*, 208 U.S. 412 (1908).

Page 124. "How have people . . . them." Margolick, "Trial by Adversity."

Chapter 27: A Revolutionary Idea

Page 126. "The genius . . . human values." Pauli Murray and Mary Eastwood, "Jane Crow and the Law: Sex Discrimination and Title VII," *George Washington Law Review*, December 1965.

Page 127. "Ruth . . . this one." Academy of Achievement, "Ruth Bader Ginsburg: Interview."

Page 128. "The law . . . aging parents." "At the U.S. Supreme Court."

Page 128. "Marty . . . take it." Academy of Achievement, "Ruth Bader Ginsburg: Interview."

Chapter 28: A First

Page 129. "The law decides . . . females." Gluck, "A Conversation."

Page 131. "sex-role pigeonholing." Ginsburg, Hartnett, and Williams, *My Own Words*, 131.

Page 132. "We're standing . . . ready to listen." C-SPAN, "Justice Ruth Bader Ginsburg Remarks," September 20, 2017.

Page 133. "We are here . . . unconstitutional." *Reed v. Reed* oral argument, October 19, 1971, https://www.oyez.org/cases/1971/70-4.

Page 133. "We feel . . . people." *Reed v. Reed* oral argument.

Page 134. "To give . . . Amendment." *Reed v. Reed*, 404 U.S. 71 (1971).

Chapter 29: Onward

Page 135. "Took great . . . ninety-three." Ginsburg, Hartnett, and Williams, *My Own Words*, 130.

Page 135. "call to arms . . . general leading." American Civil Liberties Union, *Tribute*.

Page 137. "make our laws neutral." Kirsten Sherk, "ICRW Interviews U.S. Supreme Court Justice Ruth Bader Ginsburg," International Center for Research on Women, March 18, 2016, https://www.icrw.org/news/icrw-interviews-u-s-supreme-court-justice-ruth-bader-ginsburg/.

Page 137. "so distinguished a scholar." "Ruth Bader Ginsburg discussing her post at Columbia," *New York Times*, January 26, 1972.

Page 138. "At least . . . over." Showalter, "Fighting Words."

Chapter 30: "I Ask No Favor"

Page 140. "I'm talking . . . captive audience." Weisberg, "Supreme Court Justice Ruth Bader Ginsburg."

Page 140. "I know . . . they do." Weisberg.

Page 141. "Mr. Chief Justice . . . off our necks." *Frontiero v. Richardson* oral argument, 1972, https://www.oyez .org/cases/1972/71-1694.

Page 142. "It was . . . cogent." American Civil Liberties Union, *Tribute.*

Page 142. "Were . . . listening?" Gluck, "A Conversation."

Page 142. "They were mesmerized." American Civil Liberties Union, *Tribute.*

Chapter 31: No Nonsense

Page 144. "Have . . . yet?" Von Drehle, "Redefining Fair."

Page 144. "No-nonsense" and "no humor." Von Drehle. ("no-nonsense . . . unhumourous.")

Page 145. "pull . . . it can be done." Susan Baer, "Nominee proud of her long fight against sex bias," *Baltimore Sun,* June 15, 1993.

Page 145. "zingers." Strebeigh, *Equal,* 124.

Page 145. "Professor . . . sing!" C-SPAN, "Columbia Law School Honors Justice Ginsburg," November 19, 1993, https://www.c-span.org/video/?53194-1/columbia-law-school-honors-justice-ginsburg.

Page 145. "Unless . . . night." Gluck, "A Conversation."

Chapter 32: Step by Step

Page 150. "Don't ask . . . might have won." U.S. Congress, Senate, *Nomination of Ruth Bader Ginsburg,* 410 (statement of Kathleen Peratis).

Page 150. "appreciate . . . matter." Strebeigh, *Equal,* 111.

Page 151. "present the court . . . the next." U.S. Congress, Senate, *Nomination of Ruth Bader Ginsburg,* 410.

Page 151–152. "Mrs. Ginsburg . . . isn't it?" *Kahn v. Shevin* oral argument, February 25, 1974, https://www .oyez.org/cases/1973/73-78.

Chapter 33: That Double-Edged Sword

Page 155. "Where the breadwinner . . . surviving parent." *Weinberger v. Wiesenfeld* oral argument, January 20, 1975, https://www.oyez.org/cases/1974/73-1892.

Page 156. "I have . . . accident." Carmon and Knizhnik, *Notorious RBG,* 71.

Page 156. "among . . . no sense." *Weinberger v. Wiesenfeld,* 420 U.S. 636 (1975).

Page 158. "I'm typing . . . distracting associations." "Transcript of Interview," *Ohio State Law Journal* (quoting Milicent Tryon).

Page 158. "That . . . insight." Ward, "Family Ties."

Page 160. "handled." Nina Totenberg, in Dodson, ed., *The Legacy of Ruth Bader Ginsburg.*

Page 160. "It is . . . liberation." Margolick, "Trial by Adversity."

Chapter 34: No Tokens

Page 161. "perpetuates . . . new dollar?" *Duren v. Missouri* oral argument, November 1, 1978, https://www.oyez.org/cases/1978/77-6067.

Page 162. "We won't . . . tokens." Von Drehle, "Redefining Fair."

Page 163. "Under the Constitution . . . invalid." *Duren v. Missouri* opinion announcement, January 9, 1979, https://www.oyez.org/cases/1978/77-6067.

Page 163. "If it was . . . since passed." *Duren v. Missouri*, 439 U.S. 357 (1975), quoting *Taylor v. Louisiana*, 419 U.S. 522 (1975).

Chapter 35: Be the Change

Page 164. Numbers of female judges. Mary L. Clark, "Carter's Groundbreaking Appointment of Women to the Federal Bench: His Other 'Human Rights' Record," *American University Journal of Gender, Social Policy & the Law* (2003).

Page 165. Letters in support of RBG. *Congressional Record*, June 18, 1980.

Chapter 36: Judge Ginsburg

Page 166. "I think . . . fascinating case." Bayer, *Ruth Bader Ginsburg*, 73.

Page 167. "This is . . . liberated." Greenhouse, "Word for Word."

Page 168. "Today . . . Court." "President Ronald Reagan nominates Sandra Day O'Connor," *The Arizona Republic*, July 7, 1981, https://youtu.be/1FMKYq1OW1Q.

Page 168. "Isn't . . . grand!" C-SPAN, "Justice Profile."

Page 168. "O'Connor . . . treated." Kay Mills, "A Woman Sitting on the Supreme Court: History's Place for Sandra Day O'Connor," *Los Angeles Times*, February 28, 1988.

Page 170. "The effective judge . . . restrained voice." Ginsburg, "Speaking in a Judicial Voice."

Page 170. "Don't give . . . speak calmly." CBS News, "Ruth Bader Ginsburg: Her view from the bench," October 9, 2016, https://www.cbsnews.com/news/ruth-bader-ginsburg-her-view-from-the-bench/.

Page 170. "Our fundamental . . . to come." Ginsburg, "Speaking in a Judicial Voice."

Page 171. "The equal dignity . . . legacy." Ginsburg.

Chapter 37: Journey to Justice

Page 173. "It would . . . serve society." U.S. Congress, Senate, *Nomination of Ruth Bader Ginsburg*, 54. ("It is an opportunity, beyond any other, for one of my training to serve society.")

Page 173. "If you . . . manager." Barnes, "The Question Facing Ruth Bader Ginsburg."

Page 174. "There's . . . Ginsburg." Berke, "Clinton Names Ruth Ginsburg."

Page 174. "Why . . . Ginsburg?" Toobin, *The Nine*, 116.

Page 176. "surely we can . . . about it." Ginsburg, Hartnett, and Williams, *My Own Words*, 169.

Page 176. "cloak-and-dagger" and "tickled . . . sense of humor." Ginsburg, Hartnett, and Williams, 169.

Page 176. "a wonderful visit . . . these decisions." Ginsburg, Hartnett, and Williams, 170.

Page 176. "Serving . . . free." U.S. Congress, Senate, *Nomination of Ruth Bader Ginsburg*, 54. ("Serving on this Court is the highest honor, the most awesome trust that can be placed in a judge. It means working at my craft—working with and for the law—as a way to keep our society both ordered and free.")

Page 176. "I think he liked me." Ginsburg, Hartnett, and Williams, *My Own Words*, 170.

Page 178. "I'm going . . . about this." Ginsburg, Hartnett, and Williams, 171.

Page 179. "cloud nine." Patrick Rettig, "Student interviews Justice Ginsburg," *The Californian*, March 29, 2017.

Page 180. "I am proud to nominate . . . as sons." "Transcript of President's Announcement and Judge Ginsburg's Remarks," *New York Times*, June 15, 1993.

Epilogue: Becoming RBG

Page 184. "Justice O'Connor . . . could have." Joan Biskupic, "Female Justices Attest to Fraternity on Bench," *Washington Post*, August 21, 1994.

Page 184. "My heritage as . . . my heritage." "Remarks by Ruth Bader Ginsburg, Associate Justice, Supreme Court of the United States, April 22, 2004, The Capitol Rotunda, Washington, DC. https://www.ushmm .org/remember/days-of-remembrance/past-days-of-remembrance/2004-days-of-remembrance/ruth-bader -ginsburg.

Page 184. "Call us . . . the law." David G. Savage, "BFFs Ruth Bader Ginsburg and Antonin Scalia Agree to Disagree," *Los Angeles Times*, June 22, 2015.

Page 184. "What I . . . very smart." Weisberg, "Supreme Court Justice Ruth Bader Ginsburg."

Page 185. "educated and honorable . . . leadership." *United States v. VMI*, 518 U.S. 515 (1996).

Page 185. "This should be Ruth's." Nina Totenberg, "Ruth Bader Ginsburg and Sandra Day O'Connor, 'Sisters In Law,'" NPR, September 1, 2015, https://www.npr.org/2015/09/01/436368073/ruth-bader-ginsburg-and -sandra-day-oconnor-sisters-in-law.

Page 185. "exceedingly persuasive justification." *United States v. VMI*, 518 U.S. 515 (1996).

Page 186. "It's lonely for me." "Transcript of Interview," *Ohio State Law Journal*.

Page 186. "It's almost . . . curiosity." Bazelon, "The Place of Women."

Page 187. "was meant . . . ignores today" and "The ball . . . court." *Ledbetter v. Goodyear Tire and Rubber Company*, dissent announcement, May 29, 2007, https://www.oyez.org/cases/2006/05-1074.

Page 188. "Indeed . . . complexions." U.S. Congress, Senate. *Nomination of Ruth Bader Ginsburg*, 50.

Page 191. "My explanation . . . original Constitution." Kagan and Ginsburg, "Remarks Commemorating Celebration 55.

Book cover:

"Real change . . . time." U.S. Congress, Senate, *Nomination of Ruth Bader Ginsburg*, 122.

Acknowledgments

I am thankful, once again, to Justice Ruth Bader Ginsburg, not only for being who she is but also for graciously submitting to my questions: first, before an audience of schoolchildren at the Library of Congress Young Readers Center in the spring of 2017, and second, for an interview in her chambers at the Supreme Court in the summer of 2017.

I am fortunate, once again, to have had the benefit of Ben Hoffman's keen and perceptive editing notes, immeasurably improving yet another of my books.

I am grateful to the brilliant Mary Hartnett for her careful manuscript review, her expertise in the law and on the subject of Ruth Bader Ginsburg, and for her friendship. Wendy W. Williams was also generous with her time and helped guide me away from factual errors.

My literary agent, Caryn Wiseman, keeps on going above and beyond the call of duty. I am so lucky to have her in my life.

Many thanks to the team at Simon & Schuster Children's Books—Liz Kossnar, Justin Chanda, Laurent Linn, Tom Daly, Jenica Nasworthy, Dainese Santos, Jennifer Weidman, Audrey Gibbons, and Ellen Grafton.

And thank you to the talented Whitney Gardner for the creativity and style she brought to this project.

My husband, Rick Hoffman, gets the last thank-you here, for sharing my enthusiasm for all things RBG and for his patience as my own enthusiasm caused me to repeat my favorite stories a few hundred times during the four years that I've been writing two books about her. What would you like to talk about now, Rick?—D. L.

Bringing life to the extraordinary biography of Ruth Bader Ginsburg was no easy task. I found myself often calling on her for inspiration as I captured all of her moments of frustration and triumphs. Like Ruth, I didn't have to go it alone and had an amazing team of people on my side, for whom I am exceptionally grateful.

I must thank Debbie Levy first for her amazing manuscript, and all the work she did to tell the life of a legend honestly and accurately.

Thanks to Brent Taylor for taking on his new role of head cheerleader all while being the best agent I could hope for, and to Uwe Stender and everyone at Triada US for all of their support and guidance.

To my brilliant editor, Liz Kossnar, who worked tirelessly to make the book truly remarkable. Laurent Linn's Zen-like calm kept me going when the work seemed overwhelming; his encouragement and keen eye will guide me through more than just this project. I'm so grateful I got to work with both of you.

A huge thanks to everyone at Simon & Schuster who helped make this book what it is: Justin Chanda, Ellen Grafton, Jenica Nasworthy, Audrey Gibbons, and Tom Daly, who is my book design superhero.

Thanks to Shari Chankhamma for her brilliant color work.

Many friends helped inspire and reassure me as I worked on page after page of historical drawings. I have so much appreciation for each and every one of you: Lily Anderson, John Brown, Jen Gaska, Cara Hallowell, Summer Heacock, Tini Howard, Nilah Magruder, Claribel Ortega, Dave Scheidt, Eric Smith, Brie Spangler, Blair Thornburgh, and Jeremy West.

Thanks to my family, especially my mother, Patrice Langone. Much love and thanks to my aunt Linny and sister Arielle as well.

And thank you, Roger, for holding my hand and rubbing my arm and making sure I made it through this project in one piece. I love you.—W. G.

To the dissenters and doers, the change-makers and uplifters,
traveling on their journeys to justice
—D. L.

For Grandma Pat and Grandma Alice, two women who both paved their own way and showed me
there is no one way to succeed as a woman in this world
—W. G.

SIMON & SCHUSTER BOOKS FOR YOUNG READERS
An imprint of Simon & Schuster Children's Publishing Division
1230 Avenue of the Americas, New York, New York 10020
Text copyright © 2019 by Debbie Levy
Illustrations copyright © 2019 by Whitney Gardner

SIMON & SCHUSTER BOOKS FOR YOUNG READERS is a trademark of Simon & Schuster, Inc.
For information about special discounts for bulk purchases, please contact Simon & Schuster
Special Sales at 1-866-506-1949 or business@simonandschuster.com.
The Simon & Schuster Speakers Bureau can bring authors to your live event. For more information or to book an event,
contact the Simon & Schuster Speakers Bureau at 1-866-248-3049 or visit our website at www.simonspeakers.com.
Also available in a Simon & Schuster Books for Young Readers hardcover edition
Book design by Laurent Linn, Tom Daly, and Whitney Gardner
The text for this book was set in Ruthiebaderbold.
The illustrations for this book were rendered digitally.
Manufactured in the United States of America
0919 WOR
First Simon & Schuster Books for Young Readers paperback edition November 2019
10 9 8 7 6 5 4 3 2 1
Library of Congress Cataloging-in-Publication Data
Names: Levy, Debbie, author. | Gardner, Whitney, illustrator.
Title: Becoming RBG: Ruth Bader Ginsburg's journey to justice / Debbie Levy ; illustrated by Whitney Gardner.
Other titles: Becoming Ruth Bader Ginsburg
Description: New York City : Simon & Schuster Books for Young Readers, 2019. | Includes bibliographical references. |
Audience: Ages 10 and up | Audience: Grades 4-6 | Summary: "From the New York Times bestselling author of I Dissent
comes a biographical graphic novel about celebrated Supreme Court justice Ruth Bader Ginsburg. Supreme Court justice
Ruth Bader Ginsburg is a modern feminist icon—a leader in the fight for equal treatment of girls and women in society
and the workplace. She blazed trails to the peaks of the male-centric worlds of education and law, where women had
rarely risen before. Ruth Bader Ginsburg has often said that true and lasting change in society and law is accomplished
slowly, one step at a time. This is how she has evolved, too. Step by step, the shy little girl became a child who
questioned unfairness, who became a student who persisted despite obstacles, who became an advocate who resisted
injustice, who became a judge who revered the rule of law, who became . . . RBG"—Provided by publisher.
Identifiers: LCCN 2019027792 (print) | LCCN 2019027793 (eBook) | ISBN 9781534424562 (hardcover) |
ISBN 9781534424555 (paperback) | ISBN 9781534424579 (eBook)
Subjects: LCSH: Ginsburg, Ruth Bader—Juvenile literature. | Judges—United States—Biography—Juvenile literature. |
LCGFT: Graphic novels.
Classification: LCC KF8745.G56 L478 2019 (print) | LCC KF8745.G56 (eBook) | DDC 347.73/2634 [B]—dc23
LC record available at https://lccn.loc.gov/20190277 92
LC eBook record available at https://lccn.loc.gov/2019027793